CliffsNotes®

FTCE: Elementary Education K–6

CliffsNotes®

FTCE: Elementary Education K–6

by
Janet B. Andreasen
Lee-Anne T. Spalding
and Enrique Ortiz

WILEY
Wiley Publishing, Inc.

Dedication

To my husband, Robbie, and children, Zachary and Sarah. —JBA

To the Elementary Education students at the University of Central Florida; to Brett, Graham, and Gavin for allowing me the time to reach new and greater heights in my professional career. —LTS

To my wife, Diana, and kids, Enrique G., Samuel, and Natalie. —EO

About the Authors

Janet B. Andreasen, Ph.D., is an instructor for mathematics education and coordinator of secondary education programs at the University of Central Florida. She is a former Seminole County, Florida, high school teacher and has previously authored CliffsNotes: CSET Mathematics. She lives in Winter Park, Florida, with her husband, Robbie, and two children, Zachary and Sarah.

Lee-Anne T. Spalding, M.Ed., is a former Seminole County, Florida, public school educator and is currently instructing preservice teachers at the University of Central Florida. She has previously authored 12 nonfiction library market books for elementary age students. She lives in Oviedo, Florida, with her husband, Brett, and two sons, Graham and Gavin.

Enrique Ortiz, Ed.D., is an associate professor at the College of Education, University of Central Florida. Since 1987, he has been very active in the mathematics education profession. He lives in Oviedo, Florida, with his wife, Diana, and three children, Enrique Gabriel, Samuel, and Natalie.

Editorial

Acquisitions Editor: Greg Tubach

Project Editor: Kelly D. Henthorne

Composition

Proofreader: Shannon Ramsey

Wiley Publishing, Inc. Composition Services

CliffsNotes® FTCE: Elementary Education K–6

Published by:
Wiley Publishing, Inc.
111 River Street
Hoboken, NJ 07030-5774
www.wiley.com

Table of Contents

PART I: COMPETENCY REVIEWS

PART II: FULL-LENGTH PRACTICE TESTS

General Description

The Florida Teacher Certification Examination (FTCE) Elementary Education (K–6) Subject Area Examination (SAE) is designed to assess knowledge about teaching elementary grades including the areas of Language Arts and Reading; Social Science; Music, Visual Arts, Physical Education, and Health; Science and Technology; and Mathematics. The test is comprised of approximately 225 multiple-choice questions.

Each multiple choice question contains four response options—A, B, C, and D. You will record your answer choice in a separate answer booklet by bubbling the respective letter. Your score is determined by how many questions you answer correctly. There is no penalty for incorrect answers. You are given two and one-half hours to complete the test.

The Role of the Elementary Education (K–6) Subject Area Test in Teacher Certification

The Florida Teacher Certification Examinations include three examinations: General Knowledge Test (GKT), Professional Education Examination (PEd), and Subject Area Examinations (SAEs). One part of becoming a certified teacher in the state of Florida is to pass all three examinations. The SAEs determine certification areas. The Elementary Education (K–6) Examination is a Subject Area Examination.

The Elementary Education (K–6) Competencies

The Elementary Education (K–6) test is based on a set of 32 competencies which are meant to ensure a breadth of knowledge appropriate for teaching elementary grades in Florida public schools. Competencies are areas of content knowledge. Each competency is further defined by a list of skills, behaviors which demonstrate the competency. As listed in the *Competencies and Skills Required for Teacher Certification in Florida, Fourteenth Edition* (available at http://www.fldoe.org/asp/ftce/pdf/60ElementaryEducationK-6.pdf), the competencies/skills and their approximate number of questions on the FTCE Elementary Education (K–6) SAE are the following:

Language Arts and Reading

The Language Arts and Reading competencies include 6 areas: 1) Knowledge of the reading process, 2) Knowledge of literature and literary analysis, 3) Knowledge of the writing process and applications, 4) Knowledge of reading methods and assessment, 5) Knowledge of communication, and 6) Knowledge of information and media literacy. These six competencies encompass approximately **45 questions** of the examination.

Competency 1: Knowledge of the Reading Process

1. Identify the processes, skills, and phases of word recognition that lead to effective decoding (e.g., pre-alphabetic, partial-alphabetic, full-alphabetic, graphophonemic, morphemic).
2. Identify instructional methods for promoting the development of decoding and encoding skills.
3. Identify the components of reading fluency (e.g., accuracy, automaticity, rate, prosody).
4. Identify instructional methods (e.g., practice with high-frequency words, timed readings) for developing reading fluency.

5. Identify instructional methods and strategies for increasing vocabulary acquisition (e.g., word analysis, choice of words, context clues, multiple exposures) across the content areas.

6. Identify instructional methods and strategies (e.g., summarizing, self-monitoring, questioning, use of graphic and semantic organizers, think alouds, recognizing story structure) for facilitating students' reading comprehension.

7. Identify essential comprehension skills (e.g., main idea, supporting details and facts, author's purpose, fact and opinion, point of view, inference, conclusion).

8. Identify appropriate uses of multiple representations of information (e.g., charts, tables, graphs, pictures, print and nonprint media) for a variety of purposes.

9. Identify strategies (e.g., making connections and predictions, questioning, summarizing, question generating) for developing critical-thinking skills such as analysis, synthesis, evaluation.

10. Identify instructional methods for teaching a variety of informational and literary text structures.

11. Identify the content of emergent literacy (e.g., oral language development, phonological awareness, alphabet knowledge, decoding, concepts of print, motivation, text structures, written language development).

Competency 2: Knowledge of Literature and Literary Analysis

1. Identify characteristics and elements of a variety of literary genres (e.g., realistic fiction, fantasy, poetry, nonfiction).

2. Identify terminology and appropriate use of literary devices.

3. Identify and apply professional guidelines for selecting multicultural literature.

4. Identify appropriate techniques for encouraging students to respond to literature in a variety of ways.

Competency 3: Knowledge of the Writing Process and Applications

1. Demonstrate knowledge of the developmental stages of writing.

2. Demonstrate knowledge of the writing process (e.g., prewriting, drafting, revising, editing, publishing).

3. Identify characteristics of the modes of writing (e.g., narrative, descriptive, expository, persuasive, informative, creative).

4. Select the appropriate mode of writing for a variety of occasions, purposes, and audiences.

5. Identify elements and appropriate use of rubrics to assess writing.

6. Demonstrate knowledge of writing conventions (e.g., spelling, punctuation, capitalization, syntax, and word usage).

7. Identify instructional methods for teaching writing conventions.

Competency 4: Knowledge of Reading Methods and Assessment

1. Identify measurement concepts, characteristics, and uses of norm-referenced, criterion-referenced, and performance-based assessments.

2. Identify oral and written methods for assessing student progress (e.g., informal reading inventories, fluency checks, rubrics, running records, story retelling, portfolios).

3. Interpret assessment data (e.g., screening, progress monitoring, diagnostic) to guide instructional decisions.

4. Use individual student reading data to differentiate instruction.

5. Interpret students' formal and informal assessment results to inform students and parents or guardians.

6. Evaluate the appropriateness (e.g., curriculum alignment, freedom from bias) of assessment instruments and practices.

7. Identify appropriate classroom organizational formats (e.g., literature circles, small groups, individuals, workshops, reading centers, multiage groups) for specific instructional objectives.

8. Identify instructional methods for developing emergent literacy.

9. Identify methods for the diagnosis, prevention, and intervention of common emergent literacy difficulties.

Competency 5: Knowledge of Communication

1. Demonstrate knowledge of penmanship (e.g., legibility, proper slant, spacing).

2. Demonstrate knowledge of listening and speaking strategies (e.g., questioning, paraphrasing, eye contact, voice, gestures).

3. Identify instructional methods for developing listening and speaking skills.

Competency 6: Knowledge of Information and Media Literacy

1. Demonstrate knowledge of a wide array of information and media literacy (e.g., Internet, printed material, artifacts, visual media, primary sources).

2. Demonstrate knowledge of systematic and ethical processes for collecting and presenting authentic information.

3. Identify current technology available for use in educational settings (e.g., computer software and hardware, Web tools).

Social Science

Social science is broken down into 5 competencies: 1) Knowledge of time, continuity, and change (i.e., history); 2) Knowledge of people, places, and environment (i.e., geography); 3) Knowledge of government and the citizen (i.e., government and civics); 4) Knowledge of production, distribution, and consumption (i.e., economics); and 5) Knowledge of instruction and assessment of the social sciences. These 5 competencies encompass approximately **45 questions** of the examination.

Competency 7: Knowledge of Time, Continuity, and Change (i.e., History)

1. Identify historical events that are related by cause and effect.

2. Evaluate examples of primary source documents for historical perspective.

3. Identify cultural contributions and technological developments of Africa; the Americas; Asia, including the Middle East; and Europe.

4. Relate physical and human geographic factors to major historical events and movements.

5. Identify significant historical leaders and events that have influenced Eastern and Western civilizations.

6. Identify the causes and consequences of exploration, settlement, and growth.

7. Identify individuals and events that have influenced economic, social, and political institutions in the United States.

8. Identify immigration and settlement patterns that have shaped the history of the United States.

9. Identify how various cultures contributed to the unique social, cultural, economic, and political features of Florida.

Competency 8: Knowledge of People, Places, and Environment (i.e., Geography)

1. Identify the six essential elements (i.e., the world in spatial terms, places and regions, physical systems, human systems, environment and society, uses of geography), including the specific terms for each element.

2. Interpret maps and other graphic representations, and identify tools and technologies to acquire, process, and report information from a spatial perspective.

3. Interpret statistics that show how places differ in their human and physical characteristics.

4. Identify ways in which people adapt to an environment through the production and use of clothing, food, and shelter.

5. Identify how tools and technological advances affect the environment.

6. Identify physical, cultural, economic, and political reasons for the movement of people in the world, nation, or state.

7. Identify how transportation and communication networks contribute to the level of economic development in different regions.

8. Compare and contrast major regions of the world.

Competency 9: Knowledge of Government and the Citizen (i.e., Government and Civics)

1. Identify the structure, functions, and purposes of government.

2. Demonstrate knowledge of the rights and responsibilities of a citizen in the world, nation, state, and community.

3. Identify major concepts of the U.S. Constitution and other historical documents.

4. Identify how the legislative, executive, and judicial branches share powers and responsibility.

5. Demonstrate knowledge of the U.S. electoral system and the election process.

6. Identify the structures and functions of U.S. federal, state, and local governments.

7. Identify the relationships between social, economic, and political rights and the historical documents that secure these rights.

8. Demonstrate knowledge of the processes of the U.S. legal system.

9. Identify the roles of the United States in international relations.

Competency 10: Knowledge of Production, Distribution, and Consumption (i.e., Economics)

1. Identify ways that limited resources affect the choices made by governments and individuals.

2. Compare and contrast the characteristics of different economic institutions (e.g., banks, credit unions, stock markets, the Federal Reserve).

3. Identify the role of markets from production through distribution to consumption.

4. Identify factors to consider when making consumer decisions.

5. Identify the economic interdependence between nations (e.g., trade, finance, movement of labor).

6. Identify human, natural, and capital resources and how these resources are used in the production of goods and services.

Competency 11: Knowledge of Instruction and Assessment of the Social Sciences

1. Identify appropriate resources for teaching social science concepts.

2. Identify appropriate assessment methods in teaching social science concepts.

Music, Visual Arts, Physical Education, and Health

Music, Visual Arts, Physical Education, and Health is broken down into 9 competencies. There are 5 competencies related to music and visual arts: 1) Knowledge of skills and techniques in music and visual arts; 2) Knowledge of creation and composition in music and visual arts; 3) Knowledge of cultural and historical connections in music and visual arts; 4) Knowledge of aesthetic and critical analysis of music and visual arts; and 5) Knowledge of appropriate assessment strategies in music and visual arts. Music and Visual Arts encompasses approximately **22 questions** of the examination.

There are 4 competencies related to Physical Education and Health: 1) Knowledge of personal health and wellness; 2) Knowledge of physical, social, and emotional growth and development; 3) Knowledge of community health and safety issues; and 4) Knowledge of subject content and appropriate curriculum design. Physical Education and Health encompasses approximately **23 questions** of the examination.

Competency 12: Knowledge of Skills and Techniques in Music and Visual Arts

1. Identify appropriate varieties of music (e.g., age-appropriate range and vocal ability, diverse cultures, genres, and styles).
2. Identify developmentally appropriate singing techniques (e.g., posture, breath support, tone quality, vocal range).
3. Identify correct performance techniques for rhythmic and melodic classroom instruments (e.g., nonpitched percussion, recorder, autoharp, keyboard).
4. Read and interpret simple, traditional, and nontraditional music notation (e.g., melodic, rhythmic, harmonic).
5. Select safe and developmentally appropriate media, techniques, and tools to create both two-dimensional and three-dimensional works of art.
6. Identify appropriate uses of art materials and tools for developing basic processes and motor skills.

Competency 13: Knowledge of Creation and Communication in Music and Visual Arts

1. Identify the elements of music (e.g., rhythm, melody, form, texture, timbre, dynamics) and ways they are used to express text, ideas, emotions, settings, time, and place.
2. Demonstrate knowledge of strategies for developing creative responses through music to ideas drawn from text, speech, movement, and visual images.
3. Demonstrate knowledge of strategies for developing creative responses through art to ideas drawn from text, music, speech, movement, and visual images.
4. Identify the elements of art and principles of design (e.g., line, color, shape, form, texture, balance, movement) and ways they are used in expressing text, ideas, meanings, and emotions.

Competency 14: Knowledge of Cultural and Historical Connections in Music and Visual Arts

1. Identify characteristics of style in musical selections.
2. Demonstrate knowledge of how music reflects particular cultures, historical periods, and places.
3. Identify characteristics of style in works of art.
4. Demonstrate knowledge of how visual arts reflect particular cultures, historical periods, and places.

Competency 15: Knowledge of Aesthetic and Critical Analysis of Music and Visual Arts

1. Identify strategies for developing students' analytical skills to evaluate musical performance.
2. Identify strategies for developing students' analytical skills to evaluate works of art.

Competency 16: Knowledge of Appropriate Assessment Strategies in Music and Visual Arts

1. Identify a variety of developmentally appropriate strategies and materials for assessing skills, techniques, creativity, and communication in music.
2. Identify a variety of developmentally appropriate strategies and materials for assessing skills, techniques, creativity, and communication in visual arts.

Competency 17: Knowledge of Personal Health and Wellness

1. Demonstrate knowledge of the interrelatedness of physical activity, fitness, and health.
2. Demonstrate basic knowledge of nutrition and its role in promoting health.
3. Identify the processes of decision making and goal setting in promoting individual health and wellness.
4. Demonstrate knowledge of common health problems and risk behaviors associated with them.

Competency 18: Knowledge of Physical, Social, and Emotional Growth and Development

1. Identify the principles of sequential progression of motor skill development.
2. Demonstrate knowledge of human growth and development and its relationship to physical, social, and emotional well-being.
3. Identify major factors associated with social and emotional health (e.g., communication skills, self-concept, fair play, conflict resolution, character development, stress management).
4. Identify problems associated with physical, social, and emotional health.
5. Identify factors related to responsible sexual behavior.

Competency 19: Knowledge of Community Health and Safety Issues

1. Identify factors contributing to substance use and abuse and identify signs, symptoms, effects, and strategies for the prevention of substance abuse.
2. Demonstrate knowledge of resources from home, school, and community that provide valid health information, products, and services.
3. Identify appropriate violence prevention strategies in the home, school, and community.
4. Identify appropriate injury prevention and safety strategies in the home, school, and community.

Competency 20: Knowledge of Subject Content and Appropriate Curriculum Design

1. Distinguish between developmentally appropriate and inappropriate instructional practices that consider the interaction of cognitive, affective, and psychomotor domains.
2. Identify various factors (e.g., environment, equipment, facilities, space, safety, group diversity) to consider when planning physical activities.
3. Analyze the influence of culture, media, technology, and other factors when planning health and wellness instruction.

Science and Technology

Science and Technology includes 7 competencies: 1) Knowledge of the nature of matter; 2) Knowledge of forces, motion, and energy; 3) Knowledge of earth and space; 4) Knowledge of life science; 5) Knowledge of the nature of science; 6) Knowledge of the relationship of science and technology; and 7) Knowledge of instruction and assessment. These 7 competencies encompass approximately **45 questions** of the examination.

Competency 21: Knowledge of the Nature of Matter

1. Identify the fundamental physical properties of matter (e.g., mass, volume).
2. Compare physical and chemical changes (e.g., cutting, burning, rusting).
3. Compare the characteristics of elements, compounds, and mixtures.
4. Compare the physical properties of solids, liquids, and gases (e.g., mass, volume, color, texture, hardness, temperature).
5. Compare the properties of liquids during phase change through heating and cooling (e.g., boiling, melting, freezing, evaporation, condensation).
6. Demonstrate knowledge that all matter is composed of parts too small to be seen (e.g., electrons, protons, neutrons).

Competency 22: Knowledge of Forces, Motion, and Energy

1. Demonstrate knowledge of temperature, heat, and heat transfer.
2. Identify the types and characteristics of contact forces (e.g., pushes and pulls, friction) and at-a-distance forces (e.g., magnetic, gravitational, electrostatic).
3. Apply knowledge of light and optics to practical applications (i.e., reflection, refraction, and diffusion).
4. Apply knowledge of electrical currents, circuits, conductors, insulators, and static electricity to real-world situations.
5. Distinguish between different types of energy (e.g., chemical, electrical, mechanical, electromagnetic, heat, light, sound, solar) and their characteristics as they apply to real-world situations.
6. Apply knowledge of the ability of energy to cause motion or create change.
7. Demonstrate knowledge that electrical energy can be transformed into heat, light, mechanical, and sound energy.
8. Demonstrate knowledge of potential and kinetic energy.
9. Demonstrate knowledge that motion of all matter can be changed by forces, observed, described, and measured.
10. Differentiate between balanced and unbalanced forces and how they affect objects.

Competency 23: Knowledge of Earth and Space

1. Identify characteristics of geologic formations (e.g., volcanoes, canyons, mountains) and the mechanisms by which they are changed (e.g., physical and chemical weathering, erosion, plate tectonics).
2. Identify the characteristics of soil and the process of soil formation.
3. Identify the major groups and properties of rocks and minerals, examples of each, and the processes of their formation.
4. Identify ways in which land, air, and water interact (e.g., soil absorption, runoff, water cycle, atmospheric conditions, weather patterns).

5. Differentiate among radiation, conduction, and convection, the three mechanisms by which heat is transferred through Earth's system.

6. Identify the components of Earth's solar system and compare their individual characteristics.

7. Demonstrate knowledge of Earth's place in our changing universe (e.g., history and purposes of space exploration, vastness of space).

8. Demonstrate knowledge of the phases of the Moon and the Moon's effect on Earth.

9. Identify Earth's tilt and orbital pattern and how they determine the seasons.

10. Analyze various conservation methods and their effectiveness in relation to renewable and nonrenewable natural resources.

11. Identify the sun as a star and its effect on Earth (e.g., radiant energy, heat, light).

Competency 24: Knowledge of Life Science

1. Compare and contrast living and nonliving things.

2. Distinguish among infectious agents (e.g., viruses, bacteria, fungi, parasites) and their effects on the human body.

3. Differentiate structures and functions of plant and animal cells.

4. Identify the major steps of plants' physiological processes of photosynthesis, transpiration, reproduction, and respiration.

5. Demonstrate knowledge of how plants respond to stimuli (e.g., heat, light, gravity).

6. Identify the structures and functions of organs and systems of both animals and humans.

7. Demonstrate knowledge of animals' physiological processes (e.g., respiration, reproduction, digestion, circulation).

8. Demonstrate knowledge of cell theory as the fundamental organizing principle of life on Earth.

9. Demonstrate knowledge of heredity, evolution, and natural selection.

10. Demonstrate knowledge of the interdependence of living things with each other and with their environment (e.g., food webs, pollution, hurricanes).

Competency 25: Knowledge of the Nature of Science

1. Demonstrate knowledge of basic science processes (e.g., observing, classifying, communicating, qualifying, inferring, predicting).

2. Apply knowledge of scientific inquiry (e.g., forming hypotheses, manipulating variables, recording and interpreting data) to learning science concepts.

3. Identify the appropriate laboratory equipment for specific activities.

4. Identify state safety procedures for teaching science, including the care of living organisms and the accepted procedures for the safe preparation, use, storage, and disposal of chemicals and other materials.

5. Demonstrate knowledge of basic scientific vocabulary (e.g., theory, law, hypotheses, models).

Competency 26: Knowledge of the Relationship of Science and Technology

1. Identify the interrelationship of science and technology.

2. Identify the tools and techniques of science and technology used for data collection and problem solving.

3. Identify ways in which technology can be used by students to represent understanding of science concepts.

Competency 27: Knowledge of Instruction and Assessment

1. Identify a variety of appropriate instructional strategies (e.g., cooperative learning, inquiry learning, investigations) for teaching specific topics.

2. Select manipulatives, physical models, and other classroom teaching tools for teaching specific topics.

3. Identify a variety of methods for assessing scientific knowledge, including analyzing student thinking processes to determine strengths and weaknesses.

Mathematics

Mathematics includes 5 competencies. Assessment of the mathematics competencies and skills will use real-world problems when feasible. The competencies for mathematics include: 1) Knowledge of numbers and operations; 2) Knowledge of geometry and measurement; 3) Knowledge of algebra; 4) Knowledge of data analysis; and 5) Knowledge of instruction and assessment. The mathematics competencies encompass approximately **45 questions** of the examination.

Competency 28: Knowledge of Numbers and Operations

1. Associate multiple representations of numbers using word names, standard numerals, and pictorial models for real numbers (e.g., whole numbers, decimals, fractions, integers).

2. Compare the relative size of integers, fractions, decimals, numbers expressed as percents, and numbers with exponents.

3. Apply ratios, proportions, and percents in real-world situations.

4. Represent numbers in a variety of equivalent forms, including whole numbers, integers, fractions, decimals, percents, and exponents.

5. Perform operations on rational numbers (e.g., whole numbers, fractions, decimals, integers) using multiple representations and algorithms and understand the relationships between these operations (i.e., addition, subtraction, multiplication, and division).

6. Select the appropriate operation(s) to solve problems involving ratios and percents and the addition, subtraction, multiplication, and division of rational numbers.

7. Use estimation in problem-solving situations.

8. Apply number theory concepts (e.g., primes, composites, multiples, factors, number sequences, number properties, rules of divisibility).

9. Apply the order of operations.

Competency 29: Knowledge of Geometry and Measurement

1. Analyze properties of two-dimensional shapes (e.g., area, sides, angles).

2. Apply geometric properties and relationships to solve problems (e.g., circumference, perimeter, area, volume) using appropriate strategies and formulas.

3. Apply the geometric concepts of symmetry, congruency, similarity, and transformations.

4. Identify and locate ordered pairs in a rectangular coordinate system.

5. Analyze properties of three-dimensional shapes (e.g., volume, faces, edges, vertices).

6. Compose and decompose two-dimensional and three-dimensional geometric shapes.

7. Determine how a change in length, width, height, or radius affects perimeter, circumference, area, surface area, or volume.

8. Within a given system (i.e. metric or customary), solve real-world problems involving measurement with both direct and indirect measures and make conversions to a larger or smaller unit.

9. Solve real-world problems involving estimates and exact measurements.

10. Select appropriate measurement units to solve problems.

11. Identify three-dimensional objects from two-dimensional representations of objects and vice versa.

Competency 30: Knowledge of Algebra

1. Extend and generalize patterns or functional relationships.

2. Interpret, compare, and translate among multiple representations of patterns and relationships by using tables, graphs, equations, expressions, and verbal descriptions.

3. Select a representation of an algebraic expression, equation, or inequality that applies to a real-world situation.

4. Demonstrate knowledge of one- and two-step linear equations and inequalities.

5. Apply the commutative, associative, and distributive properties to show that two expressions are equivalent.

Competency 31: Knowledge of Data Analysis

1. Demonstrate knowledge of the concepts of variability (i.e. range) and central tendency (i.e., mean, median, mode).

2. Use data to construct and analyze frequency tables and graphs (e.g., bar graphs, pictographs, line graphs).

3. Make accurate predictions and draw conclusions from data.

Competency 32: Knowledge of Instruction and Assessment

1. Identify a variety of appropriate instructional strategies (e.g., cooperative learning, peer tutoring, think alouds) for teaching specific concepts.

2. Identify ways that manipulatives, mathematical and physical models, and technology can be used in instruction.

3. Identify a variety of methods for assessing mathematical knowledge, including analyzing student thinking processes to determine strengths and weaknesses.

Types of Questions

There are seven types of questions included on the Elementary Education (K–6) SAE. All questions are multiple-choice format with four possible choices.

Scenario: Examine a situation, problem, or case study. Then answer a question, make a diagnosis, or recommend a course of action.

Direct Question: Choose the response option that best answers the question.

Command: Select the best response option.

Sentence Completion: Select the response option that best completes the sentence.

Charts, graphs, and maps: Identify or interpret a diagram by choosing the response option that best answers the question.

Graphics: Choose the option that best answers a question involving a number line, a geometric figure, graphs of lines or curves, a table, or a chart.

Word problems: Apply mathematical principles to solve a real-world problem.

Registering for the Test

You must register for the FTCE: Elementary Education (K–6) Subject Area Examination prior to taking it. The exam is administered in two forms: paper and pencil exams and computer-based exams. The forms of the test are equivalent in length and difficulty.

Paper and Pencil Examinations

Paper and pencil exams are administered on specific dates throughout the year. There are regular administration dates and supplemental administration dates. The paper and pencil exams generally are offered in January, February, April, July, September, and October. Registration for paper and pencil exams must be completed approximately 6–7 weeks prior to the test date. Late registration is allowed up to a month prior to the exam for an additional fee. Score reports are available approximately 4 weeks after administration of the paper and pencil exam.

Additional supplemental administration dates are available for an additional fee. The two supplemental administrations are usually in June and December. Registration deadline for supplemental exams is 2 weeks prior to the exam date, and score reports are available two weeks after taking the exam.

Paper and pencil examinations are administered at testing sites throughout the state of Florida. Test site options are indicated on the registration form. Test sites are assigned on a first-come, first-served basis.

Computer-based Examinations

Computer-based examinations are available on a more frequent basis. Time slots are filled on a first-come, first-served basis. Computer-based testing sites are available throughout Florida, and some out-of-state sites are also available. No registration deadlines exist for computer-based examinations; however, you are encouraged to register as early as possible for choice of time and site.

At the conclusion of the computer-based examination, you will receive an unofficial score report. Official score reports will be mailed approximately 2 weeks after completion of the examination.

Registration

Registration for the paper and pencil examinations can be done either online at http://www.fl.nesinc.com/FL_register_toc.asp or by mail. Complete registration for computer-based examinations is online. Pay test fees at the time of registration.

When you register, you will be asked for codes for school districts or colleges and universities to which you wish a copy of your score report be sent. The codes are available on the website. If you are already working in a school district or are a student in an initial teacher preparation program in which the certification examinations are required for graduation, be sure to indicate the appropriate code(s) on your registration form. You will receive an official score report regardless of whether you choose to have additional score reports sent to school districts or colleges and universities. See http://www.fl.nesinc.com/ for additional information as well as the codes and forms for registration.

Fees for Exams

As of September 1, 2009, the fee to take any Subject Area Examination for the FTCE is $200 for the first attempt. If you don't pass on the first attempt, retakes cost $220. Late registration is an additional $15 fee. Supplemental administrations are an additional $100 fee.

Day of the Test

The following items must be brought with you to the testing site:

- Your admission ticket

  This indicates what test you are taking, the test center/site, test date, and appointment time (for computer-based examinations) or reporting time (for paper and pencil examinations).

- Proper identification:

  Whether you are taking a paper-based or computer-based test, you must bring two valid and unexpired forms of identification that are printed in English.

  Government-issued identification that must have a clear photograph and your signature, such as a driver's license, state-issued identification card, United States military ID (with visible signature), or passport.

  One additional form of identification that must have either a photo or a signature, such as a Social Security card or a student ID. If you do not have proper identification, you will not be permitted to test.

- Several number-2 sharpened pencils if you are taking a paper-based test.

- If you are taking a computer-based examination, your photograph will be taken, and you will be given Guidelines for Test Takers, which is also available at http://www.fl.nesinc.com/FL_bulletinforms.asp. You will also be asked to sign the test center log book that indicates you have read the guidelines and understand the procedures, which will be used for computer-based testing.

- The following items are not allowed at any test sites:

  Smoking

  Visitors

  Weapons of any kind

  Cell phones and any other electronic communication devices, even if it has an on/off switch

  Scratch paper or notes of any kind

  Dictionaries or any other books

  Correction fluid

  Calculators

  Food or drinks, including water

You should report to the testing site at least 30–45 minutes prior to your scheduled testing time.

During the test, you may take restroom breaks as needed; however, any time you take for a restroom break is considered part of your allocated test time. You may not leave the testing room except to go to the restroom until you have been officially dismissed by a test administrator. You may not communicate in any way with any other test takers. Computer-based examinations may be videotaped.

When you have completed the examination, you can ask to be dismissed from the testing site if the time allotted is not completed yet. Your test materials will be collected and you may not return to the testing site.

How to Use This CliffsTestPrep Book

The following are some tips for you to consider during the preparation period before taking the FTCE Elementary Education (K–6) Subject Area Examination. These ideas should help you analyze and focus your preparation time as you get ready to take the test.

Develop a Focusing Process

The practice tests provided in this book will help you prepare to take the actual FTCE Elementary Education (K–6) Examination. It is a good idea that you read all the background information provided in this book and identify all the areas that the actual test covers: Language Arts and Reading; Social Science; Music, Visual Arts, Physical Education, and Health; Science and Technology; and Mathematics. Begin by taking the Diagnostic Test which follows this chapter. This test will help you to identify potential areas of weakness and strength.

Take a close look at "Competency Reviews" in Part I of this book. This section helps you to focus your studies before you take the practice tests and to prepare for taking the actual test. After reviewing these competencies, you should make a list of the competency/skill areas for which you feel you need more background or practice and for which you feel less familiar and confident. The two full-length practice exams also should help you get acquainted with the format of the FTCE Elementary Education (K–6) Subject Area Examination. Also, take a look at the glossary of important terms in the back of this book. Then, check the resources you need to start studying in more detail. Study each of the topics covered in the test, starting with the ones you need more time to study according to your diagnostic test results. At the end, you should have studied all areas, both those in which you are familiar and less familiar. Do not leave any topic out and spend sufficient time on each topic.

Setting aside time for your studies before you take the practice tests is very important. You want to have terms, formulas, concepts, and skills fresh in your mind for the practice and actual tests. Select the resources that work best for you to be used during this study time. You might also need a tutor, teacher, mentor, advisor, or a study group for support and extra help. However, you should take into account your preferences and study habits as you set a sound study plan.

After carefully studying for the test, find a quiet place (no phone, cell phone, television, radio, stereo, or other forms of electronic entertainment), take the first practice test, and spend two and one half uninterrupted hours answering the questions. You should probably use a desk for this and avoid any disruption. This gives you an idea on how to time yourself.

Remember that every person is different in terms of timing. You need to know yourself and the speed that is comfortable for you. During the actual test, do not pay attention to what others do. Remember to prepare several number-2 sharpened pencils, and write your answers in the given test answer book for later review. For any questions which require computations, you should write your solution process as you work on the questions as detailed and clearly as possible. These notes are very helpful when you start evaluating your solutions. Check the answers for the first practice test and see whether you had any problems by competency. Are there any major areas of concern or priority? This gives you another opportunity to narrow down and focus your preparation priorities. We recommend that you go back and study everything a bit more, with an emphasis on the areas of need. Once again, after carefully studying for the test, find a quiet place and take the second practice test. Check the answers for the second practice test and, if you need to, study other competencies before taking the actual test.

After these focusing exercises, you should have a better idea of how and when you are ready to take the actual FTCE Elementary Education (K–6) Subject Area Examination.

Check the Resources You Need

After you set and focus your preparation priorities, you are ready to find the resources you need. Think about your coursework background and find any college textbooks; Web links; class notes; videos; publications from local, state, and national professional organizations; or other material that might help you study for the test. We have included a list of resources in this book that you can use to help with this selection process. You should organize the resources you have in terms of your preparation priorities and use them in that order. Remember to review all the topics—even those you feel you know well.

Refer to the Solution Manual

An answer/explanation section is provided at the end of each practice test. Use this section to help you understand possible solutions and improve your test-taking ability. You should not take more than one practice exam per day. You need some time in between taking the exams to review your answers and possibly to readdress your study priorities.

Get R-E-A-D-Y before the Test!

The following are some ideas to keep in mind before you take the test:

- **R**est and sleep well several days before the test. You will not do as well if you are not rested and feel tired or tense.
- **E**at well. A nutritious and balanced breakfast and lunch (if the test is taken in the afternoon) can go a long way. If you will be taking examinations during both the morning and afternoon testing sessions, you might want to bring along something to eat during the break. Food is not allowed in the testing room.
- **A**ccessories you need for the test:

    Your admission ticket.

    Proper identification. Whether you are taking a paper-based or computer-based test, you must bring two valid and unexpired forms of identification that are printed in English. The first identification must be government issued and must have a clear photograph and your signature, such as a driver's license, state-issued identification card, United States military ID (with visible signature), or passport. The second identification, which you may be asked to produce, must have either a photo or a signature, such as a Social Security card or a student ID. If you do not have proper identification, you will not be permitted to test.

    Several number-2 sharpened pencils if you are taking a paper-based test.

- **D**ress comfortably and in layers so you can adapt to the testing room conditions. It is better to wear soft-soled shoes so that you do not disturb others if you need to leave your seat.
- **Y**ou need to relax and get **R-E-A-D-Y**. Leave plenty of time to get to the test session without pressure or anxiety. That way, you will arrive on time and be as relaxed as possible and ready to begin the test.

Get Double R-E-A-D-Y during the Test!

The following are some additional ideas to keep in mind during the test:

- **R**ead and review the directions carefully (at least twice). Make sure that you understand and follow the instructions for the test and for each item of the test. This first step is crucial. When answering multiple-choice questions, make sure that you read all of the answer choices before choosing an answer. Remember that you are selecting the best possible answer out of four choices.
- For computational problems: **E**stimate and use common sense before calculating problems; this should give you a rough idea of what the answer should be before you start to work on the problem. You can also use your estimate to check your final answer and calculation errors. Sometimes, with multiple-choice items, you can eliminate one or two of the choices that contain errors or don't make sense and then choose the best answer out of the remaining choices. You should mark an answer to the multiple-choice items, even if you are not sure of the correct answer. Your score is not reduced because of wrong answers. However, you should attempt to figure out the best answer before guessing.

- Always refer to the original directions and context of the problem, especially when an answer doesn't make sense. You might have missed something about the problem setting. The test booklet contains general directions for the examination as a whole, and specific directions for the individual questions and, in some cases, group of questions. If you do not understand a specific direction, raise your hand and ask the test administrator.

- Double-check your answer choice. Don't skip steps. Work carefully and avoid accidental computational or reasoning errors. Check the accuracy of your answers for the multiple-choice items, and make sure that they were marked appropriately. However, don't overdo your checking. Remember to time and pace yourself. Do not rush to finish.

- You can do it! You are **R-E-A-D-Y**!

Language Arts and Reading

1 Ⓐ Ⓑ Ⓒ Ⓓ
2 Ⓐ Ⓑ Ⓒ Ⓓ
3 Ⓐ Ⓑ Ⓒ Ⓓ
4 Ⓐ Ⓑ Ⓒ Ⓓ
5 Ⓐ Ⓑ Ⓒ Ⓓ

6 Ⓐ Ⓑ Ⓒ Ⓓ
7 Ⓐ Ⓑ Ⓒ Ⓓ
8 Ⓐ Ⓑ Ⓒ Ⓓ
9 Ⓐ Ⓑ Ⓒ Ⓓ
10 Ⓐ Ⓑ Ⓒ Ⓓ

11 Ⓐ Ⓑ Ⓒ Ⓓ
12 Ⓐ Ⓑ Ⓒ Ⓓ
13 Ⓐ Ⓑ Ⓒ Ⓓ
14 Ⓐ Ⓑ Ⓒ Ⓓ
15 Ⓐ Ⓑ Ⓒ Ⓓ

16 Ⓐ Ⓑ Ⓒ Ⓓ
17 Ⓐ Ⓑ Ⓒ Ⓓ
18 Ⓐ Ⓑ Ⓒ Ⓓ
19 Ⓐ Ⓑ Ⓒ Ⓓ
20 Ⓐ Ⓑ Ⓒ Ⓓ

21 Ⓐ Ⓑ Ⓒ Ⓓ
22 Ⓐ Ⓑ Ⓒ Ⓓ
23 Ⓐ Ⓑ Ⓒ Ⓓ

Social Science

1 Ⓐ Ⓑ Ⓒ Ⓓ
2 Ⓐ Ⓑ Ⓒ Ⓓ
3 Ⓐ Ⓑ Ⓒ Ⓓ
4 Ⓐ Ⓑ Ⓒ Ⓓ
5 Ⓐ Ⓑ Ⓒ Ⓓ

6 Ⓐ Ⓑ Ⓒ Ⓓ
7 Ⓐ Ⓑ Ⓒ Ⓓ
8 Ⓐ Ⓑ Ⓒ Ⓓ
9 Ⓐ Ⓑ Ⓒ Ⓓ
10 Ⓐ Ⓑ Ⓒ Ⓓ

11 Ⓐ Ⓑ Ⓒ Ⓓ
12 Ⓐ Ⓑ Ⓒ Ⓓ
13 Ⓐ Ⓑ Ⓒ Ⓓ
14 Ⓐ Ⓑ Ⓒ Ⓓ
15 Ⓐ Ⓑ Ⓒ Ⓓ

16 Ⓐ Ⓑ Ⓒ Ⓓ
17 Ⓐ Ⓑ Ⓒ Ⓓ
18 Ⓐ Ⓑ Ⓒ Ⓓ
19 Ⓐ Ⓑ Ⓒ Ⓓ
20 Ⓐ Ⓑ Ⓒ Ⓓ

21 Ⓐ Ⓑ Ⓒ Ⓓ

Music, Visual Arts, Physical Education, and Health

1 Ⓐ Ⓑ Ⓒ Ⓓ
2 Ⓐ Ⓑ Ⓒ Ⓓ
3 Ⓐ Ⓑ Ⓒ Ⓓ
4 Ⓐ Ⓑ Ⓒ Ⓓ
5 Ⓐ Ⓑ Ⓒ Ⓓ

6 Ⓐ Ⓑ Ⓒ Ⓓ
7 Ⓐ Ⓑ Ⓒ Ⓓ
8 Ⓐ Ⓑ Ⓒ Ⓓ
9 Ⓐ Ⓑ Ⓒ Ⓓ
10 Ⓐ Ⓑ Ⓒ Ⓓ

11 Ⓐ Ⓑ Ⓒ Ⓓ
12 Ⓐ Ⓑ Ⓒ Ⓓ
13 Ⓐ Ⓑ Ⓒ Ⓓ
14 Ⓐ Ⓑ Ⓒ Ⓓ
15 Ⓐ Ⓑ Ⓒ Ⓓ

16 Ⓐ Ⓑ Ⓒ Ⓓ
17 Ⓐ Ⓑ Ⓒ Ⓓ
18 Ⓐ Ⓑ Ⓒ Ⓓ
19 Ⓐ Ⓑ Ⓒ Ⓓ
20 Ⓐ Ⓑ Ⓒ Ⓓ

21 Ⓐ Ⓑ Ⓒ Ⓓ
22 Ⓐ Ⓑ Ⓒ Ⓓ

Science and Technology	Mathematics
1 Ⓐ Ⓑ Ⓒ Ⓓ	1 Ⓐ Ⓑ Ⓒ Ⓓ
2 Ⓐ Ⓑ Ⓒ Ⓓ	2 Ⓐ Ⓑ Ⓒ Ⓓ
3 Ⓐ Ⓑ Ⓒ Ⓓ	3 Ⓐ Ⓑ Ⓒ Ⓓ
4 Ⓐ Ⓑ Ⓒ Ⓓ	4 Ⓐ Ⓑ Ⓒ Ⓓ
5 Ⓐ Ⓑ Ⓒ Ⓓ	5 Ⓐ Ⓑ Ⓒ Ⓓ
6 Ⓐ Ⓑ Ⓒ Ⓓ	6 Ⓐ Ⓑ Ⓒ Ⓓ
7 Ⓐ Ⓑ Ⓒ Ⓓ	7 Ⓐ Ⓑ Ⓒ Ⓓ
8 Ⓐ Ⓑ Ⓒ Ⓓ	8 Ⓐ Ⓑ Ⓒ Ⓓ
9 Ⓐ Ⓑ Ⓒ Ⓓ	9 Ⓐ Ⓑ Ⓒ Ⓓ
10 Ⓐ Ⓑ Ⓒ Ⓓ	10 Ⓐ Ⓑ Ⓒ Ⓓ
11 Ⓐ Ⓑ Ⓒ Ⓓ	11 Ⓐ Ⓑ Ⓒ Ⓓ
12 Ⓐ Ⓑ Ⓒ Ⓓ	12 Ⓐ Ⓑ Ⓒ Ⓓ
13 Ⓐ Ⓑ Ⓒ Ⓓ	13 Ⓐ Ⓑ Ⓒ Ⓓ
14 Ⓐ Ⓑ Ⓒ Ⓓ	14 Ⓐ Ⓑ Ⓒ Ⓓ
15 Ⓐ Ⓑ Ⓒ Ⓓ	15 Ⓐ Ⓑ Ⓒ Ⓓ
16 Ⓐ Ⓑ Ⓒ Ⓓ	16 Ⓐ Ⓑ Ⓒ Ⓓ
17 Ⓐ Ⓑ Ⓒ Ⓓ	17 Ⓐ Ⓑ Ⓒ Ⓓ
18 Ⓐ Ⓑ Ⓒ Ⓓ	18 Ⓐ Ⓑ Ⓒ Ⓓ
19 Ⓐ Ⓑ Ⓒ Ⓓ	19 Ⓐ Ⓑ Ⓒ Ⓓ
20 Ⓐ Ⓑ Ⓒ Ⓓ	20 Ⓐ Ⓑ Ⓒ Ⓓ
21 Ⓐ Ⓑ Ⓒ Ⓓ	21 Ⓐ Ⓑ Ⓒ Ⓓ
22 Ⓐ Ⓑ Ⓒ Ⓓ	22 Ⓐ Ⓑ Ⓒ Ⓓ
23 Ⓐ Ⓑ Ⓒ Ⓓ	23 Ⓐ Ⓑ Ⓒ Ⓓ

The test that follows is approximately half the length of the regular FTCE: Elementary Education (K–6) Subject Area Examination. Allow yourself 1 hour and 15 minutes to complete the diagnostic test. Record your answers on the Diagnostic Test Answer Sheet. When you are finished, check your answers. The answer key will give you the competency number to which the question is related.

Language Arts and Reading

1. Which of the following is a transition word a student should use when writing about cause and effect?

   A. because
   B. and
   C. but
   D. or

2. At the beginning of the school year, Leila, a first-grade student, made approximations while reading. However, by the middle of the year, she was pointing to each word on the page as she read each book. What concept of print is Leila exhibiting?

   A. directionality
   B. voice-to-print match
   C. return sweep
   D. sight word recognition

3. Which of the following would be considered a primary source?

   A. first hand testimony
   B. a model created to depict a historical event
   C. a timeline of events in a textbook
   D. a website

4. A hyperbole is an exaggerated statement used for effect and is not meant to be taken literally. Which of the following is a hyperbole?

   A. She must have weighed 1,000 pounds!
   B. The bar of chocolate was humongous!
   C. She ran as fast as a cheetah.
   D. Her nose was red like a cherry.

5. Where can you easily access a wide array of multicultural literature, free of charge, for use in your elementary classroom?

   A. school library
   B. college library
   C. Library of Congress
   D. the Internet

6. Knowledge of individual words in sentences, syllables, onset-rime segments and the awareness of individual phonemes in words is known as

   A. phonics.
   B. phonological awareness.
   C. phoneme segmentation.
   D. phoneme manipulation.

7. During what stage of the writing process do students typically correct their writing for mechanical and spelling errors?

   A. brainstorm
   B. revision
   C. edit
   D. pre-write

8. During what stage of reading have students mastered basic concepts of print and are beginning to use various strategies for problem solving in reading?

   A. pre-reading
   B. fluent
   C. early
   D. emergent

9. What cueing system focuses on meaning that is associated with language through prior knowledge and experience?

   A. graphophonemic
   B. semantic
   C. visual
   D. auditory

10. A fable, a category of folklore, is defined as

    A. a story with a moral.
    B. a story with historical references.
    C. a story that is realistic and could happen.
    D. a poem.

11. What question might you ask to assist a student in using the semantic cueing system?

    A. Does that look right?
    B. Does that sound right?
    C. Does that make sense?
    D. What were you thinking?

12. When a student attempts to synthesize what has been read, they are

    A. making generalizations.
    B. using old ideas to create new ones.
    C. predicting and drawing conclusions.
    D. all of the above.

13. The peak of a story is known as the

    A. resolution.
    B. conclusion.
    C. climax.
    D. plot.

14. In the classic folklore story, *The Three Billy Goats Gruff*, the goats trip-trap, trip-trap over the bridge. What literary device describes the use of the words, trip-trap?

    A. irony
    B. metaphor
    C. onomatopoeia
    D. simile

15. The purpose of anecdotal notes is

    A. to make note of everything a student is doing wrong.
    B. to observe students while they work and record the observations for later study.
    C. to make notes of student work and stick strictly to your lesson plan regardless of these notes.
    D. none of the above.

16. The National Reading Panel identified five critical areas for success in reading. Which of the following is NOT one of the five critical areas?

    A. comprehension
    B. fluency
    C. motivation
    D. phonics

17. A kindergarten teacher is modeling how words on a page are read from left to right and top to bottom, using a pointer and a big book. What is the focus of this lesson?

    A. fluency
    B. concepts of print
    C. the advantages of using quality children's literature
    D. how to use a pointer

18. In order to communicate in writing, penmanship must be legible. Which of the following contributes to legible handwriting?

    A. spacing
    B. letter formation
    C. letter alignment
    D. all of the above

19. What stage of the writing process could be enhanced by six trait writing lessons?

    A. brainstorm
    B. revision
    C. edit
    D. all of the above

20. The Florida Comprehensive Assessment Test (FCAT) is a(n)

    A. norm-referenced test.
    B. informal reading inventory.
    C. performance based assessment.
    D. criterion-referenced test.

21. An example of visual media is

    A. an online article.
    B. a journal.
    C. the newspaper.
    D. an atlas.

22. Questioning and retelling enhance communication skills among students in the classroom. What critical reading skill is most enhanced by these strategies?

    A. fluency
    B. comprehension
    C. word recognition
    D. phonics

23. Which of the following is a web-based activity that could take place in the classroom?

    A. blog
    B. online newsletter
    C. Wiki page
    D. all of the above

Social Science

1. Which war was an extension of the European Seven Years War and was a battle over colonial territory and wealth by the French and the English?

   A. The French and Native American War
   B. The French and Indian War
   C. The French and English War
   D. The War of the Roses

2. Human systems refers to what essential element of teaching geography?

   A. location
   B. regions
   C. people
   D. processes that shape the Earth

3. How many voyages did Columbus make in an effort to find a route to the East?

   A. 1
   B. 2
   C. 3
   D. 4

4. The Civil War was the conflict that ended slavery in this country. What document abolished slavery when it was signed by President Lincoln in 1862?

   A. Louisiana Purchase
   B. Magna Carta
   C. Emancipation Proclamation
   D. Treaty of Paris

5. The use of what teaching strategy can assist students in synthesizing and summarizing informational text?

   A. graphic organizers
   B. fill-in-the-blank tests
   C. independent worksheets
   D. silent reading with no group discussion

6. An absolute location is defined as

   A. a formal location where street names or coordinates are used to describe the locality.
   B. an informal location.
   C. a location where local landmarks are used to describe the place.
   D. a difficult location to access.

7. What is the name of the revolution that is defined as the transition from manual labor to machine?

   A. American Revolution
   B. European Revolution
   C. Colonial Revolution
   D. Industrial Revolution

8. Human beings tend to live in environments that meet their needs. Which essential element of geography refers to the interaction between people and their surroundings?

   A. Human Systems
   B. Processes that shape the Earth
   C. World in Spatial terms
   D. Environment and Society

9. What historic document was approved by the Second Continental Congress and laid the foundation for a new government in America?

   A. Poor Richard's Almanac
   B. Preamble to the Constitution
   C. Declaration of Independence
   D. Emancipation Proclamation

10. What representation of the Earth is said to be most accurate?

   A. relief map
   B. globe
   C. thematic map
   D. political map

11. The three branches of government in the United States provide for a system of checks and balances. The three branches are:

    A. congress, president, and supreme court.
    B. legislative, judicial, and executive.
    C. first, second, and third.
    D. electorate, electoral college, and state representatives.

12. Small representations, usually shapes and pictures, of real things on a map are known as

    A. symbols.
    B. a legend.
    C. cartographers.
    D. keys.

13. When one company or institution has exclusive control of a particular good or service in a market, this is known as

    A. oligopoly.
    B. monopoly.
    C. roly-poly.
    D. capitalism.

14. How many electoral votes are required to win the presidency?

    A. 250
    B. 260
    C. 270
    D. 240

15. Electors are representatives of the people that actually elect the president and vice president. As of 2009, how many electors are there in the United States of America?

    A. 535
    B. 536
    C. 537
    D. 538

16. Policies that aid in governmental control of the economy are known as

    A. financial policy.
    B. fiscal policy.
    C. inflation policy.
    D. trade policy.

17. What article of the Constitution established the judicial branch of government in the United States of America?

    A. I
    B. II
    C. III
    D. V

18. Which of the following people advises the President on matters of foreign policy?

    A. Secretary of State
    B. Secretary of the Treasury
    C. Press Secretary
    D. First Lady

19. The Supreme Court is the highest court of appeals in the United States. One of its most important powers is the power of

    A. legislative review.
    B. judicial review.
    C. executive review.
    D. legal review.

20. What financial institution is owned, controlled, and operated by its members?

    A. federal reserve banks
    B. credit unions
    C. stock market
    D. Wall Street

21. Consumer decision making has a large effect on the supply and demand of products in this country and all over the world, therefore teaching our youth _____ skills is vital.

    A. fiscal policy
    B. economic reasoning
    C. global responsibility
    D. home economics

Music, Visual Arts, Physical Education, and Health

1. The color red orange is considered a

   A. saturated color.
   B. secondary color.
   C. primary color.
   D. tertiary color.

2. You require your students to acquire information from the Internet in your classroom. Some of your students will gather some information at home. Which of the following guidelines would NOT be appropriate to suggest to parents for Internet safety at home?

   A. Setting time limits
   B. Placing the computer in the child's bedroom
   C. Being aware of the child's login name and password
   D. Encouraging children to not give out personal information.

3. The music teacher is planning a lesson reinforcing melodic intervals by using Curwen hand signs. What type of skill is she most likely emphasizing?

   A. ability to match pitch
   B. development of vocal range
   C. development of rhythm
   D. use of good posture

4. The Centers for Disease Control recommends that children engage in how many minutes of physical activity each day?

   A. 30 minutes
   B. 45 minutes
   C. 60 minutes
   D. 90 minutes

5. Which of the following involves the volume of a sound or note?

   A. timbre
   B. dynamics
   C. tune
   D. form

6. Which of the following is NOT a category of social and emotional growth and development?

   A. Self-concept
   B. Character development
   C. Fair Play
   D. Physical growth

7. Which of the following is involved when larger periods of time are constructed from smaller rhythmic units added at the end of the previous unit?

   A. additive rhythm
   B. divisive rhythm
   C. harmonic rhythm
   D. dynamic rhythm

8. A music teacher used the following assessment activity during a recorder unit.

   The students evaluated a peer's performance of a particular song on accuracy of notes, rhythms, and fingering. The student evaluating others had a form to fill out during the performance and then wrote a short paragraph about the student's performance, including two strengths, two weaknesses, and two suggestions of how to improve. The teacher assessed the written paragraph.

   This is an example of

   A. rubric assessment.
   B. traditional assessment.
   C. authentic assessment.
   D. portfolio assessment.

9. Which of the following is NOT an example of bone strengthening activity?

   A. Running
   B. Lifting weights
   C. Swimming
   D. Jumping Rope

10. Musical, dance, and dramatic presentation are examples of

    A. teacher-centered tasks.
    B. performance-based tasks.
    C. selected-response tasks.
    D. constructed-response tasks.

11. Fill in the blank: _____ refers to how a person feels about him/herself.

   A. Self-worth
   B. Self-esteem
   C. Self-reliance
   D. Self-concept

12. The changes in music style during this era were not uniform across the board.

   A. Eighteenth century
   B. Medieval
   C. Renaissance
   D. Baroque

13. This Renaissance period music genre generally refers to unaccompanied religious texts set to music.

   A. madrigal
   B. chorale
   C. motet
   D. cantata

14. In art, the relative darkness or lightness of a color is

   A. value.
   B. texture.
   C. line.
   D. shape.

15. The nutritional category of Milk includes which of the following foods?

   A. Yogurt
   B. Beans
   C. Asparagus
   D. Beef

16. Complete the following sentence: The _____ domain deals with how one deals with emotions.

   A. Cognitive
   B. Psychomotor
   C. Affective
   D. Reactive

17. Which of the following is a nonlocomotor skill?

   A. Walking
   B. Spinning around
   C. Galloping
   D. Running

18. Which of the following is NOT a symptom of marijuana abuse?

   A. Rapid talking
   B. Dilated pupils
   C. Sleepiness
   D. Nose bleeds

19. This period was known for its intricate ornamentation.

   A. Baroque
   B. Medieval
   C. Renaissance
   D. Classical

20. A teacher had the students consider a work of art using the following areas: communication of a unique voice, appropriate use of style to express the purpose of the work of art, efforts to make the piece memorable and distinctive, and demonstration of appropriate use of technical elements. Which of the following areas is the teacher most likely emphasizing?

   A. knowledge of the principles presented in a work of art
   B. analytical skills to judge a work of art
   C. understanding of the principles presented in a work of art
   D. planning skills to generate a work of art

21. Fill in the blank: _____ is the impact of a continually changing environment on the body.

   A. Physical fitness
   B. Self-esteem
   C. Stress
   D. Conflict resolution

22. Separating material into component parts is which level of Bloom's Taxonomy?

   A. Analysis
   B. Evaluation
   C. Synthesis
   D. Application

Science and Technology

1. What are the names for the parts of the atom located inside the nucleus?

   A. molecules and protons
   B. electrons and protons
   C. electrons and neutrons
   D. protons and neutrons

2. Cells in which a nucleus exists are called _____.

   A. Prokaryotic cells
   B. Eukaryotic cells
   C. Nucleolus
   D. Ribosomes

3. A computer-based application used to facilitate the preparation, manipulation, modification, and arrangement of electronically developed text, tables, and images for reports and documents is called a

   A. social network.
   B. word processor.
   C. spreadsheet.
   D. data base.

4. What is the Earth's pull of gravity on an object called?

   A. mass
   B. weight
   C. volume
   D. density

5. Complete the sentence: The _____ is the innermost part of the earth and is solid.

   A. Outer core
   B. Mantle
   C. Crust
   D. Inner core

6. Which is the most specific level of taxonomy?

   A. Species
   B. Genus
   C. Domain
   D. Kingdom

7. Which of the following is NOT a good laboratory procedure?

   A. Washing hands frequently
   B. Eating in the laboratory
   C. Disposing of chemicals properly
   D. Wearing gloves

8. Who was the first American to be launched into space?

   A. John Glenn
   B. Neil Armstrong
   C. Alan Shepard
   D. Yuri Gagarin

9. What is the most effective method of controlling viruses?

   A. Antibiotics
   B. Radiation
   C. Balanced diet
   D. Vaccination

10. Which of the following is not considered a geologic formation?

    A. Volcanoes
    B. Earthquakes
    C. Canyons
    D. Mountains

11. A sound wave is produced by

    A. sonar.
    B. pitch.
    C. acoustic.
    D. vibrations.

12. Complete the sentence: _____ reproduction requires only one parent.

    A. Asexual
    B. Nonsexual
    C. Conjugation
    D. Sexual

13. A measure related to the average kinetic energy of the molecules of a substance is called

A. mechanical force.
B. contact force.
C. temperature.
D. heat.

14. Instruments that can be used to measure absorbance spectrum of a liquid are called

A. pressure sensors.
B. temperature probes.
C. spectrometers.
D. barometers.

15. Complete the sentence: _____ is/are the horizontal movement of air.

A. Hurricanes
B. Clouds
C. Wind
D. Tornadoes

16. This type of force requires physical contact and interaction between objects.

A. at-a-distance forces
B. contact forces
C. electrical forces
D. magnetic forces

17. Complete the sentence: _____ are the ways in which scientists answer questions and solve problems systematically.

A. Laboratories
B. Scientific methods
C. Controlled experiments
D. Hypotheses

18. Which of the following occurs when two plates intersect and force each other upward?

A. Earthquakes
B. Canyons
C. Mountains
D. Volcanoes

19. In an experiment, students are starting to write statements about the relationships among the variables that they intend to study. They are most likely involved with developing their

A. hypotheses.
B. theory.
C. laws.
D. identification of variables.

20. Which of the following forces is not considered an at-a-distance force?

A. frictional force
B. gravitational force
C. electrical force
D. nuclear force

21. Which one of the following is the correct order of methodology for an experiment?

1. Plan a controlled experiment

2. Revisit the hypothesis to answer question

3. Analyze data and draw conclusions

4. Identify a research question

5. Formulate a hypothesis

6. Collect data

A. 5, 4, 1, 6, 2, 3
B. 4, 5, 1, 6, 2, 3
C. 5, 4, 1, 6, 3, 2
D. 4, 5, 1, 6, 3, 2

22. Animals that live in water or on land in different stages of their lives are called:

A. Reptiles
B. Birds
C. Amphibians
D. Worms

23. Complete the sentence: _____ rock is formed from the cooling of magma.

A. Metamorphic
B. Sedimentary
C. Igneous
D. Compressed

Mathematics

1. A student used five blocks as part of an activity dealing with numeration. What type of representation model is the student using?

   A. word name
   B. standard numeral
   C. concrete model
   D. pictorial model

2. Find the next term in the pattern 2, 6, 18, 54,...

   A. 58
   B. 72
   C. 108
   D. 162

3. A garden is triangular and has side lengths of 3 feet, 5 feet, and 6 feet. Each side of the triangle is doubled. The perimeter of the garden has increased by how many times?

   A. 2 times
   B. 3 times
   C. 4 times
   D. 8 times

4. A bar graph using horizontal rectangular bars to show the frequency of each value involves the following representation model or models.

   A. pictorial and abstract
   B. concrete and abstract
   C. pictorial only
   D. abstract only

Use the data set that follows to answer questions 5–8.

The students in a class received the following scores in a test worth 100 points:

80, 23, 55, 58, 45, 32, 40, 55, 50

5. Find the mean of the data set (if necessary, round to the nearest whole number).

   A. 49
   B. 50
   C. 44
   D. 57

6. Find the median of the data set.

   A. 55
   B. 50
   C. 49
   D. 57

7. Find the range of the data set (round to the nearest one).

   A. 57
   B. 49
   C. 50
   D. 55

8. Find the mode of the data set.

   A. 50
   B. 49
   C. 1
   D. 55

9. Which angle in the following figure is complementary to angle ABD?

   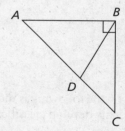

   A. Angle ABC
   B. Angle DAB
   C. Angle CBD
   D. Angle ACB

10. The number 3^{-2} is equal to

   A. 9
   B. $\frac{2}{3}$
   C. -9
   D. $\frac{1}{9}$

11. A farmer sells his crop for $5 a bushel at the farmer's market. There is a fee of $50 to have a booth at the market. How much profit will the farmer make if he sells *b* bushels at the market?

   A. 5*b* dollars
   B. 5*b* − 50 dollars
   C. 5*b* + 50 dollars
   D. 50 dollars

12. Cheyenne is 40 inches tall. She has a shadow that is 36 inches long. A tree in Cheyenne's backyard is 10 feet tall. How long will the tree's shadow be?

   A. 6 feet
   B. 9 feet
   C. 14 feet
   D. 16 feet

13. The number 465^0 is equal to

   A. 465
   B. 1
   C. 0
   D. −465

14. How many edges does a cube have?

   A. 4
   B. 6
   C. 8
   D. 12

15. Which one of the following is most appropriate to help students develop classification skills?

   A. Cuisenaire rods
   B. Algebra tiles
   C. Pattern blocks
   D. Fraction tiles

16. Which of the following statements is true?

   A. An acute triangle can be an isosceles triangle.
   B. An obtuse triangle can be an equilateral triangle.
   C. A right triangle can be an obtuse triangle.
   D. An equilateral triangle can be a scalene triangle.

17. What is the value of $2^{-6} \cdot -8$?

   A. 8
   B. $\frac{1}{8}$
   C. −8
   D. $-\frac{1}{8}$

18. Identify the coordinates of point R in the figure shown.

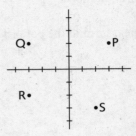

   A. (3, 2)
   B. (2, 3)
   C. (−3, −2)
   D. (−2, −3)

19. Which one of the following is least appropriate to help students develop area ideas?

   A. Geoboard
   B. Two-color chips
   C. Color tiles
   D. Pattern blocks

20. Simplify the following expression:
$30^2 - 60 \div 12 \cdot \left(\frac{1}{5} - 5^{-2}\right) \cdot 15 + 78.$

   A. 16,875.25
   B. −132
   C. 978.0375
   D. 139.875

21. Select the unit of measure that is most appropriate for the length of a pencil.

   A. Inches
   B. Feet
   C. Yards
   D. Meters

22. Solve for x: $3x - 4 + x = x + 8 + 3x - 2x$

    A. $x = 2$

    B. $x = 4$

    C. $x = 6$

    D. $x = 7$

23. Find the area of a circle with a diameter of 12 inches.

    A. 12π in^2

    B. 6π in^2

    C. 36π in^2

    D. 144π in^2

Diagnostic Test Answers

Language Arts and Reading

1. **A.** Competency 3.
2. **B.** Competency 1.
3. **A.** Competency 6.
4. **A.** Competency 2.
5. **A.** Competency 2.
6. **B.** Competency 1.
7. **C.** Competency 3.
8. **C.** Competency 1.
9. **B.** Competency 1.
10. **A.** Competency 2.
11. **C.** Competency 4.
12. **D.** Competency 1.

13. **C.** Competency 2.
14. **C.** Competency 2.
15. **B.** Competency 4.
16. **C.** Competency 1.
17. **B.** Competency 4.
18. **D.** Competency 5.
19. **D.** Competency 2.
20. **D.** Competency 4.
21. **A.** Competency 6.
22. **B.** Competency 5.
23. **D.** Competency 6.

Social Science

1. **B.** Competency 7.
2. **C.** Competency 8.
3. **D.** Competency 7.
4. **C.** Competency 7.
5. **A.** Competency 11.
6. **A.** Competency 8.
7. **D.** Competency 7.
8. **D.** Competency 8.
9. **C.** Competency 7.
10. **B.** Competency 8.
11. **B.** Competency 9.

12. **A.** Competency 8.
13. **B.** Competency 10.
14. **C.** Competency 9.
15. **D.** Competency 9.
16. **B.** Competency 10.
17. **C.** Competency 9.
18. **A.** Competency 9.
19. **B.** Competency 10.
20. **B.** Competency 10.
21. **B.** Competency 10.

Music, Visual Arts, Physical Education, and Health

1. **D.** Competency 13.
2. **B.** Competency 19.
3. **A.** Competency 12.
4. **C.** Competency 17.
5. **B.** Competency 13.
6. **D.** Competency 18.
7. **A.** Competency 12.
8. **C.** Competency 16.
9. **C.** Competency 17.
10. **B.** Competency 16.
11. **B.** Competency 18.
12. **C.** Competency 14.
13. **C.** Competency 12.
14. **A.** Competency 13.
15. **A.** Competency 17.
16. **C.** Competency 20.
17. **B.** Competency 18.
18. **D.** Competency 19.
19. **A.** Competency 14.
20. **B.** Competency 15.
21. **C.** Competency 18.
22. **A.** Competency 20.

Science and Technology

1. **D.** Competency 21.
2. **B.** Competency 24.
3. **B.** Competency 26.
4. **B.** Competency 21.
5. **D.** Competency 23.
6. **A.** Competency 24.
7. **B.** Competency 25.
8. **C.** Competency 23.
9. **D.** Competency 24.
10. **B.** Competency 23.
11. **D.** Competency 22.
12. **A.** Competency 24.
13. **C.** Competency 22.
14. **C.** Competency 26.
15. **C.** Competency 23.
16. **B.** Competency 22.
17. **B.** Competency 25.
18. **C.** Competency 23.
19. **A.** Competency 27.
20. **A.** Competency 22.
21. **D.** Competency 27.
22. **C.** Competency 24.
23. **C.** Competency 23.

Mathematics

1. **C.** Competency 28.
2. **D.** Competency 30.
3. **A.** Competency 29.
4. **A.** Competency 28.
5. **A.** Competency 31.
6. **B.** Competency 31.
7. **A.** Competency 31.
8. **D.** Competency 31.
9. **C.** Competency 29.
10. **D.** Competency 28.
11. **B.** Competency 30.
12. **B.** Competency 29.

13. **B.** Competency 28.
14. **D.** Competency 29.
15. **C.** Competency 32.
16. **A.** Competency 29.
17. **D.** Competency 28.
18. **C.** Competency 29.
19. **B.** Competency 32.
20. **C.** Competency 28.
21. **A.** Competency 29.
22. **C.** Competency 30.
23. **C.** Competency 29.

Diagnostic Test Solutions

Language Arts and Reading

1. **A.** Competency 3. A transition word a student should use when writing about cause and effect is *because*.

2. **B.** Competency 1. Voice-to-print match also known as one-to-one correspondence shows that Sheila now understands the concept of a word and word boundaries.

3. **A.** Competency 6. A primary source is a document or piece of work, which was actually written, recorded, or created during the specific time under study.

4. **A.** Competency 2. A hyperbole is an exaggerated statement used for effect and is not meant to be taken literally.

5. **A.** Competency 2. School libraries should contain a wide variety of multicultural children's literature, nonfiction resources, and various genres.

6. **B.** Competency 1. Knowledge of individual words in sentences, syllables, onset-rime segments and the awareness of individual phonemes in words is known as phonological awareness.

7. **C.** Competency 3. The teacher, if truly focusing on the content, is encouraging her students to revise and improve upon what has been written and is not yet concerned with editing for errors.

8. **C.** Competency 1. During the early stage of reading students have typically mastered basic concepts of print and are beginning to use various strategies for problem solving in reading.

9. **B.** Competency 1. The semantic cueing system focuses on meaning that is associated with language through prior knowledge and experience.

10. **A.** Competency 2. A fable is a story with a moral.

11. **C.** Competency 4. The semantic cueing system focuses on meaning (making sense) that is associated with language through prior knowledge and experience.

12. **D.** Competency 1. When students attempt to synthesize what has been read, they are making generalizations, using old ideas to create new ones, and predicting and drawing conclusions.

13. **C.** Competency 2. The climax is the highest point of interest or suspense in a story.

14. **C.** Competency 2. Onomatopoeia are words whose sound is imitative of the sound of the noise and/or action designated.

15. **B.** Competency 4. The purposes of anecdotal notes are to observe students while they work and record the observations for later study.

16. **C.** Competency 1. Phonological awareness, phonics, vocabulary, fluency, and comprehension are the five critical components to reading success.

17. **B.** Competency 4. Concepts of print includes that print conveys meaning, directionality (left to right progression, top to bottom), concept of a word (word boundaries), one-to-one correspondence, letter knowledge, phonemic awareness, and literacy language (author, illustrations, title, and so on).

18. **D.** Competency 5. Line quality (consistency of pencil strokes), spacing, letter formation, and letter alignment are all factors that impact legible handwriting.

19. **D.** Competency 2. The six trait writing lessons can enhance brainstorming, revision, and editing.

20. **D.** Competency 4. Criterion-referenced tests are assessment instruments that assess the point at which the student has achieved mastery. These tests (FCAT) enable educators in determining whether or not a student has met a predetermined goal.

21. **A.** Competency 6. Visual media is non-print media.

22. **B.** Competency 5. Comprehension, listening, and speaking skills are all enhanced by questioning and retelling.

23. **D.** Competency 6. Blogs are user-friendly web pages that allow students to post and comment on their work. Wiki pages are "mini web pages" that provide collaborative opportunities to post, add, and edit a variety of content related to a specific topic of study or group project. Online newsletters (created by teachers and/or students) could be links on a teacher's classroom web pages used to inform parents of the learning taking place in the classroom.

Social Science

1. **B.** Competency 7. The French and Indian War (1754–1763), which was an extension of the European Seven Years War, was a battle over colonial territory and wealth by the French and the English. This war resulted in effectively ending French cultural and political influence in North America. In their victory, England gained massive amounts of land but also weakened their rapport with the Native Americans. In sum, although the war strengthened England's hold on the colonies, it also worsened their relationship, which inevitably led to the Revolutionary War.

2. **C.** Competency 8. Human systems are people or inhabitants.

3. **D.** Competency 7. Columbus made four voyages in an effort to find a route to the East. During his expeditions he discovered the Bahamas, Hispaniola, Cuba, Dominica, Guadeloupe, Jamaica, Central America, and South America. As illustrations and historical accounts depict, he was greeted by Native Americans who had settled the land prior to his arrival. The Vikings also had explored the area as well.

4. **C.** Competency 7. Abraham Lincoln implemented and signed the Emancipation Proclamation in 1862.

5. **A.** Competency 11. Using graphic organizers can assist students in synthesizing and summarizing informational text.

6. **A.** Competency 8. An absolute location is defined as a formal location where street names or coordinates are used to describe the locality.

7. **D.** Competency 7. The Industrial Revolution is defined as the transition from manual labor to machine.

8. **D.** Competency 8. Environment and Society is the essential element of geography that refers to the interaction between people and their surroundings.

9. **C.** Competency 7. The Declaration of Independence was the historical document approved by the Second Continental Congress, which laid the foundation for the foundation for a new government in America.

10. **B.** Competency 8. A globe, which is a small-scale model, is said to be the most accurate representation of the Earth.

11. **B.** Competency 9. The three branches of government are legislative, judicial, and executive.

12. **A.** Competency 8. Symbols are small representations, usually shapes and pictures, of real things on a map.

13. **B.** Competency 10. A monopoly is when one company or institution has exclusive control of a particular good or service in a market.

14. **C.** Competency 9. As of 2009, there are 538 total electoral votes. In order for a candidate to receive the majority and win the presidency, they must have 270 electoral votes.

15. **D.** Competency 9. Electors are a body of elected representatives chosen by the voters in each state. While they are human beings who have their own views on whom they would prefer to become the leader of this country, they pledge in advance to vote according to the wishes of the general public.

16. **B.** Competency 10. Fiscal policies aid in governmental control of the economy.

17. **C.** Competency 9. Article III established the judicial branch of government.

18. **A.** Competency 9. The Secretary of State advises the President on matters of foreign policy.

19. **B.** Competency 10. The Supreme Court's most important power is the power of judicial review.

20. **B.** Competency 10. A credit union is a financial institution that is owned, controlled, and operated by its members.

21. **B.** Competency 10. Economic reasoning is making decisions by comparing costs and benefits. This skill is used daily by American citizens.

Music, Visual Arts, Physical Education, and Health

1. **D.** Competency 13. Primary colors are red, yellow, and blue. Secondary colors are green, orange, and purple. Tertiary colors fall between primary and secondary colors. Compound colors contain a mixture of primary colors. Complementary colors are opposite of each other on the color wheel. Saturated colors are the ones around the color wheel. Red orange falls between primary and secondary colors, which makes it a tertiary color.

2. **B.** Competency 19. Internet safety is an important aspect of safety. Children should be monitored when they are using the Internet. They should have limited time, focused tasks, and parents should be aware of children's login names and passwords. The computer should be placed in a central location, and children should be encouraged not to give out private information through the Internet.

3. **A.** Competency 12. Some effective methods to aid children in developing the ability to match pitch: songs should be sung in appropriate range; simple songs utilizing the childhood chant (so, mi, la) are easy for children to imitate; sing a melodic phrase and ask for the child to follow you; and reinforce melodic intervals by using Curwen hand signs or other indications of high and low.

4. **C.** Competency 17. The CDC recommends children engage in at least 60 minutes of physical activity daily.

5. **B.** Competency 13. Dynamics involves the volume (loudness or softness) of the sound or note.

6. **D.** Competency 18. Social and emotional growth and development can be categorized into six areas, namely communication skills, self-concept, fair play, conflict resolution, character development, and stress management. Physical growth is not an aspect of social and emotional growth and development.

7. **A.** Competency 12. Rhythm is the variation of the length and accentuation of a series of sounds or other events; for example, variations in the length of musical tones indicated by using musical notation involving various types of notes and rests. For instance, a series of strikes on a percussion instrument called rhythmic pattern or drum beat. Divisive rhythms involve dividing a larger period of time into smaller rhythmic units. Additive rhythms are involved when larger periods of time are constructed from smaller rhythmic units added at the end of the previous unit.

8. **C.** Competency 16. Authentic assessment is a form of assessment in which students are asked to perform real-world tasks that demonstrate meaningful application of important concepts and skills.

9. **C.** Competency 17. Bone-strengthening activities generally include impact activities. Running, lifting weights, and jumping rope are all types of bone strengthening activities. Swimming is an aerobic activity.

10. **B.** Competency 16. Performance-based tasks require the actual student performance such as a completed project; musical, dance, or dramatic presentation; or work that demonstrates levels of achievement.

11. **B.** Competency 18. Self-concept is a cognitive aspect of self and generally refers to the system of beliefs, attitudes, and opinions learned and that each person determines to be true. Self-esteem is an emotional aspect of self and generally refers to how one feels about him/herself.

12. **C.** Competency 14. Renaissance period (1450–1600) included a gradual change from a feudal system to the modern state and a change in people's view of the Earth and cosmos. It had an increase in secular music (madrigals and art songs), but also had sacred music (liturgical forms like mass and motels). This gradual change was not uniform.

13. **C.** Competency 12. Motet is applied to a number of highly varied choral musical compositions, which uses a polyphonic approach (a texture consisting of two or more independent melodic voices). Motet is French for "word." This style of music appeared in the thirteenth century with motet written for three voices. It combined secular and sacred text, fifteenth and sixteenth centuries (Renaissance) with contrapuntal work for four or five voices a cappella and sacred text, and Baroque and Romantic periods with a cappella and orchestral variations.

14. **A.** Competency 13. Value is a relative darkness or lightness of a color.

15. **A.** Competency 17. Yogurt is in the milk category. Beans and beef are in the meat and beans category. Asparagus is in the vegetable category.

16. C. Competency 20. Cognitive domain is how one deals with knowledge. Affective domain is how one deals with emotions. Psychomotor domain is how one deals with physical movement and skills.

17. B. Competency 18. Locomotor skills involve walking, running, and galloping. Nonlocomotor skills involve twisting and turning. Spinning around is a nonlocomotor skill.

18. D. Competency 19. Symptoms of marijuana use include rapid talking, outbursts of laughter, forgetfulness in conversation, sleepiness, and dilated pupils. Nose bleeds are not a symptom of marijuana use.

19. A. Competency 14. Baroque period (1600–1760) was known for its intricate ornamentation. The word "baroque" was derived from the Portuguese word barroco, which means "misshapen pearl" (irregular in shape).

20. B. Competency 15. In order to help students' development of analytical skills to evaluate musical performance, the students need opportunities to perform and evaluate their own musical performances and the musical performance of other students and professional musicians or singers. They can also accomplish this by analyzing the use of instruments or voices in a recording or performance.

21. C. Competency 18. Stress is defined as the impact of a continually changing environment on the body.

22. A. Competency 20. Separating material into its component parts is *analysis*.

Science and Technology

1. **D.** Competency 21. There are several fundamental physical properties of matter: mass, volume, density, and chemical change. Matter is what makes up everything in the world: rocks, people, chairs, buildings, water, oxygen, animals, and chemical substances, among others. It takes up space (volume) and has mass. It not only involves its molecules and atoms, but also subatomic particles such as protons and electrons. Protons and neutrons are the subatomic particles that are located inside the nucleus.

2. **B.** Competency 24. Prokaryotic cells have no nucleus. Eukaryotic cells contain a nucleus.

3. **B.** Competency 26. Spreadsheets allow tabulation and performance of simple and complicated calculations, mathematical manipulations, and plots and graphs on various types of data, such as numbers, names, alphabetical information, scientific measurements, statistical information, and budget information. Database software allows easy collection, access, organization, and retrieval of data, such as inventories, experiments, and records. Word processors facilitate the preparation, manipulation, modification, and arrangement of electronically developed text, tables, and images for reports and documents. Internet allows access to online resources, and faster communication and sharing of information, including social networking and online communities, such as e-mail, instant messaging, YouTube, TeacherTube, Facebook, MySpace, Twitter, LinkedIn, and Wiki, which is a Web site that uses Wiki software.

4. **B.** Competency 21. Gravity does not change the mass of the rocks. Weight is often confused with mass. The measure of the Earth's pull of gravity on an object is called weight. It is the force of gravity on objects. It is measured in pounds (English or traditional system) or grams (metric system).

5. **D.** Competency 23. The layers of the Earth are the inner core, outer core, mantle, and crust. The inner most part of the Earth is the inner core.

6. **A.** Competency 24. The levels of taxonomy are domain, kingdom, phylum, class, order, family, genus, and species. The most specific level is species.

7. **B.** Competency 25. Good laboratory procedures include washing hands frequently, disposing of chemicals properly, and wearing gloves. Eating in the laboratory is not good laboratory procedure.

8. **C.** Competency 23. John Glenn was the first American to orbit the Earth. Neil Armstrong was the first American to walk on the moon. Alan Shepard was the first American to be launched into space. Yuri Gagarin was the first human being in space.

9. **D.** Competency 24. Vaccination is the most effective method for controlling the spread of viruses.

10. **B.** Competency 23. Volcanoes, canyons, and mountains are geological formations. Earthquakes are not geological formations.

11. **D.** Competency 22. Sonar is a measuring instrument, which is used to send out an acoustic pulse in water and measures distances in terms of the time it takes the echo of the pulse to return.

    Pitch represents the perceived fundamental frequency of a sound. It is one of the three major auditory attributes of sounds along with loudness and timbre. Acoustic relates to the study of sound, ultrasound, and infrasound (all mechanical waves in gases, liquids, and solids). It is also used to describe some instruments, like classical guitars. It refers to the energy in the form of mechanical waves that is transmitted through materials (like plastic or air). The best selection is that a sound wave is produced by vibration. It is a type of mechanical energy that propagates through matter as a wave. If something vibrates at a reasonable high frequency, then it will make sound. When a vibrating object is large enough and next to air, the air will vibrate as well and produce sound.

12. **A.** Competency 24. Asexual reproduction requires one parent. Sexual reproduction requires two parents.

13. **C.** Competency 22. A mechanical force is a type of contact force. It is the application of force to bend, dent, scratch, compress, or break something; for example, machines in general multiply force or change the direction of force. Contact forces require physical contact and interaction between objects (that is, pushes and pulls, and friction). Temperature is one of the physical properties of solids, liquids, and gases. Temperature is a measure related to the average kinetic energy of the molecules of a substance. It has to do with the degree of hotness or

coldness of the substance. This is how hot or cold an object is with respect to a standard unit of measurement. This is the best selection for this item. Heat is a measurement of the total energy in a substance. That total energy is made up of the kinetic, and the potential energies of the molecules of the substance. Temperature does not tell you anything about the potential energy.

14. **C.** Competency 26. A pressure sensor measures pressure of gases or liquids, among others. Tools like spectrometers and sensors facilitate the collection of data, which might also be used with computer software to manage data. Spectrometers are instruments that can be used to measure absorbance spectrum of a liquid, conduct kinetic studies of absorbance versus time, conduct equilibrium studies of absorbance versus time and/or absorbance versus concentration, and measure emissions of gas discharge tubes or other light sources, and other experiments. Barometers are used for either weather studies or for lab experiments involving pressures close to normal atmospheric pressure. Temperature probes are used for data-collection during temperature-related experiments.

15. **C.** Competency 23. Wind is the horizontal movement of air.

16. **B.** Competency 22. Two main types of forces are contact forces (for example, frictional, tension, air resistant, applied, and mechanical forces) and at-a-distance forces (for example, magnetic, gravitational, and electrostatic forces). Contact forces require physical contact and interaction between objects. At-a-distance forces result even when the interacting objects are not in physical contact, but they exert a push or pull despite their physical separation. Electrical forces are action-at-a-distance forces. They are involved when the protons in the nucleus of an atom and the electrons outside the nucleus exert an electrical pull towards each other despite the spatial separation. Nuclear forces are also at-a-distance forces and are present in the nucleus of atoms. Nuclear force is released by fission (the breaking of a heavy nucleus into two lighter nuclei), fusion (two atomic nuclei fuse together to form a heavier nucleus), or radioactive decay (a neutron of proton in the radioactive nucleus decays spontaneously by emitting particles, electromagnetic radiation, gamma rays, or all three of them).

17. **B.** Competency 25. Scientific methods are the ways scientists answer questions and solve problems systematically.

18. **C.** Competency 23. Volcanoes occur when magma erupts above the Earth. Canyons occur when rivers erode soil away. Mountains occur when two plates intersect and force each other upward. Earthquakes occur when two continental plates shift horizontally.

19. **A.** Competency 27. The first step is to ask a question. In order to answer the question, observations are needed. Observations may include collecting observed data such as the number of a specific species of frogs in an area. Once the question is formulated and observations are conducted, a hypothesis is created. A hypothesis is a possible answer to the question. They are based on what was observed and are testable. Answers are predicted and an experiment is formulated to test the hypothesis.

20. **A.** Competency 22. At-a-distance forces result even when the interacting objects are not in physical contact, but they exert a push or pull despite their physical separation; for examples, gravitational, magnetic, electrical and nuclear forces. Frictional forces are a type of contact forces.

21. **D.** Competency 27. The correct order of the methodology for an experiment is the following:

    4. Identify a research question.

    5. Formulate a hypothesis.

    1. Plan a controlled experiment.

    6. Collect data.

    3. Analyze data and draw conclusions.

    2. Revisit the hypothesis to answer question.

22. **C.** Competency 24. Amphibians are animals that live part of their lives on land and part of their lives in water.

23. **C.** Competency 23. Metamorphic rock transforms through change in environment like burial. Sedimentary rock is formed by the accumulation of rocks that fuse together to make a new rock. Igneous rock is formed when magma cools.

Mathematics

1. **C.** Competency 28. The use of five blocks as part of an activity dealing with numeration involves the concrete representation model. A word name and standard models involve the abstract level. The pictorial model involves pictures or drawings.

2. **D.** Competency 30. Each term is 3 times the term before. The next term is $54 \times 3 = 162$.

3. **A.** Competency 29. Perimeter is the distance around a shape. The original perimeter is $3 + 5 + 6 = 14$ feet. If each side of the triangle is doubled, the sides would be 6, 10, and 12. The new perimeter is $6 + 10 + 12 = 28$ feet. This is double the original perimeter.

4. **A.** Competency 28. A bar graph using horizontal rectangular bars to show the frequency of each value involves the pictorial and abstract representation models. The horizontal rectangular bars are pictorial representations, and the numerals used for the frequency values are abstract representations.

5. **A.** Competency 31. To find the mean of this set of data, find the sum of the scores (out of 100 points), and divide by the number of score (9 in this case): $(23 + 32 + 40 + 45 + 50 + 55 + 55 + 58 + 80) \div 9 = 438 \div 9 = 48.666 \ldots$ or approximately 49 (rounded to the nearest whole number).

6. **B.** Competency 31. Order data from least to greatest: 23, 32, 40, 45, 50, 55, 55, 58, 80. The median is the middle score the data. Because we have an odd number of scores (9), the middle of the data is 5th score. Counting from left to right 50 is the 5th value, or counting from right to left 50 is still the 5th value. The median is 50.

7. **A.** Competency 31. The range is the difference between the greatest score and the least score: $80 - 23 = 57$. The range of this data set is 57.

8. **D.** Competency 31. The mode is 55, which is the one with the highest frequency (2).

9. **C.** Competency 29. Complementary angles add to 90 degrees. $\angle ABC$ is a right angle. $\angle CBD$ is complementary to $\angle ABD$.

10. **D.** Competency 28. The number 3^{-2} is equal to $\frac{1}{3}^2 = \frac{1}{9}$.

11. **B.** Competency 30. The farmer sells his bushels for \$5 each. If he sells b bushels at the market, he would obtain $5b$ dollars. It cost him \$50 to have the booth. This should be subtracted from the income of the booth to find the profit. The profit is $5b - 50$.

12. **B.** Competency 29. The shadow and the height are sides of similar triangles. Set up a proportion. $\frac{40 \text{ inches}}{36 \text{ inches}} = \frac{10 \text{ feet}}{x \text{ feet}}$. Cross multiply, so $40x = 360$. Divide both sides by 40. $x = 9$ feet.

13. **B.** Competency 28. The number 465^0 is equal to 1 because any number with a exponent of zero is equal to one. It not equal to itself, negative, or zero.

14. **D.** Competency 29. Edges are where faces intersect. A cube has six faces. A cube has 12 edges.

15. **C.** Competency 32. The most appropriate alternative to help students develop classification skills is the Pattern blocks. Cuisenaire rods are more appropriate for modeling numeration and operation activities, including whole number, fractions, decimals, addition, subtraction, multiplication and division ideas. Algebra tiles are more appropriate for representing equations and functions involving variables. Fraction tiles are more appropriate for modeling fraction concepts and operations.

16. **A.** Competency 29. Consider each choice:

    Acute triangles have all angles less than 90 degrees. Isosceles triangles have at least two sides of equal length. A triangle can be acute and isosceles.

    An obtuse triangle has one angle that is greater than 90 degrees. An equilateral triangle has all equal sides. Since all the sides of an equilateral triangle are the same, all the angles will be the same as well. Since the angles of a triangle add to 180 degrees, each angle in an equilateral triangle is 60 degrees. An equilateral triangle cannot be obtuse.

A right triangle has one angle equal to 90 degrees. The other two angles must be less than 90 degrees for the total of all three angles to be 180 degrees. An obtuse triangle has one angle that is greater than 90 degrees. A right triangle cannot be obtuse.

An equilateral triangle has all equal sides. A scalene triangle has all different side lengths. A triangle cannot be equilateral and scalene.

The only choice that is true is A.

17. **D.** Competency 28. The value of $2^{-6} \cdot -8$ is $\frac{1}{2}^6 \cdot -8 = \frac{1}{64} \cdot -8 = \frac{-8}{64} = \frac{-1}{8}$.

18. **C.** Competency 29. Point R is three units to the left and two units down from the origin (0,0). This makes the coordinates of point R (–3, –2).

19. **B.** Competency 32. Two-color chips are least appropriate manipulative to help students develop area ideas. Fraction tiles are more appropriate for developing fraction concepts and operations. Geoboard, Color tiles, and Pattern blocks are more appropriate for developing area ideas.

20. **C.** Competency 28.

$$30^2 - 60 \div 12 \cdot \left(\frac{1}{5} - 5^{-2}\right) \cdot 15 + 78$$

$$= 900 - 60 \div 12 \cdot \left(\frac{1}{5} - \frac{1}{25}\right) \cdot 15 + 78$$

$$= 900 - 60 \div 12 \cdot \left(\frac{5}{25} - \frac{1}{25}\right) \cdot 15 + 78$$

$$= 900 - 60 \div 12 \cdot \left(\frac{4}{25}\right) \cdot 15 + 78$$

$$= 900 - 5 \cdot \left(\frac{4}{25}\right) \cdot 15 + 78$$

$$= 900 - \left(\frac{4}{5}\right) \cdot 15 + 78$$

$$= 900 - (4) \cdot 3 + 78$$

$$= 900 - 12 + 78 = 966$$

21. **A.** Competency 29. A pencil is less than 1 foot long. The appropriate unit for measuring a pencil is an inch.

22. **C.** Competency 30.

$3x - 4 + x = x + 8 + 3x - 2x$

$4x - 4 = 2x + 8$ (Combine like terms.)

$2x - 4 = 8$ (Subtract $2x$ from both sides.)

$2x = 12$ (Add 4 to both sides.)

$x = 6$ (Divide both sides by 2.)

23. **C.** Competency 29. The area of a circle is πr^2. If the diameter is 12 inches, the radius is 6 inches. Therefore, the area is $\pi(6)^2 = 36\pi$ in^2.

PART I

COMPETENCY REVIEWS

Language Arts and Reading

This chapter provides a general review of Language Arts and Reading (Competencies 1–6) with sample questions and explanations at the end of the chapter. Checkpoint exercises are found throughout, giving you an opportunity to practice the skills addressed in this section. The answers to the checkpoint exercises immediately follow the set of questions. We encourage you to cover the answers as you complete the checkpoint exercises. Sample questions for the competency as a whole appear at the end of the chapter. Answers and explanations follow the sample questions.

Competency 1: Knowledge of the Reading Process

Competency Description

According to the Competencies and Skills Required for Teacher Certification in Florida, Elementary Education (available at http://www.fldoe.org/asp/ftce/pdf/60ElementaryEducationK-6.pdf) **Competency 1** for the Elementary Education (K–6) Subject Area Examination (SAE) addresses the following key indicators:

1. Identify the processes, skills, and phases of word recognition that lead to effective decoding (e.g., pre-alphabetic, partial-alphabetic, full-alphabetic, graphophonemic, morphemic).
2. Identify instructional methods for promoting the development of decoding and encoding skills.
3. Identify the components of reading fluency (e.g., accuracy, automaticity, rate, prosody).
4. Identify instructional methods (e.g., practice with high-frequency words, timed readings) for developing reading fluency.
5. Identify instructional methods and strategies for increasing vocabulary acquisition (e.g., word analysis, choice of words, context clues, multiple exposures) across the content areas.
6. Identify instructional methods and strategies (e.g., summarizing, self-monitoring, questioning, use of graphic and semantic organizers, think alouds, recognizing story structure) for facilitating students' reading comprehension.
7. Identify essential comprehension skills (e.g., main idea, supporting details and facts, author's purpose, fact and opinion, point of view, inference, conclusion).
8. Identify appropriate uses of multiple representations of information (e.g., charts, tables, graphs, pictures, print and nonprint media) for a variety of purposes.
9. Identify strategies (e.g., making connections and predictions, questioning, summarizing, question generating) for developing critical-thinking skills such as analysis, synthesis, and evaluation.
10. Identify instructional methods for teaching a variety of informational and literary text structures.
11. Identify the content of emergent literacy (e.g., oral language development, phonological awareness, alphabet knowledge, decoding, concepts of print, motivation, text structures, written language development).

Overview

Knowledge of the reading process is one, if not the most important, aspect of elementary education. Approximately **22 questions** address Competency 1. This section addresses the following areas related to **Competency 1** key indicators:

- Knowledge of the Reading Process
  - The Five Components of Reading
  - Word Recognition Skills
  - Critical Thinking Strategies
  - Reading Fluency
  - Reading Comprehension
  - Informational and Literary Text Structures
- Emergent Literacy

Knowledge of the Reading Process

The Five Components of Reading

The following are five critical skills necessary for success in reading:

1. **Phonemic awareness** is the ability to hear and manipulate the sounds of spoken language. This includes noticing rhyme and recognizing the separate, small sounds in words (phonemes).

2. **Phonics** is the understanding of the relationships between the written letters of the alphabet and the sounds of spoken language. This knowledge allows a reader to "decode" words by translating the letters into speech sounds.

3. **Fluency** is the ability to read quickly, accurately, and with proper expression. Fluent readers can concentrate on understanding what they read because they don't have to focus on decoding.

4. **Vocabulary** includes all the words the reader can understand and use. The more words a child knows, the better he or she will understand what is read. Knowing how words relate to each other is a building block that leads to comprehension.

5. **Comprehension** is the ability to understand what one has read. This includes understanding the plot of a story or the information in an article. It also includes things like recognizing the main idea of an article or being able to compare and contrast different characters in a story. (http://www.justreadflorida.com/docs/Read_to_Learn.pdf)

Word Recognition Skills

Word recognition means that the student has the ability to visually identify words in isolation or context. The goal of enhancing word recognition is to enable students to understand how words work. The phases of word recognition are pre-alphabetic, partial-alphabetic, full-alphabetic, graphophonemic, and morphemic.

Critical Thinking Strategies

- **making connections**—Teachers facilitate and encourage three types of connections to text to aid reading comprehension: text to self, text to text, and text to world. A text to self connection implies that the reader has made a connection from the reading to their own personal lives. A text to text connection implies that the reader has made a connection from the reading to another book with a similar writing style, theme, or topic. A text to world connection implies that the reader has made a connection from the reading to a topic or an event that has taken or is taking place in the world. Whatever the connection, the act of making any connection helps the reader to better remember and comprehend the text.

- **making predictions**—Making predictions about what a particular text is going to be about aids student comprehension. Prior to the reading of a particular text, the front cover, including the title and illustration or photograph, can be used by the teacher and students to predict what they think the text is going to be about. Then throughout the reading, these predictions can be affirmed or revised according to the content of the selection, written and visual.

- **questioning**—Questioning is the strategy that helps students make meaning of the text being read. Teachers must model a variety of questions for students to then internalize and implement in their own reading. Students should read with a purpose and question in mind. Questions about the content of the text, the author's intent, and questions that lead to further research about a particular topic are all appropriate. There are four key types of questions:
  - "Right there" questions (text explicit)—These are literal questions in which the answer is in the text itself.
  - "Think and search" questions (text implicit)—The answer is implicit in the text, but the student must synthesize, infer, or summarize to find the answer. Think and search questions tend to be more open-ended without set answers.

- "Reader and author" questions (text implicit or experience-based)—The answer needs the reader to combine his or her own experiences with what the text states, that is, the knowledge presented by the author.
- "On my own" questions (text implicit or experience-based)—The reader needs to generate the answer from his or her prior knowledge. The reader may not need to read the text to answer, but the answer would certainly be shaped differently after reading the text.

- **summarizing**—To summarize is to simply and concisely paraphrase what has been read. This takes place during and after the reading. Summarizing what has been read can be done orally (whole group, small group, pairs) or in writing.

Reading Fluency

Components of reading fluency include the following:

- **Accuracy**— Ability to correctly read the words in a text
- **Automaticity**—Ability to instantly recognize a large bank of words to quickly decode unfamiliar words
- **Rate**—Speed of reading
- **Prosody**—Ability to read with appropriate rhythm, intonation, and expression

To become fluent, the student must have a strong foundation in word recognition and must spend time reading. The more a student reads, the more fluent they become. Fluent readers focus on comprehension and make connections, read with expression and phrasing, decode quickly, and self-correct when their reading does not make sense.

A sampling of instructional methods that aid fluency include repetitive or repeated reading, oral reading, echo reading, choral reading, timed reading, readers theater, audio books, poetry readings, independent, and paired reading.

Reading Comprehension

The following are skills essential to reading comprehension:

Main idea	Identifying the main idea means determining the essential message of a reading selection. The main idea can be constructed from the various supporting details in the text.
Supporting details and facts	The supporting details and facts in a selection provide the reader with the vital information needed to synthesize and summarize what is being read.
Author's purpose	Identifying the author's purpose or point of view is vital to comprehension. For example, the author's purpose for writing the text could be to explain, inform, persuade, or entertain.
Fact and opinion	A fact is a piece of information that is true and accurate. An opinion is a personal judgment. Students should be able to read a selection and identify what is fact and what is someone's opinion.
Point of view	A point of view is a way of looking at something. Authors write from varying points of view. Student should be able to identify from which point of view an author is writing.
Inference	Making an inference is often referred to as "reading between the lines" or making meaning from the implied or underlying theme/point of the text. An inference often includes merging what is already known about a topic to the new information being presented.
Visualize	To visualize a text means to create mental pictures in one's mind about the content of the reading.
Conclusion	The conclusion is the end or summation of a reading selection.

The following instructional methods and skills facilitate student reading comprehension:

- **activating prior knowledge**—Students must connect what they hear, read, and view with what they already know. Making these connections to the text enables the reader to process the information and add the new knowledge to what they already know. Students can use the Think-Pair-Share technique to discuss what they already know about a topic with a partner. Teachers can use graphic organizers, like K-W-L charts, to elicit what students already know about a topic.

- **summarizing**—To summarize is to simply and concisely paraphrase what has been read. This takes place after the reading and can be done orally or in writing. This summation of the reading is often included in a retelling of the selection. Students can use the Think-Pair-Share technique to discuss their summaries with a partner.

- **self-monitoring**—Being aware of their thinking as they are reading is what self-monitoring is all about. Students must pause periodically to reflect and think about the information being presented in the text. This reflection may lead to students making adjustments to their thinking and inevitably gaining greater meaning from the text.

- **questioning**—Questioning is the strategy that helps students make meaning of the text being read. Teachers must model a variety of questions for students to then internalize and implement in their own reading. Students should read with a purpose and question in mind. Questions that clarify the content of the text and the author's intent and questions that lead to further research about a particular topic are all appropriate.

- **use of graphic and semantic organizers**—Graphic/semantic organizers are used by teachers and students to highlight the big ideas in a text and to facilitate connections. These organizers synthesize and summarize the reading to aid comprehension.

- **think alouds**–Also known as "talking to the text," this instructional method involves the teacher modeling her thoughts *aloud* while reading text (fiction and informational) aloud to her students. Teachers often incorporate vocabulary into their think alouds to pre-teach new words and their meaning. Once modeled by the teacher, think alouds can be practiced by students with a partner.

- **recognizing story structure**–Narratives or stories have a beginning, middle, and end that incorporate such literary elements as setting, characters, and plot. Teachers highlight and facilitate the analyzing of story structure through questioning techniques before, during, and after a read aloud or shared reading.

Informational and Literary Text Structures

Unlike literary or narrative text, informational or nonfiction text is structured using organizational aids called text features. The following is a list of common text features used in informational text: title, table of contents, headings, subheadings, bold and italicized words, illustrations, photographs, labeled diagrams, charts, graphs, tables, glossary, and index.

These text features usually support the body of the text and help to synthesize and summarize the information being presented. Previewing the text, paying specific attention to these features, aids the student in not only reading the body of the informational text but also the various features in place to aid their comprehension of the content. Text feature "scavenger hunts" can be performed to locate the text features present in a particular text. After reading, a variety of graphic organizers (cause and effect, venn diagrams, double entry journals, timelines, and so on) can be used to further explore the content.

Most literary text or narratives have a logical sequence. Students can be taught to recognize the beginning, middle, and end of a story through story retellings after a read aloud.

Checkpoint

1. Fill in the blank: Accuracy, rate, prosody, and automaticity are all components of reading _____.

2. True or false: "Talking to the text" is also known as a strategy called a *think aloud*.

3. True or false: Graphophonemic is a phase of word recognition in elementary age students that refers to the letter-sound relationship.

4. Fill in the blank: _____ and _____ are two essential skills related to reading comprehension.

Checkpoint Answers

1. fluency

2. True

3. True

4. Any two of the following: main idea, supporting details and facts, author's purpose, fact and opinion, point of view, inference, visualize, conclusion

Emergent Literacy

Emergent literacy is the beginning phase of literacy. Young children learn that text and pictures provide meaning. They learn to appreciate, explore, and enjoy text. During this phase, children are exposed to the structure or syntax of language and are encouraged to predict what the text may be about.

- **oral language development**—In order to enhance a child's oral language or verbal skills, children must be involved in the following, on a regular basis: open-ended (whole group, small group, and one-on-one) discussions, read alouds, echo reading, songs, nursery rhymes, storytelling, readers theater, cloze activities, poetry, role play and drama, fingerplays, and so on. Oral language is the foundation for further reading and writing achievement.

- **phonological awareness**—Phonological Awareness includes the ability of a student to identify and manipulate large parts of spoken language (words, syllables, onset/rime units) and awareness of other aspects of sound in our language like **alliteration**, intonation, and rhyming.

- **alphabet knowledge**—Alphabet knowledge requires young learners to identify and name the upper- and lowercase letters of the alphabet. Alphabet books, magnetic letters, and the use of environmental print all enhance alphabet knowledge.

- **concepts of print**—Knowledge of how print works is vital. Young learners should understand: print conveys meaning, directionality (left to right progression, top to bottom), concept of a word (word boundaries), one-to-one corresponding letter knowledge, phonemic awareness, and literacy language (author, illustrations, title, and so on).

Checkpoint

1. True or false: Emergent literacy refers to the *latter* part of the reading process.

2. True or false: Basic concepts of print include but are not limited to directionality, title page, and illustrations.

3. True or false: Oral language development can be enhanced through class and small group discussions.

Checkpoint Answers

1. False

2. True

3. True

Competency 2: Knowledge of Literature and Literary Analysis

Competency Description

According to the Competencies and Skills Required for Teacher Certification in Florida, Elementary Education (available at http://www.fldoe.org/asp/ftce/pdf/60ElementaryEducationK-6.pdf) **Competency 2** for the Elementary Education (K–6) Subject Area Examination (SAE) addresses the following key indicators:

1. Identify characteristics and elements of a variety of literary genres (e.g., realistic fiction, fantasy, poetry, nonfiction).
2. Identify terminology and appropriate use of literary devices.
3. Identify and apply professional guidelines for selecting multicultural literature.
4. Identify appropriate techniques for encouraging students to respond to literature in a variety of ways.

Overview

Knowledge of literature and the ability to analyze literature's many genres and forms is of primary importance to elementary educators. There are approximately **6 questions** that address Competency 2. This section addresses the following areas related to **Competency 2** key indicators:

- Literary Genres
- Literary Elements and Devices
- Multicultural Children's Literature
- Literature Response

Literary Genres

Children's literature can be defined as books written primarily for children. The books can be categorized into several genres or types. There are eight main genres of children's literature: poetry, folklore, fantasy, science fiction, realistic fiction, historical fiction, biography, and nonfiction (Galda & Cullinan, 2006). These genres of children's literature may be presented in picture book or chapter book form and include a wide-variety of settings, cultures, and ethnicities in hopes of broadening the readers' or listeners' horizons. The eight genres are defined here.

- **Poetry**—Contains short lines, imagery, and elements of sound, such as rhythm and rhyme
- **Folklore**—Stories that were told by word of mouth: nursery rhymes, fairy tales, **fables, myths, legends,** tall tales
- **Fantasy**—Stories that could not happen in the real world
- **Science fiction**—Stories that might happen in the future
- **Realistic fiction**—Stories focusing on events that *could* happen in the real world
- **Historical fiction**—Realistic stories set in the past
- **Biography**—Stories that tell the tale of a person's life
- **Nonfiction**—Books that present information

Checkpoint

1. True or false: Nursery rhymes, fairy tales, legends, and myths are all considered folklore.

2. Fill in the blank: Realistic stories set in the past that usually incorporate significant time periods and/or events in history are considered _____ fiction.

3. Fill in the blank: _____ are stories that tell the tale of a person's life.

Checkpoint Answers

1. True
2. historical
3. Biographies

Literary Elements and Devices

Each genre of children's literature contains **literary elements** that are specific to that type of writing. Literary elements such as setting, characters, plot, theme, and style are present in most **narratives,** and nonfiction text features like labeled diagrams and photographs present informative text in a comprehensible manner. Nonfiction text features include but are not limited to the following: titles, headings, subheadings, bold print, captions, charts, graphs, timelines, table of contents, index, glossary and drawings.

Literary elements:

- **Setting**—where the story takes place
- **Characters**—people or animals in a story, novel, or play
- **Plot**—the events that take place in a story; often includes a climax and resolution
- **Theme**—the subject or central idea of the story
- **Style**—the vocabulary and syntax the author uses to create the story

A sampling of literary devices:

- **Alliteration**—two or more words or syllables, near each other, with the same beginning consonant
- **Hyperbole**—an exaggeration used to emphasize a point
- **Onomatopoeia**—the use of words with sounds that reinforce their meaning (that is, *smash, bang, boom*)
- **Analogy**—a detailed and sometimes lengthy comparison of two ideas or events
- **Irony**—using words that mean the opposite of what the author intends
- **Personification**—giving human qualities to a thing or abstraction
- **Climax**—the point of highest dramatic interest or a turning point in the story
- **Metaphor**— a comparison of two distinctly different things suggesting a similarity between them
- **Simile**—a comparison using *like* or *as*

Checkpoint

1. Fill in the blank: The _____ is the events that take place in the story.

2. True or false: The literary element of style refers to the appearance of the words on the page.

3. True or false: *Her eyes twinkle like the stars* is an example of a metaphor.

Checkpoint Answers

1. plot
2. False; writing style and word usage
3. False; simile

Multicultural Children's Literature

Multicultural children's literature can be loosely defined as books written for children that illuminate the variety of cultures, ethnicities, and traditions present in a country of multicultural heritage (Norton, 2009). Criteria that must be considered in the selection of quality multicultural children's literature is as follows (Galda & Cullinan, 2006):

- Depicts diversity but avoids stereotyping of a particular culture
- Explores cultural differences and similarities in a sensitive manner
- Provides an accurate and positive portrayal of the culture represented
- Language and setting must be consistent with the culture and again avoid stereotyping.

Checkpoint

1. Fill in the blank: A book portraying all _____ children as being smart and disciplined would be considered stereotypical of this culture.

2. True or false: Classroom libraries should contain a wide variety of multicultural children's literature to aid in the exploration and understanding of various cultures.

Checkpoint Answers

1. Asian
2. True

Literature Response

Responding to literature in a variety of ways assists students with deeply comprehending a text. These activities help children to understand the essence of the stories they are reading. These responses can take on many forms, such as: artistic literature response, discussion, drama, inquiry, written response, and **multimedia**.

- Artistic literature response incorporates a variety of artistic mediums such as drawing, painting, collage, scratchboard, etc.
- A response that involves discussion might include **literature circles** or book clubs (face to face or online) that encourage small, temporary, and **heterogeneous** groups of students to talk about the story they are reading.
- Dramatic responses might include poetry readings, **readers theater**, or storytelling.
- Inquiry could include research about a particular author (an author study) or topic (inquiry circles).
- Written response involves readers responding to what has been read in writing. The use of independent **graphic organizers**, reading logs, learning logs, and reading response journals are all examples of written response.
- Multimedia tools such as computer software programs or online resources can enhance student reading comprehension. Students could create power point presentations, **wiki** pages, digital storytellings, or **web-quests** in response to literature.

Checkpoint

1. Fill in the blank: Responding to a piece of literature by drawing is an example of _____ literature response.

2. True or false: Small groups of students talking about a book they are reading are called book chats.

3. Fill in the blank: Reading response journals assist students with text _____.

Checkpoint Answers

1. artistic
2. False; literature circles
3. comprehension

Competency 3: Knowledge of the Writing Process and Its Applications

Competency Description

According to the Competencies and Skills Required for Teacher Certification in Florida, Elementary Education (available at http://www.fldoe.org/asp/ftce/pdf/60ElementaryEducationK-6.pdf) **Competency 3** for the Elementary Education (K–6) Subject Area Examination (SAE) addresses the following key indicators:

1. Demonstrate knowledge of the developmental stages of writing.
2. Demonstrate knowledge of the writing process (e.g., prewriting, drafting, revising, editing, publishing).
3. Identify characteristics of the modes of writing (e.g., narrative, descriptive, expository, persuasive, informative, creative).
4. Select the appropriate mode of writing for a variety of occasions, purposes, and audiences.
5. Identify elements and appropriate use of rubrics to assess writing.
6. Demonstrate knowledge of writing conventions (e.g., spelling, punctuation, capitalization, syntax, word usage).
7. Identify instructional methods for teaching writing conventions.

Overview

Knowledge of the writing process and applications is of primary importance to elementary educators. There are approximately **6 questions** that address Competency 3. This section addresses the following areas related to **Competency 3** key indicators:

- Writing: Stages, Process, Modes, and Conventions
  - Developmental Writing Stages
  - The Writing Process
  - Modes of Writing
  - Teaching Writing Conventions

Writing: Stages, Process, Modes, and Conventions

Developmental Writing Stages

The developmental stages of writing begin with scribbling and end with conventional spelling. These stages include but are not limited to: scribbling, mock handwriting, mock letters, conventional letters, invented—temporary—or phonetic spelling and conventional spelling.

The Writing Process

The writing process includes the following stages and components:

- **Prewriting**—Activating prior knowledge, gathering and organizing ideas; may include brainstorming a list of ideas and researching / reading about a topic; may include deciding upon the intended audience
- **Drafting**—Transfer of ideas to paper; focus is on getting all thoughts down (the content) rather than on spelling, grammar, and mechanics
- **Revising**—Refining and clarifying the draft; focus is on meaning and further developing the writing piece

- **Editing**—Proofreading the draft for misspelled words, grammatical and mechanical errors; focus is on the mechanics (punctuation, sentence fragments, capitalization, etc.)
- **Publishing**—Sharing a final product

Modes of Writing

The mode of writing reveals the purpose of the writing as well as the intended audience.

- **Narrative writing**—Writing that recounts a personal or fictional experience or tells a story based on a real or imagined event
- **Persuasive writing**—Writing that attempts to convince the reader that a point of view is valid or that the reader should take a specific action
- **Descriptive writing**—Writing that attempts to "paint a picture" or describe a person, place, thing, or idea
- **Expository writing**—Writing that gives information, explains why or how, clarifies a process, or defines a concept
- **Informative writing**—Writing that informs the reader in an attempt to create newfound knowledge
- **Creative writing**—Writing that uses the writer's imagination

Teaching Writing Conventions

Writing conventions include such mechanics as spelling, punctuation, capitalization, and grammar. These conventions can be taught whole group through modeled, shared, and interactive writing opportunities or to small groups and individuals during writing conferences. Students apply their knowledge of writing conventions during the editing and publishing phases of the writing process during daily writer's workshop. Teachers can provide insight into their expectations of writing by providing detailed rubrics. Rubrics assessing writing should include sections related to the writing process, mode of writing, and the importance of spelling, punctuation, capitalization, and grammar.

Checkpoint

1. True or false: The editing phase of writing requires the writer to modify his writing for content.

2. True or false: Expository writing attempts to convince the reader of a particular point of view.

3. Fill in the blank: The _____ stage of writing include brainstorming, gathering, and organizing ideas.

4. Fill in the blank: _____ is the first developmental phase of writing.

Checkpoint Answers

1. False
2. False; persuasive
3. prewriting
4. Scribbling

Competency 4: Knowledge of Reading Methods and Assessment

Competency Description

According to the Competencies and Skills Required for Teacher Certification in Florida, Elementary Education (available at http://www.fldoe.org/asp/ftce/pdf/60ElementaryEducationK-6.pdf) **Competency 4** for the Elementary Education (K–6) Subject Area Examination (SAE) addresses the following key indicators:

1. Identify measurement concepts, characteristics, and uses of norm-referenced, criterion-referenced, and performance-based assessments.
2. Identify oral and written methods for assessing student progress (e.g., informal reading inventories, fluency checks, rubrics, running records, story retelling, portfolios).
3. Interpret assessment data (e.g., screening, progress monitoring, diagnostic) to guide instructional decisions.
4. Use individual student reading data to differentiate instruction.
5. Interpret students' formal and informal assessment results to inform students and parents or guardians.
6. Evaluate the appropriateness (e.g., curriculum alignment, freedom from bias) of assessment instruments and practices.
7. Identify appropriate classroom organizational formats (e.g., literature circles, small groups, individuals, workshops, reading centers, multiage groups) for specific instructional objectives.
8. Identify instructional methods for developing emergent literacy.
9. Identify methods for the diagnosis, prevention, and intervention of common emergent literacy difficulties.

Overview

Knowledge of reading methods, assessment in the area of reading, and the instructional methods related specifically to emergent literacy is of primary importance to elementary educators. There are approximately **6 questions** that address Competency 4. This section addresses the following areas related to **Competency 4** key indicators:

- Reading Assessment
- Classroom Organizational Formats
- Emergent Literacy

Reading Assessment

Assessment is defined as the process for gathering data about students to identify areas of strength and weakness in order to guide future instruction. There are two basic types of assessment; formal and informal. Formal assessments include intelligence tests, achievement tests (norm and criterion referenced), and diagnostic tests. Informal assessments include, but are not limited to, informal reading inventories, running records, cloze tests, anecdotal notes, checklists, rubrics, portfolios, and surveys. The following are key terms and definitions related to reading assessment:

- **Norm-referenced tests**—Assessment instruments that have been administered to students of various socio-economic backgrounds and in a variety of geographic locations in order to develop *norms*. These norms are the average scores of the populations and serve as a comparison point for teachers to compare their student results with that of a similar population.
- **Criterion-referenced tests**—Assessment instruments that assess the point at which the student has achieved mastery. These tests enable educators in determining whether or not a student has met a predetermined goal. The Florida Comprehensive Assessment Test (FCAT) is a criterion-referenced test.

- **Interpreting FCAT**—FCAT math and reading is scored on a scale of 100 to 500. These scores are then expressed as a category from 1–5 (1 being the lowest, and 5 being the highest). These (1–5) are called achievement levels. FCAT writing is scored on a 6 point scale (1–6), with 1 being the lowest score and 6 being the highest. If a student either did not respond to the prompt or wrote in a foreign language, they would receive a "U" for unscorable.

- **Diagnostic assessment**—Diagnostic assessments are standardized tests (carefully constructed and field-tested) and aim to determine a student's strengths and weaknesses.

- **Performance-based assessment**—Also known as authentic assessment, this form of assessment incorporates real-life applications of what has been taught and enables the teacher to assess meaningful and complex educational products and performances.

- **Fluency checks**—Quick (usually one-minute timed readings) assessments that focus on accuracy, rate and prosody; students' WPM (words per minute) or WCPM (words correct per minute) are calculated.
  - Words Per Minute (WPM) formula: $\dfrac{\text{Number of Words} \times 60}{\text{Number of Seconds}}$

    Example: A student read a 188 word piece in 4:30. His reading rate would be as follows:

    $\dfrac{188 \times 60}{270 \text{ (seconds)}} = 41.8$ WPM. Thus, this student reads at 41.8 words per minute.
  - Words Correct Per Minute (WCPM) formula: $\dfrac{\text{Number of Words} - \text{Errors } (x - E)\ 60}{\text{Number of Seconds}}$

    Example: A student read a 188 word piece in 4:30 with 4 recorded errors. Her accuracy rate would be as

    follows: $\dfrac{188 - 4\ (x - E) \cdot 60}{270 \text{ (seconds)}} = 40.9$ WCPM. Thus, the student reads 40.9 words correct per minute.

- **Informal reading inventories**—Individual tests that generally include lists of words or sentences and leveled reading passages with accompanying questions. These inventories can be performed quickly and provide valuable information on the students' independent, instructional, and frustration reading levels. Teachers calculate the student's accuracy rate, expressed as a percentage (formula and table follows) to identify the appropriate reading level. You can use accuracy rate to determine whether the text (leveled selection) read is easy enough for independent reading, difficult enough to warrant instruction yet avoid frustration, or too difficult for the reader. Teachers then use this valuable information to guide reading instruction and provide for differentiated instruction.

  Teachers can calculate the accuracy rate by using the following formula:

  $$\dfrac{(\text{Total words read } - \text{ total errors})}{\text{Total words read}} \times 100 = \text{Accuracy rate}$$

  OR

  $$\dfrac{(TW - E)}{TW} \times 100 = AR$$

  For example:

  $$\dfrac{(120 - 6)}{120} \times 100 = \text{accuracy rate}$$

  $$\dfrac{114}{120} \times 100 = \text{accuracy rate}$$

  $$.95 \times 100 = 95\%$$

Reading level	Accuracy rate range*
Independent reading level	95–100%
Instructional reading level (appropriate for use in guided reading session)	90–94%
Frustration reading level	89% and below

Depending on the IRI being used, the percentages could vary.

- **Rubric**—A rubric is a set of scoring guidelines or criteria for evaluating student work. They often provide specific guidelines regarding teacher expectations.

- **Running records**—Informal assessments that enable the teacher to observe, score, and interpret a student's reading behaviors. Observations include:
  - **Errors (E)**—Errors are tallied during the reading whenever a child does any of the following: substitutes another word for a word in the text, omits a word, inserts a word, or has to be told a word by the person administering the running record.
  - **Self-corrections (SC)**—Self-correction occurs when a child realizes his error and corrects it. When a child makes a self-correction, the previous substitution is not scored as an error.
  - **Meaning (M)**—Meaning is part of the semantic cueing system in which the child takes her cue to make sense of text by thinking about the story background, information from pictures, or the meaning of a sentence. These cues assist in the reading of a word or phrase.
  - **Structure (S)**—Structure refers to the structure of language and is often referred to as syntax (syntactic cueing system). Implicit knowledge of structure helps the reader know whether what he reads sounds correct.
  - **Visual (V)**—Visual information (graphophonemic cueing system) is related to the look of the letter in a word and the word itself. A reader uses visual information when he studies the beginning sound, word length, familiar word chunks, and so on.
- **Analyzing a running record**—Qualitative analysis is based on observations that you make during the running record. It involves observing how the child uses the meaning (M), structural (S), and visual (V) cues to help her read. It also involves paying attention to fluency, intonation, and phrasing. When a child makes an error in a line of text, record the source(s) of information used by the child in the second column from the right on the running record form. Write M, S, and V in to the right of the sentence in that column. Then circle M, S, and/or V, depending on the source(s) of information the child used.
- **Scoring a running record**—Information gathered while doing a running record is used to determine error, accuracy, and self-correction rates. Directions for calculating these rates follow. The calculated rates, along with qualitative information and the child's comprehension of the text, are used to determine a child's reading level.

  Error rate is expressed as a ratio and is calculated by dividing the total number of words read by the total number of errors made.

  $$\frac{\text{Total words}}{\text{Total errors}} = \text{Error rate}$$

  OR

  $$\frac{TW}{E} = ER$$

  For example:

  $$\frac{120}{6} = 20$$

  The ratio is expressed as 1:20. This means that for each error made, the child read 20 words correctly.

  For information on determining the accuracy rate, see IRI.

  Self-correction is expressed as a ratio and is calculated by using the following formula:

  $$\frac{\text{Errors} + \text{self-correction}}{\text{self-correction}} = \text{Self-correction rate}$$

  OR

  $$\frac{(E + SC)}{SC} = SC \text{ rate}$$

  For example:

  $$\frac{(10 + 5)}{5} = SC$$

  $$\frac{15}{5} = SC$$

  $$3 = SC$$

  The SC is expressed as 1:3. This means that the child corrects 1 out of every 3 errors. If a child is self-correcting at a rate of 1:3 or less, this indicates that she is self-monitoring her reading.

- **Screening**—A screening instrument is used to assess students at the beginning of the year to identify the students' reading level and capabilities. This screening tool can then be compared to the progress monitoring assessments to show growth over time.

- **Progress monitoring**—A progress monitoring instrument is used throughout the year to show gains in reading achievement and to provide information to the teacher that will help guide instruction.

- **Anecdotal notes (records)**—Anecdotal notes or records are short, concise, written observations made by the teacher while students work. Their purpose is to observe and record information that may be useful in guiding reading instruction and sharing student capabilities with parents. Dating these notes and filing them in a student portfolio or lesson plan book ensures easy access to on-going informal information about the student.

- **Cueing systems**—There are three main cueing systems: semantic, syntactic, and graphophonemic. The syntactic cueing system focuses on the structure of the sentence and how language works. Students using the syntactic cueing system can identify sentences that sound correct. The teacher can ask, "Does that sound correct?" when a syntactical error is made. The semantic cueing system focuses on any meaning a student derives from a sentence that is primarily based on prior knowledge. Students using the semantic cueing system can identify sentences that make sense and those that do not. Teachers can ask, "Did that make sense?" when a semantic error is made. The graphophonemic cueing system focuses on various visual cues and knowledge about the relationship between sounds and symbols. The student's phonological awareness is very important for this cueing system. If you were using the graphophonemic cueing system, you would want to investigate how the reader applies their knowledge of phonology as they read. Teachers can ask, "Does that look right?" when a graphophonemic error is made.

- **Miscue analysis**—A technique for recording and analyzing students' oral reading errors in order to gain an insight into the reading process they employ. It is useful to ask comprehension questions or ask students to retell what they have read after the reading to determine how well students have understood the text.

- **Cloze test**—The cloze procedure involves getting students to fill in words deliberately omitted from a passage of text. This procedure assists students in the prediction and the use of context clues.

- **Response logs**—A response log is an informal assessment that documents students' reading, viewing, and listening. Students record thoughts and feelings as they read, listen to, or watch literary, factual, or media texts. It is important to encourage students to value their own responses to texts.

- **Retelling**—Retelling is a technique that involves reading, either silently or aloud, and then retelling what has been read. In the retelling, a student reveals the parts of the text that were more significant to him.

Checkpoint

1. True or false: A criterion referenced test is an example of a formal assessment.

2. True or false: The three main cueing systems are semantic, syntactic, and graphophonemic.

3. Fill in the blank: _____ are short, concise written observations made while students work.

Checkpoint Answers

1. True

2. True

3. Anecdotal notes

Classroom Organizational Formats

- Literature circles are small, temporary, and heterogeneous groups of students that gather together to discuss a book of their choice with the goal of enhancing comprehension.

- A workshop approach to literacy provides a framework for teachers and students to learn together in a meaningful way. A workshop organizational format usually begins with teacher demonstration and modeling (mini-lessons), an opportunity for guided practice of the skills and content, independent practice (individual or small group), and finally ends with opportunities for sharing. While the independent practice takes place, teachers provide small group or individual differentiated instruction to meet the needs of their students. During this time in reading, the teacher is usually providing guided reading lessons to primary students or facilitating literature circles in the intermediate grades. During a writing workshop, teachers usually conduct small group lessons or meet one on one with students to confer about their writing.

- Literacy centers/stations are essential to a balanced literacy program and offer a wide variety of learning opportunities to students. These centers allow the students time to practice and apply what they are learning in a small group setting. Examples of some literacy centers are poetry, listening, word work, writing, spelling, comprehension, literature response, vocabulary, art, independent reading, and so on.

- Small groups are groups of students working together in order to expand their knowledge. Examples of small groups are jigsaws (small groups provided a task to later share their knowledge with the whole class), literature circles, and students working at centers.

- Paired/buddy reading takes place between two students of the same or differing ages/grade levels. The pair of students usually has a copy of the same text and read chorally or take turns reading to each other.

Checkpoint

1. True or false: The workshop approach to organizing your classroom provides time to meet with small groups of students and provide differentiated instruction to meet individual and small group needs.

2. True or false: True literature circles contain many students and many different books so that students can teach each other about what they are reading independently.

Checkpoint Answers

1. True

2. False

Emergent Literacy

Emergent literacy is defined as the skills, knowledge, and attitudes that are developmental precursors to conventional forms of reading and writing (www.ed.gov, n.d.). Young children learn that text and pictures provide meaning. They learn to appreciate, explore, and enjoy text. During this phase, children are exposed to the structure or syntax of language and are encouraged to predict what the text may be about. Simply stated, students at this phase are getting to know books and learning about print. The following are terms related to emergent literacy.

- **Oral language development**—In order to enhance a child's oral language or verbal skills, children must be involved in the following, on a regular basis: open-ended (whole group, small group, and one-on-one) discussions, read alouds, echo reading, songs, nursery rhymes, storytelling, readers' theater, cloze activities, poetry, role play and drama, fingerplays, and so on.

- **Phonological awareness**—Phonological awareness includes the ability of a student to identify and manipulate large parts of spoken language (words, syllables, onset/rime units) and awareness of other aspects of sound in language like **alliteration**, intonation, and rhyming.

- **Alphabet knowledge**—Alphabet knowledge requires young learners to identify and name the upper- and lowercase letters of the alphabet. Alphabet books, magnetic letters, and the use of environmental print all enhance alphabet knowledge.

- **Concepts of print**—Knowledge of how print works is vital. Young learners should understand: print conveys meaning, directionality (left to right progression, top to bottom), concept of a word (word boundaries), letter knowledge, phonemic awareness, and literacy language (author, illustrations, title, and so on).

Repetition and routine are key components of high quality instruction for young students. Through daily read alouds, guided reading, and shared reading instruction, students can be exposed to basic concepts of print, word recognition skills, vocabulary, sight words, high frequency words, literary elements, content knowledge, narrative and expository structure, and comprehension strategies, just to name a few. This type of routine and repetitive instruction provides students the opportunity to truly internalize the necessary skills to become successful readers. Specifically, the incorporation of these basic concepts in small group guided reading settings can prevent difficulties with emergent literacy skills or intervene when these skills pose difficulty to students. This being said, consistently monitoring their growth by using various assessments is not only mandated by the state but also vital to the teacher's instructional goals. Whether formal or informal, assessments help the teacher identify student strengths and weaknesses. In order to instruct and create lesson plans that meet the varying needs of the diverse population in the classroom, teachers must employ various assessment instruments. The following are examples of various assessment instruments and how they can be used with young students:

- **Concepts of print**—Checklist that identifies basic knowledge of print conventions and overall book structure (that is, letter identification, word boundaries, book cover, and so on).

- **Checklists**—High frequency word checklists can be used as screening and progress monitoring tools to assess what words students know instantly.

- **Rubrics**—Retelling rubrics can be used to identify what important literary elements students are incorporating into their retelling.

- **Games**—Sight word bingo can be used to informally assess sight word recognition.

- **Surveys**—Interest and attitude surveys can be used to gauge attitudes about reading and identify topics of interest to the students.

- **Portfolios**—Working and/or growth portfolios can be used to collect work samples over time to gain true insight into how the students' skills have progressed.

Checkpoint

1. Fill in the blanks: Phonological awareness refers to the ability to _____ and _____ large parts of spoken language.

2. True or false: Oral language skills can be enhanced through songs, echo reading, and story retellings.

3. Fill in the blank: _____ and _____ are two informal assessment instruments.

Checkpoint Answers

1. identify and manipulate

2. True

3. Any two of the following: checklists, rubrics, games, concepts of print, surveys, portfolios

Competency 5: Knowledge of Communication

Competency Description

According to the Competencies and Skills Required for Teacher Certification in Florida, Elementary Education (available at http://www.fldoe.org/asp/ftce/pdf/60ElementaryEducationK-6.pdf) **Competency 5** for the Elementary Education (K–6) Subject Area Examination (SAE) addresses the following key indicators:

1. Demonstrate knowledge of penmanship (e.g., legibility, proper slant, spacing).
2. Demonstrate knowledge of listening and speaking strategies (e.g., questioning, paraphrasing, eye contact, voice, gestures).
3. Identify instructional methods for developing listening and speaking skills.

Overview

Knowledge of oral and written communications skills is of primary importance to elementary educators. There are approximately **6 questions** that address Competency 5. This section addresses the following areas related to **Competency 5** key indicators:

- Penmanship
- Instructional Methods and Strategies
  - Listening
  - Speaking Strategies

Penmanship

Penmanship refers to the quality or style of one's handwriting. Legible or easily read handwriting is a developmental process, somewhat like reading. In the primary grades, students are taught manuscript handwriting techniques, and the intermediate grades teach cursive. Depending on your school or district, students may be taught traditional manuscript or D'Nealian, which is a more modern form of handwriting that incorporates more strokes. Being able to transfer thoughts to paper in a legible manner is of utmost important in written communication. The following are several elements related to traditional and legible manuscript handwriting:

- **Letter formation**—Four basic strokes: circles, horizontal lines, vertical lines, and slant lines.
- **Spacing**—Should be consistent (to the eye) between letters, words, and sentences.
- **Letter size and alignment**—Should be roughly the same size on the writing lines, using the headline, midline, and baseline as instructed (that is, tall letters should touch the headline; "tail" letters should descend below the baseline; all letters should "sit" on the baseline and should not float above this designated line).
- **Line quality**—Strokes of the pencil should be of a consistent smoothness, color, and weight; line quality should not be too dark or wavy, too light or varied; smooth circles and straight lines are the goal.

Checkpoint

1. Fill in the blank: Students are taught to write in cursive in the _____ grades.

2. True or false: The element of legible handwriting that refers to consistency of the pencil strokes is letter alignment.

Checkpoint Answers

1. intermediate
2. False; line quality

Instructional Methods and Strategies

Listening and speaking opportunities should abound in elementary classrooms. Both listening and speaking are oral processes that are essential elements of high quality language arts instruction. Students must be taught to listen and speak effectively for maximum success in the school environment and later life.

Listening

Listening is the language art used most often yet it is also the one most often neglected. Listening requires the student to take in or receive what has been heard and seen, attend to what is most important, and then comprehend the message. Students must be provided multiple opportunities daily, to listen effectively in order to gain meaning from the world around them. They must also know that there are several purposes of listening. *Efferent listening* refers to listening to learn new information, and *aesthetic listening* is performed more for pleasure and enjoyment. Listening to their teachers, other authority figures at the school site, and their peers is vital to student success in school. The following lists a variety of methods and strategies that should be used to enhance listening skills in the school environment:

- **Set a purpose**—Prior to a read aloud, storytelling, or class demonstration, ensure that students understand the objective of the lesson. Making predictions prior to the lesson helps to set a purpose for listening attentively to confirm or revise what has been stated. Activating prior knowledge related to the topic enhances the listeners' ability to make connections to the new information being presented and what was already known about a particular topic. The use of visuals help to engage the listeners as well.

- **Questioning and visualizing**—Before, during, and after a reading or class discussion, students should question the content of the lesson to ascertain the important concepts and begin to organize the newly learned information. Along with questioning, students need to visualize while listening as well. The questioning and visualizing strategies enhance critical thinking skills and aid in deeper comprehension.

- **Summarizing**—Concurrently and after questioning, students should begin to synthesize the information and see relationships among key concepts. Having students pair up to discuss what has been heard as in a Think-Pair-Share, will enable them to process the information and allows for another opportunity to listen.

- **Graphic organizers**—In order to solidify that last phase of listening, comprehension, many teachers encourage students to complete graphic organizers to synthesize and then evaluate the learning that has taken place.

Speaking Strategies

Listening and speaking often go hand in hand in elementary classrooms. Allowing students to process their learning through speaking is vital to deeply understanding the concepts being presented day in and day out. Speaking to an individual or group, using eye contact, taking turns, and projecting your voice is not only useful in the classroom but necessary to effective communication in daily life. The following lists a variety of methods and strategies that should be used to enhance speaking skills in the school environment:

- **Organizational format**—A combination of whole group lessons and small group discussions provides multiple and varying speaking opportunities for students. Students in classrooms with literacy centers or stations have many opportunities to speak and process their learning. The use of small groups in guided reading and literature circles again provides students the opportunity to not just recall what is being read and learned but to critically think about the information and hear their classmates' points of view as well.

- **Questioning**—As stated, listening and speaking go hand in hand; therefore, the questioning strategy is one that can be thought but also expressed orally. Teachers model varying levels of questioning (literal, inferential, and critical), and students then begin to add these types of questions to their own repertoire.

- **Retelling**—Retelling what has been heard helps the students to organize their thoughts into a logical sequence of beginning, middle, and end. Students are encouraged to focus on the big ideas and summarize or paraphrase the less important parts.
- **Drama**—Allowing students to role play, storytell, and share readers theater scripts with an audience provides an authentic way for students to elaborate on their learning. Students can manipulate visuals to add to the performance.

Checkpoint

1. Fill in the blank: The _____ strategy is useful in both effective listening and speaking.

2. True or false: Efferent listening is listening for pleasure or enjoyment.

3. Fill in the blank: In order to foster multiple opportunities for listening and speaking in the classroom, your day should be structured to incorporate both whole group and _____ lessons.

Checkpoint Answers

1. questioning
2. False
3. small group

Competency 6: Knowledge of Information and Media Literacy

Competency Description

According to the Competencies and Skills Required for Teacher Certification in Florida, Elementary Education (available at http://www.fldoe.org/asp/ftce/pdf/60ElementaryEducationK-6.pdf) **Competency 6** for the Elementary Education (K–6) Subject Area Examination (SAE) addresses the following key indicators:

1. Demonstrate knowledge of a wide array of information and media literacy (e.g., Internet, printed material, artifacts, visual media, primary sources).
2. Demonstrate knowledge of systematic and ethical processes for collecting and presenting authentic information.
3. Identify current technology available for use in educational settings (e.g., computer software and hardware, Web tools).

Overview

Knowledge of information and media literacy has gained increasing importance in recent years in elementary education. There are approximately **6 questions** that address Competency 6. This section addresses the following areas related to **Competency 6** key indicators:

- Information and Media Literacy
- Educational Technology
  - Interactive White Boards
  - Computer Software

Information and Media Literacy

Media literacy refers to the ability of a student to interpret media messages. These media messages are provided in a variety of formats and for many purposes. These messages in the school environment are primarily meant to inform the reader. The following is a list of definitions related to information and media literacy:

- **Artifacts**—Real objects; usually representative of a particular culture or event
- **Internet**—A communication system that connects computers and their networks all over the world
- **Printed material**—Anything with printed text: books, magazines, journals, and so on
- **Primary sources**—A document or piece of work that was written, recorded, or created during a particular time period: photographs, speeches, interviews, diaries, video and audio recordings, and so on
- **Visual media**—Also known as non-print media, this refers to anything that is not literally printed: television, video, some radio broadcasts, etc.

Safely and effectively navigating the Internet and all of its many tools is an important skill for elementary age students. In this digital age, students are accessing and using mass amounts of information on the Web at younger and younger ages. The following are some basic guidelines for how elementary age students can safely interact with the Internet:

- Primary students should be provided preselected sites to choose from in order to avoid exposure to inappropriate web content.
- Intermediate students can also be provided preselected sites but should be taught advanced search skills to collect information helpful to their learning.

- Once accessed, students should be taught to critically question and evaluate the site based on its content and their needs. Questions like, "Does this site contain accurate information?" and "Does this site contain information I need for the subject I am studying?" should be considered when accessing information and media online.
- Older students must be taught proper citation skills and should understand copyright laws.

Checkpoint

1. True or false: An authentic arrowhead found on a Native American reservation is an example of an artifact.

2. True or false: Visual media refers to any print material including books, journals, and magazines.

3. True or false: The Internet is a safe environment for students of all ages.

Checkpoint Answers

1. True
2. False
3. False

Educational Technology

Interactive White Boards

Interactive white boards are becoming more and more popular in educational settings. Lessons that would have taken place on a traditional whiteboard using erasable markers are now being accessed or created using new software that allows the students to interact with the material in a digital fashion. Using this interactive white board technology, students and teachers can read, write, click, drag, hide, and save all of their work on the computer. Educators can quiz and analyze student work instantaneously.

Computer Software

- Basic programs like the Microsoft Office package include computer software that can be used to simply word process information like stories they have written (Word) or create presentations (Powerpoint).
- Programs like Kidspiration offer students the opportunity to create their own graphic organizers including but not limited to charts, timelines, and webs.
- Programs like PhotoStory, Windows MovieMaker, and iMovie enable students to create digital stories to share their learning through visual media.

Web Tools

- **E-mail**—Students can interact with other students around the country and the world using basic e-mail. Programs like Epals aid teachers in setting up electronic correspondence with other classrooms.
- **Online book clubs**—Many publishing companies offer online book clubs to motivate students to discuss the books they have been reading online with other students outside of their classrooms and sometimes even with the authors.
- **WebQuests**—WebQuests are web-based learning experiences in which students navigate through predetermined web sites to glean further insight into a topic of study. Sample webquests can be found online or teachers/students can create their own based on a topic of study.

- **Wiki sites**—Many web tools allow students to create their own "mini-web pages". Wiki and Pbworks are two examples of such tools. Students can combine text, graphics, animation, and even hyperlinks to share and extend their knowledge.

- **Video conferencing**—Programs like Skype are allowing students to communicate, via video online, with other students regarding topics of study. These online video discussions allow for greater understanding and the expansion of knowledge.

- **Blogs**—A blog, short for weblog, is a user-friendly webpage that allows students to post and comment on their work. Ongoing dialogue surrounding the work is encouraged. Classroom news blogs and literature response blogs have become common in elementary classrooms.

- **Podcasts**—Students and teachers have the ability to publish their audio recordings for all to hear, online. These podcasts, like blogs, allow students a new way to share their learning.

- **Video projects**—Creating digital stories or videos related to student learning share and expand newfound knowledge. Uploading these videos to safe video-hosting sites like TeacherTube allows students to share their knowledge with the masses.

Checkpoint

1. True or false: To aid comprehension, students can create their own graphic organizers using computer software.

2. Fill in the blank: The Internet provides such tools as _____ to promote discussion about books outside of the regular classroom.

3. True or false: Blogs tend to isolate students and do not allow for collaboration opportunities.

Checkpoint Answers

1. True
2. online book clubs
3. False

Summary

The Language Arts and Reading section (Competencies 1–6) encompasses a variety of subcompetencies related to the basic knowledge required of educators teaching elementary age students. Knowledge of the reading process entails the five components of reading: emergent literacy, word recognition skills, critical thinking strategies, comprehension skills, and informational/literary structures. Knowledge of literature and literary analysis includes genres of literature, literature response activities, multicultural children's literature, and literary devices. Knowledge of the writing process means that the teacher understands the developmental stages of writing, modes of writing, the phases of the writing process, and writing conventions. Reading methods and assessment refers to key terms and definitions related to current reading assessments and organizational formats that enhance reading instruction. Knowledge of communication entails written communication along with listening and speaking skills and instructional methods. Finally, information and media literacy highlights skills necessary for today's students and provides basic information regarding technological tools used in educational settings.

This section reflects the skills required in this area for teacher certification in Florida, Elementary Education (available at http://www.fldoe.org/asp/ftce/pdf/60ElementaryEducationK-6.pdf). You should use the information in this section to complement your previous knowledge in the areas of language arts and reading. The general review of Language Arts and Reading (Competencies 1–6) provided in this chapter should allow you to explore areas of strength and need that you might still need to review. As indicated before, sample questions for the competency area as a whole appear in the next section of the chapter. Answers and explanations follow the sample questions. These sections should provide an opportunity for further practice and analysis.

Sample Questions

1. What are the three cueing systems?

    A. emergent, early, and fluent
    B. word identification, oral language development, and letter identification
    C. graphophonemic, semantic, and syntactic
    D. pre-alphabetic, alphabetic, and conventional

2. The literary device defined as two or more words or syllables, near each other, with the same beginning consonant is

    A. hyperbole.
    B. pun.
    C. satire.
    D. alliteration.

3. There are _____ critical components for reading success.

    A. 11
    B. 5
    C. 6
    D. 4

4. A primary source document is

    A. one that was created during that time period.
    B. nonprint media.
    C. a web site.
    D. a blog.

5. During a read aloud, a kindergarten student comments that the teacher is reading the pictures and not the words in the book. This child is demonstrating a lack of understanding in

    A. letter knowledge.
    B. alphabetic principle.
    C. concepts of print.
    D. phonemic awareness.

6. Sally is experiencing reading difficulties as noted on her recent timed fluency check. Her reading speed is slow and halted. This shows a weakness in which area of fluency?

    A. rate
    B. accuracy
    C. automaticity
    D. prosody

7. The teacher has organized her classroom to allow for small groups. Students are listening to books on tape or CD, reading poetry, and responding to quality literature in writing. This is an example of what organizational format?

    A. literature circles
    B. shared reading
    C. interactive writing
    D. reading centers/stations

8. A third grade class is reading *The Miraculous Journey of Edward Tulane* by Kate DiCamillo. Rather than reading this book as a whole group, the teacher has created small groups of students who have specific discussion roles. What organizational format is being used to encourage discussion and overall comprehension of *The Miraculous Journey of Edward Tulane*?

    A. book talks
    B. guided reading
    C. literature circles
    D. independent reading

9. A teacher asks her students, "Which two words rhyme: fat, rag, cat?" Which area of emergent literacy does this illustrate?

    A. phonological awareness
    B. vocabulary
    C. concepts of print
    D. fluency

10. Mrs. Spalding's second grade class has just read an article from a *Time for Kids* magazine. Through modeled writing, she is demonstrating how to write a five sentence paragraph about the article. This is an example of what comprehension skill?

    A. visualizing
    B. making an inference
    C. summarizing
    D. author's purpose

11. A teacher encourages her students to brainstorm ideas about a topic of interest that they might like to write about. Brainstorming takes place during what phase of the writing process?

    A. drafting
    B. prewriting
    C. editing
    D. revising

12. Identify the literary device used in the following example.

Her stare was as cold as ice!

    A. onomatopoeia
    B. simile
    C. metaphor
    D. analogy

13. Graphic organizers are

    A. busy work.
    B. worksheets that require basic recall of facts.
    C. synthesizing and summarizing tools that aid comprehension.
    D. a waste of time.

14. When an author attempts to convince the reader that a point is valid, they are using what mode of writing?

    A. descriptive
    B. expository
    C. narrative
    D. persuasive

15. The Florida Comprehensive Assessment Test (FCAT) is a(n)

    A. norm-referenced test.
    B. informal reading inventory.
    C. criterion-referenced test.
    D. performance based assessment.

16. In order to communicate in writing, penmanship must be legible. Which of the following contributes to legible handwriting?

    A. spacing
    B. letter formation
    C. letter alignment
    D. all of the above

17. A student read a 200-word piece in 4:45 with 6 recorded errors. What would his accuracy rate be for that reading?

    A. 42 WCPM
    B. 40.9 WCPM
    C. 40 WCPM
    D. 41.8 WCPM

18. An example of visual media is

    A. a book.
    B. a journal.
    C. the newspaper.
    D. a television program.

19. Questioning and retelling are two strategies that enhance _____ skills.

    A. listening and speaking
    B. comprehension
    C. word recognition
    D. both A and B

20. Classroom news and literature response _____ have become common web-based activities in elementary classrooms.

    A. blogs
    B. digital stories
    C. word documents
    D. all of the above

Answer Explanations for Sample Questions

1. **C.** Competency 4. Graphophonemic (visual), semantic (meaning), and syntactic (structure) are the three cueing systems related to the reading process.

2. **D.** Competency 2. Alliteration is defined as two or more words or syllables with the same beginning consonant.

3. **B.** Competency 1. Phonological awareness, phonics, vocabulary, fluency, and comprehension are the five critical components to reading success.

4. **A.** Competencies 1 and 6. A primary source is a document or piece of work, which was actually written, recorded, or created during the specific time under study.

5. **C.** Competency 4. Concepts of print includes that print conveys meaning, directionality (left to right progression, top to bottom), concept of a word (word boundaries), letter knowledge, phonemic awareness, and literacy language (author, illustrations, title, and so on).

6. **A.** Competency 1. Rate is defined as the speed of reading and greatly influences whether or not a student can comprehend the text. Accuracy, prosody, and automaticity are also crucial elements of fluency.

7. **D.** Competency 4. Reading centers/stations allow students to construct meaning in a small group setting. For the teacher, this organizational format allows time to meet with guided reading groups and to differentiate instruction to meet the varying needs of students in the classroom.

8. **C.** Competency 2. Literature circles are small, temporary groups of students that gather together to discuss a book that each of them are reading with the goal of enhancing comprehension.

9. **A.** Competencies 1 and 4. Emergent literacy includes oral language development, print awareness, phonological awareness, and alphabet knowledge. Phonological awareness is the ability of a student to identify and manipulate large parts of spoken language (words, syllables, onset/rime units) and awareness of other aspects of sound in our language like alliteration, intonation, and rhyming.

10. **C.** Competency 1. Summarizing is to simply and concisely paraphrase what has been read.

11. **B.** Competency 3. Prewriting is the phase of the writing process that includes activating prior knowledge, gathering, and organizing ideas. Drafting, editing, and revising are all later phases in the writing process.

12. **B.** Competency 2. Each of the options are literary devices. Although an analogy is a detailed and sometimes lengthy comparison of two ideas or events, simile is the correct answer. A simile is a comparison using *like* or *as*.

13. **C.** Competency 1. Graphic organizers are synthesizing and summarizing tools that aid student comprehension. They allow students to process what they have read, heard, or viewed. Graphic organizers can be completed individually or in small groups and can be an alternative form of assessment when completed.

14. **D.** Competency 3. Persuasive writing is writing that attempts to convince the reader that a point of view is valid or that the reader should take a specific action. Descriptive, expository, and narrative are all modes of writing as well.

15. **C.** Competency 4. FCAT is a criterion-referenced test. These types of tests are assessment instruments that assess the point at which the student has achieved mastery.

16. **D.** Competency 5. Letter formation, spacing, letter size and alignment, along with line quality all contribute to legible handwriting or penmanship.

17. **B.** Competency 4. If a student read a 200-word piece in 4:45 with 6 recorded errors, his accuracy rate would be as follows: $\dfrac{200 - 6(x - E) \cdot 60}{285 \text{ (seconds)}} = 40.9$ WCPM. Thus, the student reads 40.9 words correct per minute.

18. **D.** Competency 6. Visual media is also known as non-print media and refers to anything that is not literally printed: television, video, some radio broadcasts, and so on.

19. **D.** Competency 5. Comprehension, listening, and speaking skills are all enhanced by questioning and retelling.

20. **A.** Competency 6. Blogs are user-friendly web pages that allow students to post and comment on their work.

Social Science

This chapter provides a general review of Social Science (Competencies 7–11) with sample questions and explanations at the end of the chapter. Checkpoint exercises are found throughout, giving you an opportunity to practice the skills addressed in this section. The answers to the Checkpoint exercises immediately follow the set of questions. We encourage you to cover the answers as you complete the Checkpoint exercises. Sample questions for the competency as a whole appear at the end of the chapter. Answers and explanations follow the sample questions.

Competency 7: Knowledge of Time, Continuity, and Change (History)

Competency Description

According to the Competencies and Skills Required for Teacher Certification in Florida, Elementary Education (available at www.fldoe.org/asp/ftce/pdf/60ElementaryEducationK-6.pdf) **Competency 7** for the Elementary Education (K–6) Subject Area Examination (SAE) addresses the following key indicators:

1. Identify historical events that are related by cause and effect.
2. Evaluate examples of primary source documents for historical perspective.
3. Identify cultural contributions and technological developments of Africa; the Americas; Asia, including the Middle East; and Europe.
4. Relate physical and human geographic factors to major historical events and movements.
5. Identify significant historical leaders and events that have influenced Eastern and Western civilizations.
6. Identify the causes and consequences of exploration, settlement, and growth.
7. Identify individuals and events that have influenced economic, social, and political institutions in the United States.
8. Identify immigration and settlement patterns that have shaped the history of the United States.
9. Identify how various cultures contributed to the unique social, cultural, economic, and political features of Florida.

Overview

Knowledge of history, specifically time, continuity, and change is of primary importance to elementary educators responsible for educating our youth in the social sciences. There are approximately **11 questions** that address Competency 7. This section addresses the following areas related to **Competency 7** key indicators:

- Historical Events and Figures
- Early Explorers
- Florida History

Historical Events and Figures

Today's world has been shaped by many notable occurrences and historic figures. The idea that some of these historical events are related by cause and effect is known as historic causation. The following is a list of some notable historical events and figures:

- **Columbus landing in the New World**—Christopher Columbus (1451–1506), perhaps one of the most famous early explorers, believed the Earth was a sphere. After much pleading, the King and Queen of Spain agreed to fund his expeditions. Columbus made four voyages in an effort to find a route to the East. During his expeditions he discovered the Bahamas, Hispaniola, Cuba, Dominica, Guadeloupe, Jamaica, Central America, and South America. Columbus's discoveries opened up the Western Hemisphere to economic and political development by the Europeans, namely the Spanish, English, and French.

- **French and Indian War (1754–1763)**—This war, which was an extension of the European Seven Years War, was a battle over colonial territory and wealth by the French and the English. This war resulted in effectively ending French cultural and political influence in North America. In their victory, England gained massive amounts of land but also weakened their rapport with the Native Americans. In sum, although the war strengthened England's hold on the colonies, it also worsened their relationship, which inevitably led to the Revolutionary War.

- **The American Revolutionary War (1775–1783)**—The Revolutionary War was also known as the American War of Independence. Due to rising tensions caused by the French and Indian War, colonists of the 13 original colonies (Massachusetts, Rhode Island, Connecticut, New Hampshire, New York, New Jersey, Pennsylvania, Delaware, Georgia, Maryland, North Carolina, South Carolina, and Virginia) desired to form self-governing independent states (American Revolution). These states, in order to defend their right to self-governance, fought the British. The war ended with the signing of the Treaty of Paris, which recognized the sovereignty of the United States.

- **Declaration of Independence (1776)**—This historic document written by Thomas Jefferson and adopted by the Second Continental Congress begins with a preamble or reason for the necessity of the document and then establishes the reasons why the original colonies sought freedom from British rule. This declaration laid the foundation for their new government and severed ties to Great Britain. The new nation would be called the United States of America.

- **The Industrial Revolution (1830s)**—This period of time was characterized by the transition from manual labor to the use of machines, specifically machines used in the creation of textiles, iron, and steam.

- **The Civil War (1861–1865)**—The American Civil War was a conflict between the North (the Union) and the South (the Confederacy). Eleven southern slave states wanted to secede from the union. Although noted as the deadliest war in American History, this war ended slavery (1862 Lincoln's Emancipation Proclamation), restored the union, and strengthened the role of the federal government.

- **Westward Expansion (1807–1912)**—After the War of 1812, Americans wanted to explore and settle the land to the west. This territory had been expanded due to the Louisiana Purchase. Famous explorers like Lewis and Clark, followed by pioneer families, swept westward and founded new communities. Another component of settling the west involved the removal of the Native Americans that lived there (under the authority of President Andrew Jackson). They were cruelly and violently driven from their homes and pushed to concentrated areas called reservations. By the early twentieth century, the west was settled, and the United States consisted of 48 contiguous states.

- **World War I (1914–1918)**—This First World War was initiated by a conflict between Austria-Hungary and Serbia. Soon afterward, it became a global conflict that involved major world powers. The two opposing military alliances were the Entente (Allied) Powers (Russian Empire, United Kingdom, France, Canada, Australia, Italy, the Empire of Japan, Portugal, and the United States) and the Central Powers (German Empire, the Austrian-Hungarian Empire, the Ottoman Empire (Turkey) and the Kingdom of Bulgaria). The Allied Powers were victorious, but lasting effects and repercussions from the war led to WWII.

- **World War II (1939–1945)**—The Second World War was again a global military conflict between two opposing forces: The Allies (Leaders)—Great Britain (Churchill), United States (Roosevelt/Truman), Russia (Stalin), Free France (De Gaulle), and China (Chiang Kai-shek)—and the Axis Powers (Leaders)—Germany (Hitler), Italy (Mussolini), and Japan (Hirohito). The attack on Pearl Harbor resulted in the United States' involvement in the war. In 1945 the Allies defeated the Axis with the USSR and the United States emerging as the world's superpowers. This led to the Cold War, which lasted for the next 45 years. The United Nations was formed in an effort to prevent further global conflicts.

- **Korean War (1950–1953)**—Due to a division in Korea (communist North and American-occupied South) caused by WWII, war began in 1950. The United States came to South Korea's aid but to no avail. In 1953, the war ended with a signing of a peace treaty at Panmunjom and with Korea remaining divided, just as it was at the beginning of the conflict.

- **Civil Rights Act of 1964**—This statutory law ended a 100-year quest by African Americans for racial equality. This landmark piece of legislation outlawed racial segregation in the United States. Specifically, it voided Jim Crow laws in the southern states and prohibited racial discrimination in schools, public places, and places of employment.

- **Vietnam War (U.S. involved 1959–1975)**—This war was fought between the communist North Vietnam and the government of South Vietnam. The United States, again in an effort to oppose communism, supported the South Vietnamese forces until 1973 after Congress passed the Case-Church Amendment in response to the anti-war movement. North Korea captured the capital of South Korea, Saigon (Fall of Saigon), which marked the end of the war and the beginning of a reunified Korea under communist rule.

- **Persian Gulf War (August 1990–February 1991)**—Also known simply as the Gulf War, this military conflict authorized by the United Nations was between Iraq and a coalition force made up of 34 nations. The purpose of this war was to liberate Kuwait and expel Iraqi forces. Operation Desert Storm was the name for the United States land and air operations involved in the Gulf War effort.

There have been a significant number of historical events and leaders that have helped to influence and shape Eastern and Western civilization as we know it. The following is a sampling of just a few of those leaders and events:

Historical Leaders	Influential Events
Alexander the Great	King of Macedonia in 336 B.C. Conquered the Persian Empire Founded the city of Alexandria in Egypt, a center of learning and culture Created a massive empire and restored order in Ancient Greece
Nicolaus Copernicus (1473–1543)	First astronomer to place the sun at the center of the universe
Galileo Galilei (1564–1642)	Italian physicist, mathematician, astronomer, and philosopher responsible for the birth of modern science
Isaac Newton	English physicist, mathematician, astronomer, natural philosopher, alchemist, and theologian known for defining gravity and the laws of motion
John Locke	British Enlightenment writer whose ideas influenced the Declaration of Independence, state constitutions, and the United States Constitution; believed that people are born free with certain natural rights including the right to life, liberty, and property
Thomas Jefferson	Third President of the United States; considered one of the Founding Fathers of the United States Principal author of the Declaration of Independence Played a role in the Louisiana Purchase and the Lewis and Clark Expedition

Checkpoint

1. True or false: The defeat of the Axis Powers in WWII led to the emerging of two world superpowers and inevitably the Cold War.

2. Fill in the blank: The _____ War led to the start of the American Revolutionary War.

3. True or false: Christopher Columbus discovered the New World.

4. Fill in the blank: _____ was the first astronomer to place the sun at the center of the universe.

Checkpoint Answers

1. True

2. French and Indian

3. False; the Vikings and Native Americans

4. Nicolaus Copernicus

Early Explorers

The following table provides dates, explorers, their nationality, and their most notable achievements (adapted from http://www.mce.k12tn.net/explorers/explorers.htm). This site also provides other valuable information related to American history and simple quizzes for testing your knowledge.

Date	Explorer	Nationality	Achievement
1492–1504	Christopher Columbus	Italian	Made four voyages to West Indies and Caribbean Islands
1497–1503	Amerigo Vespucci	Italian	Sailed to West Indies and South America
1497–1498	John Cabot	Italian	Explored the shores of Newfoundland, Nova Scotia, and Labrador
1498	Vasco da Gama	Portuguese	First to travel to West Indies around Africa's Cape of Good Hope
1513	Vasco de Balboa	Spanish	Led expedition across Panama and found the Pacific Ocean
1513	Juan Ponce de Leon	Spanish	Explored Florida looking for the Fountain of Youth
1520–1521	Ferdinand Magellan	Portuguese	Circumnavigated the globe with five ships and 270 men
1519–1521	Hernando Cortez	Spanish	Conquered Aztecs in Mexico
1523–1535	Francisco Pizarro	Spanish	Conquered Peru
1534–1542	Jacques Cartier	French	Traveled St. Lawrence River
1539–1541	Hernando De Soto	Spanish	Explored American Southeast; discovered the Mississippi River
1540–1542	Francisco Vazquez de Coronado	Spanish	Explored American Southwest
1577–1580	Sir Frances Drake	English	First Englishman to sail around the world; defeated the Spanish Armada; claimed California for England
1603–1616	Samuel de Champlain	French	Explored eastern coast of North America and the coast of the St. Lawrence River to Lake Huron; reached Lake Champlain
1609–1611	Henry Hudson	English	Explored Hudson Bay, Hudson River, and Hudson Strait

Checkpoint

1. True or false: John Cabot traveled around the Cape of Good Hope to reach the West Indies.

2. Fill in the blank: _____ explored Florida in search of the Fountain of Youth.

3. Fill in the blank: Hernando De Soto explored the present day American Southeast and discovered the _____ River.

Checkpoint Answers

1. False

2. Juan Ponce de Leon

3. Mississippi

Florida History

Florida history is the main topic of social studies education in fourth grade in the state of Florida. The following highlights important information regarding Florida's history:

- Initially inhabited by various tribes like the Timicuan.
- Named Florida by Juan Ponce de Leon in 1513.
- The English, Spanish, and French established settlements in Florida during the 1500s and 1600s.
- St. Augustine, founded by the Spanish, came to serve as the capitals of the British (East) and Spanish (West) colonies of Florida.
- Britain tried to develop Florida through the importation of immigrants for labor.
- Spain regained control of Florida after the American Revolutionary War.
- In 1845, Florida became the 27th state in the United States of America.
- Florida's land was intensely developed prior to the Great Depression of the 1930s.
- Florida's economy was adversely effected by WWII.
- Florida is one of the most populous states in the south.

Checkpoint

1. True or false: Juan Ponce De Leon discovered Florida.

2. True or false: Florida became the 17th state in the union in 1845.

3. Fill in the blank: Florida was inhabited by _____ prior to its later discovery by Europeans.

Checkpoint Answers

1. False
2. False
3. Native American tribes

Competency 8: Knowledge of People, Places, and Environment (Geography)

Competency Description

According to the Competencies and Skills Required for Teacher Certification in Florida, Elementary Education (available at www.fldoe.org/asp/ftce/pdf/60ElementaryEducationK-6.pdf) **Competency 8** for the Elementary Education (K–6) Subject Area Examination (SAE) addresses the following key indicators:

1. Identify the six essential elements (i.e., the world in spatial terms, places and regions, physical systems, human systems, environment and society, uses of geography), including the specific terms for each element.
2. Interpret maps and other graphic representations and identify tools and technologies to acquire, process, and report information from a spatial perspective.
3. Interpret statistics that show how places differ in their human and physical characteristics.
4. Identify ways in which people adapt to an environment through the production and use of clothing, food, and shelter.
5. Identify how tools and technological advances affect the environment.
6. Identify physical, cultural, economic, and political reasons for the movement of people in the world, nation, or state.
7. Identify how transportation and communication networks contribute to the level of economic development in different regions.
8. Compare and contrast major regions of the world.

Overview

Knowledge of geography, specifically people, places, and the environment is of primary importance to elementary educators responsible for educating our youth in the social sciences. There are approximately **11 questions** that address Competency 8. This section addresses the following areas related to **Competency 8** key indicators:

- Essential Elements of Geography
- Map and Globe Terminology

Essential Elements of Geography

Geography can be defined as the study of the Earth's surface, atmosphere, and people. The following web identifies the six essential elements of geography (Chapin, 2009):

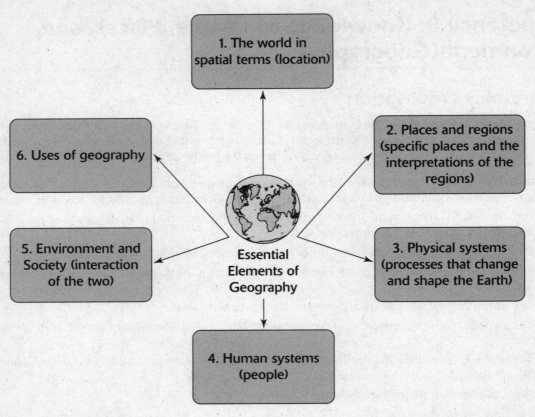

1. The world in spatial terms refers to location. Location refers to the position on the Earth's surface. These locations can be either **relative** or **absolute**. Spatial terms reference organization of people and places on Earth.

2. Places and regions refers to the physical characteristics of specific places and how they form and change.

3. Physical systems are processes that change and shape the Earth.

4. Human systems are the people or inhabitants.

5. Environment and Society refers to the relationships and interactions that take place between people and their surroundings.

6. Finally, uses of geography include interpreting the past and present along with planning for the future.

Checkpoint

1. Fill in the blank: There are _____ essential elements of geography.

2. True or false: One of the six essential elements of geography is Environment and Society.

3. Fill in the blank: A(n) _____ location is described by general terms and area landmarks.

Checkpoint Answers

1. six

2. True

3. relative

Map and Globe Terminology

Maps and globes are valuable educational tools in the elementary classroom. Teachers use maps to not only teach map skills but also to provide information to their students about places all over the world. Many maps are two-dimensional representations of a location often from an aerial viewpoint. Three-dimensional maps can be created by **cartographers**, using contour lines or lines that show the rise and fall of the land. Along with maps, graphs, diagrams, photographs, and satellite images provide valuable geographical information. These geographical representations can be used to describe natural changes (that is, volcanoes, earthquakes, floods) that occur and affect the world. In order to become adept in the use of maps and other geographical representations, students should not only be exposed to a wide variety of maps but also should create their own maps as well.

The following terms are essential to the use and understanding of maps:

- **Cartographers**—Mapmakers
- **Globe**—Small model of the Earth; considered the most accurate representation of Earth
- **Map**—Flattened out globe or portion of globe
- **Grid**—Vertical and horizontal lines on a map
- **Equator**—Horizontal, imaginary line that divides the Earth into its northern and southern halves
- **Prime Meridian**—Vertical, imaginary line that divides the Earth into its eastern and western halves; runs through Greenwich, England (1884 site of the Royal Observatory; at that time housed the most advanced geographic equipment)
- **International Date Line**—Where the date officially changes each day
- **Latitude and longitude**—The grid lines on a map; longitude lines run from the poles, north and south; latitude lines run parallel to the equator, east and west
- **Hemispheres**—Northern and southern halves of the Earth
- **Scale**—Items on map are drawn to size; when compared to each other, they are the right size and distance apart; the larger the scale, the more detail shown (for example, theme park map), the smaller the scale, the more area shown but less detail (that is, world map); shown on map in fractions or words and figures (that is, 1 inch: 16 miles; 1: 1,000)
- **Symbol**—Representations of real things on a map (for example, dots for cities, stars for capitals); usually small simple shapes and pictures
- **Legend**—Also known as the key; explains what the symbols, colors, lines, and so on mean on a map
- **Directions**—Main directions are north, south, east, and west
- **Compass rose**—Indicator of four main directions (above) and northeast, northwest, southeast, and southwest; often part of the legend
- **Continents**—Seven mainland masses on Earth: Asia, Africa, North America, South America, Antarctica, Europe, and Australia
- **Oceans**—Largest expanses of sea water on Earth: Atlantic, Pacific, Indian, Southern (identified in 2000), and Arctic
- **Relief maps**—Show the shape of the land's surface; provide detail through use of color and contour lines
- **Thematic maps**—Show specific topics or subjects (for example, human or animal populations, climate, and so on)
- **Political maps**—Show governmental boundaries of counties, states, and countries; identify major cities and significant bodies of water
- **Physical maps**—Show country borders, major cities, significant bodies of water, and major landforms like deserts, mountains, and plains
- **Regions**—A wide-ranging geographic area; usually contains similar physical features (for exmaple, caverns, deltas, deserts, hills, mesas, mountains, plains, plateaus, and so on) or unifying characteristics (for example, common language, government)

- **Deforestation**—The process of clearing the forests; destabilizes mountainous regions
- **Continental drift**—Described by the theory of plate tectonics; refers to the movement of the Earth's crust over time
- **Erosion**—The wearing away or diminishing of the Earth's surface
- **Population**—People living in a particular geographic area
- **Demography**—A branch of science concerned with the well-being of society; statistical study of human populations interested in analyzing changes in size, movement, crime rates, education levels, and so on.

Checkpoint

1. Fill in the blank: The _____ is the imaginary line that divides the Earth into its eastern and western halves.

2. True or false: Demography is the statistical study of human populations.

3. Fill in the blank: _____ maps are those that specify a particular topic or subject.

Checkpoint Answers

1. Prime Meridian

2. True

3. Thematic

Competency 9: Knowledge of Government and the Citizen (Government and Civics)

Competency Description

According to the Competencies and Skills Required for Teacher Certification in Florida, Elementary Education (available at www.fldoe.org/asp/ftce/pdf/60ElementaryEducationK-6.pdf) **Competency 9** for the Elementary Education (K–6) Subject Area Examination (SAE) addresses the following key indicators:

1. Identify the structure, functions, and purposes of government.
2. Demonstrate knowledge of the rights and responsibilities of a citizen in the world, nation, state, and/or community.
3. Identify major concepts of the U.S. Constitution and other historical documents.
4. Identify how the legislative, executive, and judicial branches share powers and responsibility.
5. Demonstrate knowledge of the U.S. electoral system and the election process.
6. Identify the structures and functions of U.S. federal, state, and local governments.
7. Identify the relationships among social, economic, and political rights and the historical documents that secure these rights.
8. Demonstrate knowledge of the processes of the U.S. legal system.
9. Identify the roles of the United States in international relations.

Overview

Knowledge of our government and what it means to be a responsible citizen is of primary importance to elementary educators responsible for educating our youth in the social sciences. There are approximately **12 questions** that address Competency 9. This section addresses the following areas related to **Competency 9** key indicators:

- Government
  - Local and State Government
  - Federal (national) Government
  - Local, State, and Federal Powers
  - Federal Court System
  - State Courts
  - Election Process/Electoral College
- Civics

Government

Government can be defined as the agency in which a governing body functions and exercises authority. The government in the United States of America is a **democracy** or government by the people. A democratic form of government provides for equality and inalienable rights of its citizens. These citizens elect officials to make important decisions on their behalves. The government is primarily responsible for administering justice, the education system, maintaining roads, maintaining statistics about society, and overseeing the national defense. The various levels of government in the United States are local, state, and federal (national).

Local and State Government

- The leader of the local government is the **mayor**. The mayor is an elected official and works in concert with the **city council**.
- The leader of the state government is the **governor**. The governor is also an elected official who works cooperatively with state senators of the **Senate** and state representatives of the **House of Representatives**.

Federal (National) Government

The three branches of government are legislative, judicial, and executive. All branches are concerned with upholding the laws set forth by the Constitution of the United States of America and representing the citizens of this country. These branches provide for a system of checks and balances (each branch has the ability to check or limit the other; see "Election Process/Electoral College") and the separation of powers (each branch has specific powers and cannot interfere with the powers of another).

- **Legislative**—**Congress**; comprised of the Senate and the House of Representatives; established by Article I of the Constitution
- **Judicial**—**Supreme Court**; can determine established laws to be unconstitutional; led by supreme court justices appointed by the President of the United States; established by Article III of the Constitution
- **Executive**—Led by the President and Vice President; leads the country and the military; appoints justices; can veto rulings made by Congress; established by Article II of the Constitution

    Concerning international relations and the executive branch of government:

- Both the Secretary of State (appointed by the president) and the National Security Council advises the president on matters of foreign policy.
- Ambassadors are also Executive branch members, who reside in other countries in order to lobby for the United States in international meetings.

Note: The Magna Carta of 1215 (England) is considered the very first modern document that sought to limit the powers of the governing body.

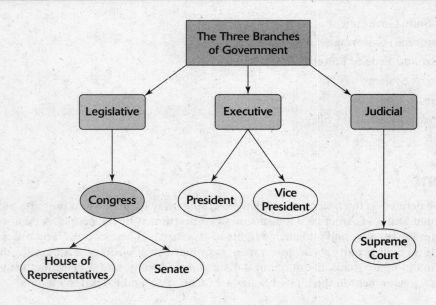

Local, State, and Federal Powers

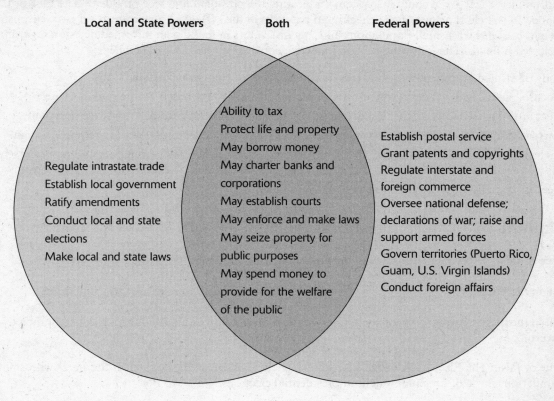

Local and State Powers   Both   Federal Powers

Regulate intrastate trade
Establish local government
Ratify amendments
Conduct local and state elections
Make local and state laws

Ability to tax
Protect life and property
May borrow money
May charter banks and corporations
May establish courts
May enforce and make laws
May seize property for public purposes
May spend money to provide for the welfare of the public

Establish postal service
Grant patents and copyrights
Regulate interstate and foreign commerce
Oversee national defense; declarations of war; raise and support armed forces
Govern territories (Puerto Rico, Guam, U.S. Virgin Islands)
Conduct foreign affairs

Federal Court System

There are three levels of federal courts in the Unites States: U.S. District Courts, U.S. Court of Appeals, and the Supreme Court. These courts are responsible for interpreting and applying the law in an effort to protect the rights and liberties of United States citizens. The following terms relate to the Unites States legal system:

- **U.S. District Courts**—Trial courts; each state has at least one district court; hears nearly all categories of federal cases including civil and criminal; 94 judicial districts
- **U.S. Court of Appeals**—One court for each of the 12 regional circuits; hears appeals from courts within its circuit
- **Supreme Court**—Highest court of appeals in the United States; established in Article III, Section 1 of the United States Constitution; consists of one chief justice and eight associate justices appointed by the president; one of its most important powers is **judicial review**

State Courts

Each state has its own independent system of courts that operates under that state's laws and constitution. The local courts in the state court system have limited jurisdiction and hear only minor cases.

Election Process/Electoral College

Knowing that the United States of America is a democracy, its citizens choose their elected officials and make decisions about laws, statutes, and referenda by voting. Citizens must register to vote and declare membership to a political party. There are many political parties in the United States, but the two main parties are the Republican and Democratic political parties. In order to become an elected official, candidates for office campaign to inform the public about the candidate's views and intentions if elected. Elections take place on a regular basis.

The Electoral College, also known as the College of Electors, was established by Article II in the United States Constitution in 1787. It is the country's system for electing the president and vice president. The Electoral College was included in Article II as one of the checks and balances in the system of government for two reasons: to give equal weight to states with small populations and to assist voters in making an informed decision regarding our highest elected officials. The following is basic knowledge related to the Electoral College:

- Body of elected representatives (electors) is chosen by the voters in each state.
- Electors pledge in advance to vote for the candidate of their party based on the popular vote.
- Meet after the citizen vote; cast ballots based on the public vote for president and vice president.
- Currently (2009) there are 538 electors in the United States; 270 electoral votes are required to win.
- Each state is assigned a number of electoral votes based on the number of senators and representatives it has (for example, Florida currently has 2 senators and 25 representatives for a total of 27 electoral votes).
- Electors actually elect the president and vice president.

Checkpoint

1. True or false: Supreme Court Justices are elected officials in the judicial branch of government.

2. Fill in the blank: The _____ government has the ability to regulate intrastate trade.

3. Fill in the blank: Article ____ of the United States Constitution established the legislative branch of government.

4. True or false: The Electoral College, also known as the College of Electors, gives the states with small populations more of an equal weight in presidential elections.

5. Fill in the blank: There are _____ U.S. District Courts.

Checkpoint Answers

1. False; appointed
2. local/state
3. I
4. True
5. 94

Civics

Civic education, also known as citizenship education, has been said to be one of the most important components of social studies education. The development of good citizens is imperative to the future of the country. Students should be exposed to social studies concepts that foster a need for becoming responsible, functioning members of their community. They should understand that they have certain rights as citizens and particular responsibilities as well.

Civic education is imperative to the democratic way of life. Because democratic society is founded on the principles set forth in the Constitution of the United States, following is a summary of that important historical document:

- Comprised of a **preamble**, seven articles, and 27 amendments
  - Article 1—Legislative Branch; includes nine sections
  - Article 2—Executive Branch; includes four sections
  - Article 3—Judicial Branch; includes three sections

- Article 4—The States; includes four sections
- Article 5—Amendments
- Article 6—Supreme Law, Oaths of Office and Debts
- Article 7—Approving the Constitution

The **Bill of Rights**, amendments (legally adopted changes) 1 through 10 of the Constitution of the United States of America, lays the foundation for the civic rights of citizens in this country and limits the power of the federal government. Briefly, the following describes the basic rights noted in the first ten amendments to the United States Constitution known as the Bill of Rights:

- First Amendment—Provides for five freedoms: religion, speech, the press, assembly, and petition
- Second Amendment—States the right of citizens to keep and bear arms
- Third Amendment—States that citizens do not have to provide housing to soldiers during peacetime
- Fourth Amendment—States the right to privacy
- Fifth Amendment—States the right to due process of the law
- Sixth Amendment—States the right to a public and speedy trial in front of an impartial jury
- Seventh Amendment—States, in civil lawsuits (that is, lawsuits dealing with significant property or money), the right to a jury trial
- Eighth Amendment—States that punishment cannot be excessive (cruel and unusual) and should fit the crime
- Ninth Amendment—States that citizens have other rights not necessarily stated in the Bill of Rights
- Tenth Amendment—Limits the national government to only the powers provided in the United States Constitution

Checkpoint

1. True or false: Civic education is not important in the overall social studies curriculum.

2. Fill in the blank: The _____ Amendment to the Constitution states that persons convicted of a crime must be mandated fair punishment that fits the crime.

3. True or false: The Bill of Rights only provides for the rights and freedoms of the citizens of the United States and does not limit governmental control.

Checkpoint Answers

1. False

2. Eighth

3. False

Competency 10: Knowledge of Production, Distribution, and Consumption (Economics)

Competency Description

According to the Competencies and Skills Required for Teacher Certification in Florida, Elementary Education (available at www.fldoe.org/asp/ftce/pdf/60ElementaryEducationK-6.pdf) **Competency 10** for the Elementary Education (K–6) Subject Area Examination (SAE) addresses the following key indicators:

1. Identify ways that limited resources affect the choices made by governments and individuals.
2. Compare and contrast the characteristics of different economic institutions (e.g., banks, credit unions, stock markets, the Federal Reserve).
3. Identify the role of markets from production, through distribution, to consumption.
4. Identify factors to consider when making consumer decisions.
5. Identify the economic interdependence among nations (e.g., trade, finance, movement of labor).
6. Identify human, natural, and capital resources and how these resources are used in the production of goods and services.

Overview

Knowledge of economics, specifically production, distribution and consumption, is of primary importance to elementary educators responsible for educating our youth in the social sciences. There are approximately **8 questions** that address Competency 10. This section addresses the following areas related to **Competency 10** key indicators:

- Economics
  - Economic Institutions

Economics

Economics is defined as the science that deals with the production, consumption, and distribution of goods and services. All categories in the social sciences are somehow related to economics. For example, significant historical events like the Great Depression (1930s) were spawned by the fall of the economy (history). Human beings have chosen locations to settle based on whether or not they were appropriate for production of goods they needed for survival and for ease of distribution (geography).

In the United States, we operate in a mixed (market) economy or one in which the government and private businesses both play vital roles. The majority of goods and services are produced by the private sector. The prices of these goods and services are determined by supply and demand for those items. When a population demands more of something, the supply increases as does the price. Often times, an increase in competition can be seen among producers of the sought after items or services. When demand for an item decreases, the supply is reduced and again, so is the price. Producers of less popular goods and services often go out of business or choose to produce other items. Along with voting for officials who help to shape economic policy, the choices consumers make regarding goods and services have a significant impact on our overall economy. Teaching youth (future consumers) problem-solving and strategic-thinking skills in relation to economics will help them to make better decisions in the modern global economy.

In an effort to simplify some of the abstract ideas related to economics, the Council on Economic Education, NCEE, created this simplified list of economic principles (www.ncee.net):

1. People choose.
2. People's choices involve costs.
3. People respond to incentives in predictable ways.

4. People create economic systems that influence individual choices and incentives.

5. People gain when they trade voluntarily.

6. People's choices have consequences that lie in the future.

In addition to the preceding information, the following are key terms related to economics:

- **production**—The creation of goods and services
- **distribution**—The dissemination or dispersing of goods and services
- **consumption**—The using and intake of goods and services
- **trade**—The act of buying and selling
- **finance**—The managing of monetary resources
- **human resources**—A person used to accomplish a goal
- **natural resources**—An available supply of something (land, water, oil) occurring in nature; often used to create wealth
- **capital resources**—Any asset used in the production of goods and services
- **limited resources**—Items that are in short supply
- **free enterprise**—Emphasizes private ownership; supply and demand
- **monopoly**—One company or institution having exclusive control of a particular good or service in a market
- **fiscal policy**—Government spending policies that affect interest rates, tax rates, and government spending; policies aid in governmental control of economy
- **Gross Domestic Product (GDP)**—Formerly known as the "gross national product;" total monetary value of all goods and services produced in a nation during a specific time frame (for example, one year)
- **inflation**—A persistent, general increase in prices over a period of time
- **stagflation**—High rate of inflation accompanied by rising unemployment
- **recession**—A slowing of economic activity
- **depression**—Long-lasting and painful recession or slowing of economic activity
- **scarcity**—Insufficient supply or shortage of goods and services; often affected by consumer decision making

Economic Institutions

Economic institutions (organizations created to pursue particular endeavors like banking by financial institutions) are vital components of our overall economy. The following table identifies various economic institutions and describes their overall purpose in our economy.

Institution	Definition and Purpose
Bank	Depository; financial institution; an establishment authorized by the government that mediates financial transactions and provides other financial services (loans, checking/savings accounts, pay interest, and so on)
Credit union	Depository; financial institution; an establishment owned, controlled, and operated by its members; provides financial services much like commercial banks but often provide lower interest rates for some of those services
Stock market	A place (virtual or physical) where stocks and bonds are exchanged; also known as the stock exchange; two largest stock exchanges are the New York Stock Exchange and the National Association of Securities Dealers Automated Quotations (NASDAQ); activity in these exchanges are an indicator of the state of the economy
Federal Reserve banks	The central bank of the United States federal banking system located in each of the 12 districts; regulates and supervises member banks in the 12 regions; maintains funds for future use, issues bank notes, controls credit, lends money, and so on; involved in the setting of national monetary policy

Checkpoint

1. True or false: The Great Depression of the 1930s was considered a long-lasting and painful slowing of the overall economy.

2. True or false: Consumer decision making has no effect on the supply and demand of products in this country and all over the world; therefore, teaching our youth **economic reasoning** skills is futile.

3. Fill in the blank: Both _____ and _____ are depository financial institutions that mediate financial transactions and provide a variety of financial services.

4. True or false: A market economy operates on the concepts of supply and demand.

Checkpoint Answers

1. True
2. False
3. banks and credit unions
4. True

Competency 11: Knowledge of Instruction and Assessment of the Social Sciences

Competency Description

According to the Competencies and Skills Required for Teacher Certification in Florida, Elementary Education (available at www.fldoe.org/asp/ftce/pdf/60ElementaryEducationK-6.pdf) **Competency 11** for the Elementary Education (K–6) Subject Area Examination (SAE) addresses the following key indicators:

1. Identify appropriate resources for teaching social science concepts.
2. Identify appropriate assessment methods in teaching social science concepts.

Overview

Knowledge of appropriate instruction and assessment methods related to vital social science concepts is of primary importance to elementary educators. There are approximately **2 questions** that address Competency 11. This section addresses the following area related to **Competency 11** key indicators:

- Instructional Resources, Methods, and Assessment

Instructional Resources, Methods, and Assessment

As you have read this chapter, you should have noticed the importance of educating youth in the social sciences. Elementary age students not only need to know about the world before they were in it but must understand the basics of how the world works today and its many facets. The foundation you provide in the elementary school will positively impact further instruction in the social sciences.

Educators must first access their state standards and then know how and where to find the resources necessary to instruct students. Resources abound for this particular content area. In this digital age, using reputable Web sites on the Internet can be one of the most efficient means of enhancing your knowledge of subject matter for topics needing to be taught to your grade level students. For example

- Government agencies have web sites and most provide valuable information for educators. (www.usa.gov)
- Specialized organizations, like the National Council for the Social Studies, have a web site and multiple links to reputable web sites to assist educators in teaching in this content area. (www.socialstudies.org) Note: Members of local, state, and national organizations often receive newsletters and journals that are valuable and current sources of information.
- Societies like National Geographic have educational divisions and publish valuable resources for children. They also have web sites with multiple links that provide quality resources for educators. (www.national geographic.com)

More resources in print will be provided in school settings along with the adopted social studies textbook. Many schools have purchased supplemental resources like guided reading books and age-appropriate magazines or newspapers that include teacher's guides to help educators teach this vital subject. Using the local, school, and school-based professional library can be advantageous to the educator. An abundance of high quality children's literature (of various genres like historical fiction and nonfiction) is available to not only young children but educators. Sharing these books with students helps to enlighten them about various ways of life, geographical locations, and historical events just to name a few.

Teacher resources often include a variety of teaching methods and strategies appropriate for learners in a content area. Please remember that many teaching strategies appropriate for teaching in the areas of reading and language arts are also appropriate for content area instruction. The following is a sampling of appropriate strategies and methods often used while teaching social studies:

- Story mapping— history frames or sequence of event charts
- Anticipation guides
- Double-entry journals
- K-W-L charts
- 5–W + H charts (Who, What, When, Where, Why, How)
- Semantic Feature Analysis charts
- Graphic organizers—Venn diagrams, sequence diagrams (timelines), and concept maps
- Learning logs
- Role playing and simulations
- Guest speakers
- Field trips and virtual field trips
- Learning centers
- Community-based, service-learning experiences
- Digital media and educational software

Assessment in the social studies classroom can be more traditional using paper and pencil tests (teacher created or published with the textbook), more technologically advanced using interactive white board quizzes for example, or more performance-based using a variety of authentic tasks and portfolios of student work to show the learning that has taken place over time. Often times, performance-based assessments include the use of rubrics that delineate the expectations set forth by the teacher. Many educators choose to have the students assist in the creation of the rubrics to help the students take an active role in their learning. Please note that many of the instructional strategies aforementioned could also be used to alternatively assess learning gains.

Whatever method of assessment is used, it is vital to incorporate pre-assessment tools to gauge what the students already know and to help guide instruction (for example, K-W-L charts and anticipation guides). High-quality educators base lesson plan development on pre-assessment results to maximize the learning opportunities for their students. Effective teachers also align assessment tools to instruction to ensure that students are being fairly assessed.

Checkpoint

1. True or false: Many government agencies and specialized organizations provide valuable resources to members.

2. Fill in the blank: The use of _____ help to synthesize and summarize informational text.

3. True or false: Many language arts and reading strategies are also appropriate for content area instruction.

4. Fill in the blank: A(n) _____ can be used as an instructional aid and assessment tool.

Checkpoint Answers

1. True

2. graphic organizers

3. True

4. anticipation guide or K-W-L chart

Summary

The Social Sciences section (Competencies 7–11) encompasses a variety of subcompetencies related to the basic knowledge required of educators teaching elementary age students. Knowledge of time, continuity, and change or the study of history involves the influences that prominent historical figures and events have had on America and the world. The knowledge of people, places, and their environment, also known as the study of geography, encompasses map and globe skills, the essential elements of geography, and how the environment has impacted human life and continues to do so today. Knowledge of the government and the citizen (civics) relates to major historical documents that have shaped the country, structure and purposes for government, and basic knowledge of how the U.S. government functions. The study of economics or production, distribution, and consumption covers basic information related to financial institutions and the role of markets in the United States and the world. Finally, this section of competencies ends with the knowledge of instruction and assessment practices that are effective in the teaching and learning of the social sciences.

This section reflects the skills required in this area for Teacher Certification in Florida, Elementary Education (available at www.fldoe.org/asp/ftce/pdf/60ElementaryEducationK-6.pdf). You should use the information in this section to complement your previous knowledge in the areas of language arts and reading. The general review of the social sciences (Competencies 7–11) provided in this chapter should allow you to explore areas of strength and need that you might still need to review. As indicated before, sample questions for the competency area as a whole appear in the next section of this chapter. Answers and explanations follow the sample questions. These sections should provide an opportunity for further practice and analysis.

Sample Questions

1. Although not the first to set foot on the land we now know as America, what early explorer opened up the Western hemisphere to economic and political development by the Europeans?

   A. Hernando Cortez
   B. Vasco da Gama
   C. Christopher Columbus
   D. John Cabot

2. Many government agencies and specialized organizations provide valuable resources related to the social sciences. Choose one such agency/organization that could be used to enhance your knowledge of subject matter in this content area.

   A. NCTM
   B. NCSS
   C. IRA
   D. NCTE

3. A market economy functions around the concepts of supply and

   A. consumer.
   B. fiscal responsibility.
   C. product.
   D. demand.

4. A primary source document is

   A. one that was created during that time period.
   B. nonprint media.
   C. a Web site.
   D. a blog.

5. Who was the first astronomer to place the sun at the center of the universe?

   A. Johannes Kepler
   B. Nicolaus Copernicus
   C. Galileo Galilei
   D. Edmund Halley

6. Power to the people is a phrase that describes the function of a republic. The Bill of Rights was not only enacted to protect the citizens of the United States but to also

   A. enhance government control.
   B. place sanctions on exporting goods.
   C. limit government power.
   D. control the choices citizens make.

7. What early explorer named Florida in the year 1513?

   A. Juan Ponce de Leon
   B. Ferdinand Magellan
   C. Sir Francis Drake
   D. Vasco de Balboa

8. In the 1930s, the United States experienced a long-lasting and painful slowing of the overall economy. This is called a

    A.   regression.
    B.   repression.
    C.   depression.
    D.   recession.

9. GDP stands for

    A.   Gross National Product.
    B.   Gross Domestic Product.
    C.   Good Dogs Play.
    D.   Good Domestic Producers.

10. In what year did the United States became involved in the Vietnam War?

    A.   1973
    B.   1959
    C.   1965
    D.   1937

11. What distinct portion of the population produces the majority of goods and services?

    A.   the public sector
    B.   the private sector
    C.   the northwest sector
    D.   the unknown sector

12. After what war did Americans want to explore and settle land to the west?

    A.   Vietnam War
    B.   French-Indian War
    C.   War of 1812
    D.   Korean War

13. What is considered to be the first modern document written to limit governmental power?

    A.   the Treaty of Paris
    B.   the United States Constitution
    C.   the Bill of Rights
    D.   the Magna Carta of 1215

14. What vocabulary term is used to describe the statistical study of human populations?

    A.   topography
    B.   biography
    C.   ethnography
    D.   demography

15. Which of the following resources can educators use to enhance the comprehension of content area material?

    A. guest speakers
    B. direct instruction
    C. literature circles
    D. storytelling

16. Which imaginary line divides the Earth into its eastern and western halves?

    A. equator
    B. Prime Meridian
    C. Tropic of Cancer
    D. Tropic of Capricorn

17. In the U.S. government, some government officials are elected by the population while others are appointed by executive officials. Of the following, which government position(s) are appointed?

    A. President of the United States
    B. mayor
    C. Supreme Court Justice
    D. senator

18. The two largest stock exchanges are the New York Stock Exchange and

    A. the National Consortium of Stocks.
    B. the National Association of Securities Dealers Automated Quotations.
    C. Wall Street.
    D. Main Street.

19. What was the name of the United States air and land operations involved in the Persian Gulf War?

    A. Operation Enduring Freedom
    B. Operation Liberation
    C. Operation United Nations
    D. Operation Desert Storm

20. Who was the King of Macedonia in 336 B.C. who was credited with conquering the Persian Empire and restoring order to Ancient Greece?

    A. Ivan the Terrible
    B. Catherine the Great
    C. Alexander the Great
    D. Louis XII

Answer Explanations for Sample Questions

1. **C.** Competency 7. Christopher Columbus's discoveries opened up the Western hemisphere to economic and political development by the Europeans, namely the Spanish, English, and French.

2. **B.** Competency 11. NCTM stands for the National Council of Teachers of Mathematics. NCSS stands for the National Council of the Social Studies. IRA stands for the International Reading Association, and finally, NCTE stands for the National Council of Teachers of English. Although most of these national organizations offer suggestions that cross the curriculum, NCSS specifically references the social science content area.

3. **D.** Competency 10. Supply and demand are the concepts that provide the foundation of a market economy.

4. **A.** Competency 11. A primary source document is one that was written during that time period or shortly thereafter. It could be for example a photograph, article, book, diary entry, and so on.

5. **B.** Competency 7. All of the provided choices are astronomers, but Nicolaus Copernicus was the first to place the sun at the center of our universe.

6. **C.** Competency 9. The Bill of Rights was not only enacted to protect the rights of U.S. citizens but also to limit the power of the government. A true republic's power lies in its people.

7. **A.** Competency 7. Juan Ponce de Leon, a Spanish explorer who was searching for the Fountain of Youth inevitably named Florida. All other choices were also early explorers of the world.

8. **C.** Competency 10. A long-lasting and painful slowing of economic activity that inevitably has negative effects on the population is known as a depression.

9. **B.** Competency 10. Gross Domestic Product (GDP), formerly known as the "gross national product," is the total monetary value of all goods and services produced in a nation during a specific time frame (for example, one year).

10. **B.** Competency 7. The United States became involved in order to prevent the communist takeover of South Vietnam in the year 1959.

11. **A.** Competency 10. The majority of goods and services are produced by the private sector.

12. **C.** Competency 7. After the War of 1812, Americans wanted to explore and settle the land to the west. This movement was known as westward expansion.

13. **D.** Competency 9. The Magna Carta of 1215 (England) is considered the very first modern document that sought to limit the powers of the governing body.

14. **D.** Competency 8. Demography, referencing the study of demographics or population data regarding, for example, the income, age, and education of a population is correct.

15. **A.** Competency 11. The use of guest speakers, field trips, virtual field trips, learning centers, community-based service-learning experiences, and digital media/educational software are all examples of resources that educators can use to enhance comprehension of content area material. The other choices are examples of teaching strategies or methods.

16. **B.** Competency 8. The Prime Meridian divides the Earth into eastern and western halves. In contrast, the equator splits the Earth into its northern and southern hemispheres.

17. **C.** Competency 9. Of the choices provided the only appointed positions are those held by Supreme Court Justices. All other officials are elected.

18. **B.** Competency 10. The two largest stock exchanges are the New York Stock Exchange and the National Association of Securities Dealers Automated Quotations (NASDAQ).

19. **D.** Competency 7. Operation Desert Storm was the name for the U.S. land and air operations involved in the Gulf War effort.

20. **C.** Competency 7. Alexander the Great was King of Macedonia in 336 B.C., conquered the Persian Empire, founded the city of Alexandria in Egypt as a center of learning and culture, and created a massive empire that restored order in Ancient Greece.

Music, Visual Arts, Physical Education, and Health

This chapter provides a general review of the area of Music, Visual Arts, Physical Education, and Health (Competencies 12–20) with sample questions and explanations at the end of the chapter. Checkpoint exercises are found throughout, giving you an opportunity to practice the skills addressed in each section. The answers to the Checkpoint exercises immediately follow the set of questions. We encourage you to cover the answers as you complete the Checkpoint exercises. Sample questions for the competency area as a whole appear at the end of the chapter. Answers and explanations follow the sample questions.

Competency 12: Knowledge of Skills and Techniques in Music and Visual Arts

Competency Description

According to the Competencies and Skills Required for Teacher Certification in Florida, Elementary Education (available at http://www.fldoe.org/asp/ftce/pdf/60ElementaryEducationK-6.pdf) **Competency 12** for the Elementary Education (K–6) Subject Area Examination (SAE) addresses the following key indicators:

1. Identify appropriate varieties of music (e.g., age-appropriate range and vocal ability; diverse cultures, **genres**, and styles).

2. Identify developmentally appropriate singing techniques (e.g., posture, breath support, tone quality, **vocal range**).

3. Identify correct performance techniques for rhythmic and melodic classroom instruments (e.g., nonpitched percussion, recorder, autoharp, keyboard).

4. Read and interpret simple, traditional, and nontraditional music notation (e.g., melodic, rhythmic, harmonic).

5. Select safe and developmentally appropriate media, techniques, and tools to create both two-dimensional and three-dimensional works of art.

6. Identify appropriate uses of art materials and tools for developing basic processes and motor skills.

Overview

Two major areas are involved in this competency: music and visual arts. **Music** is the art of arranging sounds in time in order to produce a continuous, balanced, unified, and evocative composition through such principles as **melody** (tune), harmony, **rhythm** (and its associated concepts of **tempo**, meter, and articulation), **pitch** (which governs melody and harmony), **timbre** (**tone**), and **texture**. Music is an important experience in human lives, full of cultural language that evolves over time, and a dynamic and powerful expression of human emotions. **Visual arts** are art forms focusing on the creation of works that are primarily visual in nature; for example, two-dimensional art (drawing, painting, photography, printmaking, and filmmaking) and three-dimensional art (sculpture and architecture).

This competency involves areas related to the knowledge of skills and techniques in music and visual arts. There are approximately **7 questions** that address Competency 12. This section addresses the following areas related to **Competency 12** key indicators:

- Identify Appropriate Varieties of Music and Singing Techniques
- Identify Correct Performance Techniques for Rhythmic and Melodic Classroom Instruments
- Read and Interpret Simple, Traditional, and Nontraditional Music Notation
- Select and Identify Uses of Media, Techniques, and Tools to Create Two- and Three-dimensional Works of Art, and Develop Processes and Motor Skills

Identify Appropriate Varieties of Music and Singing Techniques

The voice is the most natural, personal, and adaptable instrument of expression for people. By age four to five, children discover the difference between speaking, whispering, singing, and calling voices and should be encouraged to develop their head voice quality with proper guidance. The **vocal range** of a young child varies from child to child and should be relatively high in pitch, clear, and flute-like in quality. They should learn to use their whole bodies as the instruments, using good posture, and deep breathing for singing. Also, they should be encouraged to sing beautifully in both their speaking voice range (low register) and their head voice range. Children range is usually less than an octave for preschool children: D above middle C to A for most children and octave D by some.

Teachers should take into account the children's age-appropriate range and vocal abilities as they select vocal literature (music for singing). The following are some effective methods to aid children in developing the ability to match **pitch**: songs should be sung in appropriate range; simple songs utilizing the childhood chant (so, mi, la) are easy for children to imitate; sing a melodic phrase and ask for the child to follow you; and reinforce melodic intervals by using **Curwen hand signs** or other indications of high and low.

These are some ways to help children learn songs: using the *process of immersion* in which children hear songs sung by parents, teachers, or on recordings (as the songs become more and more familiar, they will begin to join in and sing); using *rote teaching* through imitation (usually presented sequentially and repeated back by the children); and using *note teaching* (gradually and systematically learning to read notation). The process of immersion should involve a wide variety of songs with diverse *styles* (basic musical languages) and **genres** (categories for established forms of compositions like Classical [Cantata, Concerto, Mass, Motet, Opera, Oratorio, Overture, Sonata, Suite, Symphony], Gospel, Jazz, Latin American, Blues, Rhythm and Blues, Rock, Country, Electronic, Electronic Dance, Electronica, Melodic Music, Hip Hop, Rap, Punk, Reggae, Contemporary African Music, and Dub) sung or played for children until over time they assimilate these songs and learn them, appropriate movements to accompany songs (for example, rocking, moving high and low, or patting a steady beat), good role models (for example, an adult or recordings of children's voices sung in tune with expression, quality, clear diction and a sense of good intonation), and a representation of various cultures and languages with songs sung correctly in style and diction.

Checkpoint

Fill in the blank:

1. _____ range is the span from the highest to the lowest note a person's voice can produce.

2. _____ teaching is a way to help students learn songs that involves imitation usually presented sequentially and repeated back by the children.

3. _____ are categories for established forms of compositions.

Checkpoint Answers

1. Vocal
2. Rote
3. Genres

Identify Correct Performance Techniques for Rhythmic and Melodic Classroom Instruments

Rhythm is the variation of the length and accentuation of a series of sounds or other events; for example, variations in the length of musical tones indicated by using musical notation involving various types of notes and rests. For instance, a series of strikes on a percussion instrument called *rhythmic pattern* or *drum beat*. Percussion instruments are sometimes identified as nonpitched or untuned instruments (for example, cymbals, snare drum, and whistles). These instruments may have a **pitch** that cannot be heard by the ear. *Divisive rhythms* involve dividing a larger period of time into smaller rhythmic units. *Additive rhythms* are involved when larger periods of time are constructed from smaller rhythmic units added at the end of the previous unit. The mastery of music requires practice and training. By fourth or fifth grade, students might start the study of orchestral instruments provided by a music teacher. The instruments normally included in the elementary school classroom are the following:

- Rhythmic instruments (triangles, tambourines, blocks, and sticks)
- Melodic instruments (melody bells and simple flutes)
- Harmonic instruments (chording instruments, like the autoharp)

Checkpoint

Fill in the blank.

1. _____ and _____ are types of rhythms used within a music selection.

2. _____ is another identification for some percussion instruments.

3. A tambourine is a type of _____ instrument.

Checkpoint Answers

1. Divisive and additive

2. Nonpitched or untuned

3. rhythmic

Read and Interpret Simple, Traditional, and Nontraditional Music Notation

Melodic, *rhythmic*, and *harmonic* are terms used to describe traditional and nontraditional music notation. Melodic music is a term that covers various genres of nonclassical music performed by a singer and orchestra, a single instrument, or any combination of a singer, orchestra, and instrument. It is primarily characterized by the dominance of a single strong melody line. **Rhythm**, **tempo,** and **beat** are subordinate to the melody line or tune, which is generally a short piece of instrumental music, a repeating section, played a number of times, easily memorable, and followed without great difficulty. Rhythmic notation is a term used to specify the exact **rhythm** in which to play the indicated **chords**. The chords are written above the *staff* (set of five horizontal lines and four spaces representing a different musical **pitch**), and the rhythm is indicated in the traditional manner. Harmonic notation refers to the individual pure sounds normally present as part of an ordinary musical **tone** (**timbre**). It refers to the key (major or minor) in which music is written. Sharp signs and flat signs after the clef sign in the signature are used to notate keys. Two figures are usually given, one above the other. The lower figure indicates the unit of measurement, and the upper figure indicates the number of such units in each bar. For example, a signature of 3/2 indicates that there are three half-notes in each bar; 12/8 indicates that there are 12 eighth-notes. We have twelve pitches in the musical scale.

Checkpoint

1. Fill in the blank: _____ notation is the term used to identify the key in which music is written.

2. Fill in the blank: _____ are three or more notes played together and notated above the staff.

3. True or false: Melodic music is primarily characterized by the dominance of a single strong tempo.

Checkpoint Answers

1. Harmonic

2. Chords

3. False. Melodic music is primarily characterized by the dominance of a single strong melody line, and rhythm, tempo, and beat are subordinate to the melody line or tune.

Select and Identify Uses of Media, Techniques, and Tools to Create Two- and Three-dimensional Works of Art, and Develop Processes and Motor Skills

Students should have the opportunity to express, explore, create, experiment, and experience different media, techniques, and tools involving two-dimensional and three-dimensional works of art. This process should also include different topics, themes, and subject matters, and experimentation through works of art using different mediums (for example, drawing, painting, printmaking, computer graphics, ceramics, modeling, crafts, weaving, finger painting, photography, video, Styrofoam carving, sponge painting, film animation, environmental design, jewelry making, and sculpting). The students should have the opportunity to produce a portfolio including their best work of art. This should happen at each grade level. Students use both large and small motor skills as they participate in these types of activities. Depending on the age of the students and developmental levels, art materials may include scissors, brushes, fabric, paper, film, crayons, clay, glue, beads, acrylic paint, charcoal, oil paint, pastel, pen, pencil, tempera, metal, and/or wood. Students should also explore with **line**, **color**, **shape**, **form**, **texture**, and **balance** and other design principles to express meaning and emotions. They should also have opportunities to experiment with mixing colors (primary: red, blue, and yellow; secondary: orange, purple, and green), and the color wheel to express mood and feelings.

Checkpoint

Fill in the blank.

1. Name three different mediums related to art works: _____, _____, and _____.

2. Name three principles related to art design used to express meaning and emotions: _____, _____, and _____.

3. Name three materials that could be used for art design: _____, _____, and _____.

Checkpoint Answers

1. Any combinations of drawing, painting, printmaking, computer graphics, ceramics, modeling, crafts, weaving, finger painting, photography, video, carving, sponge painting, jewelry making, and/or sculpting.

2. Any combination of line, color, shape, form, texture, and/or balance.

3. Any combination of scissors, brushes, fabric, paper, film, crayons, clay, glue, beads, acrylic paint, charcoal, oil paint, pastel, pen, pencil, tempera, metal, and/or wood.

Competency 13: Knowledge of Creation and Communication in Music and Visual Arts

Competency Description

According to the Competencies and Skills Required for Teacher Certification in Florida, Elementary Education (available at http://www.fldoe.org/asp/ftce/pdf/60ElementaryEducationK-6.pdf) **Competency 13** for the Elementary Education (K–6) Subject Area Examination (SAE) addresses the following key indicators:

1. Identify the elements of music (e.g., **rhythm**, **melody**, **form**, **texture**, **timbre**, **dynamics**) and ways they are used to express text, ideas, emotions, settings, time, and place.
2. Demonstrate knowledge of strategies for developing creative responses through **music** to ideas drawn from text, speech, **movement**, and visual images.
3. Demonstrate knowledge of strategies for developing creative responses through art to ideas drawn from text, **music**, speech, **movement**, and visual images.
4. Identify the elements of art and principles of design (e.g., **line**, **color**, **shape**, **form**, **texture**, **balance**, **movement**) and ways they are used in expressing text, ideas, meanings, and emotions.

Overview

This competency involves areas related to the knowledge of creation and communication in music and visual arts. In the area of **music**, it requires proper knowledge and identification of the elements of music and ways these elements are used to communicate text, ideas, emotions, settings, time, and place. In the area of **visual arts**, it requires proper knowledge of the elements and principles of art design and the ways they are used to communicate text, ideas, meaning, and emotions. There are approximately **5 questions** that address Competency 13. This section addresses the following areas related to **Competency 13** key indicators (one related to music and the other to visual arts):

- Identify the Elements of **Music** and Demonstrate Knowledge of Strategies for Developing Creative Responses
- Demonstrate Knowledge of Strategies for Developing Creative Responses through Art and Identify the Elements of Art and Principles of Design

Identify the Elements of Music and Demonstrate Knowledge of Strategies for Developing Creative Responses

Some of the elements involved in music are **rhythm**, **melody** (tune), **form**, **texture**, **timbre** (**tone**), and **dynamics**. These elements work together to express or communicate text, ideas, emotions, settings, time, and place. A **rhythm** involves the contrast among various lengths of musical tones. **Melody** or **tune** involves the use of a succession of notes, like ups and downs in a horizontal line. **Form** involves the structure of the song or the way the song is arranged. For example, using a refrain that is repeated, or a chorus that is repeated after a verse. **Texture** involves the context in which simultaneous sounds happen. These sounds may involve **chords** (**harmony**) or counterpoint, which involves concurrent melodies of equal importance. **Monophony**, **homophony**, and **polyphony** are types of music textures. The **timbre** or tone involves the quality of the musical sound that distinguishes voices and instruments. **Dynamics** involves the volume (loudness or softness) of the sound or note. Students should have opportunities to explore how these elements of music combine to express mood. This may be done through the analysis of stories or art pieces and using musical composition to reflect or enhance the story, conversing about the structure of songs or art pieces as they sing, move, dance, pat, and/or tap.

Checkpoint

Fill in the blank.

1. Indicate three of the possible elements involved in music: _____, _____, and _____.

2. Dynamics involves the _____ of the sound or note.

3. _____ involves the structure of a song or the way a song is arranged.

Checkpoint Answers

1. Any combination of the following: rhythm, melody (or tune), form, texture, timbre (or tone), and dynamics.

2. volume

3. Form

Demonstrate Knowledge of Strategies for Developing Creative Responses through Art and Identify the Elements of Art and Principles of Design

Students should have the opportunity to experience the creative process using different media, techniques, and tools. *Creativity* is a mental and social process that involves the production of novel and interesting ideas, concepts, products, works of art, or associations and connections between existing ideas or things. However, the emphasis should be placed on the creative and decision-making processes, not the final product alone. This creativity process could be expressed in many ways (text, music, speech, movement, and visual images). Students should have opportunities to experience and analyze models of creativity (including the teacher as a role model and using profiles of creative people and their work) and develop a sense of self-efficacy. They should also have opportunities to question assumptions, define and redefine problems or situations, generate ideas, and think across subject areas. The teacher should allow students time for creative thinking, help them to think creatively, provide ways to assess their creative efforts, and reward their production of creative ideas and products. The classroom learning environment should be one that supports and values sensible risk taking, tolerates ambiguity, allows for mistakes, and allows for identifying and overcoming problems or difficulties.

Several principles of design are very important: **line**, **unity**, **color**, **shape**, **form**, **texture**, **balance**, **repetition**, **movement,** and **value**. A **line** is a thin continuous mark from a pen, pencil, or brush applied to a surface. **Unity** is a principle of art that occurs when all of the elements of a piece combine to make a balanced, pleasing, harmonious, and complete whole or unit. **Color** is an element of art. It is the visual perceptual property corresponding to the categories that we call red, or yellow, among others. *Primary colors* are red, yellow, and blue. *Secondary colors* are green, orange, and purple. *Tertiary colors* fall between primary and secondary colors. *Compound colors* contain a mixture of primary colors. *Complementary colors* are opposite of each other on the color wheel. *Saturated colors* are the ones around the color wheel.

Shape is also an element of art. It is an enclosed space and limited to two dimensions (length and width), which boundaries are defined by other elements of art (for example, **lines**, **colors**, **values**, and **textures**). Some geometric shapes that have clear edges are circles, rectangles, squares, and triangles. Some natural shapes are leaves, amoebas, and clouds. In **music**, **form** refers to the structure of the song. As an element of art, it refers to a total structure, including all the visible aspects of structure, design, and the way they are united. It also includes all the elements of a work of art independent of their meaning. It allows us to mentally capture the work of art and understand it. For example, when viewing a work of art (like *Mona Lisa* by Leonardo Da Vinci, the Sistine Chapel by Michelangelo, *The Starry Night* by Vincent van Gogh, or *Self-Portrait with Monkey* by Frida Kahlo), the formal elements involved are color, dimension, lines, mass, shape, perspective, and others, but the emotions evoked by these works of art are products of the viewer's imagination.

In art, **texture** refers to the surface tactile quality of a shape or structure: rough, smooth, soft, hard, and glossy. It may refer to the physical texture felt with the hands or visual texture that gives the illusion of texture, like the use of paint to give the impression of rough texture when the surface remains smooth. **Balance** is another basic principle of art design. It is similar to the idea of balance in physics. It refers to the ways in which the art elements (for example, **lines**, **shapes**, colors, and textures) of a piece of art are arranged. It may be symmetrical ("formal"), asymmetrical ("informal"), radical, or horizontal. In *symmetrical balance*, the elements are given the same "weight" from an imaginary line in the middle of the work of art. For example, your eyes in relation to either side of your nose have symmetrical balance. In this case, balance does not necessarily mean geometric symmetry. In *asymmetrical balance*, the elements are placed unevenly in the work of art, but work together to produce overall harmony. In *radical balance*, the pattern appears to radiate from the center axis. In *horizontal balance*, the work of art utilizes the picture plane from left to right. In an artwork, **repetition** is created when elements like objects, patterns, shapes, space, light, direction, and lines are repeated. **Movement** refers to the combination of art elements to create the appearance of action or suggestion or implication of motion. **Value** is a relative darkness or lightness of a color.

Checkpoint

1. True or false: In asymmetrical balance, the elements are given the same "weight" from an imaginary line in the middle of the work of art.

2. Fill in the blank: _____ refers to the combination of art elements to create the appearance of action or suggestion or implication of motion.

3. Fill in the blank: _____ is a basic principle of art design that refers to the ways in which the art elements of a piece of art are arranged.

Checkpoint Answers

1. False. This is the definition of symmetrical balance.

2. Movement

3. Balance

Competency 14: Knowledge of Cultural and Historical Connections in Music and Visual Arts

Competency Description

According to the Competencies and Skills Required for Teacher Certification in Florida, Elementary Education (available at http://www.fldoe.org/asp/ftce/pdf/60ElementaryEducationK-6.pdf) **Competency 14** for the Elementary Education (K–6) Subject Area Examination (SAE) addresses the following key indicators:

1. Identify characteristics of **style** in musical selections.
2. Demonstrate knowledge of how **music** reflects particular cultures, historical periods, and places.
3. Identify characteristics of **style** in works of art.
4. Demonstrate knowledge of how visual arts reflect particular cultures, historical periods, and places.

Overview

This competency involves areas related to the knowledge of cultural and historical connections in music and visual arts. It is separated in terms of main music styles and main ones for visual arts. There are approximately **4 questions** that address Competency 14. This section addresses the following areas related to **Competency 14** key indicators (one related to music and the other to visual arts):

- Identify Characteristics of Style in Musical Selections and Demonstrate Knowledge of How Music Reflects Particular Cultures, Historical Periods, and Places
- Identify Characteristics of Style in Works of Art and Demonstrate Knowledge of How Visual Arts Reflect Cultures, Historical Periods, and Places

Identify Characteristics of Style in Musical Selections and Demonstrate Knowledge of How Music Reflects Cultures, Historical Periods, and Places

The periods of classical music are classified in six periods of music by stylistic differences (the years are approximations):

- **Medieval period (450–1450)**—The medieval music includes music written during the Middle Ages. During this period the spread of Christianity, the development of the European culture, and the influence of Islamic culture evolved. It was characterized by both secular and sacred music (for example, Gregorian chants). It began with the fall of the Roman Empire and ended around the fifteenth century before the Renaissance period started. It marked the beginning of musical notation, rise of courtly culture, and **polyphony**.

- **Renaissance period (1450–1600)**—The word "renaissance" means "rebirth." It included a gradual change from a feudal system to the modern state and a change in people's view of the Earth and cosmos. It had an increase in secular music (madrigals and art songs), but also had sacred music (liturgical **forms** like mass and motets). Some of the composers of that era were Giovanni Gabrieli, Leonel Power, Jonh Durstable, Antoni Busnois (or Busnoys), and Thomas Tallis.

- **Baroque period (1600–1760)**—This period was known for its intricate ornamentation. The word "baroque" was derived from the Portuguese word barroco, which means "misshapen pearl" (irregular in shape). Some of the composers of that era were Tomaso Albinoni, Johann Sebastian Bach, Arcangelo Corelli, George Firderic Handel, Antonio Vivaldi, and Claudio Monterverdi.

- **Classical period (1750–1820)**—The Classical period falls between the Baroque and Romantic period. This period is known for its **balance** and structure. The best known composers of that era were Joseph Haydn, Wolfgang Amadeus Mozart, and Ludwig van Beethoven. Beethoven also composed Romantic music.

- **Romantic period (1820–1910)**—This era is distinguished by being emotional, large, and programmatic. Romantic music is related to romanticism in literature, **visual arts,** and philosophy. It falls between the Classical period and the Modern period. The Romantic period tried to increase emotional expression and power to describe deeper truths, and at the same time preserve and in some cases extend the Classical period. Some of the composers of the Romantic period were Ludwig van Beethoven (German, considered by some people as the first Romantic composer), Ferdinando Carulli (Itallian, guitar), Anton Reicha (French), Bernhard Henrik Crusell (Finnish, clarinet), Johann Nepomuk Hummel (German), Fernando Sor (Spanish, classical guitar), Mauro Giuliani (Italian, guitar), Niccoló Paganini, John Field, Gioachino Rossini (Italian, composer of *The Barber of Seville*), and Franz Schubert.

- **Modern period or twentieth century (1910–present)**—This era has witnessed a phenomenal change in technologies, the advent of instantaneous global communications and sound recording, the growth and eventual decline of totalitarian culture, and the birth of a "World Music" culture. It also involved a widening gap between "art" and "popular" music. This era is limitless in **styles**, **rhythms**, **form**, harmonic combinations, and complexity, with the incorporation of new instruments, sounds, and improvisation.

The main grouping for music selections are the following, including a short description of each one:

- **Balada**—It is a type of song that narrates or contains a story using a simple repeating rhyme. Music instruments usually accompany the ballad. It forms part of folk music and dance traditions. In the twentieth century, the ballad took the meaning of a popular sentimental and romantic song.

- **Blues**—It is a music genre based on the use of the blues **chord** progression and notes. There are several blues **forms**. It came from West African spirituals and emerged at the end of the nineteenth century as a form of self-expression in African American communities of the United States. They usually express melancholy and sadness. It influenced later styles like jazz, rhythm and blues, bluegrass, and rock and roll.

- **Cantata**—It was developed in the Baroque period. It is considered the most important **genre** of vocal chamber music of that period. Compositions were written for solo and chorus voices with orchestral accompaniment with either secular or sacred lyrics. It involves several **movements**.

- **Classical music**—This is a traditional music **genre** conforming to an established **form**. It is composed and written using music notation and performed by professionally trained musicians. It is in many cases defined as relating to, or being music in the educated European tradition: art song, chamber music, opera, and symphony (distinguished from folk music, popular music, or jazz).

- **Concerto**—It is a musical **form** from the Baroque period written for one or more solo instruments with orchestra accompaniment. It is usually comprised of three movements in a fast, slow, fast arrangement.

- **Contemporary African**—It is highly diverse. It shares many characteristics of Western popular music in the mid-twentieth century. It began with the advent of recording technology and development of the recording industry. R&B, American soul music, Jamaican reggae, and other musical **forms** from the Americas have heavily influenced this **genre**.

- **Country**—This is an American **style** of popular music based on the folk style of the Southern rural United States or cowboys in the American West. Until the 1920s, it was mainly performed at home, church, or local functions on fiddles, banjos, and guitars. It eventually developed into a commercial industry. Recent performers include Johnny Cash and Willie Nelson. The topics included are family, prison, hard work, love, and religion.

- **Electronic**—It includes music involving tones originating from electronic sound and noise generators, which are used alone or combined. It also involves electro means and sound-recording equipment. In the 1950s and 1960s electronic music studios were founded in major cities, including Europe, United States, and Japan.

- **Electronic dance music or EDM**—It is electronic music that is produced primarily for use in nightclub settings or dance-based entertainment with the music managed by a disc jockey (or DJ). It is based on the 1970s disco music. Synthesizers, drum machines, and sequencers are used in the creation of this type of music.

- **Folk music**—It is music that has been passed down from generation to generation by oral tradition and shared by an entire community. It is an expression of the life of people in a community.

- **Gospel**—It is music that is composed to express personal or communal Christian life and beliefs. Its definition varies based on culture and social context. A common theme is praise and worship or thanks to God, Christ, or the Holy Spirit.

- **Hip hop**—It is a musical genre consisting of a rhythmical voice style called rap. Rap is accompanied by backing beats. It is part of what is called the hip hop culture from the Bronx, New York. It started in the 1970s among African Americans and Latin Americans.

- **Jazz**—It is a musical genre originated at the beginning of the twentieth century in Southern United States African American communities. It incorporates African and European music styles, and nineteenth and twentieth century American popular music.

- **Latin American**—It includes music from Latin America and the Caribbean and a variety of styles. It combines elements from European, African, and indigenous music. Some of these styles are Salsa, Merengue, Cumbia, and Son Cubano.

- **Mass**—It is a choral composition associated with the Roman Catholic Church service. The parts of the Mass usually set to music are the Kyrie, Gloria, Credo, Sanctus, Agnus Dei, Offertory, and Benedictus.

- **Motet**—This word is applied to a number of highly varied choral musical compositions, which uses a **polyphonic** approach (a **texture** consisting of two or more independent melodic voices). Motet is French for "word." This style of music appeared in the thirteenth century with motet written for three voices. It combined secular and sacred text, fifteenth and sixteenth centuries (Renaissance) with contrapuntal work for four or five voices a cappella and sacred text, and Baroque and Romantic periods with a cappella and orchestral variations.

- **Opera**—It is a drama (tragic or comic) with music as an essential part. It is mostly sung using recitative arias, choruses, duets, trios, orchestral accompaniment, costumes, scenery, and action. Opera is an Italian word for "work." In Florence during the Renaissance period, intellectuals trying to revive the Greek and Roman drama started this type of musical work. It has evolved through the years from grand opera or opera seria (five acts and serious in nature), *opera comique* (with spoken dialogue), *opera buffa* (comic in nature and based on a farce), and *operetta* (light and romantic in nature with a popular theme and spoken dialogue).

- **Oratorio**—It is a large-scale musical composition on a sacred or semi-sacred topic (epic or religious in nature) theme. It is composed for solo voices, chorus, and orchestra. It involves singing and a storyline and not much else, no staging, and no costuming. Some action is involved, but you never see it because a narrator narrates all of the action.

- **Overture**—It is an instrumental composition for an introduction to an extended work, like an opera, oratorio, ballet, musical comedy, or film. It is a one-movement orchestral piece, which usually has a descriptive or evocative title.

- **Punk or punk rock**—It is a rock music genre, which was developed between 1974 and 1976 in the United States, United Kingdom, and Australia. It is usually fast paced and typically with short songs, stripped-down instrumentation, and often political.

- **Rock and roll**—It is a **genre** of popular music that started in the mid 1950s. It has roots in the rhythm and blues, country music, folk music, and jazz. Its sound revolves around the electric or acoustic guitar, and a strong back beat. It uses bass guitar, drums, keyboard instruments, and synthesizers (since the1970s). It may also include saxophone and harmonica. It also has a catchy **melody**.

- **Sonata**—The word sonata is from Latin and Italian *sonare*, which means "to sound." It is a classical music composition for one or more instruments. One of the instruments is usually a keyboard. It usually consists of three or four independent movements, which vary in key, mood, and **tempo**. They are written for an instrument (for example, piano sonata, violin sonata, or cello sonata).

- **Suite**—It is an ordered set of instrumental or orchestral pieces, especially of the seventeenth or eighteenth century, which are performed in a concert setting. It can be parts from an opera, or ballet. It is a group of dances usually written for keyboard or ensemble of stringed or wind instruments in the same or related keys. It can also refer to compositions for chamber orchestras and string quartets.

- **Symphony**—It is an extended, large-scale piece in three or more movements written for a full symphony orchestra. It was fully refined in the eigtheenth century.
- **Traditional African**—It is very historically ancient, rich, and diverse. It is passed down orally and is not written. It usually has a functional intent as it is performed in celebrations, festivals, and storytelling. It relies heavily on percussion instruments of every variety, such as xylophones, drums, and **tone**-producing instruments.
- **Work song**—It is usually a rhythmical communal song to accompany repetitious work. It is usually sung a cappella by people working on physical and repetitive tasks. It is usually connected to a specific type or form of work: hunting and pastoral songs, agricultural work songs, African American work songs (originally developed during the era of slavery), sea shanties (sung by sailors), cowboy songs (Western music), and industrial folk songs.

Checkpoint

1. Fill in the blank: _____ is a drama (tragic or comic) with music as an essential part.

2. Fill in the blank: Hip hop is a musical genre consisting of a rhythmical voice style called _____.

3. Fill in the blank: _____ influenced later styles like jazz, rhythm and blues, bluegrass, and rock and roll.

4. True or false: The Renaissance music includes music written during the Middle Ages.

Checkpoint Answers

1. Opera

2. rap

3. Blues

4. False. The Medieval music includes music written during the Middle Ages, not Renaissance music.

Identify Characteristics of Style in Works of Art and Demonstrate Knowledge of How Visual Arts Reflect Cultures, Historical Periods, and Places

An art movement is a phrase used to describe a group of artists who have a specific **style** during a specific period of time (months, years, or decades). Various historical periods have been defined, which could include one or more art movements or styles. Some of these styles are listed here by period:

- **Prehistoric**—This period involves stone and bone figurines including famous images of women and birds, and cave painting by Paleolithic people in Europe, more than 20,000 years old.
- **Ancient**—This period involves many types of art that were part of cultures of ancient places, like Africa, Central America, China, India, Japan, Egypt, Greece, and Rome.
- **Medieval**—This period covers more than 1,000 years of art history in Europe, the Middle East, and Africa, including major art movements and periods: Early Christian art, Migration period art, Celtic art, Byzantine art (a style of the Byzantine Empire and its provinces, appearing in mostly religious mosaics, manuscript illuminations, and panel paintings and characterized by rigid, stylized forms with gold backgrounds), Islamic art, Pre-Romanesque and Romanesque art, and Gothic art. It also includes some national and cultural styles like Crusade art, Anglo-Saxon art, and Viking art. It includes many mediums, but very strong in sculpture, illuminated manuscripts, and mosaics. The Gothic architecture included ribbed vaulting, pointed roofs, and flying buttresses; and panel painting and paintings (often oil on a thin board).
- **Renaissance**—The Early Renaissance included religious themes. The Renaissance classicism included realistic painting. The changes in style during this era were not uniform across the board. In general, art was

more emotional and dramatic in nature; for example, Michelangelo's Sistine Chapel frescoes and sculptures of David and Moses, and Leonardo's *Mona Lisa,* and Raphael's *School of Athens* fresco.

- **Baroque**—The Early Baroque included detailed and elaborate art (often sculptures and paintings). The Roman Catholic Church encouraged this style. It included the building of opulent palaces, entrances of courts, grand staircases, and reception rooms. The Late Baroque was considered drier and less dramatic and coloristic. Bernini, Caravaggio, and Rubens were important artists of this movement.

- **Eighteenth century**—This era included the Rococo style, which involved opulence, grace, and lightness (in contrast to the Baroque era). It developed from the decorative arts and interior design. It involved furniture and decorative objects. Fragonard was an important artist of this style.

- **Nineteenth century**—This era included the following: Romanticism (idealistic style, focused on emotion rather than reason and on spontaneous expression, and painted energetically with brilliant colors; included artists like Delacroix, Gericault, Turner, and Blake), Realism (everyday characters, situations, and dilemmas), Naturalism (realistic subjects in natural settings), Impressionism (visible brushstrokes with an emphasis on light and color, and layers of oil paints added without waiting for other layers to dry; included work by Monet, Renoir, and Pissarro).

- **Twentieth century**—This era included the following: Cubism (involved total destruction of realistic depiction; included Picasso and Braque in the early twentieth century), Photorealism (photo like and lifelike art, including still lifes and landscapes), and Graffiti (marking on surfaces in private or public places using mainly spray painting).

Checkpoint

Fill in the blank.

1. The _____ style involved opulence, grace, and lightness.

2. The Early _____ included detailed, and elaborate art (often sculptures and paintings).

3. _____ was an idealistic style, which focused on emotion rather than reason and on spontaneous expression, and painted energetically with brilliant colors.

Checkpoint Answers

1. Rococo
2. Baroque
3. Romanticism

Competency 15: Knowledge of Aesthetic and Critical Analysis of Music and Visual Arts

Competency Description

According to the Competencies and Skills Required for Teacher Certification in Florida, Elementary Education (available at http://www.fldoe.org/asp/ftce/pdf/60ElementaryEducationK-6.pdf) **Competency 15** for the Elementary Education (K–6) Subject Area Examination (SAE) addresses the following key indicators:

1. Identify strategies for developing students' analytical skills to evaluate musical performance.
2. Identify strategies for developing students' analytical skills to evaluate works of art.

Overview

This competency involves areas related to the knowledge of aesthetic and critical analysis of music and visual arts. It is separated in terms of main analytical skills related to the evaluation of music performance, and main analytical skills related to the evaluation of works of art. There are approximately **2 questions** that address Competency 15. This section addresses the following areas related to **Competency 15** key indicators (one related to music and the other to visual arts):

- Identify Strategies for Developing Students' Analytical Skills to Evaluate Musical Performance
- Identify Strategies for Developing Students' Analytical Skills to Evaluate Works of Art

Identify Strategies for Developing Students' Analytical Skills to Evaluate Musical Performance

In order to help students' development of analytical skills to evaluate musical performance, the students need opportunities to perform and evaluate their own musical performances and the musical performance of other students and professional musicians or singers. They can also accomplish this by analyzing the use of instruments or voices in a recording or performance. Students should have opportunities to use their bodies, voices, and other musical instruments as means of musical expression (for example, using instruments to communicate an idea, an emotion, or a feeling), read, sing or play songs; to describe the use of various **rhythms**, **textures**, modes, **harmonies**, **textures** and **forms;** and to improvise and compose music (for example, creating a new sequence of an existing song, planning the texture for completed sequence, adding expressive qualities, such as tempo and dynamics to a sequence, and performing or recording a sequence in class and discussing choices made).

Students should have opportunities to expand their music listening skills and use music vocabulary to analyze and evaluate music. For example, evaluate the expressive qualities within music that affect its ability to communicate (such as dynamics, tempo, timbre, and pitch), use of time to communicate meaning in various musical selections (such as beat, meter, and rhythm), use of melody to convey a message (such as range of **pitches**, and **rhythm**), and use of **form** to communicate meaning in music (such as **repetition**, contrast, and variation).

Students should also have the opportunity to examine how music relates to personal development and enjoyment of life by evaluating how the study of music expands the ability to communicate with and understand others, tell how music can be a joyful part of daily activities, describe how making music helps to develop skills and success in working with others, describe how they have (personally and as a class) used music to be of service to someone, and explain how participation in music can become a lifetime pursuit. They should be able to experience how music connects us to history, culture, heritage, and community and explain how people celebrate, mourn, create, communicate ideas, help others, express feelings, come together, and enjoy themselves through music.

Checkpoint

1. True or false: Students are not ready to improvise and compose music at an early age.

2. Fill in the blank: Students' use of form to communicate meaning in music should involve _____.

3. Fill in the blank: Students should be able to experience how music connects us to _____.

Checkpoint Answers

1. False. Students should have opportunities to improvise and compose music consistent with their developmental level.

2. repetition, contrast, or variation

3. history, culture, heritage, or community

Identify Strategies for Developing Students' Analytical Skills to Evaluate Works of Art

In order to help students' development of analytical skills to evaluate works of art, the students need opportunities to create and evaluate their own art works and the art works of other students. They can also accomplish this by evaluating the work of art of professional artists, including different mediums, such as paintings, sculptures, photography, and prints.

Students should have opportunities to use different types of design principles to communicate (for example, use several principles such as **line**, **unity**, **color**, **shape**, **form**, **texture**, **balance**, **repetition**, **movement,** and **value** to communicate an idea, an emotion, or a feeling), create works of art and describe the use of various elements of design, and create works of art using different mediums (for example, drawing, painting, printmaking, computer graphics, ceramics, modeling, crafts, weaving, finger painting, photography, video, printmaking, film animation, environmental design, jewelry making, and sculpting, among others).

Students should have opportunities to expand their art appreciation skills and use art vocabulary to analyze and evaluate works of art. For example, evaluate the expressive qualities within a work of art that affect its ability to communicate (such as **line**, **unity**, **color**, **shape**, **form**, **texture**, **balance**, **repetition**, **movement** and **value**).

Students should also have the opportunity to examine how works of art relate to personal development and enjoyment of life by evaluating how the study of art expands the ability to communicate with and understand others, tell how art can be a joyful part of daily activities, describe how making art helps to develop skills and the ability to work with others effectively, describe how they have (personally or as a class) used art to be of service to someone, and explain how participation in art can become a lifetime pursuit. They should be able to experience how art connects them to history, culture, heritage, and community and explain how people celebrate, mourn, create, communicate ideas, help others, express feelings, come together, and enjoy art. In the area of cultural understanding, the students should engage with a range of images and artifacts from different contexts; recognize the varied characteristics of different cultures and use them to inform how they create and make works of art; and understand the role of the artist, craftsperson, and designer in a range of cultures, times, and contexts. In the area of critical understanding, students should explore visual, tactile, and other sensory qualities of their own and others' works of art; engage with ideas, images, and artifacts and identify how values and meanings are conveyed; develop their own views and express judgments; and analyze and reflect on works of art from diverse contexts. Students should be offered the following opportunities to enhance their engagement with art: work independently and collaboratively; take different roles in teams (cooperative learning or collaborative groups); explore areas that are new to them (including ideas, techniques, and processes); engage with contemporary art, craft, and design; work with creative individuals and in creative environments where possible; work with a variety of genres; engage in interdisciplinary and multidisciplinary practice within the arts; and make links between art design and other subjects.

Checkpoint

Fill in the blank.

1. Students should be able to experience how art connects us to _____.

2. Students should have opportunities to use different types of art design principles such as _____ and _____ to communicate.

3. Students should have opportunities to create works of art using different mediums such as _____ and _____.

Checkpoint Answers

1. history, culture, heritage, or community

2. Use any combination of the following: line, unity, color, shape, form, texture, balance, repetition, movement, and value.

3. Use any combination of the following: drawing, painting, printmaking, computer graphics, ceramics, modeling, crafts, weaving, finger painting, camera, video, Styrofoam carving, printmaking, sponge painting, film animation, environmental design, jewelry making, and sculpting.

Competency 16: Knowledge of Appropriate Assessment Strategies in Music and Visual Arts

Competency Description

According to the Competencies and Skills Required for Teacher Certification in Florida, Elementary Education (available at http://www.fldoe.org/asp/ftce/pdf/60ElementaryEducationK-6.pdf) **Competency 16** for the Elementary Education (K–6) Subject Area Examination (SAE) addresses the following key indicators:

1. Identify a variety of developmentally appropriate strategies and materials for assessing skills, techniques, creativity, and communication in music.

2. Identify a variety of developmentally appropriate strategies and materials for assessing skills, techniques, creativity, and communication in visual arts.

Overview

This competency involves areas related to the knowledge of assessment strategies in music and visual arts. It is separated in terms of main strategies and materials for assessing music and main ones for art. There are approximately **4 questions** that address Competency 16. This section addresses the following areas related to **Competency 16** key indicators:

- Identify a Variety of Strategies and Materials for Assessing Skills, Techniques, Creativity, and Communication in Music
- Identify a Variety of Developmentally Appropriate Strategies and Materials for Assessing Skills, Techniques, Creativity, and Communication in Visual Arts.

Identify a Variety of Strategies and Materials for Assessing Skills, Techniques, Creativity, and Communication in Music

Students should be evaluated in their demonstration of acceptable performer and audience etiquette; ability to compare and contrast music **styles** from a variety of cultures and time periods; ability to analyze and evaluate the difference between expressing personal preferences in music; and ability to critique a music composition or music performance. Some ways to evaluate students' growth are documenting personal growth as a musician by keeping a journal or writing reflections related to personal experiences in music and selecting a piece of their own completed work and explaining to students, teacher, and/or parents how this choice illustrates progress.

They should also be evaluated in their ability to describe music changes as they occur in recorded or live performances (such as **tempo**, meter, **harmony**, dynamics, **texture**, **form**, and instrumentation); describe the emotions and thoughts the music communicates and analyze how it does so; compare and contrast music styles from a variety of cultures and time periods, including non-Western music; and analyze and evaluate the difference between expressing personal preferences in music and critiquing a music composition or music performance. They should be able to explain what music means personally; play, sing, read, and enjoy music related to various cultures, times, and places; and tell how music connects to other subjects.

Checkpoint

Fill in the blank.

1. Students should be evaluated in their demonstration of acceptable _____ etiquette.

2. Students should be evaluated in their ability to describe music changes such as _____ and _____ as they occur in recorded or live performances.

Checkpoint Answers

1. performer or audience

2. Use any combination of tempo, meter, harmony, dynamics, texture, form, and instrumentation.

Identify a Variety of Developmentally Appropriate Strategies and Materials for Assessing Skills, Techniques, Creativity, and Communication in Art

Students should be evaluated in their demonstration of acceptable presentation of works of art to communicate with others; ability to compare and contrast artistic **styles** from a variety of cultures and time periods; and ability to analyze and evaluate the difference between expressing personal preferences in type of works of art and critiquing a work of art. Some ways to evaluate students' growth are documenting personal growth as an artist by keeping a journal or writing reflections related to personal experiences in art and selecting a piece of their own completed work and explaining to students, teacher, and/or parents how this choice illustrates progress.

They should also be evaluated in their ability to describe art design principles as they occur in works of art (for example, use several design principles such as **line**, **unity**, **color**, **shape**, **form**, **texture**, **balance**, **repetition**, **movement**, and **value**); to describe the emotions and thoughts the work of art communicates and analyze how it is done; to compare and contrast artistic styles from a variety of cultures and time periods, including non-western music; and to analyze and evaluate the difference between expressing personal preferences in art and critiquing art work. They should be able to explain what art means personally, create their own art, enjoy music related to various cultures, times, and places, and tell how art connects to other subjects.

Student art works should be displayed and evaluated in a detailed and analytical way. All the students should participate in offering critiques that are guided by the teacher. This type of assessment should increase the viewpoints from which students' artwork is evaluated and promote the analytical skills of all the students. Student responses to works of art will vary. This critique process is a way for students to learn from each other, from analyzing successful and less successful problem-solving strategies, and from finding creative and aesthetic solutions. In a similar manner, analysis of the work observed at museums, galleries, or works of art provided in class should be assessed and analyzed. Students should be able to produce imaginative images, artifacts, and other outcomes that are both valuable and original; explore and experiment with ideas, materials, tools, and techniques; take risks and learn from mistakes; investigate, analyze, design, make, reflect and evaluate effectively; and make appropriate choices about media, techniques, and processes.

Checkpoint

1. Fill in the blank: Student art works should be displayed and evaluated in a _____ and _____ way.

2. True or false: In an art class, students should not be able to take risks and learn from mistakes.

Checkpoint Answers

1. detailed and analytical

2. False. The students should be able to take risks and learn from mistakes in the art class.

Competency 17: Knowledge of Personal Health and Wellness

Competency Description

According to the Competencies and Skills Required for Teacher Certification in Florida, Elementary Education (available at http://www.fldoe.org/asp/ftce/pdf/60ElementaryEducationK-6.pdf) **Competency 17** for the Elementary Education (K–6) Subject Area Examination (SAE) addresses the following key indicators:

1. Demonstrate knowledge of the interrelatedness of physical activity, fitness, and health.
2. Demonstrate basic knowledge of nutrition and its role in promoting health.
3. Identify the processes of decision making and goal setting in promoting individual health and wellness.
4. Demonstrate knowledge of common health problems and risk behaviors associated with them.

Overview

Personal health and wellness includes knowledge of physical fitness, nutrition, and decision making skills as well as knowledge of common health issues and behaviors associated with them. There are approximately **6 questions** that address Competency 17. This section addresses the following areas related to **Competency 17** key indicators:

- Health and Fitness
- Nutrition

Health and Fitness

Maintaining a healthy weight and fitness level are important for many aspects of life. Obesity rates have grown at epic proportions. In 2007, every state had obesity rates over 15 percent, with more than half the states having obesity rates above 25 percent (CDC, n.d.). The definitions of overweight and obese are connected with **Body Mass Index** (BMI). BMI most often correlates with body fat and is calculated using an individual's height and weight. The calculations for BMI are different for adults and children. Overweight and obesity rates in children are even more staggering than in the general population. Since 1980, the prevalence of obesity in children aged 2–5 years increased from 5 to 12.4 percent, aged 6–11 years increased from 6.5 to 17 percent, and aged 12–19 years increased from 5 to 17.6 percent. Children and adolescents who are obese are at increased risk for health problems both during adulthood and in their youth. Obese children are more likely to become obese adults (CDC, n.d.). The effects of being overweight and/or obese are numerous including an increased risk for coronary heart disease, Type 2 diabetes, cancer, hypertension, stroke, and sleep apnea. The importance of health and fitness cannot be overstated.

The Centers for Disease Control and Prevention (CDC, n.d.) recommends children engage in at least 60 minutes of physical activity every day. **Physical fitness** includes three aspects: **aerobics, strength training,** and **bone strengthening**. Aerobic activities are those activities in which the body is engaged in rhythmic activity for a sustained period of time. Aerobic activities include running, biking, swimming, and walking. Aerobic activities improve cardiovascular fitness, making the heart-lung systems operate efficiently. A majority of time engaged in physical activity should be in aerobic activity. Strength training is any type of activity in which the goal is to strengthen muscles in the body. Strength training can include lifting weights as well as body-weight bearing exercise like sit-ups and push-ups. Bone strengthening activities engage the body in strengthening specific sites in bones. Bone strengthening activities are often impact activities. The impact strengthens bones. Bone strengthening activities include running, jumping rope, and lifting weights.

Checkpoint

1. What are three types of physical activity?

2. Obesity increases the risk of what medical conditions?

3. What are three examples of aerobic activity?

Checkpoint Answers

1. aerobics, strength training, and bone strengthening

2. diabetes, coronary heart disease, hypertension, stroke, and others

3. running, walking, swimming

Nutrition

Good nutrition plays a part in a healthy lifestyle. **Nutrition** is the process by which animals eat and use food. The quality of one's nutrition is a measure of the quality of food input into the body. Good nutrition includes a combination of a balance of food groups, water, dietary fat, carbohydrates, protein, vitamins, and minerals. The U.S. Department of Agriculture (USDA) has developed a **food pyramid** that gives both a visual and written representation of quantities and types of food needed for good nutrition (USDA, n.d.).

The vertical stripes of the pyramid represent different food groups. The left category is grains. The USDA recommends that adults consume at least 3 ounces of grains each day, and half the grains should be whole grains. The next category is vegetables. More dark green and orange vegetables as well as dry beans and peas are recommended. Vegetables may be raw or cooked; fresh, frozen, canned, or dehydrated; whole, cut-up, or mashed; and adults should consume 2.5 to 3 cups of vegetables each day. The third category from the left is fruits. A variety of fruit should be eaten, which can include fresh, frozen, canned, and dried fruit. Fruit juice should be limited. Adults should consume 1.5 to 2 cups of fruits each day. The next category, which is very narrow on the pyramid graphic, is oils. Nutrition oils include fish oil, nut oil, and vegetable oils. Solid fats like butter and margarine should be limited. Adults should consume 5 to 6 teaspoons of oil each day. The fifth category is milk. Milk should be low-fat or fat-free. This category also include cheeses and yogurts. Adults should consume 3 cups of milk and dairy products each day. The final category to the far right is meat and beans. Choose low-fat or lean meats and poultry that is baked, broiled, or grilled. Vary the meat and beans—include fish, beans, peas, nuts, and seeds. Adults should consume 5 to 6 ounces of meat and beans each day. Amounts recommended for children vary with age.

An additional aspect of nutrition is vitamins. Different vitamins are required for different functions of the body.

Vitamin	Recommended Daily Amounts for Adult Males	Deficiency Problems
Vitamin A	900 micrograms	Night blindness
Vitamin B (B$_1$ through B$_{12}$)	Varies	Anemia, dermatitis, birth defects
Vitamin C	90 milligrams	Scurvy
Vitamin D	1.3 milligrams	Rickets (softening of bones)
Vitamin E	15 milligrams	Anemia in newborns
Vitamin K	120 micrograms	Bleeding, non-coagulation of blood

In most cases, vitamins are obtained through food intake. In cases where vitamin deficiencies exist, supplements may be used to increase the vitamin intake. Some vitamins are obtained through other means—one form of Vitamin D is obtained by exposure to the sun. Children most often lack vitamins A, C, and D.

In all cases, a minimum number of **calories** are needed for the body to function properly. This number varies with age and gender. If too few calories are consumed, the body shuts down and retains fat, water, and calories. If too many calories are consumed, weight is gained. Physical activity burns calories, reducing the net amount of calories consumed.

Checkpoint

1. What are the food groups indicated in the food pyramid?

2. True or false: Consuming too few calories can lead to weight gain.

3. True or false: Physical activity does nothing for calorie intake.

4. What three vitamins do children most often lack?

Checkpoint Answers

1. Grains, vegetables, fruits, oils, milk, and meat and beans

2. True. Consuming too few calories causes the body to retain water, fat, and calories, causing a weight gain.

3. False. Physical activity burns calories, which reduces the net intake of calories.

4. Vitamins A, C, and D

Competency 18: Knowledge of Physical, Social, and Emotional Growth and Development

Competency Description

According to the Competencies and Skills Required for Teacher Certification in Florida, Elementary Education (available at http://www.fldoe.org/asp/ftce/pdf/60ElementaryEducationK-6.pdf) **Competency 18** for the Elementary Education (K–6) Subject Area Examination (SAE) addresses the following key indicators:

1. Identify the principles of sequential progression of motor skill development.
2. Demonstrate knowledge of human growth and development and its relationship to physical, social, and emotional well-being.
3. Identify major factors associated with social and emotional health (e.g., communication skills, self-concept, fair play, conflict resolution, character development, stress management).
4. Identify problems associated with physical, social, and emotional health.
5. Identify factors related to responsible sexual behavior.

Overview

Knowledge of physical, social, and emotional growth and development is important for elementary educators. Recognizing proper physical, social, and emotional growth is as important as recognizing the signs and symptoms of developmental problems. There are approximately **9 questions** that address Competency 18. This section addresses the following areas related to **Competency 18** key indicators:

- Motor Skills Development
- Physical Growth and Development
  - Sexual Development
- Social and Emotional Growth and Development
  - Communication Skills
  - Self-concept and Self-esteem
  - Conflict Resolution
  - Character Development
  - Stress Management

Motor Skills Development

There are two categories of motor skills—**gross motor skills** and **fine motor skills.** Gross motor skills involve the use of large muscle groups. Gross motor skills include running, galloping, and skipping. Fine motor skills are those that involve more specific and detailed movements. Fine motor skills include holding a pencil, using scissors, and coloring.

As children develop from K–6, their gross motor skill development progresses as well. In kindergarten (5–6 years old), children typically develop **locomotor, nonlocomotor,** and **manipulative** skills. Locomotor skills include efficiency in walking, running, and jumping. Children can walk, run, or jump without running into each other and can distinguish between fast and slow, for example. Nonlocomotor skills including twisting and turning. Children can roll, turn around, and balance on a low balance beam. Manipulative skills include those things in which objects are manipulated, for example, kicking or throwing a ball.

These fundamental skills are developed in kindergarten and then refined through first and second grade. The tasks involved become more difficult requiring more complex motor skills. By second grade, children should be able to combine locomotor, nonlocomotor, and manipulative skills and incorporate them into games and activities. By third grade, children's muscular strength is growing, providing for increases in motor skill abilities. Children also transition from teacher-directed to self-directed activities. By fourth grade, motor skill development is usually equalized between ages and genders. By fifth grade, girls often experience a rapid increase in fine motor skill development alongside the beginning of pre-pubescence. Boys, often later in the onset of pre-pubescence, see an increase in muscular strength and development and often see an increase in competitive sports.

Fine motor skills develop in conjunction with gross motor skills as well. By the end of first grade, children should be able to copy shapes, cut on a straight or curved line, tie shoes, zip zippers, and color inside the lines.

Checkpoint

1. What is the difference between fine motor skills and gross motor skills?

2. Fill in the blank: _____ include efficiency in walking, running, and jumping.

3. Fill in the blank: Twisting and turning are _____ skills.

Checkpoint Answers

1. Fine motor skills are specific and detailed. Gross motor skills involve large movement.

2. Locomotor skills

3. nonlocomotor

Physical Growth and Development

Child development is commonly divided into six stages: newborn, infant, toddler, preschooler, school-aged child, and adolescent. Various theories exist as to the physical growth and development of children including Piaget, Vygotsky, Erikson, and others.

Newborn and infant development is characterized by rapid physical growth. The newborn transitions from consuming small quantities of breast milk or formula and sleeping more than 15 hours each day to beginning to consume solid foods and taking 1–2 naps a day in about 6 months. By three months of age, a child should be able to raise the head and chest while lying on her stomach, open and shut hands, grab and shake toys, and bring hands to the mouth. By nine months of age, a child has usually developed to a point where he can sit without support, crawl on hands and knees, and hold a bottle. By 12 months of age, a child can say "ma-ma" and/or "da-da", pull up to stand by furniture, and locates sounds by turning the head. By 18 months of age, a child can walk unassisted, hold a cup and drink from it, feed him/herself, and say at least two words.

By the time a child turns 2 years old, she should be able to walk alone, pull a toy behind her while walking, begin to run, kick a ball, and climb up and down stairs with support. They can build a tower of blocks and scribble. By the time a child is 3 years old, she can climb, run, pedal a tricycle, and walk up and down stairs with ease. As children progress to school-age, they are able to communicate with complete sentences, run, ride a bike (sometimes without training wheels), and swing without assistance.

Milestones have been established by the American Academy of Pediatrics that represent the average age at which children typically attain a skill. Milestones are averages—some children attain that skill earlier and some later. When children do not reach one or more milestone, they are said to have a **developmental delay**. Developmental delays may be physical, emotional, social, or speech. The cause of developmental delays is varied—sometimes genetic, environmental, and sometimes unknown.

Some children with developmental delays overcome the delay before beginning school. Treatment for developmental delays may include speech therapy, physical therapy, and/or occupational therapy. Children who do not progress toward the milestones are often categorized as special needs children, sometimes with mild learning disabilities and othertimes with pervasive disabilities, including autism.

Autism Spectrum Disorder (ASD) is a developmental disorder in which children lack social development. Symptoms of autism may be seen as early as the child's third birthday. Children with ASD typically lack social development including having an inability to use nonverbal social interactions effectively and avoiding eye contact. The degree to which social development is hindered varies along the spectrum. Children with autism can also exhibit delays in communication skills. An early sign of autism risk is often a speech delay. Children with autism typically do not talk before their second birthday. Some children with autism are completely nonverbal. Autism is also typically characterized by excessive repetitive behavior including being abnormally preoccupied with certain interests as well as repetitive habits like head banging, body rocking, and "flapping." Autism rates have increased significantly. Some of that increase is probably due to screenings and more effective diagnosis. The cause of autism is unknown, and there is no cure. Treatment for autism includes speech, physical, and occupational therapies; medication; controlled diet; and behavior therapy.

Sexual Development

As children approach puberty, sexual development becomes prominent. In puberty, the body grows faster than at any other time in life except infancy. Girls will typically begin puberty between the ages of 8 and 13 while boys will typically begin puberty between the ages of 10 and 15. In boys, puberty is characterized by an increase in the production of testosterone while in girls, puberty is characterized by an increase in the production of estrogen. In both cases, growth spurts take place at rapid rates, sometimes up to 4 inches in one year. The body also changes shape. Boys' shoulders will become wider, their bodies become more muscular, and their voices deepen. Girls' bodies typically become "curvier" gaining weight on their hips and developing breasts. Girls will begin menstruating. Another sure sign of puberty is hair growth. Boys and girls both begin to grow hair under the arms and in the pubic area. Boys will eventually grow hair on the face as well.

As children progress into puberty, education about sexual choices is necessary. Parents should typically take the lead in sex education of their children, but schools may play a part as well.

Checkpoint

Fill in the blank.

1. When children do not reach one or more milestone, they are said to have _____.

2. Girls typically begin _____ between ages 8 and 13.

Checkpoint Answers

1. developmental delay

2. puberty

Social and Emotional Growth and Development

Social and emotional growth and development can be categorized into six areas, namely communication skills, self-concept, fair play, conflict resolution, character development, and stress management.

Communication Skills

Communication skills include interpersonal skills. Good communication skills are important in the social growth and development of children. Communicating well provides opportunities for sharing information and understanding other's points of view. Key elements of effective communication include active listening, "I" messages, and using win-win situations.

Active Listening

Active listening involves intentionally listening to what the other person is saying. It also includes examining non-verbal communication like gestures and facial expressions. When active listening is taking place, often the listener asks questions like "what did you mean by" or "can you explain that some more?" to indicate that they are listening to the speaker. The listener also acknowledges the feelings of the speaker.

"I" Messages

"I" messages are a way to communicate feelings to others without attacking or blaming the other party. When "I" messages are used, the feelings of the speaker are communicated without directing blame or attack. For example, in a situation in which one child takes a toy from another child, an "I" message approach may be to say "I feel sad when you take the toy without asking" as opposed to a "you" message of "You took that toy and didn't even ask!" The use of the "I" message allows for the feelings of the speaker to be communicated without eliciting defensive responses from the listener.

Win-win Situations

In order to resolve conflicts, win-win situations can often be used. This type of resolution to conflict takes place when both parties involved feel their needs are being met. Negotiation takes place in order to resolve the conflict so that both parties "win," and it is not a winner-loser situation. Active listening and brainstorming solutions can be helpful in order to discover a win-win resolution. Sometimes developing a win-win resolution involves the use of an outside mediator as well.

Self-concept and Self-esteem

Self-concept and **self-esteem** relate to one's own identity. Self-concept is a cognitive aspect of self and generally refers to the system of beliefs, attitudes, and opinions learned and that each person determines to be true. Self-esteem is an emotional aspect of self and generally refers to how one feels about himself.

Conflict Resolution

Conflict resolution is an aspect of good communication skills and is included in win-win situations.

Character Development

Character development includes standards of character, which form a foundation for ethics and ethical decision making. There are **six pillars of character,** which are multi-faceted. It is not enough to just have one pillar of character—all six work together to allow the individual to make ethical decisions. The six pillars are trustworthiness, respect, responsibility, fairness, caring, and citizenship.

Stress Management

Stress is the impact of a continually changing environment on the body. There are physical and emotional effects of stress, and stress can create both positive and negative feelings. Stress can compel action, resulting in a new perspective on a situation. It can also, however, result in feelings of rejection or anger and lead to health problems including headaches, upset stomach, insomnia, and ulcers. Stress management needs to be included in any discussion of emotional and social growth and development.

The first aspect of stress management is identifying the stressor and the individual's reaction to that stressor. Once the stressor is identified, the individual must recognize what, if anything, can be changed to alleviate the stress. In some situations, the individual can do nothing to alleviate the stress; however, they can address the situation in ways which seek to lessen the impact of the stressor.

Exercise can be a physical response to stress. Eating a healthy diet and exercising regularly can help to moderate the impact of stress in one's life. Additionally, supportive relationships can help to emotionally deal with stress.

Checkpoint

1. What are three key elements of effective communication?

2. What are the six pillars of character?

Checkpoint Answers

1. active listening, "I" messages, and using win-win situations

2. trustworthiness, respect, responsibility, fairness, caring, and citizenship

Competency 19: Knowledge of Community Health and Safety Issues

Competency Description

According to the Competencies and Skills Required for Teacher Certification in Florida, Elementary Education (available at http://www.fldoe.org/asp/ftce/pdf/60ElementaryEducationK-6.pdf) **Competency 19** for the Elementary Education (K–6) Subject Area Examination (SAE) addresses the following key indicators:

1. Identify factors contributing to substance use and abuse and identify signs, symptoms, effects, and strategies for the prevention of substance abuse.

2. Demonstrate knowledge of resources from home, school, and community that provide valid health information, products, and services.

3. Identify appropriate violence prevention strategies in the home, school, and community.

4. Identify appropriate safety and injury prevention strategies in the home, school, and community.

Overview

Knowledge of community health and safety issues includes an understanding of risky behavior in children and adolescents as well as knowledge of prevention strategies and resources. There are approximately **4 questions** that address Competency 19. This section addresses the following areas related to **Competency 19** key indicators:

- Substance Abuse
  - Signs and Symptoms
  - Prevention
- Health and Safety Resources

Substance Abuse

Substance abuse is overindulgence in and dependence on an addictive substance, especially alcohol or narcotic drugs. The substance may be an illegal drug such as marijuana or cocaine, or legal substances used improperly like prescription drugs, nail polish, glue, or spray paint. General signs and symptoms of substance abuse include ceasing familiar activities like sports, homework, or hobbies; sudden changes in school attendance and quality of work; doing things you would not normally do like borrowing money or stealing; taking uncharacteristic risks; attitude change; changes in physical appearance and grooming; engaging in suspicious behavior; and feeling exhausted, depressed, hopeless, or suicidal.

Signs and Symptoms

Different drugs have different signs of abuse.

Marijuana	Rapid talking Outbursts of laughter Forgetfulness in conversation Sleepiness Dilated pupils
Stimulants Cocaine Amphetamines Methamphetamines	Dilated pupils Dry mouth and nose Bad breath Lack of interest in food or sleep Irritability Talkative, but lacking continuity in conversation Nose bleeds
Depressants Barbiturates Benzodiazepines	Symptoms of alcohol use without odor on breath Lack of facial expression Slurred speech
Narcotics Heroin Codeine Morphine Vicodin	Lethargy Constricted pupils Red and raw nostrils Track marks Slurred speech
Hallucinogens	Dilated pupils Warm skin Excessive perspiration Distorted sense of sight, hearing, touch Mood changes Flashback episodes
Dissociative Anesthetics (PCP)	Unpredictable mood swings Disorientation Fear Rigid muscles Dilated pupils
Inhalants Glue Vapor producing solvents Propellants	Runny nose Watery eyes Drowsiness Poor muscle control

Prevention

There are various school-based programs for teaching substance abuse prevention. Education has been shown to be the most effective prevention for substance abuse. This education should include both the effects of substance abuse as well as the development of skills to resist social pressures and encourage anti-drug attitudes.

Checkpoint

1. What is substance abuse?

2. What are two symptoms of substance abuse?

3. What are the symptoms of marijuana use?

Checkpoint Answers

1. Overindulgence in and dependence on an addictive substance, especially alcohol or narcotic drugs.

2. Ceasing familiar activities like sports, homework, or hobbies; sudden changes in school attendance and quality of work; doing things you would not normally do like borrowing money or stealing; taking uncharacteristic risks; attitude change; changes in physical appearance and grooming; engaging in suspicious behavior; and feeling exhausted, depressed, hopeless, or suicidal.

3. Rapid talking, outbursts of laughter, forgetfulness, sleepiness, dilated pupils.

Health and Safety Resources

Various resources exist for implementing health and safety in school, at home, and in the community.

The U.S. Food and Drug Administration (FDA) has established a standard for food labels. Every item of food sold in the United States must include a food label. The food labels must include the amount per serving of calories, fat, cholesterol, dietary fiber, and other nutrients. Reference values, know as % Daily Value, must also appear, giving the consumer an idea of how this food fits into an overall diet.

The Surgeon General is the head of the U.S. Public Health Service and is responsible for ensuring public awareness about health and nutrition. Surgeon General warnings are on some items, which are legal to purchase (sometimes at a specific age) but may be hazardous to the health of the user. The most well-known item that contains a Surgeon General Warning is cigarettes.

School-based prevention programs also exist for various issues including school violence prevention programs like conflict resolution and peer mediation and substance abuse prevention as discussed in the preceding section.

Personal safety is an important aspect of education, particularly in science labs. Goggles and an apron should be worn at all times when working with chemicals, hot liquids, or Bunsen burners. Students should know the location of safety equipment in the classroom including fire extinguishers, eye wash station, safety shower, first-aid kit, fire alarm switch, and a method for calling the main office.

Safety at home is becoming a larger issue, particularly with children spending more time online. Safety issues in the home can include locking toxic materials (like cleaners) away from children, teaching children about 911, anchoring dressers and bookcases to the wall to prevent them from falling on a child, and so on. An increasing issue of safety at home is Internet safety. Children should not use the Internet unsupervised. The computer should be placed in a central location like the living room. Children should have a reason for going online. They should not be allowed to "surf" the Internet. Using the Internet for a school project or for finding specific information is helpful and necessary. Shopping, chatting, and playing games on the Internet can be allowed, but it is helpful to have discussions with children as to the purpose of their use of the Internet. Time limits should be set, and children's online activities should be monitored. The parent should also know the child's screen name and ensure that their children do not give out personal information through their screen name.

An additional aspect of health and safety is community safety. Children should be taught to look both ways before crossing the street, not to touch stray animals, and not to talk to strangers. Children need to be taught a definition of stranger. The first time a child meets a friend of their parents, they could be considered a stranger; however, the child should not necessarily view them as a person to fear. Children should be taught their full name, address, and how to use the telephone early. Additionally, children should be educated about appropriate and inappropriate touching.

Checkpoint

1. Fill in the blank: _____ must include the amount per serving of calories, fat, cholesterol, dietary fiber, and other nutrients.

2. What are two strategies to use for Internet safety?

Checkpoint Answers

1. Food labels

2. supervise children on the Internet; place computer in central location

Competency 20: Knowledge of Subject Content and Appropriate Curriculum Design

Competency Description

According to the Competencies and Skills Required for Teacher Certification in Florida, Elementary Education (available at http://www.fldoe.org/asp/ftce/pdf/60ElementaryEducationK-6.pdf) **Competency 20** for the Elementary Education (K–6) Subject Area Examination (SAE) addresses the following key indicators:

1. Distinguish between developmentally appropriate and inappropriate instructional practices that consider the interaction of cognitive, affective, and psychomotor domains.
2. Identify various factors (e.g., environment, equipment, facilities, space, safety, group diversity) to consider when planning physical activities.
3. Analyze the influence of culture, media, technology, and other factors when planning health and wellness instruction.

Overview

Knowledge of content and curriculum design for health and physical education are important. The knowledge of incorporating health and physical education into instruction on a day-to-day basis is important for elementary teachers. There are approximately **4 questions** that address Competency 20. This section addresses the following area related to **Competency 20** key indicators:

- Instructional Practices

Instructional Practices

Bloom's Taxonomy (Bloom et al., 1956) was developed as a means of identifying educational goals and objectives. Bloom's Taxonomy can be thought of in three areas: cognitive (knowledge), affective (attitude), and psychomotor (skills). An update was made to Bloom's Taxonomy by Anderson and Krathwohl (2001).

The cognitive domain involves knowledge and the development of intellectual skills. There are six major categories for the cognitive domain, namely Knowledge, Comprehension, Application, Analysis, Synthesis, and Evaluation. These are listed from the simplest to the most complex, and they must be mastered sequentially.

Category	Definition	Key Words
Knowledge	Recall data or information	Define, describe, identify, list, name
Comprehension	Understand the meaning, translation, or interpretation of instructions and problems; state in own words	Comprehend, defend, distinguish, explain, generalize, summarize
Application	Use a concept in a new situation; apply learning in novel situations	Apply, construct, demonstrate, discover, predict, show, use
Analysis	Separate material into component parts to understand its structure	Analyze, compare, contrast, distinguish, infer
Evaluation	Make judgments about the value of ideas or materials	Compare, conclude, critique, defend, interpret, support
Synthesis	Put parts together to form a whole and create new meaning	Combine, compile, create, design, generate, revise, rewrite, summarize

The affective domain includes how one deals with emotions including feelings, values, motivations, and attitudes. There are five categories listed from least to most complex in the affective domain, namely receiving phenomena, responding to phenomena, valuing, organization, and internalizing values.

Category	Definition	Example
Receiving phenomena	Awareness and willingness to hear	Listen to a lecture on a given topic
Responding to phenomena	Active participation; reacts to stimuli; shows new behavior as result of experience	Answer questions about a lecture on a given topic
Valuing	Attaches worth or value to an object, stimuli, or behavior	Demonstrates belief in democratic process; values diversity
Organization	Integrates new value into value system	Revises judgment or changes behavior in light of new evidence
Internalizing values	Value system controls behavior; behavior is consistent and predictable	Shows self-reliance

The psychomotor domain includes physical movement, coordination, and use of motor skills. There are seven categories listed in order from least to most complex, namely perception, set, guided response, mechanism, complex overt response, adaptation, and origination.

Category	Definition	Example
Perception	Uses sensory cues to guide motor activity	Detects non-verbal communication cues; estimates where a ball will land after it is thrown
Set	Ready to act	Acts upon a sequence of steps; recognizes abilities and limitations
Guided response	Imitation and trial and error in learning new complex skill	Follows directions to build a model
Mechanism	Intermediate stage in learning a complex task; responses become habitual and proficient	Uses a computer; drives a car
Complex overt response	Performs motor skills with complex patterns; Similar to mechanism, but faster and more effective	Operates a computer efficiently and accurately
Adaptation	Patterns can be modified to fit special requirements	Responds effectively to unexpected experiences
Origination	Creates new patterns to fit a situation or problem	Creates a dance routine or a new way to solve a mathematical problem

These aspects of Bloom's Taxonomy should be taken into consideration when planning activities. Additionally, other factors should be taken into account when planning physical activities. In addition to considering the needs of the individual and maximizing the opportunities for learning, special considerations should also be taken into account to reduce the possibility of accidents or damage. These include establishing boundaries for play which are away from walls, furniture, and other children; restricting running and combat activities; increase time on task; establish expectations for listening and following directions; ensure adequate ventilation; plan ahead for movement of classroom furniture; and modify equipment if necessary.

Checkpoint

1. What are the three domains of Bloom's Taxonomy?

2. What are the levels of the cognitive domain of Bloom's Taxonomy?

3. Fill in the blank: One aspect of safety in the classroom is establishing expectations for _____.

Checkpoint Answers

1. Cognitive, Affective, and Psychomotor
2. Knowledge, Comprehension, Application, Analysis, Evaluation, and Synthesis
3. listening and following directions

Summary

The Music, Visual Arts, Physical Education, and Health section (Competencies 12–20) encompasses a variety of subcompetencies related to the basic knowledge required of educators teaching elementary age students. Knowledge of skills and techniques in music and visual arts encompasses varieties of music, singing techniques, music interpretation, and appropriate use of art materials. Knowledge of creation and composition in music and visual arts involves understanding the elements of art and music as well as strategies for developing creative responses to art and music. Knowledge of cultural and historical connections in music and visual arts includes the connection between history, music, and art. Knowledge of aesthetic and critical analysis of music and visual arts encompasses the development of analytical skills for music and art. Knowledge of appropriate assessment strategies in music and visual arts involves understanding assessment techniques applicable to the music and art classrooms. Knowledge of personal health and wellness includes understanding health, fitness, and nutrition. Knowledge of physical, social, and emotional growth and development involves an understanding of child and adolescent development not only physically, but socially and emotionally as well including signs of developmental problems. Knowledge of community health and safety issues involves recognizing resources for health and safety and community involvement. Knowledge of subject content and appropriate curriculum design entails understanding developmental appropriateness of curriculum and issues of physical education.

This section reflects the skills required in this area for Teacher Certification in Florida, Elementary Education (available at www.fldoe.org/asp/ftce/pdf/60ElementaryEducationK-6.pdf). You should use the information in this section to compliment your previous knowledge in the areas of music, visual arts, physical education, and health. The general review of Music, Visual Arts, Physical Education, and Health section (Competencies 12–20) provided in this chapter should enable you to explore areas of strength and need that you might still need to review. As indicated before, sample questions for the competency area as a whole appear in the next section of this chapter. Answers and explanations follow the sample questions. These sections should provide an opportunity for further practice and analysis.

Sample Questions

1. During a unit on physical fitness, a student recorded the following log of physical activities: swimming, running, and riding a bike. In which type of physical activity is this student engaged?

   A. strength training
   B. bone strengthening
   C. aerobics
   D. flexibility

2. Triangles, tambourines, blocks, and sticks are examples of

   A. tuning instruments.
   B. rhythmic instruments.
   C. harmonic instruments.
   D. melodic instruments.

3. A music composition that involves a number of highly varied choral musical compositions and uses a polyphonic approach from the thirteenth century is most likely

   A. an Opera.
   B. an Oratorio.
   C. a Motet.
   D. an Overture.

4. A parent asks their child's teacher for recommendations related to the child's Internet use at home. Which of the following should be recommended?

   A. placing the computer in a central location
   B. allowing unlimited computer usage
   C. allowing the child to create his own email address and password
   D. allowing the child to chat with others

5. Which of the following is not one of the six pillars of character?

   A. respect
   B. sportsmanship
   C. fairness
   D. trustworthiness

6. The perceived fundamental frequency of a sound is

   A. timbre.
   B. rhythm.
   C. texture.
   D. pitch.

7. Students in Mr. Ortiz's class were asked to keep track of the foods they ate over a two-day period. Marie logged the following foods in her chart: milk, cheese, apple juice, ground beef, chicken, strawberries, salad, and yogurt. To meet her daily nutritional needs, she should add servings from which food group?

   A. milk
   B. grains
   C. fruits
   D. meat and beans

8. The Jazz and Baroque music styles share which of the following characteristics?

   A. instrumentation
   B. tempo style
   C. improvisation
   D. harmony style

9. The categories for established forms of compositions are called

   A. textures.
   B. forms.
   C. genres.
   D. melodies.

10. Which of the following is NOT a fine motor skill?

    A. using scissors
    B. coloring
    C. walking
    D. holding a pencil

11. Which of the following will cause an individual to lose weight?

    A. consuming too many calories
    B. consuming too few calories
    C. exercising more
    D. exercising less

12. A teacher wants to enhance the fourth-grade class's understanding of the volume of sounds and notes by listening to several songs. Which of the following music elements is she most likely emphasizing?

    A. melody
    B. dynamics
    C. form
    D. texture

13. Which of the following is a nonlocomoter skill?

    A. twisting
    B. running
    C. skipping
    D. walking

14. The best procedure for enhancing student safety in physical education class is to

    A. only allow students to climb on equipment when the teacher is spotting them.
    B. have the children get equipment out of the closet.
    C. instruct the children on the rules of play prior to beginning the game.
    D. allow students to create their own rules.

15. The music teacher is planning a lesson in which children hear songs sung by her, and as the songs become more and more familiar, the children will begin to join in and sing. What type of teaching is she using?

    A. process of immersion
    B. rote teaching
    C. note teaching
    D. introductory teaching

16. A second grade student is unable to tie her shoes. To remediate the problem, the teacher should

    A. tie her shoes for her.
    B. encourage her parents to buy shoes that do not tie.
    C. have another student tie her shoes.
    D. help the student practice tying her shoes and related activities.

Use the picture to answer the question that follows:

17. What type of balance is the artist most likely using?

    A. symmetrical balance
    B. radical balance
    C. horizontal balance
    D. asymmetrical balance

18. Which of the following is not an appropriate educational practice to support students' creativity?

    A. Students work together to develop a mural for the school.
    B. Students work independently to make an original card for a friend.
    C. Students work as teams to copy as exactly as possible a drawing given by the teacher.
    D. Students work as teams to create a collage.

Answer Explanations for Sample Questions

1. **C.** Competency 17. The physical activities include swimming, running, and riding a bike. Strength training includes activities designed to strengthen muscles. Although swimming, running, and riding a bike will strengthen muscles, that is not their primary objective. Bone strengthening activities are those that include impact and strengthen specific bones in the body. Again, these activities will do that, but not as their primary objective. The primary objective of swimming, running, and riding a bike is aerobic—increasing the heart rate and promoting cardiovascular fitness

2. **B.** Competency 12. Triangles, tambourines, blocks, and sticks are examples of rhythmic instruments. Melody bells and simple flutes are examples of melodic instruments. Chording instruments, like autoharps, are harmonic instruments. Tuning instruments is not one of the types of instruments.

3. **C.** Competency 14. A music composition that involves a number of highly varied choral musical compositions and uses a polyphonic approach from the thirteenth century is most likely a Motet.

4. **A.** Competency 19. Use of the Internet is a safety issue. Recommendations for safe use of the Internet include having the computer in a central location, monitoring computer use, knowing children's screen names and passwords, and limiting time on the Internet.

5. **B.** Competency 18. The six pillars of character are trustworthiness, respect, responsibility, fairness, caring, and citizenship. Sportsmanship is not a pillar of character.

6. **D.** Competency 12. The perceived fundamental frequency of a sound is pitch. It is one of the principles of music that governs melody and harmony.

7. **B.** Competency 17. The foods listed include the food groups of milk, fruits, vegetables, and meat. She is missing grains.

8. **C.** Competency 13. The Jazz and Baroque music styles share improvisation as a common characteristic.

9. **C.** Competency 12. The categories for established forms of compositions are called genres.

10. **C.** Competency 18. Fine motor skills involve precise movement. Gross motor skills involve large movement. Walking is a gross motor skill.

11. **C.** Competency 17. Consuming too many calories will lead to weight gain. Consuming too few calories will also lead to weight gain in that the body will retain water, fat, and calories. Exercising less will burn fewer calories. Exercising more will lead to lower net calorie intake, allowing an individual to lose weight.

12. **B.** Competency 13. She is most likely emphasizing the dynamics of the songs, which involve the volume (loudness or softness) of the sounds or notes.

13. **A.** Competency 18. Nonlocomotor skills are twisting and turning.

14. **C.** Competency 20: To enhance safety, the rules of play should be explained prior to beginning the game. This is the best procedure to enhance the safety of all the children.

15. **A.** Competency 12. Process of immersion is the one that involves hearing songs sung by parents, teachers, or on recordings, and as the songs become more and more familiar, students will begin to join in and sing. Rote teaching is done through imitation, which is usually presented sequentially and repeated back by the children. Note teaching involves the gradual and systematic learning to read music notation.

16. **D.** Competency 18. The teacher should help the student learn to tie her shoes.

17. **B.** Competency 15. The type of balance the artist is most likely using in this painting is radical balance. In this type of balance, the pattern appears to radiate from the center axis.

18. **C.** Competency 16. Students working as teams to copy as exactly as possible a drawing is not an appropriate educational practice that supports students' creativity. The development of students' artistic creativity requires more flexibility. The other alternatives are more appropriate for this purpose.

Science and Technology

This chapter provides a general review of the area of Science and Technology (Competencies 21–27) with sample questions and explanations at the end of the chapter. Checkpoint exercises are found throughout, giving you an opportunity to practice the skills addressed in each section. The answers to the Checkpoint exercises immediately follow the set of questions. We encourage you to cover the answers as you complete the Checkpoint exercises. Sample questions for the competency area as a whole appear at the end of the chapter. Answers and explanations follow the sample questions.

Competency 21: Knowledge of the Nature of Matter

Competency Description

According to the Competencies and Skills Required for Teacher Certification in Florida, Elementary Education (available at http://www.fldoe.org/asp/ftce/pdf/60ElementaryEducationK-6.pdf) **Competency 21** for the Elementary Education (K–6) Subject Area Examination (SAE) addresses the following key indicators:

1. Identify the fundamental physical properties of **matter** (e.g., **mass**, **volume**).
2. Compare physical and chemical changes (e.g., cutting, burning, rusting).
3. Compare the characteristics of **elements**, **compounds**, and **mixtures**.
4. Compare the physical properties of solids, liquids, and **gases** (e.g., **mass**, **volume**, color, texture, hardness, temperature).
5. Compare properties of **liquids** during **phase change** through heating and cooling (e.g., boiling, melting, freezing, evaporation, condensation).
6. Demonstrate knowledge that all matter is composed of parts too small to be seen (e.g., **electrons**, **protons**, **neutrons**).

Overview

Knowledge of the nature of **matter** is a very important area of science education. The word science comes from the Latin word "scientia", which means knowledge. Science uses study, observation, experimentation, and practice to acquire knowledge in an organized manner. There are approximately **3 questions** that address Competency 21. This section addresses the following areas related to **Competency 21** key indicators:

- Physical and Chemical Properties of Matter
- Classification of Matter
- Phase Change

Physical and Chemical Properties of Matter

There are several fundamental physical properties of matter: **mass**, **volume**, **density,** and **chemical change**. **Matter** is what makes up everything in the world: rocks, people, chairs, buildings, water, oxygen, animals, and chemical substances, among others. It takes up space (**volume**) and has **mass**. It not only involves its **molecules** and **atoms**, but also subatomic particles such as **protons** and **electrons**. The mass of objects is always the same and is independent of gravity; for example, two rocks with the same amount of mass, which are placed on a pan balance here on Earth, will also be balanced on the moon even though the gravitational pull on the rocks is different. *Gravity* does not change the mass of the rocks. Weight is often confused with mass. The measure of the Earth's pull of gravity on an object is called **weight**. It is the force of gravity on objects. It is measured in pounds (English or traditional system), or grams (metric system). The weight of a rock on Earth would be different on the Moon. The gravitational pull would be different on Earth than it is on the Moon.

Volume is another property of matter together with **mass**. The amount of cubic space that an object occupies is called **volume**. **Density** (symbol: ρ, which is the Greek "rho") is defined as mass per unit of volume, or the ratio of total mass (m) to total volume (V): $\rho = \frac{m}{V}$ (for example, kilogram per cubic meter or kg/m^3, and grams per cubic centimeter or g/cm^3). In other words, it defines how closely the molecules are packed together. It depends on the *type of matter* you are using but not the *amount of matter* you are using. For example, an object made of iron, which is very dense, will have less volume than an object of equal mass made of some less dense substance like water. The higher an object or a substance density is, the higher the ratio of total mass to total volume would be. To calculate an object's density, you need to use a balance to measure its mass and then measure its volume (multiply together the object's length, width, and height if it is rectangular). The volume of an object may also be measured by seeing how much water it displaces when it is submerged in water. You will need to measure the water in the container before and after the object is submerged in the water, and then calculate the difference between these two numbers, which results in the volume of the object. An object's *buoyancy* is directly related to its density. An object will sink in a liquid or gas if it is denser than the liquid or gas that surrounds it. An object will float in a liquid or gas if its density is less than the density of the liquid or gas that surrounds it.

Matter is in constant change. A **physical change** does not produce a new substance (for example, freezing and melting water), and a **chemical change** or **reaction** does produce one or more substances. The following are examples of **physical changes**:

- Water boils out of a metal pot.
- Water condenses on a cold glass.
- A metal pot is put on a burner and gets hot.
- Dry ice is altered from a solid to a gaseous form of carbon dioxide.
- Gold melts or solidifies.
- Sand is mixed in with salt.
- A piece of chalk is ground to dust.
- A glass breaks.
- An iron rod gets magnetized.
- A lump of sugar dissolves into water.

The *physical* and *chemical properties* of matter describe the appearance and behavior of substances. The physical properties may be observed without altering the identity of a substance or its molecular structure (for example, changes in size, form, or appearance of the substance or object). These **physical changes** may include melting, bending, or cracking. The chemical properties of a substance indicate the ability of a substance to be altered into new ones, and involve changes in the molecular structure of the substance or object. These chemical changes may include burning, rusting, and digestion. Under some conditions, a chemical reaction may involve breaking apart, combining, recombining, or decomposing substances. For example, baking powder is chemically altered as it changes into carbon dioxide gas during the baking process. Chemical equations may be used to represent chemical reactions. The following are examples of chemical changes (the left side of the arrow is called reactants, and the right side of the arrow is called products):

- The silver in a silver spoon combines with sulfur in the air to produce silver sulfide, which is the black material we call tarnish: $2\,Ag + S \rightarrow Ag_2S$
- The iron in an iron bar combines with oxygen in the air to produce rust: $4\,Fe + 3\,O_2 \rightarrow 2\,Fe_2O_3$
- As it burns, methane combines with oxygen in the air to produce carbon dioxide and water vapor: $CH_4 + 2\,O_2 \rightarrow CO_2 + 2\,H_2O$

Checkpoint

1. If an object is denser than the liquid that surrounds it, will it sink or float in the liquid?

2. True or false: A physical change reaction produces one or more substances.

3. True or false: A glass broken into pieces is an example of a physical change.

Checkpoint Answers

1. If an object is denser than the liquid that surrounds it, then it will sink in the liquid.

2. False. A **physical change** does not produce a new substance. A chemical change or reaction does produce one or more substances.

3. True. This is an example of a **physical change** because the physical properties of the glass may be observed without altering the identity of the glass or its molecular structure.

Classification of Matter

The classification of matter also involves **elements**, **compounds**, **mixtures**, and **solutions**. An element is a substance that consists of only one type of **atom** and is represented by a symbol consisting of one or two letters. An element cannot be broken down into other substances of that element. For example, oxygen (O), iron (Fe), and carbon (C) are elements. An atom is the smallest particle of the element, which retains the properties of that element. It is the basic building blocks of matter. The atoms of each element are the same, but different from the atoms of other elements. Under most conditions, they are indivisible, but they may be split or combined during atomic reactions to form new atoms. It changes the number of protons and neutrons of an atom. Atomic reactions may take place in the sun, nuclear power reactors, nuclear bombs, and radioactive decay. Atoms are made of three components of subatomic particles: **protons**, **neutrons**, and **electrons**. The **protons** and **neutrons** are in the nucleus (or solid center) of the atom. **Electrons** are in the outer part of the atom. A **molecule** is the smallest particle of substance that may exist independently and maintains all the properties of the substance. The molecules of most elements are made of one atom, but the molecules of oxygen, hydrogen, nitrogen, and chlorine are made of two atoms each.

The three main states or phases of matter are **gas**, **liquid,** and **solid**.

- **Gas** is distinguished from **liquid** and **solid** by its relatively low **density** and viscosity, relatively great expansion and contraction with changes in pressure and temperature, ability to diffuse easily, and spontaneous tendency to distribute uniformly throughout space. It has no definite volume or shape; for example, water vapor or steam.

- **Liquid** is distinguished from **gas** and **solid** by its readiness to flow, little or no tendency to disperse in the air, and relatively high difficulty to compress. It has a definite volume, but no shape; for example, water.

- **Solid** is not gaseous or **liquid**. It is firm or compact in substance. It has definite volume and shape; for example, ice. Other phases are crystal, glass, and plasma.

At the elementary school level, children should have many opportunities to observe and describe a variety of objects, focusing on the object's physical properties, as well as what the object is made of and demonstrate knowledge that all mater is composed of parts too small to be seen; for example, **electrons**, **protons**, and **neutrons**. An activity that might help with this is to have children view salt under varied magnifications. They should observe salt with the naked eye, under a hand lens, a microscope, and the electron microscope (the electron image is available via the Internet). This way they can begin to construct the understanding that materials may be composed of parts that are too small to be seen with or without magnification, make detailed observations, and discover the unexpected details at smaller scales. This type of discovery prepares them for learning that all **matter** is made up of **atoms**, tiny moving parts too small to be seen.

A **compound** is matter that combines atoms chemically in definite weight proportions. Water (represented by the short-hand formula H_2O) is an example of a compound that has the ratio of two hydrogen molecules (represented by the subscript after the H, which tells the number of hydrogen atoms) and one oxygen molecule (represented by O, notice that no subscript is written in this case, which implies that the number of oxygen atoms is 1). A **mixture** is any combination of two or more substances, not chemically combined and without any definite weight proportions. In this case, the substances keep their own chemical properties. For example, milk is a mixture of water and butterfat particles. There are *homogeneous* and *heterogeneous mixtures*. *Homogeneous mixtures* are called **solutions**. They are uniform and consistent throughout. For example, seawater is a solution containing water and salt, which could be separated through the evaporation process. *Heterogeneous mixtures* contain dissimilar elements or parts. The following table provides a comparison between compounds and mixtures.

Category	Compounds	Mixtures
Number of elements	Two or more	Two or more
Type of particles	One kind	Two or more kinds
Chemical changes	Chemically combined	Not formed by chemical changes
Elements' chemical properties	Elements lose their individual entities	Elements keep their own chemical properties
Weight proportions	Combine in definite weight proportions	Combine without any definite weight proportions
Amount	Specific amount for each element	Does not have a definite amount for each element
Examples	Acids (vinegar, lemons), bases, salts, oxides, water	Seawater, milk

Checkpoint

Fill in the blank.

1. _____ is a substance that consists of only one type of atom.

2. The three main states of matter are _____, _____ and _____.

3. _____ is matter that combines atoms chemically in definite weight proportions.

Checkpoint Answers

1. Element

2. gas, liquid, solid

3. Compound

Phase Change

There are several *transitions* that take place within all the three main phases of **matter**. They might not be apparent by just looking at a substance. The transformations are processes that take place over time and might develop slowly. The different phases of matter are related to each other in terms of changes in temperature and/or pressure. Therefore, matter can undergo a **phase change** through heating and cooling, shifting from one form to another; for example, melting (changing from a solid to a liquid), freezing (changing from a liquid to a solid), evaporating (changing from a liquid to a **gas**), boiling (past the boiling point, which is the temperature at which a **liquid** boils at a fixed pressure; for example boiling of water to form steam), and condensing (changing from a gas to a liquid). For example, when the temperature of a **solid** is raised enough or the pressure is reduced enough, the result is a **liquid**.

The following table presents the transitions between the solid, liquid, and gaseous phases of matter due to the effect of temperature and/or pressure.

Transformation From	To		
	Solid	Liquid	Gaseous
Solid	Solid–solid transformation	Melting/fusion	Sublimation
Liquid	Freezing	N/A	Boiling/evaporation
Gaseous	Deposition	Condensation	N/A

Checkpoint

Fill in the blank.

1. _____ is a phase change that involves changing from a liquid to a solid.

2. _____ happens when the temperature of a solid is raised enough and the result is a liquid.

3. The transition between water and steam of phase change due to the effect of temperature is _____.

Checkpoint Answers

1. Freezing
2. Melting
3. boiling

Competency 22: Knowledge of Forces, Motion, and Energy

Competency Description

According to the Competencies and Skills Required for Teacher Certification in Florida, Elementary Education (available at http://www.fldoe.org/asp/ftce/pdf/60ElementaryEducationK-6.pdf) **Competency 22** for the Elementary Education (K–6) Subject Area Examination (SAE) addresses the following key indicators:

1. Demonstrate knowledge of **temperature, heat,** and heat transfer.
2. Identify the types and characteristics of contact forces (e.g., pushes and pulls, **friction**) and **at-a-distance forces** (e.g., magnetic, gravitational, electrostatic).
3. Apply knowledge of **light** and **optics** to practical applications (i.e., reflection, refraction, and diffusion).
4. Apply knowledge of **electrical currents, circuits, conductors, insulators,** and static electricity to real-world situations.
5. Distinguish between different types of energy (e.g., chemical, electrical, **mechanical**, electromagnetic, heat, light, sound, solar) and their characteristics as they apply to real-world situations.
6. Apply knowledge of the ability of energy to cause motion or create change.
7. Demonstrate knowledge that electrical energy can be transformed into heat, light, mechanical, and sound energy.
8. Demonstrate knowledge of **potential** and **kinetic energy.**
9. Demonstrate knowledge that motion of all matter can be changed by **forces,** observed, described, and measured.
10. Differentiate between **balanced** and **unbalanced forces** and how they affect objects.

Overview

Knowledge of **forces**, motion, and **energy** is very important for understanding science. Students need to be able to identify the difference between **heat** and **temperature** in order to have an appropriate understanding of **energy**. There are approximately **10 questions** that address Competency 22. This section addresses the following areas related to **Competency 22** key indicators:

- Temperature, Heat, and Heat Transfer
- Contact Forces and At-a-Distance Forces
- Light and Optics
- Electrical Currents, Circuits, Conductors, Insulators, and Static Electricity
- Types of Energy
- Balanced and Unbalanced Forces

Temperature, Heat, and Heat Transfer

The concepts of **heat** and **temperature** are not the same. **Temperature** is a measure related to the average **kinetic energy** of the molecules of a substance. It has to do with the degree of hotness or coldness of the substance. This is how hot or cold an object is with respect to a standard unit of measurement. A common type of thermometer is the one that uses a glass tube containing mercury or a liquid, such as colored alcohol. Temperature is not energy, but it is a number that relates to the kinetic energy possessed by the molecules of a substance (measured in Kelvin, Fahrenheit, or Celsius degrees). This measure is directly proportional to the average kinetic energy of the molecules. In the Celsius scale, the freezing point of water is set to zero degrees, and the boiling point to 100 degrees. The Celsius symbol is C. In the Kelvin scale, absolute zero is set at 0 degrees (the theoretical absence of all thermal energy), the freezing point of water at 273.15 degrees, and the boiling point of water at 373.15 degrees. The Kelvin symbol is K. In the Fahrenheit scale, the freezing point of water is set at 32 degrees, and the boiling point of water at 212 degrees. The Fahrenheit symbol is F.

Heat is a measurement of the total energy in a substance. That total **energy** is made up of the kinetic, and the potential energies of the molecules of the substance. Temperature does not tell you anything about the potential energy. When heat (or energy) goes into a substance one of two things may happen: the substance can experience a raise in temperature (the heat can be used to speed up the molecules of the substance), or the substance can change state (for example, if the substance is ice, it can melt into water). The faster the molecules of the substance are moving, the hotter the temperature becomes.

Checkpoint

1. Fill in the blank: _____ is a measurement of the total energy in a substance..

2. Fill in the blank: _____ is a measure related to the average kinetic energy of the molecules of a substance.

3. True or false: The concepts of heat and temperature define the same thing.

Checkpoint Answers

1. Heat

2. Temperature

3. False. The concepts of heat and temperature do not define the same.

Contact Forces and At-a-Distance Forces

Dynamics is the branch of mechanics that studies the relationship between motion and the forces affecting motion of bodies. **Force** is a pull or a push upon an object that results from the object's interaction with another object. If there is interaction between objects, then there is a force upon each of the objects. When the interaction is over, so is the force. It is necessary to make a machine work. When a force is unbalanced (or *kinetic friction*), the object accelerates (there is relative motion between the surfaces); for example, the thrust of an airplane's engine moves the airplane forward. When a force is a balanced net force on the object (or *static force*), the object does not accelerate by remaining still or continuing movement at the same speed. Two main types of forces are **contact forces** (for example, frictional, tension, air resistant, applied, and **mechanical** forces), and **at-a-distance forces** (for example, magnetic, gravitational, and electrostatic forces).

Contact forces require physical contact and interaction between objects. **Mass** is different than **weight**. An object's mass gives the object a reluctance to change its current state of motion and a measure of its resistance to acceleration. An object's weight on Earth is the **force** that Earth's gravity exerts on an object with a specific mass. **Friction** is the force involved when surfaces that touch each other have a certain resistance to motion. In a machine, friction reduces the mechanical advantage, or the ratio of output to input. For instance, an automobile uses one-quarter of its energy on reducing friction; but also friction in the tires and clutch allows the car to stay on the road and makes it possible to drive. **Mechanical force** is the application of **force** to bend, dent, scratch, compress, or break something; for example, machines in general multiply force or change the direction of **force**. An *applied force* is a force that is applied to an object by a person or another object. For example, when a person is pushing a desk across the room there is an applied force exerted upon the object.

At-a-distance forces result even when the interacting objects are not in physical contact, but they exert a push or pull despite their physical separation.

- *Gravitational forces* are involved when the sun and planets exert a gravitational pull on each other despite their large spatial separation. The gravitational pull is still present even when you have no physical contact with the Earth. **Centripetal force** is also involved when an object moves in a circular path, and force is directed toward the center of the circle in order to keep the motion going; for example, centripetal force keeps a satellite circling Earth.

- *Electrical forces* are action-at-a-distance forces. They are involved when the protons in the nucleus of an atom and the electrons outside the nucleus exert an electrical pull towards each other despite the spatial separation.

- *Magnetic forces* are action-at-a-distance forces. They are involved when two magnets can exert a magnetic pull on each other even when a short distance separates them.

- *Nuclear force* is present in the nucleus of atoms. It is released by fission (the breaking of a heavy nucleus into two lighter nuclei), fusion (two atomic nuclei fuse together to form a heavier nucleus), or radioactive decay (a neutron of proton in the radioactive nucleus decays spontaneously by emitting either particles, electromagnetic radiation or gamma rays, or all of them).

Checkpoint

Fill in the blank.

1. _____ forces result even when the interacting objects are not in physical contact, but they exert a push or pull despite their physical separation.

2. _____ forces are the result of the physical interaction between objects.

3. _____ forces are involved in the application of force to bend, dent, scratch, compress, or break something.

Checkpoint Answers

1. At-a-distance

2. Contact

3. Mechanical

Light and Optics

Light is a type of **energy** that has a comparatively low level of physical **weight** or **density**. It is considered an *electromagnetic radiation* that has a wavelength (*electromagnetic waves*); for example, radiant waves, X-rays, radio waves, and ultraviolet rays. The sun provides radiant energy. The constancy and universality of the speed of light in a vacuum is recognized to be 299,792,458 meters per second or 186,000 miles per second, which is faster than the speed of sound. It can go through some materials like *transparent* materials (such as air, water, and clear glass), but not through others like *opaque* materials (a brick wall that allows the passage of no light), or only partially through *translucent* materials (like frosted glass that allows the passage of some light). Light travels in a straight line. It can change direction, but still keeps traveling in a straight line; for example, when a light ray strikes a mirror, it changes direction, but continues traveling in a straight line. In this case, the mirror *reflects* light. Each surface reflects light differently. Rough surfaces tend to scatter light in many directions, and smooth surfaces tend to reflect light in one direction. *Refraction* occurs when light passes through a transparent material like water at a slant angle, the ray of light bends or changes speed. *Diffraction* occurs when a ray of light bends around the edges of object; the ray of light has been diffracted.

Optics is a branch of physics that studies the physical properties of light. It provides information about the behavior and properties of light and its interaction with **matter**. A **lens** is a piece of transparent and curved material; for example, glass. **Light** bends when it passes through this material. *Convex lenses* are thicker in the middle and are used as magnifying glasses and to help correct the vision of nearsighted persons. This vision correction is accomplished by using the concave lens to spread the light rays before they enter the eyes and allow the light rays to merge farther back in the eye to form a clear image on the retina. Lenses are used for monocular, binoculars, telescopes, microscopes, cameras, and projectors. A *prism* is a transparent object with flat polished surfaces that refracts or diffuses (breaks apart) light. The exact angles between the surfaces depend on the application or possible use of the prism. They are usually triangular prisms with a triangular base and rectangular sides and are made out of glass (other transparent materials can be used). They can also be used to break light up into its constituent spectral colors (the colors of the rainbow).

Checkpoint

Fill in the blank.

1. _____ is a branch of physics that studies the physical properties of light.

2. A type of energy that has a comparatively low level of physical weight or density is called _____.

3. A _____ is a piece of transparent and curved material.

Checkpoint Answers

1. Optics

2. light

3. lens

Electrical Currents, Circuits, Conductors, Insulators, and Static Electricity

Electricity is a physical occurrence related to stationary and moving **electrons** and **protons**. The electric energy is made available by the flow of electric charge through a **conductor**. A **conductor** allows electricity to flow freely through it (for example, copper is a good conductor of electricity). On the other hand, an **insulator** does not allow the electrons to flow freely (for example, glass, rubber, and air). It can be used to transform the chemical make up of a substance; for example, passing electricity through water to break the water down into hydrogen and oxygen **gases**. **Atoms** may transmit electrical energy. *Neutral atoms* contain an equal number of protons and electrons because they cancel each other out and provide no net charge. Atoms with negative charge contain more electrons than protons, and atoms with a positive charge contain fewer electrons than protons. When two objects are rubbed against each other, electrons transfer from one object to the other, and leave both of them charged. **Electric current** is the flow of electricity through a **conductor**. Electrical cables are usually made of conductors (for example, copper) and insulation (for example, rubber on the outside part). An electrical circuit is a path or combination of paths that allow the flow of the electrical current from one place to another. *Series circuits* use only one electrical path. *Parallel circuits* use several electrical paths. For example, this type of circuit allows the distribution of the electric current throughout a house. Circuit breakers could be used in a house to monitor its electric flow, and if there is an overload of electricity the flow of electricity will stop.

An **electrical circuit** must have a continuous flow of electricity going through a complete loop (circuit), returning to their original position and cycling through again. An example that illustrates the necessity of a complete loop utilizes a battery, a small light bulb, and a connecting wire. Students should observe the effect of connecting and disconnecting a wire in a simple arrangement of the battery, light bulb, and wire. If appropriate connections are made, then the light bulb will light up. The lighting of the bulb should occur immediately after the final connection is made appropriately. There should be no perceivable time delay between when the last connection is made and when the light bulb is perceived to light up. If the light bulb lights up and remains lit, this is evidence that charge is flowing through the light bulb filament and that an electric circuit has been established. A circuit is a closed loop through which electrical charges can continuously move. Students should explore different ways to set up the electric circuit by rearranging the placement of the wire, battery, and light bulb.

Using **friction** can produce **static electricity**. Static electricity refers to the accumulation of excess electric charge in a region that has poor electrical conductivity (like an insulator). It refers to the build up of electric charge on the surface of objects (stationary electric charges). For example, a plastic stick that is rubbed with silk will become electrically charged and will attract small pieces of paper. Electrically charged objects share the following characteristics: like charges repel one another, opposite charges attract each other, and charge is conserved.

Checkpoint

Fill in the blank.

1. A _____ is a closed loop through which electrical charges can continuously move.

2. The accumulation of excess electric charge in a region that has poor electrical conductivity is called _____ electricity.

3. A _____ allows electricity to flow freely through it.

Checkpoint Answers

1. circuit

2. static

3. conductor

Types of Energy

Several types of **energy** are presented in this section. Notice that many energy sources might produce more than one form of energy. For example, the sun produces **light** and **heat**, a light bulb also produces some heat energy, and an oven also produces some light energy. Also, notice that energy cannot be created or destroyed, but it can be transformed from one form of energy to another. This process is called energy transformation, which occur everyday and everywhere. The following are some examples of energy transformations:

- A person uses mechanical energy to clap producing sound energy.
- The sun provides light energy to help plants produce chemical energy.
- The mechanical energy used to rub our hands together is transformed into heat or thermal energy.
- The wind provides mechanical energy, which can be transformed into electrical energy.
- A battery is chemical energy that becomes electrical energy in a CD player; the CD player emits sound energy.
- Electrical energy is transformed into heat energy in an oven.
- Wood provides chemical energy, which changes to light energy and heat energy in a fire.
- A plane uses chemical energy from gasoline to fly (mechanical energy).
- A person uses chemical energy from food to ride a bike (mechanical energy).
- A car transforms chemical energy (gasoline) and/or electrical energy (battery in hybrid cars) to mechanical energy.
- A man uses mechanical energy to ring the doorbell, producing sound energy.

- The windmills turn mechanical energy from the wind into electrical energy.
- The traffic signal turns electrical energy into light energy.
- A lightening bolt's electrical energy transforms into light energy and sound energy.
- Light energy could be transformed to electrical energy via solar panels.

The students should also demonstrate knowledge that forces can change motion of all matter, observed, described, and measured. They should have opportunities to observe airplanes, baseballs, planets, or people, and analyze how the motion of all bodies is governed by the same basic rules. They also need multiple opportunities to experience, observe, and describe (in words and pictures) motion, including the factors (pushing and pulling) that affect motion. They should have opportunities to

- measure and record changes (for example, vary the height of a ramp and roll spheres down, measure the speed or the distance the sphere rolls, and collect data)
- investigate the effects of adding or removing mass to an object on its motion (for example, use different sizes and masses of objects dropped from the same height at the same time to explore the force of gravity, or roll a metal sphere and a wooden sphere down a ramp, and collect data to explore the impact of mass on speed and distance traveled)
- explain how force causes movement (for example, describe and predict the path of moving objects, identify the variables that change the direction and rate of moving objects, and use common sport activities to demonstrate how the rate of motion is affected by the strength of a push or pull)
- use tools to collect data (for example, design an experiment where the amount of force applied to an object is the independent variable and time or distance traveled is the dependent variable, drag a tub full of metal washers and a tub full of cotton balls a certain distance, and use a spring scale to measure the force needed to move the two masses)

The following are some examples of different types of energy:

- **Chemical**—It is the energy stored in the chemical bonds of molecules; for example, the combustion (burning) of gasoline provokes a chemical reaction that releases chemical energy. The molecules are broken to produce heat and light. Combustion is used to power automobiles and other machines. Examples of chemical energy include food, gasoline, oil, wood, and coal.

- **Electrical**—It is the energy made available by the flow of electric charge through a conductor. Moving electrons produces it. It is energy stored in electric fields that results from the presence of electric charges. The stream of electrons moving through a conductor is an electric current. It is the source of what we call electricity, which is an application of electrical energy that we use to operate telephones, televisions, and computers, among others. Lightning is a natural result of an increase of electrical energy in the atmosphere. Power plants transform chemical, mechanical, or other forms of energy to electrical energy. By connecting electricity to a machine, you are converting it to another type of energy:
  - motor-electrical energy to mechanical energy (with heat energy byproduct)
  - lamp-electrical energy to light energy (with heat energy byproduct)
  - heater coil-electrical energy to heat energy (with light energy byproduct)
  - oven-electrical energy to heat energy
  - speaker-electrical energy to sound energy (with heat energy byproduct)

  In most cases, energy changes produce heat, even when they are not the intended target energy. This is because the machines do not work completely efficient, and some energy is lost as heat in the transformation process.

- **Magnetic**—It is the force (pull or push) of a magnet. It is **energy** stored in magnetic fields that is produced by moving electric charges. If the poles of two magnets near each other are alike, then they will repel each other. If the poles of two magnets near each other are different, then they attract each other. For example, a compass is a navigational tool for determining direction relative to the Earth's magnetic poles, which consists of a magnetized pointer free to align itself with Earth's magnetic field. This tool greatly improved the safety and efficiency of travel.

- **Mechanical**—It is the energy of the moving parts of machines or humans; for example, a moving bike or handshake. It is the energy that machines create. It is the sum of **potential** (stored energy of position) and **kinetic energy** (energy of motion) of a mechanical system. It also describes the energy of an object if it is moving, or if it has the *potential* to move. For example, a moving car and a car stopped on a hill both have mechanical energy. The moving car has kinetic energy (energy of motion), and the stopped car has potential energy because gravity can pull the car down the hill. Or, a moving baseball has mechanical energy because of both its high speed (kinetic energy) and its vertical position above the ground (gravitational potential energy). Other examples of mechanical energy include a moving windmill and a book resting on a shelf.

- **Nuclear**—It is present in the nucleus of atoms. Dividing, combining, or colliding of nuclei can result in the release of nuclear energy. It is released by fission (the breaking of a heavy nucleus into two lighter nuclei), fusion (two atomic nuclei fuse together to form a heavier nucleus), or radioactive decay (a neutron or proton in the radioactive nucleus decays spontaneously by emitting either particles, electromagnetic radiation or gamma rays, or all of them).

- **Radiant or light**—It is the energy transmitted in the form of electromagnetic waves or radiation; for example, visible light that the brain interprets as color, radio waves, infrared rays, ultraviolet rays, and X-rays.

- **Solar**—It is the energy from the sun that may be converted into thermal or electrical energy. It can have the form of electromagnetic waves (or "light"). Daylight is a result of solar energy. The sun warms the Earth. Energy from the sun enables plants to synthesize food, and allows for evaporation. *Solar power* is the conversion of sunlight into electricity.

- **Sound or acoustic**—It is the energy in the form of mechanical waves transmitted through materials (like plastic or air). They can be audible or inaudible waves. The brain interprets audible wave sounds as they enter through the ears. It is less intense as it moves farther and farther from the source. For example, a telephone changes sound energy into electrical energy and then back into sound energy.

- **Thermal**—It is considered the most internal energy of objects, which is created by vibration and movement. It is a form of kinetic energy and transferred as heat. It manifests itself as an increase in temperature. Heat is thermal energy that is transferred due to a difference in temperature between two objects.

Checkpoint

1. Fill in the blank: The combustion (burning) of gasoline provokes a reaction that releases _____ energy.

2. Fill in the blank: _____ energy is considered the most internal energy of objects, which is created by vibration and movement.

3. Fill in the blank: Daylight is a result of _____ energy.

4. True or false: The motion of all bodies is governed by the same basic rules.

Checkpoint Answers

1. chemical

2. Thermal

3. solar

4. True.

Balanced and Unbalanced Forces

The development of **force** involves a push or a pull. This process can give energy to an object causing it to start moving, stop moving, or change its motion. Forces occur in pairs and can be either balanced or unbalanced. **Balanced forces** do not cause a change in motion. They are in opposite directions and equal in size.

For example, if Person A arm wrestles against Person B, and Person A is just about as strong as Person B, then there will probably be a time when both of them are pushing as hard as they can, but their arms stay in the same place. In other words, the force exerted by each person is equal, but they are pushing together in opposite directions. Because the force that each of them is exerting is equal, the two forces cancel each other out and the resulting force is zero, which produces no change in motion; as illustrated by the following two arrows:

Person A's force	Person B with equal force, in an opposite direction	
→	←	Stay in the same place, and the force exerted by each person is equal.

Similarly, balanced forces could be in action during a tug of war, but in this case the forces are pulling away from each other. Like in arm wrestling, if Team A and Team B have equal strength or force, then the rope will stay at about the same place, the resulting force is zero, and there will be no change in motion; as illustrated by the following two arrows:

Team A's force	Team B with equal force, in an opposite direction	
←	→	Stay in the same place, and the force exerted by each Team is equal

In contrast to **balanced forces**, **unbalanced forces** always cause a change in motion. They are often in opposite directions and not equal in size. When two unbalanced forces are exerted in opposite directions, their combined force is equal to the difference between the two forces, and exerted in the direction of the larger force. For example, if Person A arm wrestles against Person C, but this time Person C is a stronger person, the arms of Person A with less arm strength will move in the direction of Person C, who is pushing with a stronger force. The resulting force is equal to the force of Person C minus the force of Person A; as illustrated by the following arrows:

Person A with less strong force	Person C with stronger force	Difference between forces with the direction of stronger person	
→	←	=	←

Similarly, two teams are having a tug of war against each other, with Team C being stronger than Team A. The less strong team will move in the direction the stronger team is pulling with a force that is equal to the stronger team's force minus the force of the other person; as illustrated by the following arrows:

Team A with less strong force	Team C with stronger force	Difference between forces with direction of stronger team	
←	→	=	→

Unbalanced forces can also happen with forces in the same direction, and still cause movement. For example, a car breaks down on the road and people have to push it out of the way. If the two people push the car, the resulting force on the car will be the sum of two people's forces and in the direction they are applying the force; as illustrated by the following arrows:

Person 1	Person 2		Sum of the two forces with the same direction
→	———→	=	—————————→

Notice that when working with balanced and unbalanced forces, the strength of forces moving in the same direction are combined by adding them, and the strength of forces moving in opposite directions are combined by subtracting the smaller one from the larger one. If two forces are of equal magnitude and in opposite directions, then they balance each other. In this case, the object is said to be at equilibrium, with no unbalanced force acting upon it and thus maintains its state of motion.

Checkpoint

1. True or false: Unbalanced forces can only happen with two forces in opposite directions.

2. True or false: Balanced forces do not cause a change in motion.

3. Fill in the blank: When working with balanced and unbalanced forces, the strength of forces moving in the same direction are combined by _____ them.

Checkpoint Answers

1. False. Unbalanced forces can also happen with forces in the same direction.

2. True. Balanced forces do not cause a change in motion.

3. adding

Competency 23: Knowledge of Earth and Space

Competency Description

According to the Competencies and Skills Required for Teacher Certification in Florida, Elementary Education (available at http://www.fldoe.org/asp/ftce/pdf/60ElementaryEducationK-6.pdf) **Competency 23** for the Elementary Education (K–6) Subject Area Examination (SAE) addresses the following key indicators:

1. Identify characteristics of geologic formations (e.g., **volcanoes, canyons, mountains**) and the mechanisms by which they are changed (e.g., physical and chemical weathering, **erosion, plate tectonics**).

2. Identify the characteristics of soil and the process of soil formation.

3. Identify the major groups and properties of rocks and minerals, examples of each, and the processes of their formation.

4. Identify ways in which land, air, and water interact (e.g. soil absorption, **runoff,** water cycle, atmospheric conditions, weather patterns).

5. Differentiate among **radiation, conduction,** and **convection,** the three mechanisms by which heat is transferred through Earth's system.

6. Identify the components of Earth's solar system and compare their individual characteristics.

7. Demonstrate knowledge of the Earth's place in our changing universe (e.g., history and purposes of space exploration, vastness of space).

8. Demonstrate knowledge of the phases of the Moon and the Moon's effect on Earth.

9. Identify Earth's tilt and orbital pattern and how they determine the seasons.

10. Analyze various conservation methods and their effectiveness in relation to renewable and nonrenewable natural resources.

11. Identify the sun as a star and its effect on Earth (e.g., radiant energy, heat, light).

Overview

Knowledge of Earth and space includes an understanding of the systems of the Earth (geology) as well as those interacting in space. The interactions of the Earth within the Solar System are important. There are approximately **11 questions** that address Competency 23. This section addresses the following areas related to **Competency 23** key indicators:

- Earth Science
  - Geologic Formations
  - Rocks and Minerals
  - Water, Air, and Land
  - Heat Transfer

- Space Science
  - Planets
  - Celestial Bodies

- History

Earth Science

Earth science encompasses all aspects of knowledge of **geology** and the Earth. This includes geologic formations; rocks and minerals; the interactions of land, air, and water; and heat transfer.

Geologic Formations

The Earth is divided into three main layers—**the core, the mantle,** and **the crust**. The core is the innermost part of the Earth. It is approximately 1800 miles below the surface of the Earth. The core is made up of iron and nickel and is divided into two sections—the **inner core** and the **outer core**. The inner core is solid and approximately 780 miles thick. It is made up of iron, nickel, and other light elements. The pressure in the inner core is so great that, despite the high temperatures, it will not melt. The outer core is always **molten**, or melted. The outer core is made up of mostly iron with some nickel and other elements and makes up the remainder of the core, approximately 1300 miles. Since the Earth rotates, the outer core rotates while the inner core does not due to its solid nature, creating the Earth's magnetism.

The layer above the core is called the mantle. The mantle begins about 6 miles under the ocean's crust and 19 miles below the continent's crust. The mantle makes up a majority of the Earth's volume.

The top layer of the Earth is called the crust. The crust is the hard outer shell of the Earth and is the thinnest layer of the Earth. The crust floats on the mantle and is solid material. Nevertheless, there are two types of crusts—**oceanic crust** and **continental crust**. The oceanic crust is that part of the crust under the oceans. The oceanic crust is 4–7 miles thick. The rock in the oceanic crust is generally younger and consists mainly of basalt. Seventy-one percent of the Earth's surface is oceanic crust. The continental crust, the remaining 29 percent, is that part of the crust which contains the **continents**. There are six regions, called continents, namely Eurasia (Europe and Asia), Africa, North America, South America, Antarctica, and Australia.

Because the core is so hot, heat develops a current which radiates to the Earth's crust through **convection currents**. These currents cause the plates of the Earth's crust to move, called **plate tectonics**. Plate tectonics move the continents around the surface of the Earth and cause geological formations to occur. Due to plate tectonics, the continents have changed over time. Alfred Wegener proposed a theory that the continental plates have been joined into one plate at different periods in time, forming a supercontinent, one of which was called **Pangea**.

Geologic formations include volcanoes, canyons, and mountains.

Volcanoes form when hot material called **magma** rises from below the Earth's surface to break through the Earth's crust. Magma gathers in a reservoir called the **magma chamber**. In many cases, this reservoir eventually erupts onto the surface of the Earth, creating the volcano. When the magma reaches the surface of the Earth, it is then called **lava**. As the lava cools, it creates a cone of rock, the volcano.

Canyons form when erosion changes the face of the Earth's surface. In canyons, the erosion occurs due to water, often rivers, running through a dry region. The rocks in the dry region provide resistance which causes the canyon to be created. In some cases, the water removes rock material and transports it to a different location. As this happens, the river digs deeper into the Earth's crust, forming a canyon. As the plates of the Earth shift, there is a phenomenon called uplift which causes the plateau to rise, causing the river to be lower relative to the surface of the plateau.

When plates of the Earth's surface intersect, different phenomena may occur depending on the type of intersection and the type of plate. **Mountains** are formed when two continental plates collide with each other and force both plates upward. **Earthquakes** occur when plates slide against each other in opposite directions. As the plates slide, pressure is created. When this pressure is released, an earthquake occurs. The point on the Earth's surface where the earthquake begins is called the **epicenter**. The amount of energy released during the earthquake is measured by a **seismometer** and uses the **Richter Scale**. When an earthquake occurs under water, it often causes a **Tsunami**, or tidal wave.

Rocks and Minerals

There are various types of rocks which are formed in different ways. These include **igneous rocks, sedimentary rocks,** and **metamorphic rocks**.

Igneous rocks are formed from the cooling of magma. As the magma cools, the magma changes from a liquid to a solid state. Igneous rocks are named by composition and texture. Igneous rocks are usually coarse and make up the majority of the Earth's crust. Examples of igneous rocks include granite and basalt.

Sedimentary rocks cover igneous rocks with loose sediment. Sedimentary rocks are created when layers of debris, or sediment, are compacted and fuse together. Sedimentary rocks are called secondary due to their being made when small pre-existing rocks accumulate together. There are three types of sedimentary rocks—**clastic, chemical, and organic**. Clastic rocks are basic sedimentary rocks and are accumulations of broken pieces of rocks. Chemical rocks form when standing water evaporates and leaves dissolved minerals behind. Organic rocks are formed by organic material such as calcium from shells, bones, and teeth.

Metamorphic rocks form when a pre-existing rock is moved into an environment in which the minerals that make up the rock become unstable, often burial. The rock changes form as it seeks to regain equilibrium, forming a new rock. Common metamorphic rocks are slate, gneiss, and marble.

Soil is formed by the weathering of rocks and minerals. As rocks at the surface of the Earth are broken down by weathering, the smaller pieces mix with organic material like mosses and eventually create soil. Decaying matter adds to the thin layer of soil, creating a rich environment for plants to grow.

Water, Air, and Land

The interaction of water, air, and land determine many aspects of weather.

Water

Water is not a renewable resource—there is a limited amount of water on the Earth. The water that is present on the Earth follows a cycle called the Water Cycle. It is made up of four steps—**Evaporation, Condensation, Precipitation,** and **Collection**.

Evaporation occurs when the sun heats up the water on the surface of the Earth. This water turns into steam and goes into the air.

Condensation occurs when the water vapor in the air cools and changes back into liquid, forming clouds.

Precipitation occurs when the amount of water that has condensed in the air is too much for the air to hold. The clouds that hold the water become heavy and the water falls back to the surface of the Earth in the form of rain, hail, sleet, or snow.

Collection occurs when the water returns to the surface of the Earth and falls back into water sources like oceans, lakes, or rivers. When the water falls back to land, it either soaks into the earth and becomes ground water or runs over the soil and returns back to the water sources.

Air

Air masses determine weather patterns. In the United States, five types of air masses determine the weather—**Continental Arctic, Continental Polar, Maritime Polar, Maritime Tropical,** and **Continental Tropical**.

- Continental Arctic air masses bring extremely cold temperatures and little moisture. They generally originate in the Arctic Circle and move south across Canada and the United States during winter.
- Continental Polar air masses bring cold and dry weather, but not as cold as Continental Arctic masses. They generally form south of the Arctic circle and affect the weather in the United States in the winter. In the summer, Continental Polar air masses affect only the northern portion of the United States.

- Maritime Polar air masses are cool and moist and bring cloudy, damp weather to the United States. They form over the northern Atlantic and Pacific oceans and can form at any time of the year. They are usually warmer than Continental Polar air masses.

- Maritime tropical air masses bring warm temperatures and moisture. They are most common over the eastern U.S. and are created over the southern Atlantic Ocean and Gulf of Mexico. They can form year round but are most common in the summer.

- Continental Tropical air masses form over the Desert Southwest and northern Mexico in the summer. They begin over the equator where moist air is heated and rises. As this air moves away from the equator, it begins to cool causing precipitation in the tropics and leaving the air dry. This dry air then forms a Continental Tropical air mass creating the deserts of the Southwest and Mexico. These air masses rarely form in the winter but keep temperatures in the Southwest above 100 degrees in the summer.

An additional aspect of weather patterns is wind. **Wind** is the horizontal movement of air. The equator receives direct rays from the sun. The moist air is heated and rises, leaving low-pressure regions called **doldrums**—regions of little steady air movement. As this air moves north and south of the equator, it begins to cool and sink. Some of that air moves back toward the equator forming **trade winds**—warm, steady breezes that blow continuously. Trade winds act as the steering force for tropical storms. The remaining winds move towards the poles. They appear to curve to the east. Since they come out of the west, they are called **prevailing westerlies**. These winds are responsible for many of the weather movements in the United States and Canada. As the winds continue to travel north and south, prevailing westerlies join with polar easterlies that originate from the poles.

As winds and air interact, they form clouds. There are four main types of clouds—**Stratus, Cumulus, Cirrus,** and **Nimbus**. Most clouds are a combination of the three types.

- Stratus clouds are horizontal, layered clouds that appear to blanket the sky. Stratus clouds form where warm, moist air passes over cool air.

- Cumulus clouds are puffy and look like cotton balls. They generally form when warm, moist air is forced upward. As the air rises it cools. The size of a cumulus cloud depends on the force of upward movement. These clouds produce heavy thunderstorms in the summer.

- Cirrus clouds are wispy and feathery. They only form at high altitudes and are composed of ice crystals.

- Nimbus clouds produce precipitation.

Land

As water interacts with the land, various phenomena can occur.

Runoff occurs when rain water falls to land and moves across the land to rivers, streams, or other water sites. Runoff occurs when the quantity of rainfall exceeds the rate at which the soil can absorb the water.

Percolation is the downward movement of water through the soil and rock in the ground.

Leaching is the process by which materials in the soil are transferred into the water.

Sinkholes are formed when cavities form under the surface of the Earth. These cavities are formed when water filling the space is removed through evaporation or absorption. The weight of the soil or other material above the cavity collapses it, forming a sinkhole. Sinkholes are very common in Florida.

The **aquifer** is a formation that transmits water under the surface of the Earth. When digging a well, the aquifer is the water source.

A **reservoir** is a lake-like area where water is kept until needed. These may be canals or retention ponds and may be naturally-formed or man-made.

Heat Transfer

There are three ways heat is transferred through the Earth's system—**radiation, conduction,** and **convection**.

Radiation is when heat is transferred through electromagnetic waves. Examples of radiation are the heating of the skin by the sun and the heat of a bonfire. The heat is transferred through the movement of electromagnetic waves.

Conduction occurs when heat transfers through molecular movement. For example, when you pick up a metal bar, it is cold. As you hold it, the warmth of your body conducts heat to the metal bar.

Convection occurs through the movement of masses, either air or water. Convection occurs when hot air rises, cools, and then falls. This cycle is what makes ceiling fans warm the air in the winter. The ceiling fan forces the cooler air in the lower parts of the room to move towards the ceiling, pushing the warm air from the ceiling downward warming the room.

Checkpoint

1. What are the four stages of the water cycle?

2. True or false: Trade Winds form at the poles.

3. What are three methods for heat transfer?

Checkpoint Answers

1. evaporation, condensation, precipitation, and collection

2. False. Trade winds form at the equator.

3. radiation, conduction, and convection

Space Science

Space science includes the study of the solar system. The solar system consists of various elements. Our solar system is called **The Milky Way,** which is made up about 100,000 million stars. The shape of the Milky Way is spiral with arms extending out from the center. Within the Milky Way there are planets and other celestial bodies.

Planets

There are eight planets—Mercury, Venus, Earth, Mars, Jupiter, Saturn, Uranus, and Neptune.

Mercury is the smallest planet and is closest to the sun. It has no moons. The planet has hardly any atmosphere and is most like the Moon's surface.

Venus is the second plant from the sun. Venus is very hot due to thick gases in the atmosphere causing a greenhouse effect.

The Earth is the third planet from the sun. Oceans cover nearly three quarters of the Earth's surface. The Earth has one moon.

Mars is the fourth planet from the sun. It has the nickname of the Red Planet because it is covered with rusty colored soil. Mars has two moons called Phobos and Diemos.

Jupiter is the fifth planet from the sun and by far the largest. Jupiter has small rings and is known for its large red spot.

Saturn, the sixth planet from the sun, is the second largest planet. Saturn has about 20 moons and is known for its rings.

Uranus is the seventh planet from the sun and is the third largest. It is a bluish-green gas planet made up of hydrogen, helium, and methane. It has nine faint rings that are made up of rocks and dust. Its poles point sideways, and it has an angle of 98 degrees. Uranus has five large moons and 10 small moonlets.

Neptune is the eighth planet from the Sun and the fourth largest.

The planets orbit around the sun in elliptical orbits. In addition, many planets, including Earth, are tilted on their own axis. The tilt of the Earth accounts for the seasons. The intensity of the rays from the sun change as the Earth orbits the sun, making spring, summer, fall, and winter. The seasons are opposite in the **Northern Hemisphere** than in the **Southern Hemisphere**. In June, July, and August, the Northern Hemisphere is exposed to more direct sunlight making the temperatures warmer, so it is summer time in the Northern Hemisphere. At the same time, the Southern Hemisphere is exposed to less direct sunlight making it cooler, so it is winter in the Southern Hemisphere.

Celestial Bodies

Pluto was once considered a planet. It is now considered to be a dwarf planet. It is smaller than Earth's moon. It is yellowish in color. Pluto's orbit around the sun is tilted unlike the other planets whose orbits are elliptical with the sun in the center. As a result, there are times that Pluto is closer to the sun than Neptune.

Comets are bodies in space made of rocks, frozen water, frozen gases, and dust. Comets orbit the sun and contain a tail that follows the comet. The most famous comet is Halley's comet.

Asteroids are made up of rock, metal, or ice and are like planets in that they orbit the sun. A belt of asteroids exists between Mars and Jupiter and separates the planets.

Meteors are objects that rotate around the sun but are too small to be called asteroids or comets. They are made from bits and pieces of the solar system that have fallen into Earth's atmosphere.

Stars are made up entirely of gases and are mostly made of hydrogen. Stars are born in hot gas and dust. Color, temperature, and size depend on the star's mass. Star colors can vary from slightly reddish, orange, and yellow to white and blue. These colors are easy to see especially on dark nights. The sun is a mid-sized star and is the closest to the Earth. The sun is the center of our solar system and provides heat and light to Earth.

Moons are satellites of planets. They generally orbit around a planet. Some planets have a large number of moons. The Earth has one moon. There are phases of the moon, and the moon and Earth interact through gravitational pull. The moon is subjected to the gravitational pull of the Earth, keeping it in orbit around the Earth. Additionally, the moon's pull on the Earth affects the tides of the oceans.

The phases of the moon are a result of sunlight hitting the moon's surface and then reflecting toward Earth. The moon does not create its own light. The amount of moon that is visible through reflection is measured by the lunar phase. A full moon occurs when the moon and sun are on opposite sides of the Earth, giving a full reflection of the moon's surface. A new moon occurs when the moon and sun are on the same side of the Earth, giving no reflection of the moon's surface toward the Earth. The time between full moons is approximately 29 days. Between a New Moon and a Full Moon is a First Quarter Moon in which the right 50 percent of the moon's surface is visible. Between a Full Moon and a New Moon, is a Last Quarter Moon in which the left 50 percent of the moon's surface is visible. The side of the moon that is visible is reversed for the Southern Hemisphere.

History

The beginnings of space exploration began in 1914 when Robert Goddard received two patents for rockets. Prior to that, publications had been made by Newton and others that indicated space travel was theoretically possible. In 1926, Robert Goddard successfully applied his rocketry theories and launched the first liquid fueled rocket in Massachusetts. The rocket, called "Nell," was 4-foot high and reached an altitude of 41 feet and a speed of about 60 miles per hour. The flight lasted $2\frac{1}{2}$ seconds. This began the long road that continues today into exploration of space.

Date	Country	Accomplishment
1942	Germany	Launched first rocket to reach sub-orbital spaceflight
1946	United States	Launched American-made rocket in White Sands, NM
1957	Soviet Union	Launched Sputnik, the first satellite to be placed into orbit; Sputnik transmitted radio signals back to Earth for a short time
1957	Soviet Union	Launched Sputnik 2, which housed a dog contained in a pressurized container with food supplies and an atmosphere; showed it was possible to survive in space
1958	United States	Launched first satellite, Explorer 1
1958	United States	National Aeronautics and Space Administration (NASA) was created
1961	Soviet Union	Cosmonaut Yuri Alekseyevich Gagarin became the first human in space; made one complete orbit around the Earth and his flight lasted 1 hour 48 minutes
1961	United States	Astronaut Alan Shepard was launched into space and completed a sub-orbital flight of 15 minutes; experienced weightlessness for about 5 minutes
1962	United States	Astronaut John Glenn became first American to orbit the Earth; made three orbits
1966	Soviet Union followed by United States	Landed unmanned spacecraft on the moon
1967	United States	Gus Grissom, Ed White, and Roger Chaffee were killed during a routine test on the launch pad when a spark caused a fire to start in the crew compartment of the command module
1968	United States	Apollo 7 becomes first manned mission; orbited Earth once
1968	United States	Apollo 8 is first manned spacecraft to orbit the moon; makes 10 orbits on 6 day mission
1969	United States	Apollo 11 lands on the moon; Neil Armstrong and Edwin Aldrin, Jr., become first human beings to walk on the moon
1970	United States	Apollo 13 aborts mission to the moon after explosion of oxygen tanks; Astronauts James A. Lovell, Jr., John L. Swigert, Jr., and Fred W. Haise, Jr., return safely
1971	Soviet Union	First space station, Salyut 1, placed in orbit
1971	United States	Apollo 15 astronauts become first to drive a rover on the surface of the moon
1973	United States	First U.S. Space Station, SkyLab, placed in orbit
1981	United States	First Space Shuttle, Columbia, launched in Space Transportation System-1 (STS-1)
1983	United States	Space Shuttle Challenger makes first mission; First American space walk in 9 years
1983	United States	Sally Ride becomes first woman Astronaut on Challenger mission STS-7
1984	United States	Space Shuttle Discovery launches first mission
1985	United States	Space Shuttle Atlantis launches first mission
1986	United States	Space Shuttle Challenger explodes during liftoff killing all crew
1986	Soviet Union (Russia)	Space Station Mir is successfully placed into Earth's orbit

1990	United States	Hubble Space Telescope is deployed in order to image space
1992	United States	Space Shuttle Endeavor launches first mission
1995	United States/Russia	Space Shuttle Atlantis rendezvous with Space Station Mir
2001	United States	100th U.S. Spacewalk
2003	United States	Space Shuttle Columbia breaks up in the atmosphere over Texas on re-entry, killing the entire crew.
2005	United States	Space Shuttle Discovery returns to flight after 2 year hiatus as a result of the Columbia disaster; Changes to space protocol are enacted to increase safety

Checkpoint

1. What are four phases of the moon?

2. What two space shuttles were destroyed during missions?

3. In which Apollo mission did Armstrong and Aldrin walk on the moon?

Checkpoint Answers

1. New Moon, First Quarter Moon, Full Moon, Last Quarter Moon

2. Challenger and Columbia

3. Apollo 11

Competency 24: Knowledge of Life Science

Competency Description

According to the Competencies and Skills Required for Teacher Certification in Florida, Elementary Education (available at http://www.fldoe.org/asp/ftce/pdf/60ElementaryEducationK-6.pdf) **Competency 24** for the Elementary Education (K–6) Subject Area Examination (SAE) addresses the following key indicators:

1. Compare and contrast living and nonliving things.
2. Distinguish among infectious agents (e.g., viruses, bacteria, fungi, parasites) and their effects on the human body.
3. Differentiate structures and functions of plant and animal cells.
4. Identify the major steps of plants' physiological processes of **photosynthesis, transpiration,** reproduction, and respiration.
5. Demonstrate knowledge of how plants respond to stimuli (e.g., heat, light, gravity).
6. Identify the structures and functions of organs and systems of both animals and humans.
7. Demonstrate knowledge of animals' physiological processes (e.g., respiration, reproduction, digestion, circulation).
8. Demonstrate knowledge of cell theory as the fundamental organizing principle of life on Earth.
9. Demonstrate knowledge of **heredity, evolution,** and **natural selection.**
10. Demonstrate knowledge of the interdependence of living things with each other and with their environment (e.g., food webs, pollution, hurricanes).

Overview

Knowledge of life science includes an understanding of the systems of the body as well as how plants and animals interact in the world. There are approximately **10 questions** that address Competency 24. This section addresses the following areas related to **Competency 24** key indicators:

- Living and Nonliving Things
- Cells
  - Eukaryotic Cells
- Prokaryotes
  - Viruses and Bacteria
- Eukaryotes
  - Protists
  - Fungi
  - Plants
  - Animals
- Heredity, Evolution, and Natural Selection

Living and Nonliving Things

In order to be considered a living thing, six criteria must be met:

1. Made up of cells
2. Obtain and use energy
3. Grow and develop
4. Reproduce
5. Respond to stimuli in environment
6. Adapt to environment

Nonliving things may have some of the criteria of living things, but if they do not meet all six criteria, they are not living things. For example, a crystal can grow and develop, but it is not made up of cells, so it is not living.

Living things can be further categorized. **Taxonomy** is the classification of living things into categories based on physical characteristics. The taxonomical classification was originally seven levels developed by Carolus Linnaeus—Kingdom, Phylum, Class, Order, Family, Genus, Species—which are listed from the broadest to the most specific. Recently, an additional level, Domain, was added to the structure based on molecular analysis, which was previously impossible.

Domains	Archaea	Bacteria	Eukarya			
Kingdoms	Archaebacteria	Eubacteria	Protists	Fungi	Plants	Animals

Checkpoint

1. What are the eight levels of taxonomy?

2. What are the three domains?

3. What are the six characteristics of living things?

Checkpoint Answers

1. Domain, Kingdom, Phylum, Class, Order, Family, Genus, and Species

2. Archaea, Bacteria, and Eukaroyta

3. Made up of cells; obtain and use energy; grow and develop; reproduce; respond to stimuli in environment; adapt to environment

Cells

All living things are made up of cells. Cells are the smallest unit of living things and were not discovered until microscopes were invented in the mid-1600s. Cells come in many different shapes and sizes and can perform different functions, but they all have many parts in common. All cells contain **cell membranes, cytoplasm, organelles, and DNA.**

Cell membranes surround the cell and provide a protective layer that covers the surface of the cell and acts as a barrier to its environment. The cell membrane controls what materials go into and out of the cell. Inside the cell is a fluid called the **cytoplasm.**

Within cells are **organelles,** which carry out the life processes within the cell. Organelles perform specific functions within the cell and different cell types have different organelles. Some organelles float in the cytoplasm; others have membranes; still others are attached to membranes or other organelles.

All cells contain DNA, the genetic material that contains information needed to make new cells. DNA is passed from parent cells to new cells and determines the type and function of a cell. In some cells the DNA is enclosed inside an organelle called the **nucleus**. These cells are called **eukaryotes**. In other cells, a nucleus does not exist. These cells are called **prokaryotes**.

Eukaryotic Cells

Eukaryotic cells can have **cell walls**, a rigid structure that gives support to the cell. The cell wall is the outermost part of the cell. Cell walls in plants and algae are made up of **cellulose**, a complex sugar that animals cannot digest without help. Cell walls in plants allow the plants to stand upright. When a plant droops over, it is often due to the cells lacking water causing the cell walls to collapse and the plant to droop. In cells without a cell wall, the cell membrane is the outermost part of the cell. In cells with a cell wall, the cell membrane is just inside the cell wall.

The cell membrane of eukaryotic cells contains **proteins, lipids,** and **phospholipids**. Proteins and lipids control the movement of larger materials into and out of the cell. Small nutrients and water move into the cell while wastes move out of the cell by diffusion. The web of proteins inside the cytoplasm is called the **cytoskeleton**. The cytoskeleton acts both as muscles and a skeleton for the cell. It keeps the cell membrane from collapsing and helps cells move.

Eukaryotic cells also contain a nucleus, a large organelle containing the cell's DNA. The cell's DNA contains the information on how to make the cell's proteins. The proteins are not made in the nucleus; instead the instructions for making the protein are copied from the DNA and sent out through pores in the nucleus. The nucleus of many cells contains the **nucleolus**, a dark area in which the cell begins to make **ribosomes**. Ribosomes are the smallest of all organelles. Some ribosomes float in the cytoplasm while others are attached to membranes or the cytoskeleton. Ribosomes are not covered by a membrane. In all cases, ribosomes build proteins which are made of **amino acids**. All cells need proteins to live, so all cells have ribosomes.

Chemical reactions take place in a cell, many of which take place on the **endoplasmic reticulum**, or ER, a system of folded membranes in which proteins, lipids, and other materials are made. The folded membranes contain many tubes and passageways for delivering substances to different parts of the cell. There are two types of ER, rough and smooth. **Rough ER** is covered in ribosomes and is usually found near the nucleus. **Smooth ER** does not contain ribosomes, makes lipids, and breaks down toxic material that could damage the cell.

The power source of the cell is the **mitochondrion**, the organelle in which sugar is broken down to produce energy. Mitochondria are covered by two membranes, the outer membrane and the inner membrane. Mitochondria make a substance called **ATP** the form of energy that cells can use. Most of a cell's ATP is made in the inner membrane of the mitochondria.

The organelle that packages and distributes proteins is called the **Golgi Complex**. The Golgi complex looks like smooth ER, but its job is to take the lipids and proteins made from the ER and deliver them to the other parts of the cell. The Golgi complex might modify lipids and proteins to do different jobs. The final product is enclosed in a piece of the Golgi complex's membrane that then pinches off in a small bubble called a **vesicle,** which transports the lipids and proteins to other parts of the cell or outside the cell. The vesicles responsible for digestion inside a cell are called **lysosomes**. Lysosomes are organelles that contain digestive enzymes that destroy worn out or damaged organelles, get rid of waste, and protect the cell from invaders. **Vacuoles** are large vesicles. In plant and fungal cells, some vacuoles act like large lysosomes by storing digestive enzymes and aiding in digestion within the cell. Other vacuoles in plant cells store water and other liquids.

Plant cells contain **chloroplasts,** which animal cells do not. Chloroplasts are organelles present in plant and algae cells and allow the plant to harness energy from the sun. **Photosynthesis** takes place in the chloroplasts. The process of photosynthesis allows plants and algae to use sunlight, carbon dioxide, and water to make sugar and oxygen. Chloroplasts are green because they contain **chlorophyll**, a green pigment found inside the inner membrane of a chloroplast. Chlorophyll traps the energy from sunlight which is then used in photosynthesis to make the sugar glucose. Glucose is then used by the mitochondria to make ATP.

Checkpoint

1. True or false: Cells are present in all living things.

2. What parts do all cells contain?

3. Fill in the blank: Cells which have a nucleus are called _____.

Checkpoint Answers

1. True

2. cell membranes, cytoplasm, organelles, and DNA

3. eukaryotes

Prokaryotes

Prokaryotes are single-celled organisms. They are small and simple cells that do not have a nucleus or membrane-bound organelles. Prokaryotes are divided between two domains—**Archaea** and **Bacteria**.

Viruses and Bacteria

Archaeabacteria are single-celled microorganisms. They have no cell nucleus or complex organelles, but their cells contain DNA and ribosomes to carry on the functions of life. They are similar in shape to bacteria, but have some notable differences. They live in a variety of harsh, oxygen-deprived habitats including hot springs, salt lakes, soils, oceans, and marshlands.

Eubacteria are large groups of single-celled organisms that grow in nearly every environment on Earth. They are typically micrometers in length and can be classified based on their shape, type of cell wall, methods of movement, or way of obtaining energy. In terms of shape, bacteria can be spheres (**cocci**), rods (**bacilli**), or spirals (**spirilla**).

Bacteria have three basic roles in nature. They act as decomposers in order to return raw materials and nutrients to the soil for other life. Bacteria will also be nitrogen fixers, meaning that they can turn nitrogen in the atmosphere into nitrogen that is in a form useful for life. These bacteria form a symbiotic relationship with a plant in which the bacteria consume nutrients and produce nitrogen that the plant needs, but cannot create on its own. Lastly, bacteria that cause disease are called pathogens. Examples of human diseases include tetanus, syphilis, leprosy, and tuberculosis. Each pathogen produces specific diseases when interacting with the host human body. Staphylococcus and Streptococcus are two common bacteria that cause skin infections, pneumonia, meningitis, and other minor and serious diseases. These same bacteria, however, are commonly found on the skin and are not pathogenic at all. Infections caused by bacteria can usually be treated with antibiotics.

Another major infectious agent is the virus. Viruses and bacteria are similar in some ways, but also different. Bacteria can live outside a host; viruses cannot. Bacteria are made of cells; viruses use the cells they infect and do not have cells of their own. Instead they are made of a protein coat that surrounds either DNA or RNA. Viruses spread in many ways including human contact, air-borne contact, and surface contact. Viruses are the cause of diseases such as the common cold, influenza, chickenpox, Ebola, AIDS, and SARS. Viruses cannot be treated with antibiotics. Because viruses live in the host cell and take it over, the virus cannot be killed without killing the host cell. This is not always practical, so some viruses are never eliminated from the body. The most effective method of controlling viruses is vaccination. The body's immune system must eliminate the virus. Vaccination gives the body's immune system a boost in fighting viruses.

Checkpoint

1. True or false: Viruses can be treated with antibiotics.

2. True or false: Bacteria can live outside a host.

Checkpoint Answers

1. False. Only bacterial infections can be treated with antibiotics

2. True.

Eukaryotes

Eukaryotes are organisms whose cells contain complex structures including membrane-bound organelles and a nucleus containing DNA. These cells are typically much larger than prokaryotes. Eukaryotic cells are still microscopic, but they are about 10 times larger than bacteria. All living things that are not eubacteria or archaebacteria are made up of eukaryotic cells. Most eukaryotes are multi-cellular, although some are single-cellular. Eukaryotes include protists, fungi, plants, and animals.

Protists

Protists are organisms that are similar to plants, fungi, and animals, but do not fit neatly into those kingdoms. They come in many shapes and sizes, but they have a few traits in common. All protists are eukaryotic. Most protists are single-celled organisms, but some are multi-cellular and others live in colonies. Some protists produce their own food while others eat other organisms or decaying matter. Some protists control their own movement while others cannot. Protists are less complex than other eukaryotic organisms. They do not have specialized tissues.

Protists obtain food in many ways—some create their own food; others eat other organisms. Protists that produce their own food have special structures called chloroplasts. Similar to plants, chloroplasts provide the structure to capture energy from the sun through photosynthesis. Some protists consume food in their environment. These protists are **heterotrophs**. Protist heterotrophs eat small living organisms like bacteria, yeast, or other protists. Some are decomposers that get energy from breaking down dead organic matter. Other protist heterotrophs are **parasites**, namely organisms that invade other organisms called hosts to obtain the nutrients it needs.

Protists reproduce in several ways. Some protists reproduce asexually while others reproduce sexually. In **asexual reproduction**, offspring come from one parent and are an identical copy of the parent. Asexual reproduction in protists occurs through fission. **Sexual reproduction** requires two parents and often involves a process called **conjugation** in which two individuals join together and exchange genetic material using a second nucleus. They then divide to produce four protists that have new combinations of genetic material.

Protists can be divided into three types—plant-like protists, which act as producers; animal-like protists; and fungus-like protists.

There are two categories of plant-like protists, those that are unicellular and the **algae**. All algae have chlorophyll and most have other pigments giving them color. Most algae live in water. Red algae have a pigment making them red allowing them to absorb the light deep in clear water. Green algae can be unicellular or multicelluluar and live in water or moist soil. Brown algae are found in cool climates. Free-floating single-celled protists are called **phytoplankton**. Phytoplankton are microscopic and usually float near the water's surface and produce much of the world's oxygen.

Animal-like protists are heterotrophs and are called **protozoans**. Amoebas are an example of a protozoan. They are found in fresh and salt water and as parasites in animals. They appear shapeless but are actually highly structured. Many amoebas eat bacteria and small protists, but some are parasites. Amoebas move with **pseudopodia**, or false feet. To move, an amoeba stretches out a pseudopod from the cell. The cell then flows into the pseudopod, providing movement. They also use pseudopodia to catch food. Another protozoan is the **zooflagellate**. Zooflagellates move with **flagella**, whiplike strands extending out from the cell, back and forth to move. Some zooflagellates are parasites that cause disease while others are mutualists. **Ciliates** are complex protists that have hundreds of tiny, hairlike structures called **cilia,** which beat back and forth causing the ciliate to move. They also use cilia for obtaining food. The most common ciliate is the paramecium.

Fungus-like protists are heterotrophs that are similar to fungi but do not fit in the fungi kingdom. They can be parasites that do not move about or move only at certain phases of life. Spore forming protists are parasites that absorb nutrients from their host. They have no cilia or flagella and cannot move on their own. Water molds are also heterotrophs that do not move. Water molds live in water, moist soil, and other organisms. Slime molds move only at certain phases of their life cycle. They live in cool, moist places in the woods. When environmental conditions are favorable, slime mold use pseudopodia to move. When environmental conditions are unfavorable, slime mold form spores that do not move.

Fungi

Fungi are eukaroytoic hetertrophs that have rigid cell walls and no chlorophyll. Fungi come in a variety of shapes, sizes, and colors. Fungi are heterotrophs (find food in their environment), but they cannot catch or surround food. They must live on or near their food supply. Most fungi are consumers and obtain nutrients by dissolving food with digestive juices. Many fungi are decomposers and feed on dead plant or animal matter. Others are parasites. Still others are mutualists.

Fungi are made up of eukaryotic cells. Multi-cellular fungi are made up of chains of cells called **hyphae**. Most of the hyphae that make up a fungus grow together to form a **mycelium**, a twisted mass of hyphae. The mycelium makes up most of the fungus, but is hidden from view underground.

Reproduction in fungi is either asexual or sexual. Asexual reproduction occurs in two ways—breaking apart or producing **spores,** which form new fungi. Sexual reproduction in fungi happens when **sex cells** are formed and then joined together to make sexual spores that grow into new fungi.

There are four main groups of fungi, classified based on their shape and how they reproduce.

Threadlike fungi live in soil and are decomposers. Some are parasites. They reproduce both asexually using spore cases called **sporangia** and sexually when hypha from one individual joins with hypha from another individual. A common example of threadlike fungi is black break mold.

Sac fungi include yeasts, mildews, truffles, and morels. Sac fungi reproduce both asexually though a sac called an **ascus** and sexually through spores developed within the ascus. Many sac fungi are helpful to humans. Yeasts are used in making bread and alcohol through fermentation. Some antibiotics and vitamins come from sac fungi. Some sac fungi are not helpful to humans, however. Many sac fungi are parasites that can cause plant diseases.

Club fungi are most commonly recognized as mushrooms. They produce sexually. Some club fungi are edible, but others are not. There are other forms of club fungi as well. Bracket fungi grows outward from wood to form shelves. Smuts and rusts are common plant parasites and often attack crops.

Imperfect fungi include all other species of fungi. These fungi reproduce asexually. Most are parasites that cause disease in plants and animals. Athlete's foot is caused by imperfect fungi. Penicillin derives from penicillium, an imperfect fungi.

Plants

A plant is a eukaryotic, multicellular **autotroph**. Almost all food originates from plants, whether the food is the plant itself or animals that eat the plants; therefore, plants form the basis of many food webs. Plants come in various shapes and sizes, but they all have several characteristics in common. Plants are **autotrophs**—meaning they create their own food—have a two stage life cycle, and have cell walls..

The two stages of a plant's life cycle are the **sporophyte** stage and the **gametophyte** stage. During the sporophyte stage, plants make spores, which then can grow in a suitable environment. During the gametophyte stage, male and female parts make gametes. The female gametophytes produce eggs and male gametophytes produce sperm. Sperm must fertilize the egg which then grows into a sporophyte creating spores.

Plants are classified into two major groups—**nonvascular plants** and **vascular plants.** Nonvascular plants do not have specialized tissues to move water and nutrients through the plant. Mosses, liverworts, and hornworts are nonvascular plants. Nonvascular plants must rely on **diffusion** to move materials from one part of the plant to another. As a consequence, nonvascular plants are very small. Vascular plants have tissues, called **vascular tissues**, which move water and nutrients from one part of the plant to another. Vascular tissues can move water and nutrients to any part of the plant, so vascular plants can be very large. There are two types of vascular tissues, **xylem** and **phloem**. Vascular plants are divided into **seedless plants, nonflowering seed plants,** and **flowering seed plants**. Seedless plants include ferns, horsetails, and club mosses. Nonflowering seed plants are called **gymnosperms**. Flowering seed plants are called **angiosperms.** Angiosperms are then divided into monocots and dicots.

Nonvascular	Vascular			
Mosses Liverworts Hornworts	Seedless plants	Seed plants		
	Ferns	Gymnosperm	Angiosperms	
		Cone bearing plants	Flowering plants	
			Monocots	Dicots

Plant cells contain **chlorophyll**, a green pigment that captures energy from sunlight. Plants use the energy from sunlight to make food from carbon dioxide and water in a process called **photosynthesis**. Plants are protected by a **cuticle**, a waxy layer that coats the surfaces of plants which are exposed to air. The cuticle prevents the plant from drying out. Plant cells contain rigid cell walls which keep the plant upright.

Photosynthesis

Photosynthesis is the process by which plants make food. Plants use chlorophyll to capture energy from the sun. The light energy captured by chlorophyll helps form glucose molecules. In the process, oxygen is given off. Photosynthesis is represented by the following chemical equation:

$$6\,CO_2 + 6\,H_2O \longrightarrow C_6H_{12}O_6 + 6\,O_2$$

Carbon dioxide and water are used to form sugar and oxygen. The sugar is used for food by the plant, and the oxygen is released from the leaves.

Transpiration

In order for photosynthesis to occur, carbon dioxide must be absorbed by the plant. Plant surfaces above ground are covered by a waxy cuticle that protects the plant from water loss. Carbon dioxide enters the plant's leaves through **stomata**, openings in the leaf's surface which can open and close. When stomata are open, carbon dioxide enters the leaf, oxygen produced during photosynthesis exits the leaf, and water vapor exits the leaf. The loss of water through leaves is called **transpiration**. Water absorbed through the roots replaces the water lost through transpiration.

Reproduction

Plants can reproduce with either sexual or asexual reproduction.

In flowering plants, sexual reproduction occurs within the flowers. The male part of the flower is the **stamen,** which is made of the **anther** that makes pollen, and the **filament** that holds up the anther. The female part of the flower is the **pistil,** which is made of the **stigma, style**, and **ovary**. Pollination occurs when pollen is moved from **anthers** to **stigmas**. This movement often happens through wind or animals. Pollen contains sperm. Once pollen lands on the stigma, a tube grows from the pollen through the **style** to an **ovule** which is inside the **ovary**. Each ovule contains an egg. When the sperm fuses with the egg, **fertilization** occurs. Once fertilization occurs, the ovule develops into a seed containing a tiny, undeveloped plant. The ovary surrounding the ovule becomes a fruit that swells and ripens to protect the developing seeds. Once the seeds are developed, the young plant inside the seed stops growing. When the seed is dropped or planted in a suitable environment, the seed sprouts and forms a new plant. This process is called **germination**.

Flowering plants may also reproduce asexually without flowers. This may occur through **plantlets**, **tubers,** or **runners**. Plantlets occur when tiny plants grow along the edges of a plant's leaves. The plantlets then fall off and grow new plants. Tubers are underground stems that can produce new plants. Runners are above-ground stems that form new plants.

Respiration

Cellular respiration is the process by which plants convert the energy that is stored in glucose molecules into energy that cells can use. This happens in the mitochondria. Plant cells use oxygen in this process and they create carbon dioxide and water as waste. Any excess glucose that is not used in cell respiration is converted into sucrose, another sugar, or stored as starch. Cell respiration is not unique to plant cells. All eukaryotic organisms need to convert energy storage molecules like sugars into usable energy (ATP).

Responses to Environment

Plants have various responses to their environment. When a plant is placed so that light only comes from one direction, the plant tips will most likely bend towards the light. Plant growth also changes with the direction of gravity. Roots will grow toward the center of the Earth and shoots will grow upward away from the center of the Earth. If a plant is placed on its side, the shoots will begin to move upward and the roots will begin to move downward relative to the new position. Plants also respond to environmental changes through the seasons. Plants living in regions with cold winters can detect the change in seasons. As the seasons change, so do the length of days and nights. As fall and winter approach, days get shorter and nights get longer. Plants respond to the changes in length of day/night and will begin reproducing at the appropriate time of the year. All trees lose their leaves; however, some will lose some of their leaves year-round but keep most of them (**evergreen trees**) while others will lose all of their leaves at specific times of the year, typically fall (**deciduous trees**). The loss of leaves allows the plants to survive cold temperatures or long dry spells.

As deciduous trees prepare to lose their leaves, their leaves often change color. The green chlorophyll breaks down, so the color of the leaves changes to orange or yellow.

Animals

Animals are eukaryotic, multicellular heterotrophs that come in various shapes and sizes. Some animals are microscopic. Others are bigger than a car. Unlike plant cells, animal cells do not have cell walls. Animal cells are surrounded only by cell membranes.

There are two types of animals—**vertebrates** and **invertebrates**. Vertebrates are animals that have a backbone. Vertebrates include fish, amphibians, reptiles, birds, and mammals. Invertebrates do not have a backbone. Invertebrates include insects, snails, jellyfish, worms, and sponges. Less than 5% of animals are vertebrates.

An animal's body is formed by distinct parts that have different functions. Some cells are skin cells. Others are muscles cells, nerve cells, or bone cells. When different kinds of cells combine, they become **tissues**. Most animals also have **organs**, a group of tissues that carry out a specific function within the body. Each organ has a unique role in the function of the body.

Most animals can move from place to place. They may move differently—fly, run, or swim, for example. Animals cannot make their own food; movement often assists in the search for food. They survive by eating other organisms.

Invertebrates

Animals without a backbone are called invertebrates. Invertebrates have three basic body symmetries—**bilateral, radial,** or **asymmetry**. Most animals have bilateral symmetry, meaning the two sides of the body mirror each other. Radial symmetry occurs when the body is organized around a center. Asymmetry occurs when there is no symmetry in the structure of the body. Invertebrates are classified into six distinct categories, with three categories of worms.

Sponges	Cnidarians	Worms			Mollusks	Echinoderms	Arthropods
		Flatworms	Roundworms	Segmented Worms			

Sponges are the simplest invertebrates. They are asymmetrical and have no tissues. They are marine animals.

Cnidarians have stinging cells. They are more complex than sponges. They have complex tissues and a simple network of nerve cells. Jellyfish, sea anemone, and coral are cnidarians.

Flatworms are the simplest kind of worms. Flatworms have bilateral symmetry. There are three types of flatworms: planarians and marine flatworms, flukes, and tapeworms. Planarians live in freshwater lakes and streams or in damp places on land. Most planarians eat other animals. Flukes are parasites that have suckers and hooks allowing them to attach to animals. Tapeworms are similar to flukes and are also parasites. They live and reproduce in other animals and feed on these animals. Tapeworms, however, do not have a gut. They attach to the intestines of another animal and absorb nutrients.

Roundworms have bodies that are long, slim, and round. They have bilateral symmetry and a simple nervous system. Most species of roundworms are small and they typically break down dead tissues of plants and animals. Many roundworms are also parasites.

Segmented worms have bilateral symmetry but are more complex than flatworms and roundworms. They have a closed circulatory system and a complex nervous system. Segmented worms can live in salt water, fresh water, or on land. They eat plant material or animals and are grouped into earthworms, marine worms, and leeches.

Most **mollusks** live in the ocean, but some live in fresh water and some live on land. Mollusks fit into three categories: gastropods, bivalves, and cephalopods. Gastropods include slugs and snails. Bivalves include clams and shellfish that have two shells. Cephalopods include squids and octopuses.

Echinoderms are spiny-skinned invertebrates that include sea stars, sea urchins, and sand dollars. They are marine animals and live on the sea floor. Adult echinoderms have radial symmetry.

Arthropods are the largest group of animals. At least 75 percent of all animal species are arthropods. All arthropods have a segmented body with specialized parts, jointed limbs, an **exoskeleton**, and a well-developed nervous system. The segmented body includes structures such as wings, claws, and antennae. There are three main body parts: the head, thorax, and abdomen. Arthropods include centipedes, millipedes, crustaceans (lobsters), arachnids (spiders), and insects.

Vertebrates

Vertebrates are animals with a backbone. Vertebrates include **fish, amphibians, reptiles, birds,** and **mammals**.

There are two main types of vertebrates—**endotherms** and **ectotherms**. Endotherms are warm-blooded animals. They are able to regulate their own body temperature. Birds and mammals are endotherms. Ectotherms are cold-blooded animals. They are unable to regulate their own body temperature and rely on the environment to regulate their temperature. Amphibians, reptiles, and fish are ectotherms.

There are more than 25,000 species of **fish,** but all share several characteristics. All fish live in water. Fish have strong muscles attached to their backbone which allows them to swim quickly. They have **fins** that are fan-shaped structures that help them to steer, stop, and balance in the water. Many fish have **scales** covering their bodies to protect them and lower friction as they swim through the water. Fish have a brain that keeps track of information obtained through **senses**, of which all fish have at least three—vision, hearing, and smell. Fish breathe using **gills**, an organ that removes oxygen from the water. Water passes through the gills and the oxygen in the water passes through a membrane into the blood which then carries the oxygen to the rest of the body. Most fish reproduce by external fertilization. The female lays unfertilized eggs into the water and the male drops sperm onto the eggs in order to fertilize them. Some species of fish reproduce by internal fertilization in which the male deposits sperm inside the female. The female then usually lays fertilized eggs called **embryos**, although some embryos develop inside the female fish. There are three types of fish—**jawless fish, cartilaginous fish,** and **bony fish.** Jawless fish include hagfish and lampreys; they are typically eel-like. Cartilaginous fish include sharks and rays. Bony fish are the largest group and include goldfish, tuna, trout, catfish, and cod.

Amphibians are animals that live in water or on land during different stages of their life cycle. Unlike fish, they have **lungs** and legs as adults. The lungs allow the amphibian to get oxygen from the air and the lungs deliver that oxygen to the blood. Most amphibians live part of their life in water and part on land. Amphibian eggs do not have a shell or protective membrane so they must be laid in a moist environment in order to prevent dehydration. Embryos must also develop in wet environments and most amphibians continue to live in water after hatching. Later, they develop into adults that live on land. The skin of amphibians is thin, smooth, and moist. Water helps amphibians to regulate their body temperature and moisture content of their skin. Amphibians do not drink water; instead they absorb it through the skin. Due to their double life, amphibians change dramatically as they grow. For example, a frog or toad embryo becomes a **tadpole** that must live in water. Tadpoles obtain oxygen through gills like fish and have a long tail for swimming. As the tadpole develops, it loses its gills and tail and develops lungs and limbs so that it can live on land as a frog or toad. This transformation is referred to as **metamorphosis**.

There are more than 5,400 species of amphibians and they are categorized into three groups: **caecilians, salamanders,** and **frogs and toads**. Caecilians live in tropical areas of Asia, Africa, and South America and look like earthworms or snakes; however, they have the thin, moist skin of amphibians. Salamanders generally live in the woods of North America. They have four strong legs and a long tail. Frogs and toads encompass about 90% of all amphibians. Toads are actually a type of frog and frogs and toads live all over the world. They are found in regions from deserts to rain forests. They have strong leg muscles for jumping and well-developed ears and vocal cords for hearing and calling.

Reptiles live entirely on land. All reptiles have lungs to breathe air and have thick, dry skin. Their skin has a watertight layer that keeps cells from losing water by evaporation. The eggs of reptiles are called **amniotic eggs** and they hold a fluid that protects the embryo. They also have a shell, allowing the eggs to be laid under rocks or in the ground. Reptiles reproduce by internal fertilization. The egg is fertilized inside the female and a shell is formed prior to the female laying her eggs. In a few cases, reptiles do not lay eggs and instead the embryo develops inside the mother and the young are born alive. There are four groups of reptiles: **turtles and tortoises, crocodiles and alligators, lizards and snakes,** and **tuataras**. Turtles and tortoises have a shell, making it hard to outrun predators. Many turtles can pull their head and legs into the shell to protect themselves. Tortoises live on land and turtles spend all or much of their live in water. Some turtles, like the sea turtle, come on land to lay eggs. Crocodiles and alligators spend most of their time in the water. They have a flat head and their eyes and nostrils are on top of their head. They are meat eaters with their diet consisting of invertebrates, fish, turtles, birds, and mammals. Snakes and lizards are the most common reptiles today. Snakes are **carnivores,** and their tongue allows them to smell. Some snakes kill their prey by squeezing it until it suffocates while others have fangs that inject venom into their prey. Snakes can open their mouths extremely wide, providing for ways to swallow whole animals that are larger than the snake is. Lizards are generally **carnivores,** eating primarily insects and worms, but some eat plants. Lizards do not swallow their prey whole. Tuataras live only on a few islands off the cost of New Zealand. They look similar to lizards, but are classified into a different group. They do not have visible ear openings like lizards do.

Birds share many characteristics with reptiles—their legs and feet are covered by scales, and their eggs have an amniotic sac like reptiles. However, bird eggs have harder shells, and birds have feathers and wings. They can usually fly and can regulate their own body temperature. Birds require a lot of energy to fly, so their body breaks down food quickly to generate energy. Most birds eat insects, nuts, seeds, or meat. To enable flight, birds have wings and have lightweight bodies. Birds can be grouped into four categories—**flightless birds, water birds, perching birds,** and **birds of prey.** Flightless birds do not have the muscles for flight. They often run very fast or are skilled swimmers. Flightless birds include penguins, ostriches, and kiwi. Water birds have webbed feet for swimming or long legs for wading. Water birds fly, are comfortable in the water, and find food on land and in water. They include cranes, ducks, geese, swans, pelicans, and loons. Perching birds have adaptations for resting on branches. They include songbirds like robins and sparrows. Their feet are able to wrap around a branch when they land in a tree. Birds of prey hunt and eat mammals, fish, reptiles, and birds. They have sharp claws and a sharp beak. Birds of prey include owls, ospreys, eagles, and hawks.

Mammals live in almost every climate on Earth. All mammals have hair and **mammary glands**, which are structures that make milk. Although all mammals have mammary glands, only mature females actually produce milk. Mammals have lungs to get oxygen from the air. The hair on mammals helps them to regulate their body temperature. Mammals that live in cold climates have thick coats of hair, called **fur**. Mammals that live in warmer climates do not need as much hair, but all mammals have hair. Mammals also have teeth with different shapes and sizes for different jobs. All mammals reproduce sexually, and in most cases, mammals give birth to live young. A mammal's brain is larger than most other animals, allowing the mammal to learn and think quickly. Mammals have five senses—vision, hearing, smell, touch, and taste—which allow them to examine the world around them. There are three categories of mammals—**placental mammals, monotremes,** and **marsupials.** The embryos of placental mammals develop inside the mother's body and are attached to the mother through a placenta. Most mammals are placental including rodents, rabbits, bats, walruses, elephants, giraffes, whales, and apes. Monotremes are mammals that lay eggs. These include echidnas and the platypus. Marsupials carry their young in a pouch. They give birth to live young, that are underdeveloped and finish their development in a pouch for several more months. Marsupials include koalas, opossums, and kangaroos.

Physiological Processes

Two or more tissues working together to carry out a specific function of the body form an **organ**. Different organs work together to create an **organ system**. There are 11 organ systems in the human body: **Integumentary System, Muscular System, Skeletal System, Cardiovascular and Circulatory System, Respiratory System, Urinary System, Reproductive System, Nervous System, Digestive System, Lymphatic System,** and **Endocrine System.**

System	Function
Integumentary	Skin, hair, and nails which protect the tissue beneath them; skin has two main layers—**epidermis** (the top layer) and **dermis** (the bottom layer)
Muscular	Three types of muscle cause movement in the body: **Skeletal muscles** attach to bones with tendons for body movement; **smooth muscles** move food through the digestive system; and **cardiac muscle** is in the heart
Skeletal	Provides the frame for the body and protects body parts; made up of **bones, cartilage, and ligaments**
Cardiovascular and Circulatory	Transports materials in the blood around the body. The heart pumps blood throughout vessels in the body, namely **arteries**, **capillaries**, and **veins**. Blood is pumped to the lungs in order to pick up oxygen and remove carbon dioxide.
Respiratory	Air moves down the **trachea** to the **lungs** for the absorption of oxygen into the blood and removal of carbon dioxide waste from the blood; oxygen goes into the blood for transport to the cells of the body for cell respiration.
Urinary	The **kidneys** filter waste from the blood and send the urine into the **bladder** to await removal. The kidneys also regulate the body's water balance.
Reproductive	Provides the components for creating new life
Nervous	Senses the environment and controls the body. It receives and sends electrical signals throughout the body along **neurons**; two parts—**central nervous system** (brain and spinal cord) and **peripheral nervous system** (nerves of the body that connect all parts of the body to the central nervous system and sense organs)
Digestive	Digests food into small particles in the mouth, stomach, and small intestines so that nutrients can be absorbed in the small intestines; the large intestines absorb water and vitamins while preparing waste for removal.
Lymphatic	Lymphatic vessels remove excess fluid from around cells and return it to the circulatory system while eliminating bacteria and viruses; contains **lymph nodes**, small bean-shaped masses of tissue that remove pathogens from the **lymph**.
Endocrine	Glands that send out hormones, chemical messengers, which control body functions (e.g., pituitary, thyroid, ovaries, testes, and adrenal glands)

Checkpoint

1. What are the four categories of eukaryotes?

2. What do plant cells have that animal cells do not have?

3. True or false: Eukaryotes have a nucleus.

4. Fill in the blank: _____ is the process by which plants make food.

5. What are the two types of animals?

6. What are the five categories of vertebrates?

7. Which organ system removes waste from the body?

Checkpoint Answers

1. protists, fungi, plants, and animals

2. chloroplasts and cell walls

3. True

4. Photosynthesis

5. vertebrates and invertebrates

6. fish, amphibians, reptiles, birds, and mammals

7. urinary system

Heredity, Evolution, and Natural Selection

Heredity is the passing of traits from parents to their offspring. The principles of heredity used today were discovered by **Gregor Mendel**. Mendel began his work by selectively mating pea plants. He examined traits of the parents and traits of their offspring by studying one characteristic (for example, flower color) at a time and examining how the parents' traits were passed on to the offspring. He determined that there were factors that were passed from one generation to the next that, when combined, created either **dominant traits** or **recessive traits**. For example, when Mendel bred a purple-flowered plant with a white-flowered plant, he discovered that all of the offspring had purple flowers. Purple flowers are a dominant trait. However, when he crossed the first generation purple-flowered plants with themselves, then the white flowers reappeared, meaning that white flowers are a recessive trait or one that is hidden by factors that cause a dominant trait. The factors that Mendel investigated are now called **genes**. One set of genes is given from each parent to their offspring. The characteristics of the offspring are then determined by the dominant and recessive **alleles** received from the parents. An allele is a form that a gene can take, e.g., there is a gene for flower color where the dominant allele is for purple flowers and the recessive allele is for white flowers.

In asexual reproduction, one parent cell is needed. The structures of the cell are copied identically in a process called **mitosis**. Most cells in the body make copies of themselves through this process when they need to divide (e.g., skin cell growth). In sexual reproduction, two **gametes** (for example, egg and sperm) join together to form an offspring that is different from both parents. Each parent cell contributes half of its genetic material to the gamete. In sexual reproduction, gametes are made through a process called **meiosis**. In meiosis, cells are produced that contain half the genetic material of the parent sex cells.

As species reproduce, various traits are passed from parents to children. Some traits are advantageous to the species in that they help the organism survive and reproduce in its environment. This trait, which is advantageous to the species, is known as an **adaptation**. As species adapt over time, they can turn into a new species in a process called **evolution**. Scientists use **fossils**, imprints of once-living organisms found in rock layers, to examine changes in species over time. The **fossil record** is the timeline of life gathered from examining fossils. As scientists examine the fossil record they make conclusions about the ancestry of species and how they have adapted over time. The most famous scientist who created the theory of evolution was **Charles Darwin**. Darwin examined plants and animals in varying places around the world on his voyage on the H.M.S. Beagle and noticed that animals and plants in different places had similar adaptations, but also had differences. As a result of his observations, he developed a theory of **natural selection** to explain how evolution occurs over time to create new species from existing species. The theory of natural selection proposes that nature selects those species best fit to survive and reproduce because they are the most fit to do so, i.e., they have the best adaptations or **survival of the fittest**. Over geologic time new species will arise from pre-existing ones as organisms continue to adapt to a changing environment.

Checkpoint

1. What are the two ways cells can divide?

2. Who was the father of modern genetics?

3. Who was the father of evolution?

Checkpoint Answers

1. mitosis and meiosis

2. Gregor Mendel

3. Charles Darwin

Competency 25: Knowledge of the Nature of Science

Competency Description

According to the Competencies and Skills Required for Teacher Certification in Florida, Elementary Education (available at http://www.fldoe.org/asp/ftce/pdf/60ElementaryEducationK-6.pdf) **Competency 25** for the Elementary Education (K–6) Subject Area Examination (SAE) addresses the following key indicators:

1. Demonstrate knowledge of basic science processes (e.g., **observing, classifying, communicating,** qualifying, **inferring, predicting**).

2. Apply knowledge of **scientific inquiry** (e.g., forming **hypotheses,** manipulating variables, recording and interpreting data) to learning science concepts.

3. Identify the appropriate laboratory equipment for specific activities.

4. Identify state safety procedures for teaching science, including the care of living organisms and the accepted procedures for the safe preparation, use, storage, and disposal of chemicals and other materials.

5. Demonstrate knowledge of basic scientific vocabulary (e.g., **theory,** law, **hypotheses,** models).

Overview

Knowledge of the nature of science includes scientific processes, inquiry, and procedures for teaching science. There are approximately **5 questions** that address Competency 25. This section addresses the following areas related to **Competency 25** key indicators:

- Scientific Processes and Inquiry
- Laboratory Safety and Procedures

Scientific Processes and Inquiry

Scientific methods are ways in which scientists answer questions and solve problems systematically. The steps for any scientific method are the same; the order may differ based on what is needed to answer the question posted. The scientific method includes the following steps: 1) ask a question, 2) make observations, 3) hypothesize, 4) predict, 5) test, and 6) conclude.

The first step is to ask a question. In order to answer the question, observations are needed. Observations may include collecting observed data such as the number of a specific species of frogs in an area. Once the question is formulated and observations are conducted, a **hypothesis** is created. A hypothesis is a possible answer to the question. Hypotheses are not based on blind guessing; they are based on what was observed and are testable. Answers are predicted and an experiment is formulated to test the hypothesis. **Controlled experiments** are designed so that there is an experimental group and a control group. The two groups are identical except for one factor, the **variable,** which is used with the experimental group. This allows for conclusions to be made that are directly related to the factor being tested. Once the experiment is conducted, analysis of the data is done, and conclusions are made based on the results of the experiment.

Checkpoint

1. What are the six steps in any scientific method?

2. What two groups are in a controlled experiment?

Checkpoint Answers

1. ask a question, make observations, hypothesize, predict, test, and conclude

2. experimental and control

Laboratory Safety and Procedures

When conducting experiments in laboratory settings, safety procedures must be followed. Procedures should be clearly explained to students prior to engaging in laboratory experiments. The teacher should have experience with the laboratory situation. It is recommended that teachers perform any experiment prior to asking students to conduct it.

Students must be taught how to properly use tools in experiments including microscopes, graduated cylinders, two balance scales, thermometers, scalpels, and Bunsen burners.

Eye protection should be worn during all laboratory experiments. Safety goggles that are shared among students should be sterilized between uses. When using heat sources, long hair should be tied back and loose clothing should be secured.

Laboratory space should contain safety equipment including eye wash stations, shower stations, emergency blankets, first aid kits, and fire extinguishers. Students should not be allowed to eat or drink in the laboratory. Laboratory space should be well ventilated. When using chemicals, they should be stored and disposed of properly. Hazardous chemicals should be stored in locked cabinets that are low to the ground. Students must wash their hands after handling any type of plant or animal. Gloves should be worn to protect the skin from chemicals used in preserved specimens, and gowns should be worn to protect the student's clothing and body.

Most science supply companies have resources that can assist teachers with educating children for laboratory safety and procedures.

Checkpoint

1. True or false: Hair should be tied back when conducting science experiments.

2. True or false: Safety goggles can always be shared among students.

3. True or false: It is okay to have a fire extinguisher in the classroom next door to the laboratory.

Checkpoint Answers

1. True

2. False. Safety goggles can be shared only if they are sterilized between uses.

3. False. A fire extinguisher should be in the laboratory.

Competency 26: Knowledge of the Relationship of Science and Technology

Competency Description

According to the Competencies and Skills Required for Teacher Certification in Florida, Elementary Education (available at http://www.fldoe.org/asp/ftce/pdf/60ElementaryEducationK-6.pdf) **Competency 26** for the Elementary Education (K–6) Subject Area Examination (SAE) addresses the following key indicators:

1. Identify the interrelationship of science and technology.
2. Identify the tools and techniques of science and technology used for data collection and problem solving.
3. Identify ways in which technology can be used by students to represent understanding of science concepts.

Overview

Knowledge of the relationship of science and technology. There are approximately **3 questions** that address Competency 26. This section addresses the following areas related to **Competency 26** key indicators:

- Interrelationship and Tools and Techniques of Science and Technology
- Technology Use by Students in Science

Interrelationship of Science and Technology

Science is the systematic and logical investigation of observable events. Its goals include to identify and establish principles and theories that may be used in the solution of problems, and accomplish these by using formal techniques, such as systematic studies, observations, experimentations, and inquiry methods. In order to establish knowledge, scientific findings must be repeatable, susceptible to disagreement and change, disprovable, and submitted to a rigorous peer-reviewed process. It also involves the development of theories, laws, and hypotheses. Their development is driven by the quality of data that is available and how it is interpreted at a given time. The following is description of theory, hypothesis, and law as defined in science:

- A theory is a well-validated and well-supported explanation of some aspect of the natural world; for example, Theory of Relativity, Quantum Mechanics, Germ Theory of Disease, and Theory of Evolution.
- A hypothesis is a tentative and testable insight into the natural world, which is not yet verified but if it were found to be true it would explain certain aspects of the natural world, and might become a scientific theory.
- A law is a truthful explanation of different events that happen with uniformity under certain conditions; for example, laws of nature, laws of gravitation, Kepler's three laws of planetary motion, laws of thermodynamics. It is a description of how things behave, but does not necessarily explain why they behave the way they do.

The use of scientific and inquiry-based methods is very important. These methods refer to techniques used to investigate phenomena, acquire new knowledge, or correct and integrate previous knowledge. Methods of inquiry must be based on gathering observable, empirical, and measurable evidence subject to specific principles of ethics and reasoning. A scientific method consists of the collection of data through observation and experimentation, and the formulation and testing of hypotheses (new researchable questions or hypotheses usually come out of the testing of hypotheses, and the process is carried out all over again). The issues of validity and reliability of data, findings, and interpretations need to be considered:

- *Validity* refers to the degree to which a measure accurately assesses the specific concept it is designed to measure.
- *Reliability* refers to the consistency of a set of measurements or measuring instrument. This can refer to whether the measurements of the same instrument provide the same measurement (test-retest), or whether two independent investigators give consistently similar scores (this is called inter-rater reliability).

Note that an instrument could be reliable but not valid. A reliable instrument might be measuring something consistently, but not necessarily what it is supposed to be measuring validly. Reliability refers to the precision of the instrument, and validity refers to the accuracy of the instrument.

Technology Use by Students in Science

Technologies are not usually exclusive products of or tools for science. The development of technology limits or expands the development of scientific discoveries. Technology has to satisfy their own utility, usability, and safety requirements, among others, which take time, money and effort. Engineers are an important factor when it comes to the interrelationship between science and technology. Engineering is more goal-oriented or result-oriented process for the design, improvement, and development of tools and systems. One of its goals is to investigate natural observable events for practical human means. In many cases, it uses and integrates results and techniques from science, but it draws knowledge from many areas, such as scientific, engineering, mathematical, linguistic, social, and historical. In many cases, technology is a combination of science and engineering, but as a human activity technology precedes science and engineering. For instance, when studying the flow of electrons in electrical conductors, scientists might use already existing tools and knowledge, and then engineers might use the newfound knowledge to develop and improve tools.

Students' use of technology gets them ready to participate in tomorrow's rapidly evolving world. They should learn to analyze and intervene creatively to improve the quality of life. Science requires that students become independent and creative problem solvers, individually and as team members. Students must have opportunities to respond and develop a range of ideas, and develop science products and systems. These opportunities should combine practical skills, understanding of aesthetics, social and environmental issues, and industrial practices. Students should also analyze and evaluate uses and effects of present and past technologies. They should also become discriminating and informed consumers of scientific products, but also become innovators using science as a tool.

An example of the interrelationship of science and technology is how the late 1600s development of the technology to make precision magnifying lenses helped scientists discover the existence of tiny organisms, such as bacteria. Lately, a great deal of attention has been given to nanotechnology. Advances in nanoscale science and technology have revolutionized manufacturing procedures, medicine, and energy discoveries. "Nano" comes from the Latin word "nanus" that means dwarf, and is used to describe very small quantities of mass, time, and length. It indicates a scaling factor in exponential notation of 10^{-9} or one billionth; for example, a nanogram (one billionth of a gram), nanosecond (one billionth of a second), and nanometer (one billionth of a meter). In general, nanoscience studies the chemical and physical consequences of manipulating materials on the nanometer (nm) length scale, is concerned with the development of tools for manipulating materials on this scale, and exploit these tools for the development of new products and processes.

Computer software and hardware are very important in the collection, manipulation, and analysis of data; for example:

- Word processors facilitate the preparation, manipulation, modification, and arrangement of electronically developed text, tables, and images for reports and documents.
- Spreadsheets allow tabulation and performance of simple and complicated calculations, mathematical manipulations, and plots and graphs on various types of data, such as numbers, names, alphabetical information, scientific measurements, statistical information, and budget information.
- Database software allows easy collection, access, organization, and retrieval of data, such as inventories, experiments, and records.
- Online databases allow access to essential tools for research in science and other areas, including scientific associations and scientists from around the world, massive bibliographic databases, print material, and interlibrary loans.
- Internet allows access to online resources, and faster communication and sharing of information, including social networking and online communities, such as e-mail, instant messaging, YouTube, TeacherTube, Facebook, MySpace, Twitter, LinkedIn, and Wiki, which is a Web site that uses Wiki software.

Graphing calculators also provide an incredible tool for this purpose when placed in the hands of students. Also, tools like spectometers and sensors facilitate the collection of data, which might also be used with computer software to manage data. Spectometers are instruments that can be used to measure absorbance spectrum of a liquid, conduct kinetic studies of absorbance versus time, conduct equilibrium studies of absorbance vs. time and/or absorbance vs. concentration, and measure emissions of gas discharge tubes or other light sources, and other experiments. Sensors are also instruments used to collect data; for example:

- Accelerometers are small devices that can be mounted on moving objects to study one-dimensional motions, such as the motion of a car, elevator, mass on a string undergoing simple harmonic motion, or amusement park rides.
- Barometers are used for either weather studies or for lab experiments involving pressures close to normal atmospheric pressure.
- Blood pressure sensors are designed to measure human blood pressure.
- Temperature probes are used for data-collection during temperature-related experiments.

Checkpoint

Fill in the blank.

1. A _____ is a well-validated and well-supported explanation of some aspect of the natural world.

2. A _____ is a truthful explanation of different events that happen with uniformity under certain conditions.

3. _____ allows access to online resources, and faster communication and sharing of information, including social networking and online communities.

4. A _____ is a tentative and testable insight into the natural world.

Checkpoint Answers

1. theory
2. law
3. Internet
4. hypothesis

Competency 27: Knowledge of Instruction and Assessment

Competency Description

According to the Competencies and Skills Required for Teacher Certification in Florida, Elementary Education (available at http://www.fldoe.org/asp/ftce/pdf/60ElementaryEducationK-6.pdf) **Competency 27** for the Elementary Education (K–6) Subject Area Examination (SAE) addresses the following key indicators:

1. Identify a variety of appropriate instructional strategies (e.g., cooperative learning, inquiry learning, investigations) for teaching specific topics.
2. Select manipulatives, physical models, and other classroom teaching tools for teaching specific topics.
3. Identify a variety of methods for assessing scientific knowledge, including analyzing student thinking processes to determine strengths and weaknesses.

Overview

Knowledge of instruction and assessment. There are approximately **3 questions** that address Competency 27. This section addresses the following areas related to **Competency 27** key indicators:

- Instructional Classroom Teaching Tools
- Instructional Strategies and Methods of Assessment

Students should be evaluated in their demonstration of acceptable scientific ethics and procedures; ability to identify inventions; ability to analyze and evaluate data collected or found in data bases, and critiquing scientific findings and reports. Some ways to evaluate students' growth are the following: documenting experiments by keeping notes or writing reflections related to personal experiences in science, and presenting findings from experiments using valid and reliable data. They should also be evaluated in their ability to describe findings using inquiry-based methods. They should be able to explain what science means personally, and tell how science connects to society and other subjects.

Instructional Strategies and Classroom Teaching Tools

Students should be evaluated in their demonstration of acceptable presentation of scientific work, ability to communicate with others, and ability to analyze and evaluate scientific work. Some ways to evaluate students' growth are the following: documenting personal growth by keeping scientific notes, collecting data, or writing reflections related to personal experiences in science. They should also be evaluated in their ability to describe scientific principles as they occur in experiments to describe data findings.

Student scientific findings should be displayed and evaluated in a detailed and analytical way. All the students should participate in offering critiques that are guided by the teacher. This type of assessment should increase the viewpoints from which students' scientific work is evaluated and promote the inquiry-based skills of all the students. Student responses to scientific work will vary. This critique process is a way for students to learn from each other, learn from analyzing successful and less successful problem solving strategies, and find creative and aesthetic solutions to scientific issues or problems.

The *National Science Education Standards* reported, "Scientific inquiry refers to the diverse ways in which scientists study the natural world and propose explanations based on the evidence derived from their work. Inquiry also refers to the activities of students in which they develop knowledge and understanding of scientific ideas, as well as an understanding of how scientists study the natural world" (NSES, 1996, National Academy Press, Washington, DC, p. 23). The inquiry process involves

- observation (close analysis of information, procedures, and evidence)
- measurement (involving quantitative description of evidence, and value placed on precision and accuracy)
- experimentation (testing questions and ideas)
- communication (relaying results, writing, speaking, and explaining)
- mental processes (inductive reasoning, formulating hypotheses, analogy, extrapolation, classification, prediction, inference, synthesis, and deductive reasoning)

The inquiry-based learning approach is more focused on using and learning content as a means to develop information-processing and problem-solving skills. The process should be more of a student-centered approach, as opposed to a teacher-centered approach. In this type of process, the teacher becomes a facilitator of learning. It also places more emphasis on "how we come to know" and less emphasis on "what we know." Students need to be more involved, motivated, engaged, and responsible as they construct knowledge through active involvement. The more involved, motivated, engaged, and responsible students are by a subject, experiment or project, the more likely they will be able to construct in-depth knowledge of a subject, experiment, or project. An inquiry-based learning environment must model appropriate scientific processes, allow for creative thinking, provide flexibility, use effective questioning strategies, and empower thinking skills and content. Teachers should encourage students to explain and justify their answers using data, and manipulate data to distinguish patterns and trends (graphs, tables, and charts), and explain what they see, including, if needed, the possibility of outliers.

When trying to use an inquiry-based approach as part of the learning process, you should provide opportunities for students to use relevant data to answer research questions by analyzing the data. It is not enough that the students collect data or use equipment. For example, constructing a molecular solar system scale model is not an inquiry-based activity in itself, unless they also involve research questions and discussion of findings. Drill and practice activities for a particular concept or skill are not considered inquiry-based activities.

The *5-Step Experiential Learning Cycle* has been suggested as method to support science learning. It may be repeated as needed for different scientific concepts. The five steps are presented and discussed here:

- *Exploration* ("Do it"): Perform an activity with limited or no help from the teacher; for example, making products or models, role playing, presenting findings, problem solving, or playing a game.
- *Sharing* ("What Happened?"): Publicly share the results, reactions, and observations, talk freely about experiences, share reactions and observations, and discuss feelings generated by the experience (as a group or individually.
- *Processing* ("What's Important?"): Discuss, analyze, and reflect about how the experience was carried out, how issues were brought out by the experience, how specific problems or issues were addressed, what personal experiences were involved, and what recurring themes were encountered.
- *Generalizing* ("So What?"): Connect the experience with real world examples, find general trends or common truths in the experience, identify "real life" principles that surfaced, and list key terms that capture the learning.
- *Application* ("Now What?"): Apply what was learned to a similar or different situation, learn from past experiences, discuss how new learning can be applied to other situations, discuss how issues raised can be useful in the future, discuss how more effective behaviors can develop from the new learning, and develop a sense of ownership for what was learned.

Another suggested method to support science learning is the 5-E's Learning Cycle. It is a method of structuring science lessons that is based on cognitive psychology and constructivist learning theory. Bybee (1997, *Achieving Science Literacy: From Purposes to Practices*. Portsmouth, NH: Heinemann) described what this five step learning cycle involves: *Engagement, Exploration, Explanation, Elaboration,* and *Evaluation*. Note that *Evaluation* is not the last step of this cyclical process. It is more like a recurring step within all other four stages of this learning cycle. Examples of the evaluation aspects for each stage are given for each description here.

- **Engagement**—The cyclical process starts with engagement. At this stage, the teacher presents the problem, pre-assesses the students, helps students make connections, and informs students of the research questions, relevant information, procedures, goals, and objectives of the activity. The evaluation of students' engagement revolves around the pre-assessment, and students' proper understanding of the activity, and motivation to engage in the activity. The context of the activity and students' mastery of prior knowledge and prerequisites are very important at this point. This evaluation could involve teacher's field notes and observations (formal or informal), and students' oral and written responses. Note that the effectiveness of the activity is directly related to the level of students' engagement.

- **Exploration**—In this phase, students should be actively engaged in the activity collecting or finding data to solve the problem, and the teacher should make sure the students are doing these effectively and appropriately. Evaluation during this stage should focus on the process itself; including students' proper and logical use of data collection and recording procedures instead of focusing on the product resulting from their data collection.

- **Explanation**—At this point, students should use the data they have collected to solve the problem, answer research questions, and report their procedures and thinking process as they solve the problem. The teacher could also introduce new vocabulary, ideas, concepts, skills, phrases, or sentences to label what the students have already figured out. Evaluation during this stage should focus on the process the students are using, including how well they use the collected information and develop new ideas. The teacher could ask comprehension questions dealing with new vocabulary and concepts.

- **Elaboration**—It is the last step of the cycle, and before it goes back to the engagement stage. Students are given new information questions, and problems in order to extend what they have learned in the earlier parts of the learning cycle, and posed problems that students solve by applying what they have learned, including examples and non-examples. Evaluation during this stage should focus on the overall performance and final application problems, answers to and discussion of research questions, product, report, or presentation (individually or as small groups).

Instructional Strategies and Methods of Assessment

Assessment can be used for a variety of purposes. Each purpose presents its own opportunities and challenges. Five most common types of assessment are

- **Diagnostic assessment** (pretests) used to help determine what students know when they begin any educational task
- **Formative assessment** used to help guide day-to-day classroom activities
- **Student outcome** or **summative assessment** used to find out what students have learned and mastered in their individual programs
- **Comparative assessment** used to determine how an individual's or a group's outcome compares to another group's outcome
- **Student assessment** used to help determine the effect of a program, curriculum innovation, pedagogic strategy, professional development, or policy initiative

Other terms used to describe assessment are the following:

- **Traditional assessment** involves students selecting responses from a multiple-choice, true/false list or matching list, or working out the full solution of an equation.

- **Standardized testing** involves the administration of tests under controlled conditions and using consistent scoring procedures.

- **Performance assessment** involves the direct, systematic observation of an actual student's performance and rating of that performance according to pre-established performance criteria or rubric, and assessment of both the results and process.

- **Alternative assessment** involves students' derived responses to a task or question; for example, demonstrations, exhibits, portfolios, oral presentations, or essays; not traditional assessment.

- **Authentic assessment** involves presenting tasks that reflect the kind of mastery demonstrated by experts or in real-world situations.

As part of an inquiry-based learning environment, assessment is focused on determining students' progress and development in reasoning skills, in addition to content understanding. Inquiry-based learning is concerned with in-school success, and students' preparation as life-long learners. Inquiry-based classrooms are open learning environments in which students search and make use of resources beyond the classroom and the school, and use technology to connect appropriately with local and world communities. Students learn to use an inquiry approach to help them connect science with the scientific method.

Abstract concepts like **potential** and **kinetic energy** are difficult to understand by students. Studies have shown that one of the most effective ways to introduce and reinforce abstract scientific concepts is by using **manipulatives** (blocks, rods, bean and sticks, among others). They include objects that can be touched and moved around by students in ways that enable descriptions to come alive; for example, using race vehicles powered by springs or rubber bands down a ramp to illustrate potential and kinetic energy. Students should have opportunities to investigate ways to solve problems, and share and discuss their solutions and procedures. They should also have opportunities to make sound connections between new information and previously acquired information. An effective way to provide the possibility of making this type of connections is the use of small groups of students working cooperatively or collaboratively with manipulatives. Activities like this one allow students to design and experiment with their own vehicles in an environment that encourages social interaction and active learning. They allow for cooperation and collaboration, creativity, self-esteem, and self-efficacy. Also, physical models can be used to develop an intuition related to fundamental scientific ideas and processes. Physical models can serve as the basis for short, in-class demonstrations or for course projects.

Recently, many "virtual" versions of **manipulatives** (called virtual manipulatives or applets) and simulations of activities are now available in a number of Websites, and used in science and mathematics education. Virtual manipulatives are interactive, Web-based visual representation of objects that provide opportunities for constructing mathematical or scientific knowledge. Some virtual manipulatives are available online from the following sources: *National Library of Virtual Manipulatives*, and *National Council of Teachers of Mathematics* (NCTM) *Illuminations*. They could be used to help students learn some of the underlying ideas of mathematics modeling and computer simulation. They should be used carefully and not just as a substitute for real concrete manipulatives, models, or simulations. We can find static and dynamic virtual models on the Internet. Static virtual models are not considered true virtual manipulatives. They are pictorial representations of the physical concrete manipulatives that cannot be manipulated. Virtual manipulatives should be more than pointing and clicking to get results in the computer and providing answers at an abstract level. For example, virtual manipulative should provide some control by allowing slides, flips, turns, and/or rotations.

Computer simulations are the technique of representing the real world via a computer program. They can represent real or imaginary situations, and may allow users to study or try things that would be difficult or impossible to do in real life. They should imitate the internal processes and not merely the results of what they are simulating. Some simulations are available online from the following sources:

- Lions and Antelopes (by Jo Edkins, 2004: explores the relationship between predator, herbivores, and vegetation)
- Plants-in-motion (by Roger P. Hangarter, 2000: using time lapsed photography to show the movement of Arabidopsis plants in response to stimuli, and that plants are living organisms)
- Science Simulations on the Internet from Kent County Council (biology, physics, health, astronomy, and virtual experiments)

Checkpoint

Fill in the blank.

1. _____ learning should be of a more student-centered approach, than a teacher-centered approach.

2. _____ assessment is used to help determine what students know when they begin any educational task.

3. A type of assessment used to help guide day-to-day classroom activities is called _____ assessment.

4. _____ refers to the precision of an assessment instrument.

5. _____ refers to the accuracy of an assessment instrument.

6. True or false: Gloria constructed a reliable instrument for her experiment. She concluded that since her instrument is reliable it would also be a valid instrument.

Checkpoint Answers

1. Inquiry or Inquiry-based

2. Diagnostic

3. formative

4. Reliability

5. Validity

6. False: A reliable instrument might be measuring something consistently, but not necessarily what it is supposed to be measuring validly. Reliability refers to the precision of the instrument, and validity refers to the accuracy of the instrument. They do not depend on each other.

Summary

The Science and Technology section (Competencies 21–27) encompasses a variety of sub-competencies related to the basic knowledge required of educators teaching elementary age students. Knowledge of the nature of matter entails understanding the physical properties of matter, physical and chemical change, and properties of solids, liquids, and gases. Knowledge of forces, motion, and energy includes understanding forces, temperature change, light, electricity, and energy. Knowledge of Earth and space means that the teacher understands the structure of the Earth, geological processes, the Earth's place in the solar system, and interactions of the sun, planets, and other celestial bodies. Knowledge of life science entails understanding living and non-living things, the structure of plants and animals, and the interaction of living things with their environment. Knowledge of the nature of science entails understanding scientific inquiry and use of laboratory equipment. Knowledge of the relationship of science and technology includes understanding the use of technology in scientific experimentation and instruction. Finally, knowledge of instruction and assessment entails the understanding of methods for assessing scientific understanding in the classroom.

This section reflects the skills required in this area for Teacher Certification in Florida, Elementary Education (available at http://www.fldoe.org/asp/ftce/pdf/60ElementaryEducationK-6.pdf). You should use the information in this section to compliment your previous knowledge in the areas of science and technology. The general review of Science and Technology (Competencies 21–27) provided in this chapter should allow you to explore areas of strength and need that you might still need to review. As indicated before, sample questions for the competency area as a whole appear in the next section of the chapter. Answers and explanations follow the sample questions. These sections should provide an opportunity for further practice and analysis.

Sample Questions

1. The topmost layer of the Earth is called the

   A. crust.
   B. inner Core.
   C. outer Core.
   D. mantle.

2. Which of the following is a component of evolution?

   A. global warming
   B. greenhouse gases
   C. hurricanes
   D. natural selection

3. The geological phenomena of plate tectonics is most likely caused by

   A. solar energy heating the crust of the Earth.
   B. the mantle of the Earth shrinking and cooling.
   C. convection currents in the core.
   D. ocean currents moving the plates.

4. Pam says that CO_2 is matter. Is she correct?

   A. She is not correct because CO_2 is a gas.
   B. She is not right because CO_2 does not have a specific shape like a rock.
   C. She is correct because CO_2 is composed of molecules, and molecules are matter.
   D. She is not right because you can't see CO_2.

5. Rocks formed when existing rocks undergo change are called

   A. sedimentary rocks.
   B. metamorphic rocks.
   C. igneous rocks.
   D. river rocks.

6. Which organ system breaks down food into nutrients for the body?

   A. Muscular System
   B. Skeletal System
   C. Digestive System
   D. Respiratory System

7. It is summer in the Northern Hemisphere from June through August. What is the cause of this?

   A. the Earth moving closer to the sun causing the sun's rays to be more intense
   B. the tilt of the Earth causing the sun's rays to hit the northern hemisphere directly
   C. the rotation of the Earth causing the northern hemisphere to be closer to the sun
   D. the sun becoming hotter between June and August

8. Ralph is on a diet. Which of the following is he trying to lose with this diet?

   A. density
   B. mass
   C. weight
   D. buoyancy

9. MySpace is a type of

   A. social network.
   B. instant messaging.
   C. electronic mail.
   D. spreadsheet.

10. Jonathan is conducting an experiment to test whether or not the sun has an effect on the growth of a particular plant. He sets up an experiment in which he has two plants that are identical. One plant is exposed to the sun while the other is not exposed to the sun. What type of experiment is Jonathan conducting?

    A. controlled experiment
    B. single-subject experiment
    C. descriptive experiments
    D. disection

11. A tugboat exerts a force of 4500 newtons on a large boat and another tugboat exerts a force of 6300 newtons in the opposite direction on the same large boat. What is the combined force of these two tugboats on the large boat?

    A. 4500 newtons
    B. 6300 newtons
    C. 10800 newtons
    D. 1800 newtons

12. Which of the following is NOT a component of every cell?

    A. cell membrane
    B. cell wall
    C. DNA
    D. cytoplasm

13. The first American to be launched into space was

    A. John Glenn.
    B. Neil Armstrong.
    C. James Lovell.
    D. Alan Shepard.

14. Hector is concerned with the precision of a thermometer he is using for an experiment. His concern is related to

    A. the validity of the instrument.
    B. the clarity of the instrument.
    C. the reliability of the instrument.
    D. the acceptability of the instrument.

15. Mrs. Spalding is conducting a scientific experiment with her fourth grade class. She is heating water to boiling to begin her experiment. Which of the following should Mrs. Spalding be sure to do with her students?

    A. allow her students to run in the laboratory room
    B. leave the fire extinguisher in the room next door
    C. require all her students to wear safety goggles
    D. allow the students in the back of the room to not wear safety goggles

Answer Explanations for Sample Questions

1. **A.** Competency 23. The layers of the Earth are, from center to surface, the inner core, the outer core, the mantle, and the crust.

2. **D.** Competency 24. Natural selection is a component of evolution.

3. **C.** Competency 23. Plate tectonics is caused by convection currents which radiate from the core of the Earth. These currents cause the plates to move.

4. **C.** Competency 21. Yes, she is correct because CO_2 is composed of molecules, and molecules are matter, even when they are not easily seen.

5. **B.** Competency 23. Sedimentary rocks are formed when layers of debris fuse together. Igneous rocks form when magma cools. Metamorphic rocks are formed when existing rocks undergo change, often due to burial.

6. **C.** Competency 24. The digestive system breaks down food for nutrients.

7. **B.** Competency 23. The seasons are caused by the tilt of the Earth. In the summer months in the Northern Hemisphere, the sun's rays are more direct, causing it to be warmer.

8. **B.** Competency 22. Ralph is most likely on a diet because he wants to reduce the amount of matter on his body. He most likely wishes to lose mass. If he wishes to lose weight, he would need to go to another planet.

9. **A.** Competency 26. MySpace is a type of social network.

10. **A.** Competency 25. Jonathan has set up an experimental group and a control group. This is a controlled experiment.

11. **D.** Competency 22. Since the tugboats provide unbalanced forces in opposite directions, you need to subtract 4500 from 6300, which provides a difference of 1800 newtons.

12. **B.** Competency 24. All cells contain a cell membrane, cytoplasm, organelles, and DNA.

13. **D.** Competency 23. John Glenn was the first American to orbit the Earth. Neil Armstrong was the first American to walk on the moon. James Lovell piloted Apollo 13. Alan Shepard was the first American to be launched into space.

14. **C.** Competency 27. Hector's concern is related to the reliability of the instrument, which involves the precision of the instrument. Validity refers to the accuracy of the instrument.

15. **C.** Competency 25. Safety goggles should be worn by all students at all times.

Mathematics

This chapter provides a general review of the area of Mathematics (Competencies 28–32) with sample questions and explanations at the end of the chapter. Checkpoint exercises are found throughout, giving you an opportunity to practice the skills addressed in each section. The answers to the Checkpoint exercises immediately follow the set of questions. We encourage you to cover the answers as you complete the Checkpoint exercises. Sample questions for the competency area as a whole appear at the end of the chapter. Answers and explanations follow the sample questions.

Competency 28: Knowledge of Numbers and Operations

Competency Description

According to the Competencies and Skills Required for Teacher Certification in Florida, Elementary Education (available at http://www.fldoe.org/asp/ftce/pdf/60ElementaryEducationK-6.pdf) **Competency 28** for the Elementary Education (K–6) Subject Area Examination (SAE) addresses the following key indicators:

1. Associate multiple representations of numbers using word names, standard numerals, and pictorial models for **real numbers** (e.g., **whole numbers**, **decimals**, **fractions**, **integers**).

2. Compare the relative size of integers, fractions, decimals, numbers expressed as percents, and numbers with **exponents**.

3. Apply ratios, proportions, and percents in real-world situations.

4. Represent numbers in a variety of equivalent forms, including whole numbers, integers, fractions, decimals, percents, and exponents.

5. Perform operations on rational numbers (e.g., whole numbers, fractions, decimals, integers) using multiple representations and algorithms and understand the relationships between these operations (i.e., addition, subtraction, multiplication, and division).

6. Select the appropriate operation(s) to solve problems involving ratios and percents and the addition, subtraction, multiplication, and division of rational numbers.

7. Use estimation in problem-solving situations.

8. Apply number theory concepts (e.g., primes, composites, multiples, factors, number sequences, number properties, rules of divisibility).

9. Apply the order of operations.

Overview

Knowledge of **numbers** and **operations** is one of the most important areas of mathematics education. It involves different types of **cognitive levels** (concrete, pictorial, and abstract), number sets and their equivalent forms, estimation, problem solving, and number theory. There are approximately **11 questions** that address Competency 28. This section addresses the following areas related to **Competency 28** key indicators:

- Associate Multiple Representations of Real Numbers
- Compare the Relative Size of Numbers
- Apply Ratios, Proportions, and Percents
- Represent Numbers in a Variety of Equivalent Forms
- Select and Perform Operations to Solve Problems
- Use Estimation in Problem Solving Situations
- Apply Number Theory Concepts
- Apply the Order of Operations

Associate Multiple Representations of Real Numbers

Real numbers include **rational** and **irrational numbers** and can be expressed as a ratio of two integers, $\frac{a}{b}$, where $b > 0$. You can basically have three forms of representing or modeling a number (and other mathematical concepts and skills): **concrete**, **pictorial** (also known as **representational** and graphic representations), and **symbolic** (also known as **abstract**) levels. Children seem to learn best when early learning experiences start with the use of concrete materials, such as toys, cubes, and other objects to represent numerical ideas. However, concrete activities should not be used exclusively. They should also have experiences involving the representational and abstract levels. The representational level involves pictorial representations of the manipulative materials or objects used for learning.

Number lines, pie graphs, bar graphs, and charts can also be used as representation of numerical values. The abstract level involves the use of symbols to represent ideas.

For example, the idea of number can be modeled in a way that children come to understand and know it. At the concrete level, manipulative materials can be used to facilitate this learning. The manipulative materials could be cubes, pencils, books, or people they count to find how many they have in a set or group. In this manner, students find the numberness or cardinality of the set. Other counting number-related ideas are equality, more than, less than, combining groups, and separating groups, which could be modeled similarly. At the pictorial level and in a similar way, pictures (or pictorial representations) or drawings could be used to model number ideas. The symbolic form of numbers is called numerals. The cardinality of a set with three objects is represented by using the numeral "3" at the symbolic level. The number name "three" is also considered to be at the symbolic level. The abstract level is involved when you say words, and read or write symbols. Children's ability to transfer ideas from one mode or level of a number idea demonstrates their degree of understanding of the idea.

Examples of Multiple Representations of Numbers			
Set of Numbers	**Word Name**	**Standard Numeral**	**Pictorial Model**
Whole Numbers	Five	5	Let each square equal one unit:
Integers	Negative five	−5	Let gray represent negative, and white positive numbers: Note that $^{+}1 + -1 = 0$:
Fractions	One-fifth	$\frac{1}{5}$	Let the each square equal one out five pieces:
Decimals	Five-tenths	0.5	Let each square equal one out of ten pieces:

Checkpoint

1. Fill in the blank: The _____ cognitive level is involved when children are trying to find out how many crayons are contained in a box of crayons.

2. Peter wrote the following symbol on the board: 3. Is he writing a number or a numeral?

3. True or false: A number is a symbolic representation of a numerical quantity.

Checkpoint Answers

1. Concrete

2. He is writing a numeral on the board.

3. False. A number is an idea represented symbolically by a numeral or number name.

Compare the Relative Size of Numbers

The **exponential notation** is a way to represent repeated multiplication in a simple format. In this sense, **exponents** are used to indicate the number of times an expression is multiplied by itself. For example, $5 \times 5 \times 5$ can be written in exponential form as 5^3, indicating the number of times 5 is multiplied by itself three times. The number 5,329 can be expressed using expanded notation using number name form as 5 thousands, 3 hundreds, 2 tens, and 9 ones; using numeric form as $4 \times 1000 + 3 \times 100 + 2 \times 10 + 9 \times 1$, and using exponential form as $4 \times 10^3 + 3 \times 10^2 + 2 \times 10^1 + 9 \times 10^0$, where $10^0 = 1$. These are other examples of expressions with exponents: $y^2 = y \cdot y$ ("$\cdot$" is used to express multiplication), $\frac{1}{a \cdot a} = \frac{1}{a^2} = a^{-2}$, $a^3 \cdot a^2 = a^5$ (add exponents), $(a^2)^3 = a^6$, and $\sqrt{a} = a^{\frac{1}{2}}$.

When you compare numbers, you need to keep in mind the equivalent ways a quantity could be represented. For example, $\frac{1}{2}$ is a fraction that could be expressed as $\frac{2}{4}$ using an equivalent fraction, 0.5 or 0.50 using decimals, and 50% using percents. The following are other examples of multiple representations of numbers:

$$\sqrt{144} = \sqrt{12^2} = 12$$

$$200 = 200.0 = \frac{400}{2} = 200\% = 2 \times 100 = 2 \times 10^2$$

A fraction can be converted into a decimal by dividing the **numerator** by the **denominator**. For example, $\frac{3}{4}$ is equivalent to 0.75 because 3 divided by 4 is equal to 0.75. Similarly, $9\frac{3}{4}$ is equivalent to 9.75. The decimal numbers are terminating or non-terminating repeating decimals. A non-terminating non-repeating number is called an irrational number, which is a subset of the real numbers (the square root of 2 is an example of an irrational number). A simple fraction can be converted into a terminating (for example, 0.45, 0.5, and 0.010), or a non-terminating repeating decimal (for example, 0.66... or $0.\overline{6}$, where the line on top of the 6 indicates that 6 is repeating). A terminating decimal can be converted into a fraction by writing the decimal number as a fraction with the denominator as a power of 10, and then simplifying this fraction to lowest terms. For example, 0.245 is equivalent to $\frac{245}{1000}$ (use as many zeroes as digits in the decimal part of the number, in this case 3 zeroes for 3 digits in 0.245). This can be simplified to 49/200 by dividing the numerator and denominator by 5 (the greatest common factor of 245 and 1000).

A decimal (or fraction after being converted into a decimal) can be converted into a percent by shifting the decimal point two places to the right and adding the percent sign (%) to it. For example, 0.39 can be written as 39%, 0.436 as 43.6%, 5.49 as 549%, or .005 as 0.5%. The process of converting a percent to a decimal is the reverse of converting a decimal to a percent. You can convert a percent to a decimal by shifting the decimal point two places to the left without the percent sign. For example, 78% can be written as 0.78, 978% as 9.78, 65.7% as 0.657, and 0.6% as 0.06.

Checkpoint

1. Order the following numbers from least to greatest: 60%, 1, –0.75, 0.64, –1.5, $\frac{7}{9}$, 2^{-2}, and 1×10^{-2}.

2. Express 83,476 in exponential notation. $8 \times 10^4 + 3 \times 10^3 + 4 \times 10^2 + 7 \times 10^1 + 6 \times 10^0$

3. Is $-\frac{1}{4}$ an integer? Explain.

4. Convert $\frac{5}{8}$ into a percent. 62.5%

5. Convert 0.54 into a fraction. $\frac{54}{100}$

Checkpoint Answers

1. -1.5, -0.75, 1×10^{-2}, 2^{-2}, 60%, 0.64, $\frac{7}{9}$, and 1.

   $1 \times 10^{-2} = 1 \times 1/10^2 = 1 \times 1/100 = 1 \times 0.01 = 0.01$,

   $2^{-2} = \frac{1}{2^2} = \frac{1}{4} = 0.25$,

   $60\% = 0.6 = 0.60$,

   $\frac{7}{9} = 0.777\ldots$ or $0.\overline{7}$

2. $8 \times 10^4 + 3 \times 10^3 + 4 \times 10^2 + 7 \times 10^1 + 6 \times 10^0$

3. No, because not all fractions are integers. Negative and positive fractions are not integers unless they are equivalent to whole numbers or their negative counterpart. In this case, $-\frac{1}{4}$ (or -0.25 in decimal form) cannot be expressed as a whole number or the negative of a whole number.

4. Since $5 \div 8 = 0.625$, then $\frac{5}{8}$ is equal to 62.5%.

5. $0.54 = \frac{54}{100} = \frac{27}{50}$

Apply Ratios, Proportions, and Percents

A **ratio** is another way to represent or use fractions. Ratios are involved when you compare two numbers or quantities. The following are four real-world examples of ratios: four bicycles cost $480.00, the map scale is 1 centimeter per kilometer, the speed limit is 70 miles per hour, the sale tax for the sofa is 7% (notice that a **percent** is a type of ratio). A **rate** is a specific case of ratios. A rate is involved when the measuring units in describing two quantities being compared are different. For example, speed situations: I ran 200 meters in 25 seconds, or I bought a six-pack of cola for $1.50. The **unit rate** is involved when the second term in the rate is equal to 1. For example, Lourdes can type 36 words per minute, or Paul earns $15.00 per hour.

A **proportion** involves a statement that indicates that two ratios are equal. For example, at the market today, four apples cost $1.20, then eight apples should cost $2.40. This could be stated in the following proportion:

$$\frac{4}{1.20} = \frac{8}{2.40}$$

Notice that the relationship between quantities in each side of the proportion (or for each ratio) is presented in the same manner: number of apples to number of dollars. This order could be changed as long as you do the same on both sides of the proportion. For example, an equivalent form of this proportion using the ratio of dollars to apples is the following:

$$\frac{1.20}{4} = \frac{2.40}{8}$$

Checkpoint

1. Does the following statement represent a proportion?

   $$\frac{4}{20} = \frac{8}{50}$$

2. What value of x would make the following proportion true?

   $$\frac{4}{8} = \frac{x}{24}$$

3. David said that 20% is a unit rate. Is he right?

4. Find the item with the best unit price:

> $1.45 for 12 ounces
>
> $1.90 for 15 ounces
>
> $4.34 for 45 ounces

Checkpoint Answers

1. No, this statement does not represent a proportion because the two ratios are not equivalent.

2. $x = 12$

3. No, he is not right. It is a rate but is not a unit rate.

4. Find the unit price for each situation:

   $1.45 for 12 ounces: $1.45 \div 12$ is about $0.12 per ounce

   $1.90 for 15 ounces: $1.90 \div 15$ is about $0.13 per ounce

   $4.34 for 45 ounces: $4.34 \div 45$ is about $0.10 per ounce

   The best unit price is $4.34 for 45 ounces.

Represent Numbers in a Variety of Equivalent Forms

Besides multiple representations of number quantities using word names and standard numerals, we can also represent numbers in different equivalent forms using whole numbers, fractions, decimals, percents, and exponents. The following table offers some examples.

Examples of Equivalent Forms of Numbers		
Form	**Two hundred thirty-four cubes in a set**	**Seven eighths of a region**
Whole Numbers	234	
Integers	234 or +234	
Fractions	$\frac{234}{1}$	$\frac{7}{8}$
Decimals	234.0	0.875
Percent	23400%	87.5%
Exponential	$2 \times 10^2 + 3 \times 10^1 + 4 \times 10^0$	$8 \times 10^{-1} + 7 \times 10^{-2} + 5 \times 10^{-3}$

Checkpoint

Complete the following table by expressing the numbers in their equivalent forms:

Form	One hundred sixty-eight pencils in a box	One fourth of a region	Five eighths of a region
Whole Numbers			
Integers			
Fractions			
Decimals			
Percent			
Exponential			

Checkpoint Answers

Form	One hundred sixty-eight pencils in a box	One fourth of a region	Five eighths of a region
Whole Numbers	168		
Integers	168 or +168		
Fractions	$\dfrac{168}{1}$	$\dfrac{1}{4}$	$\dfrac{5}{8}$
Decimals	168.0	0.25	0.675
Percent	16800%	25%	67.5%
Exponential	$1 \times 10^2 + 6 \times 10^1 + 8 \times 10^0$	$2 \times 10^{-1} + 5 \times 10^{-2}$	$6 \times 10^{-1} + 7 \times 10^{-2} + 5 \times 10^{-3}$

Select and Perform Operations to Solve Problems

The major operations on rational numbers are addition, subtraction, multiplication, and division. When solving word problems, it is important to take the time to select the appropriate operation involved in the problem. This requires the ability to translate the word problem into a mathematical sentence and solving the mathematical sentence accordingly. Some word problems might require multiple steps and operations. The examples provided in this section involve only whole numbers, but decimals or fractions could be used in a similar manner. Make sure you practice operations with integers, fractions, decimals, ratios, and percents.

For addition and subtraction, we have four types of problems: *join*, *separate*, *part-part-whole*, and *compare*. *Join problems* involve adding or joining elements to a set. Three quantities are involved: *the starting amount*, *the change amount,* and *the resulting amount*. Variations of the join problems include situations when the result is unknown, the change amount is unknown, or the starting amount is unknown. A *separate problem* involves removing elements from a set. Similar to join problems, we have three quantities involved, and three variations of the separate problems. *Part-part-whole problems* involve no action or change over time like what happens with join and separate problems, and focus on the relationship between a set and its two subsets (or a whole and two parts). Variations of these problems involve situations when *the whole is unknown*, or *part of the whole is unknown*. *Compare problems* also involve no action, but involve comparisons between two different sets. These comparisons can be made in terms of how much *more* or how much *less* is one set than another set. Variations of the compare problems are *difference unknown*, *larger amount unknown*, and *smaller amount unknown*. For any of these types of problems, always remember to relate your answer back to the initial question of the problem. The following tables provide examples for each type of problem (Carpenter, et al., 1999; Carpenter & Moser, 1992; Cathcart, et al., 2001; Greer, 1992).

Addition and Subtraction Problems That Involve Actions			
Type of Problem	**Example of Problems**	**Mathematical Sentences**	**Solutions**
Join	Result unknown: Carla had 29 apples and Frank gave her 56 apples. How many apples does Carla have now?	29 + 56 = ___	Carla has 85 apples now.
	Change unknown: Carla had 29 apples, and Frank gave her some more apples. If Carla has 85 apples now, how many apples did Frank give her?	29 + ___ = 85	Frank gave her 56 apples.
	Start unknown: Carla had some apples, and Frank gave her 56 more apples. If Carla has 85 apples now, how many apples did she have to start with?	___ + 56 = 85	Carla started with 29 apples.
Separate	Result unknown: Mary had 85 apples. If she gave 29 apples to Albert, how many apples does she have left?	85 – 29 = ___	Mary has 56 apples left.
	Change unknown: Mary had 85 apples. If she gave some apples to Albert and now she has 29 apples left, how many apples did Mary give to Albert?	85 – ___ = 29	Mary gave 56 apples to Albert.
	Start unknown: Mary had some apples. If she gave 56 apples to Albert and now she has 29 apples, how many apples did Mary have to start with?	___ – 56 = 29	Mary had 85 apples to start with.
Addition and Subtraction Problems That Involve No Actions			
Part-Part-Whole	Whole unknown: Samuel has a combination of 29 red apples and 56 green apples in a box. How many apples does he have altogether in the box?	29 + 56 = ___	Samuel has 85 apples in the box.
	Part unknown: Samuel has a total of 85 apples in a box, with 29 of them being red apples and the rest green apples. How many green apples does he have?	29 + ___ = 85	Samuel has 56 green apples.
Compare	Difference unknown: Samuel has 85 apples and Frank has 56 apples. How many more apples does Samuel have than Frank? Or How many less apples does Frank have than Samuel?	56 + ___ = 85, or 85 – 56 = ___	Samuel has 29 more apples than Frank.
	Larger unknown: Frank has 56 apples, and Samuel has 29 more apples than Frank. How many apples does Samuel have?	56 + 29 = ___	Samuel has 85 apples.
	Smaller unknown: Samuel has 85 apples. Samuel has 29 more apples than Frank. How many apples does Frank have?	29 + ___ = 85, or 85 – 29 = ___	Frank has 56 apples.

For multiplication and division, the types of problems are fundamentally different than the ones for addition and subtraction. The types of problems are *equal groups* or *repeated addition*, *area and array*, *multiplicative comparison*, and *combination*. *Equal groups problems* involve making a certain number of equal-sized groups. The three numbers involved are the number of groups (factor), size of the groups (factor), and total number of the objects (product). For example, 3×6 is 3 groups of 6 objects each. Equal groups can also be interpreted in relation to repeated additions: $3 \times 6 = 6 + 6 + 6$. *Partitive or sharing division* and *measurement or subtractive division* are two models for division modeling related to equal groups problems. *Area and array problems* involve finding the area of a rectangular area or arrangement. For example, it could involve finding the area of a rectangle that is 3 feet wide by 6 feet long, or the number of chairs involved in a 3 rows by 6 columns chairs arrangement. The *multiplicative comparison problems* involve the comparison of two quantities multiplicatively. They involve finding "how many times as much" of one quantity is compared in another quantity, or "stretching" the original quantity by a certain quantity. The *combination problems* involve different combinations that can be made from two sets like shirts and pants. The table on the next page provides examples for each type of problem.

Multiplication and Division Problems			
Type of Problem	**Example of Problems**	**Mathematical Sentences**	**Solutions**
Equal Groups or Repeated Addition	Multiplication: Oscar has 5 bags of apples with 17 apples in each bag. How many apples does Oscar have altogether?	$5 \times 17 =$ ___	Oscar has 85 apples altogether.
	Partitive or sharing division: Oscar has 85 apples. He arranges the apples into 5 bags with the same amount of apples in each bag. How many apples are contained in each bag?	$85 \div 5 =$ ___	Oscar will have 17 apples contained in each bag.
	Measurement or subtractive division: Oscar has 85 apples. He arranges the apples into bags of 17 apples each. How many bags of apples did he make?	$85 \div 17 =$ ___	Oscar will have 5 bags of 17 apples each.
Area and Array	Multiplication: Oscar has a farm of apple trees planted in 5 rows of 17 apples each arrangement. How many apple trees does he have in his farm?	$5 \times 17 =$ ___	Oscar has 85 apple trees in his farm.
	Division: Oscar planted 85 palm trees in his farm. He wants to plant the trees in 5 equal rows of palm trees. How many palm trees would he plant in each row?	$85 \div 5 =$ ___	Oscar would plant 17 palm trees in each row.
Multiplicative Comparison	Multiplication: Oscar has 17 apples and Tom has 5 times as many apples as Oscar does. How many apples does Tom have?	$5 \times 17 =$ ___	Tom has 85 apples.
	Division: Tom has 85 apples. This is 5 times as many as what Oscar has. How many apples does Oscar have?	$85 \div 5 =$ ___	Oscar has 17 apples.
Combination	Multiplication: How many combinations of shirts and pants can be made out of 5 shirts and 17 pants?	$5 \times 17 =$ ___	You can have 85 combinations.
	Division: If you have 5 shirts, how many pants are needed to make 85 combinations of pants and shirts?	$85 \div 5 =$ ___	You need 17 pants.

Checkpoint

Write a mathematical sentence, and solve each problem.

1. Gloria has 120 basketballs. She wants to put 30 basketballs into each box. How many boxes does she need?

2. Bob has 12 times as many baseball cards as his friend Carlos. Carlos has 34 baseball cards. How many baseball cards does Bob have?

3. Nancy has 123 papers and Mary has 67 papers. How many less papers does Mary have than Nancy?

4. Martha has 108 M&M's to be shared equally between her and her eight friends. How many M&M's would each one get?

Checkpoint Answers

1. $120 \div 30 = 4$. Gloria needs 4 boxes.

2. $12 \times 34 = 408$. Bob has 408 baseball cards.

3. $123 - 67 = 56$. Mary has 56 papers less than Nancy.

4. $108 \div 9 = 12$. Martha and her friends would get 12 M&M's each.

Use Estimation in Problem Solving Situations

Estimation is a very important part of problem solving. It can be used to test the reasonableness of possible solutions to problems, calculator results, and mental calculations. This is especially relevant for multiple choice items like the ones included in the FTCE. Five types of estimation strategies are described in this section: *front-end*, *rounding*, *clustering*, *compatible numbers*, and *special numbers*. The *front-end strategy* involves the left-most or highest place value digits. For example, you can estimate the sum of 345 + 675 by adding the front-end digits of these numbers, in this case 3 + 6 = 9, and estimating 900 for the sum. Using the *rounding strategy*, this same exercise would round 345 as 300 (the number is closer to 300 than to 400) and 675 as 700 (the number is closer to 700 than to 600), and find the estimated sum to be 1000 instead. The *clustering strategy* works well when the set of numbers involved are close together. For example, you can estimate the sum of 37 + 68 + 13 by noticing that 37 + 13 is equal to 50. As a result, the sum is close to 50 + 70 (by rounding 68), and the estimated sum is 120. In the *compatible* (or "friendly") *numbers strategy* you adjust the numbers in order to make them easier to work with. For instance, when dividing numbers, you would need to adjust the divisor, the dividend, or both in order to make them easier to work with mentally. For example, to estimate the answer to 73 ÷ 5 using this strategy, you need to notice that 70 is close to 73 and divisible by 5, then solve 70 ÷ 5, which is equal to 15 and your estimate. With the *special numbers strategy*, you need to look for numbers that are close to "special" values that are easy to work with, like one-half, one-fourth, or powers of ten. For example, to estimate 54% of 243, you could notice that 54% is close to one-half (or 50%), one-half of 243 is about 120.

Checkpoint

Estimate the answers to the following problems:

1. 16 + 11 + 24 + 35

2. 25 + 44 + 35 + 80 + 57 + 60

3. 367 + 532

4. 37 + 41 + 39 + 39 + 44 + 42

Checkpoint Answers

1. Using the compatible numbers strategy, 16 + 24 = 40, 40 + 35 = 75, and 75 + 11 = 86. Or, 11 + 24 = 35, 35 + 35 = 70, and 70 + 16 = 86.

2. Using the compatible numbers strategy, 25 + 80 is about 100, 44 + 57 is about 100, and 35 + 60 is about 100. So your estimate would be about 300.

3. Using the front-end strategy, 3 + 5 = 8, and the estimate would be 800. Using the rounding strategy, we would have 400 + 500 = 900.

4. Using the clustering strategy, notice that the numbers are close to 40, so a good estimate would be 6 × 40, or 240.

Apply Number Theory Concepts

Factors and **multiples** are important ideas related to number theory. Factors are any of the numbers or symbols that you multiply together to get another number or product. For example, 5 and 6 are factors of 30, because 5 × 6 = 30; similarly, 1 and 30 are factors of 30 because 1 × 30 = 30. Other possible factors of 30 are 2, 3, 10, and 15. This is because 2 × 15 = 30, and 3 × 10 = 30. So all the possible whole number factors of 30 are 1, 2, 3, 5, 6, 10, 15, and 30. Like is the case with 30, 1 and the number itself are always factors of a given number. In a similar manner, you can say that 30 is a multiple of 5 because 5 × 6 is equal to 30. So 30 is a multiple of 1, 2, 3, 5, 6, 10, 15, and 30. The number itself is always a multiple of a number. For example, the multiples of 5 are 5, 10, 15, 20, 25, 30, … There is an infinite number of multiples for a given number.

A number with exactly two whole-number factors (1 and the number itself) is considered a **prime number**. The first few prime numbers are 2, 3, 5, 7, 11, 13, and 17. On the other hand, **composite numbers** are numbers composed of several whole-number factors. For example, 30 is a composite number because it is composed of several whole-number number factors other than 1 and itself, like 2, 3, 5, 6, 10, and 15. The number 1 is not considered a prime or a composite number because it only has one whole-number factor, itself.

The **greatest common factor** (GCF) of a set of numbers is the largest number that is a factor of all the given numbers. For example, find the GCF of 30 and 20, or GCF (30, 20). First, find the factors of 30: 1, 2, 3, 5, 6, 10, 15, and 30. Second, find the factors of 20: 1, 2, 4, 5, 10, and 20. The GCF of 30 and 20 is 10, which is the largest common factor that divides both numbers evenly. The least common multiple (LCM) of a set of numbers is the smallest non-zero multiple that is divisible by all of the given numbers. For example, find the LCM of 30 and 20, or LCM (30, 20). First, find the non-zero multiples of 30: 30, 60, 90, 120,... Second, find the non-zero multiples of 20: 20, 40, 60, 80, 100, 120, ... As you can see, the least common multiple of 30 and 20 is 60. There are other common multiples of 30 and 20 like 120, but only 60 is the least common multiple of these two numbers.

The *rules of divisibility* are also important in the area of number theory. The following is a list of the most common ones:

- Division by zero is undefined or not possible.
- Only whole numbers ending in 0, 2, 4, 6, or 8 are divisible by 2. For example, 256 is divisible by 2 because it ends in 6, and 257 is not divisible by 2 because it does not end in 0, 2, 4, 6, or 8.
- Only whole numbers ending in 0 or 5 are divisible by 5. For example, 255 is divisible by 5 because it ends in 5, and 257 is not divisible by 5 because it does not end in 0 or 5.
- Only whole numbers whose digits add up to a number divisible by 3 are also divisible by 3. For example, to check if 234 is divisible by 3, add 2 + 3 + 4, which is equal to 9. Since 9 is divisible by 3, then 234 is also divisible by 3.
- Only whole numbers whose digits add up to a number divisible by 9 are also divisible by 9. For example, to check if 234 is divisible by 9, add 2 + 3 + 4, which is equal to 9. Since 9 is divisible by 9, then 234 is also divisible by 9.
- A number is divisible by 6 if it is divisible by both 2 and 3. For example, 252 has digits that add up to 9, which is divisible by 3, which makes 252 divisible by 3; it ends in 2, which makes it divisible by 2. So it is divisible by both 2 and 3, which makes it also divisible by 6.
- A number is divisible by 4 if the last two digits of the number are evenly divisible by 4. For example, 3480 has 80 as its last two digits, and 80 is divisible by 4. Therefore, 3480 is also divisible by 4.
- A number is divisible by 8 if the last three digits are evenly divisible by 8. For example, 3480 has 480 as its last digits, and 480 is divisible by 8. Therefore, 3480 is also divisible by 8.
- Only whole numbers ending in 0 are divisible by 10. For example, 250 is divisible by 10 because it ends in 0, and 257 is not divisible by 10 because it does not end in 0.

Number properties are another important aspect of number theory. The following is a list of some of the number properties for addition, subtraction, multiplication, and division:

Commutative property:	Addition: $a + b = b + a$	Multiplication: $ab = ba$
Associative property:	Addition: $a + (b + c) = (a + b) + c$	Multiplication: $a(bc) = (ab)c$
Identity property:	Additive Identity: $a + 0 = a$	Multiplicative Identity: $a \cdot 1 = a$
Inverse property:	Additive Inverse: $a + (-a) = 0$	Multiplicative Inverse: $a \cdot \left(\dfrac{1}{a}\right) = 1$
Distributive property:	Multiplication over addition:	$a(b + c) = ab + bc$

Checkpoint

1. Find the whole-number factors of 240.

2. Find the first five multiples of 35.

3. What is the GCF and LCM of 45 and 15?

4. If the GCF $(a, b) = 1$, then the LCM $(a, b) = $ _____

Checkpoint Answers

1. The whole-number factors of 240 are 1, 2, 3, 4, 5, 6, 12, 15, 16, 20, 40, 48, 60, 80, 120, and 240.

2. The first five multiples of 35 are 35, 70, 105, 140, and 175.

3. The factors of 45 are 1, 3, 5, 9, 15, and 45; and the factors of 15 are 1, 3, 5, and 15. The common factors of 45 and 15 are 1, 5, and 15. The GCF of 45 and 15 is 15, and the LCM of 45 and 15 is 45 ($5 \times 9 = 45$).

4. If the GCF $(a, b) = 1$, then the LCM $(a, b) = a \cdot b$ or ab.

Apply the Order of Operations

The order of operations must be followed when several operations are involved in mathematical sentences or algebraic expressions:

- Simplify inside the grouping characters such as parentheses, brackets, square roots, fraction bars, and others.
- Multiply out expression and exponents. You should treat exponential expressions ("powers") as multiplication.
- Do multiplication or division as you find them from left to right.
- Do addition or subtraction as you find them from left to right.
- Be careful with operations on integers, fractions, and decimals. Pay special attention to the sign (positive or negative value) of the answers.
  - For addition and subtraction, the rules are the following:
  - Adding or subtracting when at least one negative number is involved, you may think of adding as gaining, subtracting as losing, positive numbers as credits, and negative numbers as debits. Adding or gaining -8 is actually losing 8: $-4 + 9 = 5$, $4 + -9 = -5$.
  - For multiplication and division, the rules are the following:
  - Multiplying or dividing two positive or two negative numbers gives a positive value.
  - Multiplying or dividing a positive by a negative gives a negative number: $-4 \times 8 = -32$, or $-45 \div 5 = -9$.

For example, solving the expression $25 + 9 \times 5 - 7$ requires that you multiply 9×5 before performing addition and subtraction from left to right: $25 + 45 - 7 = 63$. This is different when parentheses are involved: $(25 + 9) \times 5 - 7$ requires that you add $25 + 9$, then multiply this sum by 5, and finally subtract 7: $34 \times 5 = 170$, $170 - 7 = 163$.

Checkpoint

Solve the following expressions:

1. $5^3 - 4x - 9$

2. $34 - 12 \times 3^2 - 4(3 - 7 \times 5)$

Checkpoint Answers

1. $5^3 - 4x - 9 = 125 - 4x - 9 = 116 - 4x$

2. $34 - 12 \times 3^2 - 4(3 - 7 \times 5)$

$$= 34 - 12 \times 9 - 4(3 - 35)$$
$$= 34 - 108 - 4(-32)$$
$$= 34 - 108 - (-128)$$
$$= -74 - -128$$
$$= 54$$

Competency 29: Knowledge of Geometry and Measurement

Competency Description

According to the Competencies and Skills Required for Teacher Certification in Florida, Elementary Education (available at http://www.fldoe.org/asp/ftce/pdf/60ElementaryEducationK-6.pdf) **Competency 29** for the Elementary Education (K–6) Subject Area Examination (SAE) addresses the following key indicators:

1. Analyze properties of two-dimensional shapes (e.g., area, sides, angles).
2. Apply geometric properties and relationships to solve problems (e.g., circumference, perimeter, area, volume) using appropriate strategies and formulas.
3. Apply the geometric concepts of symmetry, congruency, similarity, and transformations.
4. Identify and locate ordered pairs in a rectangular coordinate system.
5. Analyze properties of three-dimensional shapes (e.g., volume, faces, edges, vertices).
6. Compose and decompose two-dimensional and three-dimensional geometric shapes.
7. Determine how a change in length, width, height, or radius affects perimeter, circumference, area, surface area, or volume.
8. Within a given system (metric or customary), solve real-world problems involving measurement with both direct and indirect measures and make conversions to a larger or smaller unit.
9. Solve real-world problems involving estimates and exact measurements.
10. Select appropriate measurement units to solve problems.
11. Identify three-dimensional objects from two-dimensional representations of objects and vice versa.

Overview

Geometry is the study of shapes. Knowledge of geometry also includes spatial sense. In elementary grades, knowledge of geometry includes identification of **attributes**, **classifications**, and **properties** of shapes as well as connections between geometry and other areas of mathematics such as algebraic ideas of the **coordinate system**. **Measurement** is the assignment of a numerical value to an attribute of an object (that is, **length**, **area**, **perimeter**, **distance**, **volume**). Measurement is practical and pervasive in aspects of everyday life. Development measurement ideas also provide opportunities to connect concepts in mathematics together. There are approximately **16 questions** which address Competency 29. This section will address the following areas related to **Competency 29** key indicators:

- Geometry
  - Attributes, Properties, and Classifications
  - Congruence and Similarity
- Measurement
  - Geometric Measurement
  - Scientific Measurement

Geometry

Geometry is defined as "the branch of mathematics that deals with the deduction of the properties, measurement, and relationships of points, lines, angles, and figures in space from their defining conditions by means of certain assumed properties of space" (geometry, n.d.). Aspects of geometry in elementary grades include:

- Identification of attributes, properties, and classifications of two and three dimensional shapes
- Similarity and congruency

Attributes, Properties, and Classifications

Attributes are those aspects of a shape that are particular to a specific shape. For example, in the figure shown below, attributes may include that both shapes have four sides. The shape on the left is large and grey while the shape on the right is small and black.

Properties are those aspects of a shape that define the shape. For example, a property of the shapes shown above is that they each have four sides, making them both quadrilaterals. Properties define a type of shape (for example, rectangle, square, circle, and so on). Properties are true for any shape falling into that shape-type. All rectangles have right angles. All squares have four equal sides.

Classifications use the properties of shapes to lead to a hierarchical structure. Classifications are those names given which use properties to classify but also take into account the relationships between different classifications of shapes. An example of the hierarchical structure can be seen in quadrilaterals. All quadrilaterals have four sides, a defining property for the classification of a quadrilateral; however, there are also more specific names for quadrilaterals which use different defining properties. A trapezoid is a specific type of quadrilateral in which exactly one set of sides is parallel. This is a defining property for the classification of trapezoid. Likewise, parallelogram is a specific type of quadrilateral in which exactly two sets of sides are parallel. This is a defining property for the classification of parallelogram and makes parallelograms different from trapezoids.

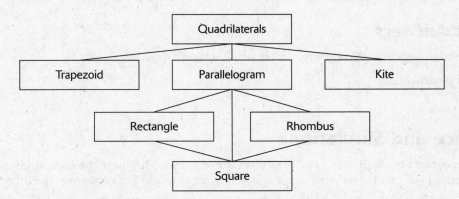

The most common classification for shapes is a **polygon** which is then further classified by the number of sides. A **polygon** is a two dimensional figure which is closed and contains at least three straight sides which meet only at corners. Under polygons, classifications are determined solely based on how many sides the shape contains, not any particular relationship between the sides (that is, they don't have to be all the same length).

Name	Number of Sides
Triangle	3
Quadrilateral	4
Pentagon	5
Hexagon	6
Heptagon	7

Name	Number of Sides
Octagon	8
Nonagon	9
Decagon	10
Dodecagon	12

All other polygons are named based on the number of sides. For example, an 11 sided polygon is an 11-gon. An 18 sided polygon is an 18-gon.

Under Triangles and Quadrilaterals, there are more specific classifications. Triangles include classifications based on angles (**acute, obtuse, right**) and on sides (**scalene, isosceles, equilateral**). Quadrilaterals include **trapezoid, kite, parallelogram, rectangle, rhombus,** and **square**.

Three dimensional figures are classified as **polyhedron** (plural polyhedra) or non-polyhedron. Polyhedra are three-dimension figures whose **faces** are all polygons. Where faces intersect are **edges**. Where edges intersect are **vertices**.

Polyhedra are divided into **prisms** and **pyramids**. **Prisms** are polyhedra which have two congruent and parallel faces. The other faces are rectangles or parallelograms. A prism is named by the shape of its base (for example, triangular prism, rectangular prism). **Pyramids** are polyhedra which have one base with all other faces intersecting at one point. Pyramids are also named by the shape of their base (for example, triangular pyramid, rectangular prism).

Nonpolyhedra include **cylinders, cones,** and **spheres.** Cylinders can be thought of as prism-like with circular bases. Cones can be thought of as pyramid-like with a circular base.

Checkpoint

1. What is the difference between attributes and properties?

2. What are the two special types of polyhedra?

3. How many sides does a nonagon have?

Checkpoint Answers

1. Attributes are to a specific shape. Properties define a set of shapes.

2. Prisms and pyramids

3. Nine

Congruence and Similarity

Two shapes are **congruent** (≅) if all aspects of the shapes are identical. They have the same side lengths, same angle measurements, area, etc. If you were to cut one shape out, it would fit exactly over the other. Same shape, same size.

Two shapes are **similar** (~) if the side lengths are proportional. Angle measurements are the same in both shapes, but the sides are proportional. Same shape, different size.

Similarity can also be thought of as a **dilation**. **Dilation** is one of four geometric transformations which include **translation** (slide), **reflection** (flip), **rotation** (turn), and **dilation.**

When shapes are congruent, side lengths and angles can be determined by examining the figures themselves. For example, if $\triangle ABC \cong \triangle DEF$, then $AB = DE$, $BC = EF$, and $AC = DF$. Likewise, $\angle A \cong \angle D$, $\angle B \cong \angle E$, and $\angle C \cong \angle F$.

Example: If $\triangle ABC \cong \triangle DEF$, find the value of x, y, and z as well as the measure of $\angle C$, $\angle D$, $\angle E$, and $\angle F$.

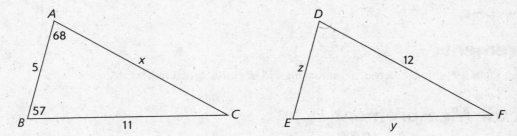

Solution: Since $\triangle ABC \cong \triangle DEF$, then $AB = DE$, $BC = EF$, and $AC = DF$. Then $x = 12$, $y = 11$, and $z = 5$. The measure of $\angle C$ can be found by using the fact that the angles of a triangle add up to 180 degrees. There are two angles given – 57 degrees and 68 degrees. These total to 125 degrees. The total is 180 degrees, so m$\angle C = 180 - 125 = 55$ degrees. Since the triangles are congruent, m$\angle D = 68$, m$\angle E = 57$, and m$\angle F = 55$.

When shapes are similar, side lengths can be determined by establishing and solving a proportion. Angle pairs are still congruent.

Example: If $\triangle ABC \sim \triangle DEF$, find the value of x and y as well as the measures of $\angle A$, $\angle B$, $\angle D$, and $\angle F$.

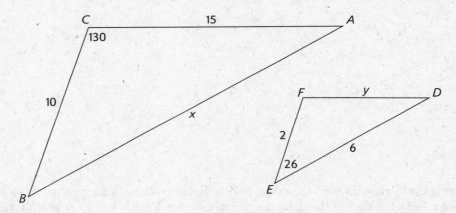

Solution: Since $\triangle ABC \sim \triangle DEF$, the sides are proportional. Set up ratios for each side and set them equal to each other. Be sure to remain consistent with the ratios. The three side ratios are: $\frac{10}{2}$, $\frac{15}{y}$, and $\frac{x}{6}$. Set these ratios equal to each other in pairs. $\frac{10}{2} = \frac{15}{y}$. If you look at the first ratio, 10 is 5 times 2. Therefore, 5 times y would be 15.

This gives $y = 3$. Similarly, $\frac{10}{2} = \frac{x}{6}$. Since 10 is 5 times 2, then x is 5 times 6, so $x = 30$. The angles are congruent in pairs. Therefore, m$\angle B = 26$ and m$\angle F = 130$. To find the measures of $\angle A$ and $\angle D$, use the fact that the angles of a triangle add to 180 degrees. So, $26 + 130 + $ m$\angle A = 180$. This gives $156 + $ m$\angle A = 180$, so measure of $\angle A = 24$. m$\angle D$ is also 24 degrees.

Checkpoint

1. True or false: The angles in similar figures are proportional.

2. Fill in the blank: Congruent shapes are_____ size and _____ shape.

3. Fill in the blank: Similar shapes are _____ size and _____ shape.

Checkpoint Answers

1. False. Sides are proportional. Angles are congruent.

2. same; same

3. different; same

Measurement

Measurement includes both geometric measurement and scientific measurement.

Geometric Measurement

Geometric measurement includes perimeter, circumference, area, and volume.

Perimeter is the distance around a polygon. It can be found by adding the lengths of all the sides of the polygon together.

Example: Find the perimeter of the shapes shown below (not drawn to scale).

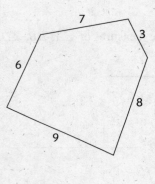
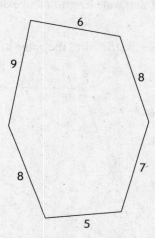

Solution: Perimeter is the distance around the shape. For the figure on the left, the perimeter is 6 + 7 + 3 + 8 + 9 which totals **33 units**. For the figure on the right, the perimeter is 6 + 8 + 7 + 5 + 8 + 9 which totals **43 units**.

Circumference is the distance around a circle. Circumference can be thought of as perimeter for circles. The ratio of the circumference to the diameter of a circle is defined as π, so $\frac{c}{d} = \pi$. This gives $C = \pi d = 2\pi r$ The value of π is approximately 3.14. For an exact value, leave the answer in terms of π (that is, 5 π units).

Example: Find the circumference of the circle shown below.

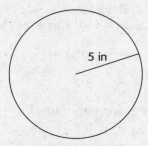

Solution: Circumference is the distance around the circle. The radius of the circle is 5 inches.
$C = 2\pi r = 2\pi(5) = 10\pi$ inches.

Area is the amount of surface which a shape covers. Area is measured in square units.

There are many formulas for finding the area of various shapes.

Rectangles: The area of a rectangle can be found by multiplying the **base** times the **height**. For any figure, the height must form a right angle with the base.

Parallelograms: If a triangle is cut off the end of a rectangle, it can be shifted to the opposite side and a parallelogram is created. The area has not changed, so the formula for the area of a parallelogram is also base times height.

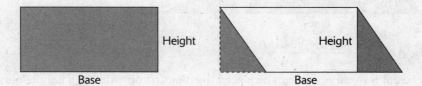

Triangles: If a diagonal is drawn in a parallelogram, two identical triangles are formed. The area of each triangle is half of the area of the parallelogram. Therefore, the formula for the area of a triangle is the base times the height divided by 2.

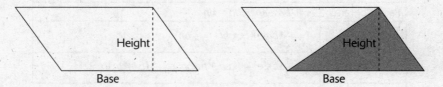

Trapezoids: The area of a trapezoid can be found by breaking the trapezoid into figures for which we know how to find the area. There are multiple ways to do this.

The figure can be divided into two triangles. The formula would then be $A = \frac{1}{2}(base_1)(height) + \frac{1}{2}(base_2)(height)$.

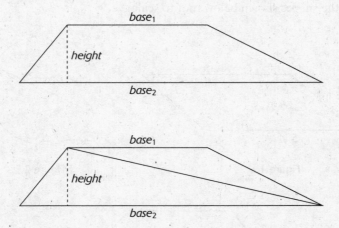

Alternatively, a rectangle can be cut out from the center of the trapezoid, leaving two triangles. If these two triangles are connected together, we can find the area of each piece to find the area of the trapezoid.

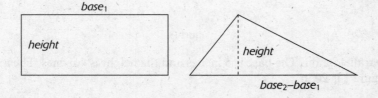

Then the area will be $A = (base_1)(height) + \frac{1}{2}(base_2 - base_1)(height)$.

One can also make a copy of the original trapezoid and connect it together with the original. This makes a parallelogram whose area is twice that of the trapezoid.

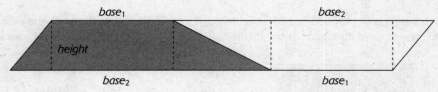

Then the area will be $A = \frac{(base_1 + base_2)(height)}{2}$.

Circles: A circle can be cut into slices that can be placed together to approximate a parallelogram. The area is then $A = \pi r^2$.

Shape	Area Formula
Rectangle	$A = (base)(height) = bh$
Parallelogram	$A = (base)(height) = bh$
Triangle	$A = \frac{1}{2}(base)(height) = \frac{1}{2}bh$
Trapezoid	$A = \frac{1}{2}(base_1 + base_2)(height) = \frac{1}{2}(b_1 + b_2)h$
Circle	$A = \pi r^2$

The areas of other shapes can often be found by breaking down the figure into shapes of which there are known formulas.

Example: Find the area of the shapes shown below (not to scale).

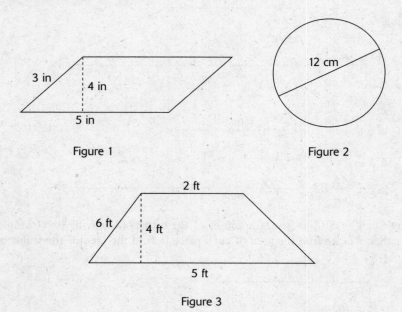

Figure 1

Figure 2

Figure 3

Solution: Figure 1 is a parallelogram. The base is 5 inches and the height is 4 inches. The area is the base times the height, so the area of figure 1 is 20 in².

Figure 2 is a circle. The diameter of the circle is 12 cm. The radius is half of the diameter, so the radius is 6 cm. The area of figure 2 is $A = \pi(6)^2 = 36\pi$ cm^2.

Figure 3 is a trapezoid. The bases are 2 feet and 5 feet. The height is 4 feet. There area is then

$$A = \frac{1}{2}(2+5)(4) = 14 \text{ ft}^2.$$

Volume is the amount of space a shape contains. Volume is measured in cubic units.

The volume of a prism can be thought of as stacking smaller prisms. The volume of the prism would then be $V = Bh$ where B is the Area of the Base and h is the height of the prism.

If a pyramid and a prism have the same base and same height, 3 pyramids will fit inside the prism. Therefore, the volume of a pyramid is $V = \frac{1}{3}Bh$.

A cylinder is similar to a prism. The base is a circle, so the volume of a cylinder is $V = (\pi r^2)h$.

A cone is similar to a pyramid. The base is a circle, so the volume of a cone is $V = \frac{1}{3}(\pi r^2)h$.

Checkpoint

1. Find the volume of a cone with a height of 4 cm and a diameter of 6 cm.

2. Find the perimeter and area of a rectangle with base 4 cm and height 8 cm.

3. Find the volume of a prism whose base is a triangle with base 3 cm and height 6 cm and the height of the prism is 7 cm.

Checkpoint Answers

1. $V = \frac{1}{3}(\pi r^2)h = \frac{1}{3}(\pi(3)^2)4 = \frac{1}{3}(9\pi)4 = 12\pi$ cm^3

2. $P = 4 + 8 + 4 + 8 = 24$ cm; $A = (b)(h) = (4)(8) = 32$ cm^2

3. $V = Bh = \left(\frac{1}{2}(3)(6)\right)(7) = (9)(7) = 63$ cm^3

Scientific Measurement

Measurement can be direct or indirect. The concept of measurement with tools like a ruler involve creating a counting unit and then repeating that unit in a countable way. If a length is said to be 3 inches long, then 1 inch is the unit and it is repeated 3 times to get a length of 3 inches. Standard measurement includes dimensions of inches, feet, yards, and miles. Metric measurement includes dimensions of centimeters, meters, and kilometers. Conversions can be made both within and between standards and metric measurement. The following conversions are helpful to know.

12 inches = 1 foot	3 feet = 1 yard	5280 feet = 1 mile
60 minutes = 1 hour	60 seconds = 1 minute	24 hours = 1 day
1 cup = 8 fluid ounces	1 pint = 2 cups	1 quart = 2 pints
1 gallon = 4 quarts	1 lb = 16 ounces	1 ton = 2000 lbs
1000 mg = 1 g	1000 g = 1 kg	1000 mL = 1 L
100 cm = 1 m	1000 mm = 1 m	1000 m = 1 km

To convert within a system of measurement, use the conversion and either multiply or divide by the conversion factor. Whether you multiply or divide is dependent upon what unit you begin with compared to what unit you would like to end with. For example, if the measure was given in feet with a goal of inches, you would multiply the number of feet by 12 inches per foot. You can think of this as multiplying by 1 as well. The units must match in the numerator and denominator to cancel themselves out.

Example: How many inches are in 4 feet?

$$4 \text{ ft} \times \frac{12 \text{ in}}{1 \text{ ft}} = 48 \text{ in}$$

Since 12 inches = 1 foot, the fraction $\frac{12 \text{ in}}{1 \text{ ft}}$ is equivalent to 1. Since the unit of feet is in both the numerator and the denominator, the unit cancels itself out.

Checkpoint

1. Convert 3 hours to minutes.

2. How many milligrams (mg) are in 3 grams (g)?

3. How many gallons are 32 cups?

Checkpoint Answers

1. $3 \text{ hours} \times \dfrac{60 \text{ minutes}}{1 \text{ hour}} = 180 \text{ minutes}$

2. $3 \text{ grams} \times \dfrac{1000 \text{ mg}}{1 \text{ g}} = 3000 \text{ mg}$

3. $32 \text{ cups} \times \dfrac{1 \text{ pint}}{2 \text{ cups}} = 16 \text{ pints}$; $16 \text{ pints} \times \dfrac{1 \text{ quart}}{2 \text{ pints}} = 8 \text{ quarts}$; $8 \text{ quarts} \times \dfrac{1 \text{ gallon}}{4 \text{ quarts}} = 2 \text{ gallons}$

Competency 30: Knowledge of Algebra

Competency Description

According to the Competencies and Skills Required for Teacher Certification in Florida, Elementary Education (available at www.fldoe.org/asp/ftce/ftcecomp.asp#fourteenth) **Competency 30** for the Elementary Education (K–6) Subject Area Examination (SAE) addresses the following key indicators:

1. Extend and generalize patterns or functional relationships.
2. Interpret, compare, and translate multiple representations of patterns and relationships by using tables, graphs, equations, expressions, and verbal descriptions.
3. Select a representation of an algebraic expression, equation, or inequality that applies to a real-world situation.
4. Demonstrate knowledge of one- and two-step linear equations and inequalities.
5. Apply the commutative, associative, and distributive properties to show that two expressions are equivalent.

Overview

Algebraic reasoning begins in elementary grades with continuing and generalizing repeating and growing patterns, identifying and using properties to show that expressions are equivalent, and representing linear equations and inequalities in real-world settings. There are approximately **6 questions** that address Competency 30. This section addresses the following areas related to **Competency 30** key indicators:

- Linear Relationships
- Properties

Linear Relationships

A relationship is linear if the relationship between two **variables** is a constant rate of change of one variable in relation to another. For example, a rate of 55 miles per hour is a constant rate of change. For each hour, the distance changes by 55 miles. Relationships can be represented in multiple ways, the most common of which are tables, graphs, and equations/expressions. Many of these relationships are first displayed as patterns.

Example: For the following pattern, find the perimeter (P) of the train in terms of the number of octagons (n).

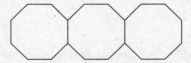

Solution: This pattern can be thought of in numerous ways. We can represent the pattern visually. If you separated each of the octagons, there would be 8 sides for each figure. This gives a perimeter of 8n for n octagons. When the octagons are connected together, two sides are lost at each connection. There is one less connection than the number or octagons. This gives a formula of $P = 8n - 2(n-1)$.

This can also be thought of visually by looking at the end shapes and the middle shapes. Each of the end shapes has 7 sides. That gives 14 sides. The shapes in the middle give 6 more sides each. There are two less octagons in the middle than the total. This gives the formula of $P = 14 + 6(n-2)$.

A table could also be used. The table may look like the following:

# octagons (n)	Perimeter (P)
1	8
2	14
3	20
4	26

For each additional octagon, the perimeter increases by 6. This means the **slope** (or rate of change) is 6. The value for 1 octagon is 8, which is 2 more than the slope, so the formula would become $P = 6n + 2$.

Checkpoint

1. A square garden measures $n \times n$. The gardener wants to place a tile border around the garden, which is 1 tile wide. How many 1×1 tiles are needed?

2. Find the number of squares (S) in the nth figure:

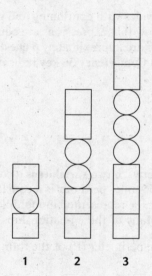

Checkpoint Answers

1. $4n + 4$; There are n tiles for each side of the garden, so 4 sides of length n. There are also 4 corners of the border that are not sides of the garden.

2. The number of squares is twice the figure number. Therefore, $S = 2n$.

Properties

There are three main properties that are necessary for symbolic manipulation of algebraic expressions.

The **commutative property** says that the order in which you add two terms together or multiply two terms together does not affect the sum or product. If the numbers are a and b, then $a + b = b + a$ and $a \times b = b \times a$. This property only applies to addition and multiplication.

The **associative property** says that when more than two terms are added together or multiplied together, the order in which the terms are paired does not affect the sum or product. If the numbers are a, b, and c, then $(a + b) + c = a + (b + c)$ and $a(bc) = (ab)c$. This property only applies to addition and multiplication.

The **distributive property** says when a sum or difference is multiplied by a common term, each part of the sum or difference can be multiplied by the common term and then added or subtracted. If the numbers are *a, b,* and *c,* then $a(b + c) = ab + ac$ and $a(b - c) = ab - ac$.

These properties can be used to demonstrate that two expressions are equivalent.

Example: Show that the expressions given to the octagon train problem are equivalent.

Solution: The equations were: $P = 8n - 2(n - 1)$, $P = 14 + 6(n - 2)$, and $P = 6n + 2$.

In the first expression, the distributive property can be used first, followed by the associative property in combining like terms $P = 8n - 2(n - 1) = 8n - 2n + 2 = 6n + 2$. The same can be done on the second expression, so $P = 14 + 6(n - 2) = 14 + 6n - 12 = 6n + (14 - 12) = 6n + 2$. These three expressions are all equivalent to each other.

These properties can also be used to solve one- and two-step linear equations and inequalities. The first approach to solving linear equations and inequalities is the idea of balance. When two expressions are equivalent, we must change them in the same ways or they do not remain equivalent. Therefore, if you subtract something from one expression, for it to continue to be equal to the other expression, you must subtract it from the second expression as well. The commutative, associative, and distributive properties can continue to be used in these situations as well.

Example: Solve $3x + 8 = 14$ for x.

First, the term with x must be isolated. In order to eliminate $+8$, 8 needs to be subtracted from each side. If you only subtracted 8 from $3x + 8$, the expressions would no longer be equal. Once $3x$ is isolated, the multiplication needs to be undone through division.

$$3x + 8 = 14$$
$$3x + 8 - 8 = 14 - 8$$
$$3x = 6$$
$$\frac{3x}{3} = \frac{6}{3}$$
$$x = 2$$

Checkpoint

1. True or false: The commutative property can be used with subtraction.

2. Fill in the blank: The associative property says that $(5 + 2) + 8 = 5 + ($_____$)$.

3. Solve: $7x = 2x + 35$ for x.

Checkpoint Answers

1. False. The commutative property only applies to addition and multiplication.

2. $2 + 8$. The associative property is used to regroup the expression.

3. $7x = 2x + 35$; Subtract $2x$ from each side, so $7x - 2x = 2x + 35 - 2x$. Then simplify $5x = 35$. Then divide both sides by 5. $\frac{5x}{5} = \frac{35}{5}$. Then simplify, so $x = 7$.

Competency 31: Knowledge of Data Analysis

Competency Description

According to the Competencies and Skills Required for Teacher Certification in Florida, Elementary Education (available at www.fldoe.org/asp/ftce/ftcecomp.asp#fourteenth) **Competency 31** for the Elementary Education (K–6) Subject Area Examination (SAE) addresses the following key indicators:

1. Demonstrate knowledge of the concepts of variability (i.e., **range**) and central tendency (i.e., **mean, median, mode**).
2. Use data to construct and analyze **frequency tables** and graphs (e.g., **bar graphs, pictographs, line graphs**).
3. Make accurate predictions and draw conclusions from data.

Overview

This section provides a look at important applications of mathematics. It involves the ideas of variability, central tendency, use of data and graphs, making predictions, and drawing conclusions. There are approximately **8 questions** that address Competency 31. This section addresses the following areas related to **Competency 31** key indicators:

- Concepts of Variability and Central Tendency
- Frequency Tables and Graphs

Concepts of Variability and Central Tendency

The range is a measure of variability. The range of a set of scores or quantities is a measure of the spread or variation of the number. It is the difference between the highest score and lowest score in the data set. The measures of central tendency of a set of quantities include the **mean, mode,** and **median**. The mean is the sum of a set of quantities divided by the total number of quantities. The median is the middle score of a set of quantities when arranged according to size (or numerical order); for an even number of scores or quantities, the median is the **average** of the middle two scores. The mode is the number that occurs with the greatest **frequency** in a set of scores. There may be one or more modes or no mode for a set of data. A data set with two modes is bimodal.

Checkpoint

This is a data set based on test scores:

78	78	67	85	92	78	95	72	72	74	85
60	95	78	92	85	65	92	66	78	78	92

Using the following set of data, find each of the following:

1. Range

2. Mode

3. Mean

4. Median

Checkpoint Answers

Order data from least to greatest: 60, 65, 66, 67, 72, 72, 74, 78, 78, 78, 78, 78, 78, 85, 85, 85, 92, 92, 92, 92, 95, 95

1. Range: 95 − 60 = 35. The range is 35.

2. Mode: 78 has the highest frequency with 6.

3. Mean: (60 + 65 + 66 + 67 + 2(72) + 74 + 6(78) + 3(85) + 4(92) + 2(95)) ÷ 22 = 1570 ÷ 22 = 71.3636 …

4. Median: The middle of the data is 11th (22 ÷ 2 = 11). Since the number of values for this data set is an even number, the median is the **average** of the middle two scores. Counting from left to right 78 is the 11th value, and counting from right to left 78 is also the 11th value. Since they are the same value, the middle number is 78. Then the median is 78.

Frequency Tables and Graphs

Frequency tables are used to organize a set of data. They show the number of pieces of data that fall within given intervals or categories. The information in the frequency table can be used to organize the data in graphs. **Bar graphs**, **line graphs**, and **pictographs** are types of statistical graphs. Bar graphs are used to compare quantities. It may be made up of all vertical bars or all horizontal bars. This type of graph is used mainly for purposes of comparison. Line graphs involve lines to show how values change over time. Pictographs are diagrams or graphs that involve pictured objects, icons, or symbols to convey ideas, or information.

Checkpoint

1. Make a frequency table using the data set given in the previous checkpoint.

2. Construct a bar graph using this data set.

Checkpoint Answers

1. Frequency table:

Scores	Frequency
60	1
65	1
66	1
67	1
72	2
74	1
78	6
85	3
92	4
95	2

2. Construct a bar graph using this data set.

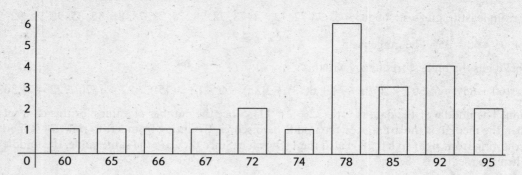

Competency 32: Knowledge of Instruction and Assessment

Competency Description

According to the Competencies and Skills Required for Teacher Certification in Florida, Elementary Education (available at http://www.fldoe.org/asp/ftce/pdf/60ElementaryEducationK-6.pdf) **Competency 32** for the Elementary Education (K–6) Subject Area Examination (SAE) addresses the following key indicators:

1. Identify a variety of appropriate instructional strategies (e.g., **cooperative learning**, **peer tutoring**, **think alouds**) for teaching specific concepts.
2. Identify ways that manipulatives, mathematical and physical models, and technology can be used in instruction.
3. Identify a variety of methods for assessing mathematical knowledge, including analyzing student thinking processes to determine strengths and weaknesses.

Overview

This section provides a look at important instructional strategies and methods. There are approximately **4 questions** that address Competency 32. This section addresses the following areas related to **Competency 32** key indicators:

- Instructional Strategies for Teaching
- Methods for Assessing Mathematical Knowledge

Instructional Strategies for Teaching

An important aspect of teaching mathematics is the ability to identify appropriate instructional strategies. These strategies provide ways to accommodate and meet students' needs, differences, and interests. **Cooperative** or **collaborative** learning are ways of organizing the classroom, supporting and facilitating students' development. In these approaches, the classroom is organized in small groups of two to five students each. The students are also assigned roles or duties to perform during activities. A more **learner-centered instruction** is being advocated and supported by the **constructivist learning theory** as framework. This is based on the premise that the student actively constructs knowledge, not in a passive manner. The process of solving problems and applying mathematics ideas becomes very relevant. The teacher's role is to facilitate the active learning of students. Students should have opportunities to answer questions involving classifying, hypothesizing, specializing (giving examples of how something works), generalizing, convincing, and analyzing. **Educational coaching** or **scaffolding** are used to provide guidance and support to a student as he or she learns, without limiting the student's investigation abilities. Other strategies are the following: **think alouds**, **peer tutoring**, problem-based instruction, simulations, games, and role playing.

Manipulatives are tools used to help students internalize mathematics concepts and skills. They help students work with abstract ideas at a concrete level. They are designed as a means to help understand mathematical abstractions. The following table provides a list of some manipulatives available for different mathematical ideas. Many of these manipulatives are now available as virtual manipulatives (also know as Applets): National Council of Teacher of Mathematics (NCTM) Illuminations (http://illuminations.nctm.org/), and National Library of Virtual Manipulatives (NLVM) (http://nlvm.usu.edu/en/nav/vLibrary.html). Calculators and computers are other important teaching tools. Geometer's Sketchpad (http://www.dynamicgeometry.com) and GeoGebra (http://www.geogebra.org) are dynamic geometry software. They allow students to construct or draw dynamic (allowing for animation and movement) geometric shapes with points, vectors, segments, lines, polygons, conic sections, and functions.

Examples of Manipulatives and Mathematical Concepts	
Manipulative	**Mathematical Concepts**
Algebra tiles	factoring, equations, estimation, integers, inequalities, operations, polynomials, similar terms, …
Attribute blocks	classifying, congruence, geometry, investigation of attributes (size, shape, color, thickness), logical reasoning, organization of data, patterns, problem solving, sequencing, similarity, sorting, symmetry, thinking skills, …
Balance scale	equality, equations, estimation, inequality, measurement, operations, mass, weight, …
Base-ten blocks	area, classification, comparing, computation (whole numbers and decimals), decimal-fractional-percent equivalencies, perimeter, metric measurement, number concepts, ordering, place value, square and cubic numbers, polynomials, sorting, …
Capacity containers	capacity, estimation, geometry, measurement, volume, …
Centimeter cubes	area, decimals, equations, fractions, mass, measurement, operations, patterns, volume, …
Chronometers	decimals, fractions, measurement, speed, time, …
Clocks	fractions, modular arithmetic, measurement, multiplication, time, weight, …
Color tiles	area, color, counting, equality, estimation, even and odd numbers, inequality, integers, measurement, number concepts, operations, patterns, percent, perimeter, probability, proportion, ratio, shapes, square numbers, spatial visualization, …
Compasses	angle measurement, constructions, geometry, measurement, proof, …
Cubes	area, averages, classification, colors, counting, cubic numbers, equalities, even and odd numbers, frequencies, graphs, inequalities, median, mean, mode, number concepts, operations, patterns, percent, perimeter, prime and composite numbers, probability, proportion, ratio, sorting, spatial visualization, square numbers, surface area, symmetry, Transformational geometry, volume, …
Cuisenaire rods	classification, comparisons, common factors and multiples, counting, decimals, estimation, even and odd numbers, factors, fractions, greatest common factors, least common multiple, logical reasoning, multiples, number concepts, operation concepts, ordering, patterns, place value, prime and composite numbers, proportions, ratios, sorting, …
Decimal squares	decimals—classification, comparing, number concepts, place value, operations, ordering, sorting, …
Fraction Tiles and Circles	fractions, operations, computation, …
Geoboards	geometric concepts, measurement, …
Hands on Equations	algebra, equations, functions, operations, …
Multilinks	area, averages, classification, colors, counting, cubic numbers, equalities, even/odd numbers, frequencies, graphs, inequalities, median, mean, mode, number concepts, operations, patterns, percent, perimeter, prime/composite numbers, probability, proportion, ratio, sorting, spatial visualization, square numbers, symmetry, transformational geometry (flips, turns, slides), volume, …
Pattern Blocks	patterns, numeration, sorting, classifying, geometry, measurement, …
Tangrams	area, geometry, measurement, …
Two-Color Chips	integers, number combinations, operations, …
Unifix cubes	area, averages, classification, colors, counting, cubic numbers, equalities, even and odd numbers, frequencies, graphs, inequalities, median, mean, mode, number concepts, operations, patterns, percent, perimeter, prime and composite numbers, probability, proportion, ratio, sorting, spatial visualization, square numbers, surface area, symmetry, Transformational geometry, volume, …

Checkpoint

Fill in the blank.

1. _____ learning is a way of organizing a classroom to support and facilitate students' development.

2. _____ help in making visible the mental processes that might be invisible to students in the reading or problem solving process.

3. _____ are concrete level tools used to help students internalize mathematics concepts.

Checkpoint Answers

1. Cooperative or Collaborative

2. Think alouds

3. Manipulatives

Methods for Assessing Mathematical Knowledge

In the *Assessment Standards for School Mathematics Assessment*, NCTM (1995) indicates that assessment is "the process of gathering evidence about a student's knowledge of, ability to use, and disposition toward mathematics and of making inferences from that evidence for a variety of purposes" (p. 3). In this manner, it should support and enhance the learning of important mathematics, and provide valuable information to both teachers and students. This implies that assessment should be more than just a score on a test. Instead, assessment should involve a more holistic view of each student's understanding, skills, and readiness. Assessment should:

- reflect the mathematics that all students need to know
- enhance mathematics learning
- be a means of fostering growth toward high expectations
- promote equity
- be an open process
- promote valid inferences about mathematics learning (NCTM)

This assessment process involves the use of valid and reliable assessment measures, and making valid inferences from the data collected. Different types of assessment and evaluative techniques should be considered and selected according to the situation at hand. One type of assessment might be appropriate for one situation and not for another. The students should be considered as a whole. Teachers should always be aware of the students' backgrounds. For example, a student may know the concept but not the words. The teachers should make sure the student understands the question or task. A variety of types of assessment, evaluative techniques, and sources of information should be considered and used with students as necessary:

- Observation (including observational checklists)
- Considerations of family life variables
- Consideration of student's readiness
- Review of school records and student files
- Oral responses
- Dramatizations
- Drawings
- Interviews
- Student's demonstrations
- Projects or project-based activities

- Checklists
- Rubrics
- Games
- Application items
- Problem solving items
- Peer evaluation
- Student writing and journals
- Self-assessment
- Portfolios
- Multiple-choice items
- Regular classroom tests
- Fill-in-the-blank with word bank

There are different useful types of assessment. The following are some of these types of assessment:

- *Objective assessment* refers to testing that requires the selection of one item from a list of choices provided with the question. This type of assessment includes true-false responses, yes-no answers, and questions with multiple-choice answers.

- *Alternative assessment* refers to other (non-traditional) options used to assess students' learning. When using this type of assessment, the teacher is not basing student progress only on the results of a single test or set of evidence. Some of the forms of this type of assessment include the portfolios, journals, notebooks, projects, and presentations.

- *Authentic assessment* is a form of alternative assessment that incorporates real-life functions and applications.

- *Performance assessment* (often used interchangeably with authentic assessment) requires the completion of a task, project, or investigation, communicates information, or constructs a response that demonstrates knowledge or understanding of a skill or concept.

- *Naturalistic assessment* involves evaluation that is based on the natural setting of the classroom. It involves the observation of students' performance and behavior in an informal context.

- *Achievement test battery* is composed of sub-tests of mathematics concepts and skills and usually includes technical aspects of mathematics.

- *Standardized tests* include content areas, and provide useful information about students' mathematics skills. Their validity and reliability depends on three basic assumptions: students have been equally exposed to the test content in an instructional program, students know the language of the test directions and the test responses, and students just like those taking the test have been included in the standardization samples to establish norms and make inferences.

- *Diagnostic tests* are used within the diagnostic-prescriptive teaching of mathematics. This process is an instructional model that consists of diagnosis, prescription, instruction, and on-going assessment. The diagnostic test results could help identify specific problem areas. The tests can be teacher-made or commercially developed.

A note of clarification might be important at this point. We should also consider what any type of assessment and learning of mathematics model is not:

- Learning mathematics is not mastering a fixed set of basic skills, and, as a result, mathematics assessment should not focus on whether students have mastered these basic skills or not.

- Problem solving and application of mathematics does not come only after mastery of skills. The application of mathematics and the implementation of interesting contexts should be used to motivate and engage students. A natural learning should provide the basis for teaching, learning, and assessment.

- We should not teach then assess. Assessment should be ongoing and summative. The best assessment also instructs and the best instructional tasks are rich diagnostic opportunities.

Checkpoint

1. Fill in the blank: _____ assessment is a form of alternative assessment that incorporates real-life functions and applications.

2. True or false: Problem solving and application of mathematics should come only after mastery of skills.

3. True or false: Assessment should be more than just a score on a test.

Checkpoint Answers

1. Authentic

2. False. Problem solving and application of mathematics does not come only after mastery of skills.

3. True.

Summary

The Mathematics section (Competencies 28–32) encompasses a variety of sub-competencies related to the basic knowledge required of educators teaching elementary age students. Knowledge of numbers and operations entails an understanding of types of numbers including whole numbers, rational numbers, decimals, and integers and their use in solving mathematical problems. Performing operations on all types of numbers is included as well. Knowledge of geometry and measurement includes aspects of spatial reasoning including recognizing and categorizing two and three dimensional shapes, using geometric properties like similarity and congruence, and computing geometric and scientific measurement in the form of perimeter, area, volume, and the relationships between systems of measurement. Knowledge of algebra entails an understanding of the development of algebraic ideas including patterning, representations, solving equations, and the use of properties of numbers. Knowledge of data analysis entails using data to draw conclusions by constructing and analyzing graphic representations of data and measures of central tendency. Finally, knowledge of instruction and assessment highlights aspects of classroom interactions related to best practices in mathematics teaching and mathematics assessment.

This section reflects the skills required in this area for Teacher Certification in Florida, Elementary Education (available at http://www.fldoe.org/asp/ftce/pdf/60ElementaryEducationK-6.pdf). You should use the information in this section to complement your previous knowledge in the areas of mathematics. The general review of Mathematics (Competencies 28–32) provided in this chapter should allow you to explore areas of strength and need that you might still need to review. As indicated before, sample questions for the competency area as a whole appear in the next section of the chapter. Answers and explanations follow the sample questions. These sections should provide an opportunity for further practice and analysis.

Sample Questions

1. $\sqrt{144} =$ _____

   A. 720
   B. 288
   C. 72
   D. 12

2. The dimensions of a rectangular garden are 14 feet by 12 feet. What will happen to the area of the garden if the length is doubled and the width is tripled?

   A. 2 times larger
   B. 3 times larger
   C. 5 times larger
   D. 6 times larger

3. $(5^4)^2 =$ ___

   A. 5^2
   B. $\sqrt{5}$
   C. 5^8
   D. 5^6

4. What is the 8th term in the following pattern: 2, 4, 8, 16, ...?

   A. 32
   B. 64
   C. 128
   D. 256

5. $\frac{3}{10} \times \frac{5}{9} =$ _____

   A. $\frac{15}{9}$
   B. $\frac{8}{19}$
   C. $\frac{8}{90}$
   D. $\frac{1}{6}$

6. $5.03 \times 4.9 =$ ___

   A. 9.93
   B. 246.47
   C. 24.647
   D. 2.4647

7. Alternative assessment may include

   A.   multiple choice items.
   B.   portfolios.
   C.   true/false items.
   D.   all of the above.

8. What is the least common multiple of 60 and 90?

   A.   30
   B.   180
   C.   360
   D.   90

9. Mike made the following table based on the number of hours he worked per day last month. Find the median number of hours he worked last month.

Number of Hours	Tally	Frequency
7	### ### //	12
8	///	3
9	//	2
10	### //	7

   A.   7 hours
   B.   8 hours
   C.   7.5 hours
   D.   2.5 hours

10. Select the most appropriate unit for measuring the height of an adult basketball player.

   A.   centimeters
   B.   feet
   C.   inches
   D.   kilometers

11. Change the fraction $\frac{3}{8}$ to a decimal.

   A.   0.375
   B.   0.0375
   C.   37.5
   D.   3.75

12. A rectangle can also be called which of the following?

   A.   Parallelogram
   B.   Pentagon
   C.   Trapezoid
   D.   Triangle

13. What is the greatest common factor of 60 and 90?

   A. 10
   B. 6
   C. 15
   D. 30

14. Find the mean for the data set given in the following table. Round your answer to the closest hundredth.

Number of Hours	Frequency
1	23
2	13
3	2
4	7

   A. 20.75 hours
   B. 2.5 hours
   C. 11.25
   D. 1.84 hours

15. A mason was tiling a living room. To add to the appearance of the floor, the designer decided to use similar triangles within the tile.

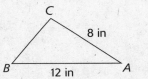

Given $\triangle ABC \sim \triangle DEF$, find the length of DF.

   A. 2 inches
   B. 4 inches
   C. 6 inches
   D. 8 inches

16. $(3^2)^3 =$ ___

   A. 729
   B. 18
   C. 2187
   D. 27

17. Which of the following expressions is NOT equivalent to $4 + 2(x + 5)$.

   A. $4 + 2x + 10$
   B. $2(x + 5) + 4$
   C. $4 + 2x + 5$
   D. $4 + 2(5 + x)$

18. Solve $2x - 6 = 14$.

   A. $x = 10$
   B. $x = 4$
   C. $x = 20$
   D. $x = 16$

19. Tom is a first grade student playing with pattern blocks and making geometric patterns. Tom is working at the _____ cognitive level.

   A. concrete
   B. representational
   C. abstract
   D. symbolic

Answer Explanations for Sample Questions

1. **D.** Competency 28. This question is about finding the square root of 144, which means that you need to find a number that when multiplied by itself you get 144. The number is 12 because $12 \times 12 = 144$.

2. **D.** Competency 29. The area of the original garden is 14 feet $\times$ 12 feet = 168 feet^2. If the length is doubled and the width is tripled, the dimensions would then be 28 feet $\times$ 36 feet. This gives an area of 1008 feet^2. 1008/168 = 6 times. Alternately, the area of a rectangle is (length) $\times$ (width). This would become (2 $\times$ length) $\times$ (3 $\times$ width). Using the associative property, this can be written as $2 \times 3 \times$ length $\times$ width = $6 \times$ length $\times$ width.

3. **C.** Competency 28. In this case, you multiply the exponents $4 \times 2 = 8$.

4. **D.** Competency 30. Each term is doubled of the term before, so the next four terms are 32, 64, 128, and 256. The eighth term in the pattern is 256.

5. **D.** Competency 28. $\frac{3}{10} \times \frac{5}{9} = \frac{(3 \times 5)}{(10 \times 9)} = \frac{15}{90}, \frac{(15 \div 15)}{(90 \div 15)} = \frac{1}{6}$, or $\frac{3}{10} \times \frac{5}{9} = \frac{(3 \times 5)}{(10 \times 9)} = \frac{\overset{1}{\cancel{3}}}{\underset{2}{\cancel{10}}} \times \frac{\overset{1}{\cancel{5}}}{\underset{3}{\cancel{9}}} = \frac{1}{6}$.

6. **C.** Competency 28. One way to solve this problem is by estimating the answer: $5 \times 5 = 25$. The closest answer to 25 is 24.647.

7. **B.** Competency 32. The question asks about a type of alternative assessment so the only choice of this type is portfolios. The others are traditional types of assessment.

8. **B.** Competency 28. The multiples of 60 are 60, 120, 180, 240, 300, 360, ... The multiples of 90 are 90, 180, 270, 360, ... The least common multiple is 180. Or, using prime factorization: $60 = 2^2 \times 3 \times 5$, and $90 = 2 \times 3^2 \times 5$. The least common multiples are $2^2 \times 3^2 \times 5 = 4 \times 9 \times 5 = 180$.

9. **C.** Competency 31. The median is a measure of central tendency of data. The median of a set of data is the middle number of the ordered data, or the mean of the middle two numbers:

7, 7, 7, 7, 7, 7, 7, 7, 7, 7, 7, **7, 8,** 8, 8, 9, 9, 10, 10, 10, 10, 10, 10, 10

The median divides the data in half. In this case, the middle of the data is between the 11th and the 12th number because we have 24 numbers: $(7+8)/2 = 7.5$. The median number of hours that Mike worked last month is 7.5 hours.

10. **B.** Competency 29. Feet is the best unit to measure the height of an adult basketball player. Centimeters and inches are smaller than necessary. Kilometers are longer than necessary.

11. **A.** Competency 28. Divide 3 by 8 to get the decimal, which is equal to 0.375.

12. **A.** Competency 29. A rectangle is a special type of parallelogram. A pentagon has five sides. A trapezoid only has one set of parallel sides. A triangle has three sides.

13. **D.** Competency 28. The factors of 60 are 1, 2, 3, 4, 5, 6, 10, 12, 15, 20, 30, and 60. The factors of 90 are 1, 2, 3, 5, 6, 9, 10, 15, 18, 30, 45, and 90. The greatest common factor of 60 and 90 is 30. Or, using prime factorization:

$60 = 2^2 \times 3 \times 5$, and $90 = 2 \times 3^2 \times 5$. The common factors are $2 \times 3 \times 5 = 30$.

14. **D.** Competency 31. To find the mean, multiply each number of hours by its frequency, add the products, and divide the sum by the total frequency (in this case 45). $(23 \cdot 1 + 13 \cdot 2 + 2 \cdot 3 + 7 \cdot 4) \div 45 = 83 \div 45 \approx 1.84$ (to the closest hundredth). The mean is 1.84 hours.

15. **B.** Competency 29. Since the triangles are similar, the sides are proportional in length. The length of a side in the smaller triangle (triangle *DEF*) is half the length of the corresponding side of the larger triangle (triangle *ABC*). Since side *AC* corresponds with side *DF*, *DF* is half of *AC*. *AC* is 8 inches, so *DF* is 4 inches.

16. **A.** Competency 28. $(3^2)^3 = (3 \times 3)^3 = 9^3 = 9 \times 9 \times 9 = 729$.

17. **C.** Competency 30. Choice A uses the distributive property $2(x + 5) = 2x + 2 \times 5 = 2x + 10$. Choice B uses the commutative property in switching the order of adding 4 and $2(x + 5)$. Choice D uses the commutative property to switch the order of $x + 5$. Choice C does not use the distributive property correctly.

18. **A.** Competency 30. First add 6 to both sides, so $2x = 20$. Then divide both sides by 2, so $x = 10$.

19. **A.** Competency 32. Since the student is using pattern blocks, which are concrete objects, he is working at the concrete level.

PART II

FULL-LENGTH PRACTICE TESTS

Practice Test 1

The test which follows is approximately the length of the FTCE: Elementary Education (K–6) Subject Area Examination. Allow yourself 2 hours and 30 minutes to complete the practice test. Record your answers on the Answer Sheet. When you are finished, check your answers. Detailed solutions follow the test.

Language Arts and Reading

1. Ⓐ Ⓑ Ⓒ Ⓓ
2. Ⓐ Ⓑ Ⓒ Ⓓ
3. Ⓐ Ⓑ Ⓒ Ⓓ
4. Ⓐ Ⓑ Ⓒ Ⓓ
5. Ⓐ Ⓑ Ⓒ Ⓓ
6. Ⓐ Ⓑ Ⓒ Ⓓ
7. Ⓐ Ⓑ Ⓒ Ⓓ
8. Ⓐ Ⓑ Ⓒ Ⓓ
9. Ⓐ Ⓑ Ⓒ Ⓓ
10. Ⓐ Ⓑ Ⓒ Ⓓ
11. Ⓐ Ⓑ Ⓒ Ⓓ
12. Ⓐ Ⓑ Ⓒ Ⓓ
13. Ⓐ Ⓑ Ⓒ Ⓓ
14. Ⓐ Ⓑ Ⓒ Ⓓ
15. Ⓐ Ⓑ Ⓒ Ⓓ
16. Ⓐ Ⓑ Ⓒ Ⓓ
17. Ⓐ Ⓑ Ⓒ Ⓓ
18. Ⓐ Ⓑ Ⓒ Ⓓ
19. Ⓐ Ⓑ Ⓒ Ⓓ
20. Ⓐ Ⓑ Ⓒ Ⓓ
21. Ⓐ Ⓑ Ⓒ Ⓓ
22. Ⓐ Ⓑ Ⓒ Ⓓ
23. Ⓐ Ⓑ Ⓒ Ⓓ
24. Ⓐ Ⓑ Ⓒ Ⓓ
25. Ⓐ Ⓑ Ⓒ Ⓓ
26. Ⓐ Ⓑ Ⓒ Ⓓ
27. Ⓐ Ⓑ Ⓒ Ⓓ
28. Ⓐ Ⓑ Ⓒ Ⓓ
29. Ⓐ Ⓑ Ⓒ Ⓓ
30. Ⓐ Ⓑ Ⓒ Ⓓ
31. Ⓐ Ⓑ Ⓒ Ⓓ
32. Ⓐ Ⓑ Ⓒ Ⓓ
33. Ⓐ Ⓑ Ⓒ Ⓓ
34. Ⓐ Ⓑ Ⓒ Ⓓ
35. Ⓐ Ⓑ Ⓒ Ⓓ
36. Ⓐ Ⓑ Ⓒ Ⓓ
37. Ⓐ Ⓑ Ⓒ Ⓓ
38. Ⓐ Ⓑ Ⓒ Ⓓ
39. Ⓐ Ⓑ Ⓒ Ⓓ
40. Ⓐ Ⓑ Ⓒ Ⓓ

41. Ⓐ Ⓑ Ⓒ Ⓓ
42. Ⓐ Ⓑ Ⓒ Ⓓ
43. Ⓐ Ⓑ Ⓒ Ⓓ
44. Ⓐ Ⓑ Ⓒ Ⓓ
45. Ⓐ Ⓑ Ⓒ Ⓓ
46. Ⓐ Ⓑ Ⓒ Ⓓ
47. Ⓐ Ⓑ Ⓒ Ⓓ
48. Ⓐ Ⓑ Ⓒ Ⓓ
49. Ⓐ Ⓑ Ⓒ Ⓓ

Social Science

1. Ⓐ Ⓑ Ⓒ Ⓓ
2. Ⓐ Ⓑ Ⓒ Ⓓ
3. Ⓐ Ⓑ Ⓒ Ⓓ
4. Ⓐ Ⓑ Ⓒ Ⓓ
5. Ⓐ Ⓑ Ⓒ Ⓓ
6. Ⓐ Ⓑ Ⓒ Ⓓ
7. Ⓐ Ⓑ Ⓒ Ⓓ
8. Ⓐ Ⓑ Ⓒ Ⓓ
9. Ⓐ Ⓑ Ⓒ Ⓓ
10. Ⓐ Ⓑ Ⓒ Ⓓ
11. Ⓐ Ⓑ Ⓒ Ⓓ
12. Ⓐ Ⓑ Ⓒ Ⓓ
13. Ⓐ Ⓑ Ⓒ Ⓓ
14. Ⓐ Ⓑ Ⓒ Ⓓ
15. Ⓐ Ⓑ Ⓒ Ⓓ
16. Ⓐ Ⓑ Ⓒ Ⓓ
17. Ⓐ Ⓑ Ⓒ Ⓓ
18. Ⓐ Ⓑ Ⓒ Ⓓ
19. Ⓐ Ⓑ Ⓒ Ⓓ
20. Ⓐ Ⓑ Ⓒ Ⓓ
21. Ⓐ Ⓑ Ⓒ Ⓓ
22. Ⓐ Ⓑ Ⓒ Ⓓ
23. Ⓐ Ⓑ Ⓒ Ⓓ
24. Ⓐ Ⓑ Ⓒ Ⓓ
25. Ⓐ Ⓑ Ⓒ Ⓓ
26. Ⓐ Ⓑ Ⓒ Ⓓ
27. Ⓐ Ⓑ Ⓒ Ⓓ
28. Ⓐ Ⓑ Ⓒ Ⓓ
29. Ⓐ Ⓑ Ⓒ Ⓓ
30. Ⓐ Ⓑ Ⓒ Ⓓ
31. Ⓐ Ⓑ Ⓒ Ⓓ
32. Ⓐ Ⓑ Ⓒ Ⓓ
33. Ⓐ Ⓑ Ⓒ Ⓓ
34. Ⓐ Ⓑ Ⓒ Ⓓ
35. Ⓐ Ⓑ Ⓒ Ⓓ
36. Ⓐ Ⓑ Ⓒ Ⓓ
37. Ⓐ Ⓑ Ⓒ Ⓓ
38. Ⓐ Ⓑ Ⓒ Ⓓ
39. Ⓐ Ⓑ Ⓒ Ⓓ
40. Ⓐ Ⓑ Ⓒ Ⓓ

Music, Visual Arts, Physical Education, and Health

1. Ⓐ Ⓑ Ⓒ Ⓓ
2. Ⓐ Ⓑ Ⓒ Ⓓ
3. Ⓐ Ⓑ Ⓒ Ⓓ
4. Ⓐ Ⓑ Ⓒ Ⓓ
5. Ⓐ Ⓑ Ⓒ Ⓓ
6. Ⓐ Ⓑ Ⓒ Ⓓ
7. Ⓐ Ⓑ Ⓒ Ⓓ
8. Ⓐ Ⓑ Ⓒ Ⓓ
9. Ⓐ Ⓑ Ⓒ Ⓓ
10. Ⓐ Ⓑ Ⓒ Ⓓ
11. Ⓐ Ⓑ Ⓒ Ⓓ
12. Ⓐ Ⓑ Ⓒ Ⓓ
13. Ⓐ Ⓑ Ⓒ Ⓓ
14. Ⓐ Ⓑ Ⓒ Ⓓ
15. Ⓐ Ⓑ Ⓒ Ⓓ
16. Ⓐ Ⓑ Ⓒ Ⓓ
17. Ⓐ Ⓑ Ⓒ Ⓓ
18. Ⓐ Ⓑ Ⓒ Ⓓ
19. Ⓐ Ⓑ Ⓒ Ⓓ
20. Ⓐ Ⓑ Ⓒ Ⓓ
21. Ⓐ Ⓑ Ⓒ Ⓓ
22. Ⓐ Ⓑ Ⓒ Ⓓ
23. Ⓐ Ⓑ Ⓒ Ⓓ
24. Ⓐ Ⓑ Ⓒ Ⓓ
25. Ⓐ Ⓑ Ⓒ Ⓓ
26. Ⓐ Ⓑ Ⓒ Ⓓ
27. Ⓐ Ⓑ Ⓒ Ⓓ
28. Ⓐ Ⓑ Ⓒ Ⓓ
29. Ⓐ Ⓑ Ⓒ Ⓓ
30. Ⓐ Ⓑ Ⓒ Ⓓ
31. Ⓐ Ⓑ Ⓒ Ⓓ
32. Ⓐ Ⓑ Ⓒ Ⓓ
33. Ⓐ Ⓑ Ⓒ Ⓓ
34. Ⓐ Ⓑ Ⓒ Ⓓ
35. Ⓐ Ⓑ Ⓒ Ⓓ
36. Ⓐ Ⓑ Ⓒ Ⓓ
37. Ⓐ Ⓑ Ⓒ Ⓓ
38. Ⓐ Ⓑ Ⓒ Ⓓ
39. Ⓐ Ⓑ Ⓒ Ⓓ
40. Ⓐ Ⓑ Ⓒ Ⓓ

41. Ⓐ Ⓑ Ⓒ Ⓓ
42. Ⓐ Ⓑ Ⓒ Ⓓ
43. Ⓐ Ⓑ Ⓒ Ⓓ
44. Ⓐ Ⓑ Ⓒ Ⓓ
45. Ⓐ Ⓑ Ⓒ Ⓓ

Science and Technology

1 Ⓐ Ⓑ Ⓒ Ⓓ
2 Ⓐ Ⓑ Ⓒ Ⓓ
3 Ⓐ Ⓑ Ⓒ Ⓓ
4 Ⓐ Ⓑ Ⓒ Ⓓ
5 Ⓐ Ⓑ Ⓒ Ⓓ
6 Ⓐ Ⓑ Ⓒ Ⓓ
7 Ⓐ Ⓑ Ⓒ Ⓓ
8 Ⓐ Ⓑ Ⓒ Ⓓ
9 Ⓐ Ⓑ Ⓒ Ⓓ
10 Ⓐ Ⓑ Ⓒ Ⓓ
11 Ⓐ Ⓑ Ⓒ Ⓓ
12 Ⓐ Ⓑ Ⓒ Ⓓ
13 Ⓐ Ⓑ Ⓒ Ⓓ
14 Ⓐ Ⓑ Ⓒ Ⓓ
15 Ⓐ Ⓑ Ⓒ Ⓓ
16 Ⓐ Ⓑ Ⓒ Ⓓ
17 Ⓐ Ⓑ Ⓒ Ⓓ
18 Ⓐ Ⓑ Ⓒ Ⓓ
19 Ⓐ Ⓑ Ⓒ Ⓓ
20 Ⓐ Ⓑ Ⓒ Ⓓ
21 Ⓐ Ⓑ Ⓒ Ⓓ
22 Ⓐ Ⓑ Ⓒ Ⓓ
23 Ⓐ Ⓑ Ⓒ Ⓓ
24 Ⓐ Ⓑ Ⓒ Ⓓ
25 Ⓐ Ⓑ Ⓒ Ⓓ
26 Ⓐ Ⓑ Ⓒ Ⓓ
27 Ⓐ Ⓑ Ⓒ Ⓓ
28 Ⓐ Ⓑ Ⓒ Ⓓ
29 Ⓐ Ⓑ Ⓒ Ⓓ
30 Ⓐ Ⓑ Ⓒ Ⓓ
31 Ⓐ Ⓑ Ⓒ Ⓓ
32 Ⓐ Ⓑ Ⓒ Ⓓ
33 Ⓐ Ⓑ Ⓒ Ⓓ
34 Ⓐ Ⓑ Ⓒ Ⓓ
35 Ⓐ Ⓑ Ⓒ Ⓓ
36 Ⓐ Ⓑ Ⓒ Ⓓ
37 Ⓐ Ⓑ Ⓒ Ⓓ
38 Ⓐ Ⓑ Ⓒ Ⓓ
39 Ⓐ Ⓑ Ⓒ Ⓓ
40 Ⓐ Ⓑ Ⓒ Ⓓ

41 Ⓐ Ⓑ Ⓒ Ⓓ
42 Ⓐ Ⓑ Ⓒ Ⓓ
43 Ⓐ Ⓑ Ⓒ Ⓓ
44 Ⓐ Ⓑ Ⓒ Ⓓ
45 Ⓐ Ⓑ Ⓒ Ⓓ

Mathematics

1 Ⓐ Ⓑ Ⓒ Ⓓ
2 Ⓐ Ⓑ Ⓒ Ⓓ
3 Ⓐ Ⓑ Ⓒ Ⓓ
4 Ⓐ Ⓑ Ⓒ Ⓓ
5 Ⓐ Ⓑ Ⓒ Ⓓ
6 Ⓐ Ⓑ Ⓒ Ⓓ
7 Ⓐ Ⓑ Ⓒ Ⓓ
8 Ⓐ Ⓑ Ⓒ Ⓓ
9 Ⓐ Ⓑ Ⓒ Ⓓ
10 Ⓐ Ⓑ Ⓒ Ⓓ
11 Ⓐ Ⓑ Ⓒ Ⓓ
12 Ⓐ Ⓑ Ⓒ Ⓓ
13 Ⓐ Ⓑ Ⓒ Ⓓ
14 Ⓐ Ⓑ Ⓒ Ⓓ
15 Ⓐ Ⓑ Ⓒ Ⓓ
16 Ⓐ Ⓑ Ⓒ Ⓓ
17 Ⓐ Ⓑ Ⓒ Ⓓ
18 Ⓐ Ⓑ Ⓒ Ⓓ
19 Ⓐ Ⓑ Ⓒ Ⓓ
20 Ⓐ Ⓑ Ⓒ Ⓓ
21 Ⓐ Ⓑ Ⓒ Ⓓ
22 Ⓐ Ⓑ Ⓒ Ⓓ
23 Ⓐ Ⓑ Ⓒ Ⓓ
24 Ⓐ Ⓑ Ⓒ Ⓓ
25 Ⓐ Ⓑ Ⓒ Ⓓ
26 Ⓐ Ⓑ Ⓒ Ⓓ
27 Ⓐ Ⓑ Ⓒ Ⓓ
28 Ⓐ Ⓑ Ⓒ Ⓓ
29 Ⓐ Ⓑ Ⓒ Ⓓ
30 Ⓐ Ⓑ Ⓒ Ⓓ
31 Ⓐ Ⓑ Ⓒ Ⓓ
32 Ⓐ Ⓑ Ⓒ Ⓓ
33 Ⓐ Ⓑ Ⓒ Ⓓ
34 Ⓐ Ⓑ Ⓒ Ⓓ
35 Ⓐ Ⓑ Ⓒ Ⓓ
36 Ⓐ Ⓑ Ⓒ Ⓓ
37 Ⓐ Ⓑ Ⓒ Ⓓ
38 Ⓐ Ⓑ Ⓒ Ⓓ
39 Ⓐ Ⓑ Ⓒ Ⓓ
40 Ⓐ Ⓑ Ⓒ Ⓓ

41 Ⓐ Ⓑ Ⓒ Ⓓ
42 Ⓐ Ⓑ Ⓒ Ⓓ
43 Ⓐ Ⓑ Ⓒ Ⓓ
44 Ⓐ Ⓑ Ⓒ Ⓓ
45 Ⓐ Ⓑ Ⓒ Ⓓ

Language Arts and Reading

1. When a teacher performs a think aloud, he is essentially

   A.   asking questions after the reading.
   B.   asking questions before the reading.
   C.   "talking to the text" during the reading.
   D.   none of the above

2. Which of the following would not be considered Folklore?

   A.   Nursery rhymes
   B.   fairy tales
   C.   biography
   D.   myths

3. When an author attempts to convince the reader that a point is valid, they are using what mode of writing?

   A.   descriptive
   B.   expository
   C.   narrative
   D.   persuasive

4. After a Kindergarten student named Amy draws a picture in her daily journal, she uses a string of random letters to communicate in writing, what she has drawn. The next step in her development as a writer would be

   A.   labeling her drawing with appropriate initial letters.
   B.   writing a paragraph about what she has drawn.
   C.   writing a complete sentence.
   D.   copying words from around the room that have nothing to do with her drawing.

5. Which of the following would be considered a formal assessment?

   A.   anecdotal notes
   B.   running record
   C.   quiz
   D.   criterion-referenced test

6. Classroom news and literature response _____ have become common web-based activities in elementary classrooms.

   A.   pdf files
   B.   digital stories
   C.   blogs
   D.   all of the above

7. Questioning and retelling are two strategies that enhance _____ skills.

   A.   listening and speaking
   B.   comprehension
   C.   word recognition
   D.   both A and B

8. Visual media refers to

   A.   any print material including books, journals, and magazines.
   B.   anything that is not literally printed; television, video, some radio broadcasts, etc.
   C.   illustrations created by an artist.
   D.   the newspaper.

9. A group of third graders are finishing up *All About Me* stories as an introductory assignment at the beginning of the year. To encourage them to revise their work and include appropriate content, the teacher provides each child with a rubric. Which of the following rubrics would assist students in the revision of their content?

   A.   a rubric focusing on punctuation and grammar
   B.   a rubric focusing on the traits of writing like organization, word choice, and the use of supporting details
   C.   a rubric that ensures each sentence has subject-verb agreement
   D.   a rubric that encourages them to check all words for correct spelling

10. During a read aloud, a kindergarten student comments that the teacher is reading the pictures and not the words in the book. This child is demonstrating a lack of understanding in

    A. letter knowledge.
    B. alphabetic principle.
    C. concepts of print.
    D. phonemic awareness.

11. Which of the following is an example of onset-rime segments?

    A. sh-ut
    B. butter-fly
    C. tell-ing
    D. pre-view

12. Which of the following is not a basic concept of print?

    A. directionality
    B. title page
    C. illustrations
    D. captions

13. Knowledge of individual words in sentences, syllables, onset-rime segments, and the awareness of individual phonemes in words is known as

    A. phonics.
    B. phonological awareness.
    C. phoneme segmentation.
    D. phoneme manipulation.

14. A grapheme is defined as

    A. the first consonant or groups of consonants that come before the first vowel in a syllable.
    B. the first vowel sound and any others that follow it in a syllable.
    C. a letter or group of letters representing one sound.
    D. a graphic organizer used for comprehension.

15. The literary device defined as two or more words or syllables, near each other, with the same beginning consonant is

    A. hyperbole.
    B. alliteration.
    C. satire.
    D. pun.

16. The teacher has organized her classroom to allow for small groups. Students are listening to books on tape or cd, reading poetry, and responding to quality literature in writing. This is an example of what organizational format?

    A. literature circles
    B. shared reading
    C. interactive writing
    D. reading centers/stations

17. An authentic arrowhead found on a Native American reservation is

    A. a valuable teaching tool.
    B. an example of a primary source.
    C. an artifact.
    D. all of the above

18. In what grade are students typically taught to write in cursive?

    A. first
    B. third
    C. fourth
    D. Kindergarten

19. The local school board has announced that they plan to do away with music classes in all of the district's elementary schools. The students and teachers at each school are outraged. What would be the best form of written communication to share their feelings and wishes with the school board?

    A. narrative
    B. descriptive
    C. persuasive
    D. expository

20. The workshop approach to organizing your classroom provides time to

    A. meet with small groups of students to meet individual and small group needs.
    B. work on your lesson plans.
    C. offer a great deal of whole group instruction.
    D. meet briefly with every student in your classroom.

21. True literature circles consist of four to six children

    A. all reading the same book they each chose based upon interest.

    B. completing worksheets about a book they are reading while sitting at a round table.

    C. all reading a text on the same reading level, with teacher assistance.

    D. reading different books but talking about them in a small group.

22. A teacher encourages her students to brainstorm ideas about a topic of interest that they might like to write about. Brainstorming takes place during what phase of the writing process?

    A. drafting
    B. revising
    C. editing
    D. prewriting

23. Indentify the literary device used in the following example:

She crawled as slow as a turtle.

    A. pun
    B. hyperbole
    C. simile
    D. alliteration

24. During the editing phase of writing the writer should

    A. edit his work for content.
    B. edit his work for mechanical and grammatical errors.
    C. simply read over his work with no intention of making changes.
    D. copy the draft exactly to create a final, published piece.

25. Text explicit questions are also known as

    A. think and search questions.
    B. inferences.
    C. right there questions.
    D. reader and author questions.

26. Which of the following instructional methods aid fluency?

    A. repetitive or repeated reading
    B. echo reading
    C. choral reading
    D. all of the above

27. More than 70% of a second grade class scored at high risk on an oral reading fluency check. The teacher would be wise to incorporate which of the following instructional methods into her daily lesson plans?

    A. daily independent silent reading
    B. round robin reading
    C. popcorn reading
    D. repeated readings of familiar text

28. The element of legible handwriting that refers to consistency of the pencil strokes is

    A. letter alignment.
    B. line quality.
    C. letter formation.
    D. vertical orientation.

29. A student read a 200 word piece in 4:45 with 6 recorded errors. What would her accuracy rate be for that reading?

    A. 42 WCPM
    B. 40.9 WCPM
    C. 40 WCPM
    D. 41.8 WCPM

30. To summarize either orally or in written form is to

    A. concisely paraphrase what has been read.
    B. expand upon the author's main idea.
    C. infer the author's purpose.
    D. none of the above

31. What are the three cueing systems?

    A. Emergent, Early, and Fluent
    B. Word identification, oral language development, and letter identification
    C. Graphophonemic, semantic, and syntactic
    D. Pre-Alphabetic, Alphabetic, and Conventional

32. Historical Fiction is defined as

    A. realistic stories set in the past that usually incorporate significant time periods and/or events in history.
    B. autobiographical text.
    C. informational text usually found in textbooks.
    D. primary source documents used in the social studies classroom.

33. Mr. Lowe's third grade class has just read an article from a *National Geographic Kids* magazine. Through modeled writing, he is demonstrating how to write a five sentence paragraph about the article. This is an example of what comprehension skill?

    A. visualizing
    B. making an inference
    C. summarizing
    D. author's purpose

34. Kidspiration is a popular

    A. computer software used in classrooms to create assignments in a technological fashion.
    B. children's television show.
    C. children's organization.
    D. basal reading series.

35. Which of the following is not a narrative literary element?

    A. theme
    B. plot
    C. style
    D. author's purpose

36. There are _____ critical components for reading success.

    A. 10
    B. 7
    C. 6
    D. 5

37. An example of a primary source document is

    A. a diary entry written by Martin Luther King, Jr.
    B. a biography written about the life of Martin Luther King, Jr.
    C. an illustration of Martin Luther King, Jr., drawn by a child during Black History month.
    D. none of the above

38. All of following should be included in a classroom library except

    A. books from a variety of genres.
    B. a plethora of nonfiction resources.
    C. books that promote stereotypes of various races and ethnicities.
    D. a wide array of multicultural children's literature.

39. A word that is recalled by memory only is known as a(n)

    A. sight word.
    B. high frequency word.
    C. alliterative phrase.
    D. phonogram.

40. Which of the following words contains a vowel digraph?

    A. car
    B. cause
    C. catch
    D. care

41. In order to foster multiple opportunities for listening and speaking in the classroom, your day should be structured to incorporate

    A. both whole group and small group lessons.
    B. a great deal of independent seatwork.
    C. multiple technology stations.
    D. none of the above

42. Accuracy, rate, prosody, and automaticity are all components of reading _____.

    A. comprehension
    B. fluency
    C. speed
    D. words correct per minute

43. Which of the following choices are essential elements of reading comprehension?

   A. inferring and questioning
   B. understanding author's purpose and point of view
   C. visualizing the text
   D. all of the above

44. Sheila, a Kindergarten student, made approximations while reading at the beginning and middle of the school year. However, by the end of the year, she was pointing to each word on the page as she read her guide reading books. What concept of print is Sheila exhibiting?

   A. directionality
   B. voice-to-print match
   C. return sweep
   D. sight word recognition

45. Which of the following choices would be considered a consonant blend?

   A. ch
   B. th
   C. wh
   D. bl

46. John is experiencing reading difficulties as noted on his recent timed, fluency check. His reading speed is slow and halted. This shows a weakness in which area of fluency?

   A. prosody
   B. accuracy
   C. automaticity
   D. rate

47. Making predictions about what a [...] is going to be about aids student [...]

   A. automaticity.
   B. sight word recognition.
   C. analysis of cause and effect.
   D. comprehension.

48. A teacher asks her students, "Which two wor[ds] rhyme: far, stick, car?" Which area of emergen[t] literacy does this illustrate?

   A. phonological awareness
   B. vocabulary
   C. concepts of print
   D. fluency

49. During a whole group lesson, a first grade teacher asks her students to do the following task: "I am going to segment a word into parts and pause between each sound. I want you to say the whole word together."

   Which progress monitoring assessment is the teacher using?

   A. test of nonsense word fluency
   B. informal reading inventory
   C. test of phonological awareness
   D. test of alphabet knowledge

Social Science

1. The two world superpowers that emerged from World War II were

   A. China and Japan
   B. England and France
   C. USSR and the USA
   D. none of the above

2. Prior to Christopher Columbus's arrival, who had discovered the land we once called the New World?

   A. Vasco da Gama
   B. Nicolaus Copernicus
   C. Hernando de Soto
   D. the Vikings and Native Americans

3. What famous Spanish explorer searched the land now known as Florida for the Fountain of Youth?

   A. Juan Ponce de Leon
   B. Hernando Cortes
   C. Francisco Pizarro
   D. Vasco de Balboa

4. To create interest and motivate students to retain content area information, a variety of instructional methods must be employed. Which of the following instructional methods or strategies would NOT entice learners in the Social Studies classroom?

   A. use of guest speakers
   B. use of role play and simulation activities
   C. use of learning centers (stations)
   D. sole use of the textbook and chapter tests

5. Human systems refers to what essential element of teaching geography?

   A. location
   B. regions
   C. people
   D. process that shapes the Earth

6. Hernando De Soto explored the present day American Southeast and discovered what river?

   A. Missouri River
   B. Nile River
   C. Potomac River
   D. Mississippi River

7. The purpose of the Persian Gulf War was to

   A. liberate Kuwait and expel Iraqi forces.
   B. liberate Iraq.
   C. liberate Kenya.
   D. none of the above

8. Operation Desert Storm was

   A. the name for the United States land and air operations involved in the Gulf War effort.
   B. the other name for the Gulf War.
   C. the name the media used for the Persian Gulf War.
   D. the name for a video game and had nothing to do with the Gulf War effort.

9. Which of the following statements describes the historical figure Thomas Jefferson?

   A. Invented bifocals and the Franklin stove
   B. Considered one of the Founding Fathers of our country and the principal author of the Declaration of Independence
   C. Implemented and signed the Emancipation Proclamation
   D. Led the nursing effort for the North during the Civil War and formed the American Red Cross after the war

10. During the Gilded Age, or the years following the Civil War, the Industrial Revolution made it possible for "robber barons" to accumulate gigantic fortunes. Which of the following people were considered "robber barons" during this time period?

    A. Andrew Carnegie
    B. John D. Rockefeller
    C. Cornelius Vanderbilt
    D. All of the above

11. Which of the following can NOT be used as an instructional aid and assessment tool in the Social Studies classroom?

   A. anticipation guide
   B. K-W-H-L chart
   C. venn diagram
   D. chapter test

12. An absolute location is defined as

   A. an informal location
   B. a location where local landmarks are used to describe the place
   C. a formal location where street names or coordinates are used to describe the locality
   D. a difficult location to access

13. Who was the first astronomer to place the sun at the center of the universe?

   A. Isaac Newton
   B. Nicolaus Copernicus
   C. Galileo Galilei
   D. John Locke

14. Human beings tend to live in environments that meet their needs. Which essential element of geography refers to the interaction between people and their surroundings?

   A. Environment and Society
   B. Human Systems
   C. Process that shapes the Earth
   D. World in Spatial terms

15. Small representations, usually shapes and pictures, of real things on a map are known as

   A. a legend
   B. cartographers
   C. symbols
   D. keys

16. Which of the following is the horizontal, imaginary line that divides the Earth into its northern and southern halves?

   A. Prime Meridian
   B. Tropic of Capricorn
   C. International Date Line
   D. Equator

17. What article of the Constitution ... judicial branch of government in the U... States of America?

   A. I
   B. III
   C. X
   D. V

18. The Supreme Court is the highest court of appeals in the United States. One of its most important powers is the power of

   A. legislative review.
   B. executive review.
   C. judicial review.
   D. legal review.

19. On a theme park map, features like bathrooms and restaurants are drawn the right size and distance apart in an effort to represent, in a smaller form, the park's amenities accurately. This map is known as being drawn to _____.

   A. legend
   B. scale
   C. coordinates
   D. hemispheres

20. Electors are representatives of the people that actually elect the president and vice president. As of 2009, how many electors are there in the United States of America?

   A. 538
   B. 536
   C. 537
   D. 535

21. _____ refers to the physical characteristics of specific places and how they form and change.

   A. Landmarks and symbols
   B. Legends and keys
   C. Places and regions
   D. Maps and globes

22. What representation of the Earth is said to be most accurate?

   A. relief map
   B. thematic map
   C. political map
   D. globe

23. Policies that aid in governmental control of the economy are known as

    A. financial policy.
    B. fiscal policy.
    C. inflation policy.
    D. trade policy.

24. What financial institution is owned, controlled, and operated by its members?

    A. federal reserve banks
    B. credit unions
    C. stock market
    D. Wall Street

25. Consumer decision making has no effect on the supply and demand of products in this country and all over the world, therefore teaching our youth _____ skills is futile.

    A. fiscal policy
    B. economic reasoning
    C. global responsibility
    D. home economics

26. _____ (is) are appointed officials in the judicial branch of government.

    A. Supreme Court Justices
    B. The President of the United States
    C. The Vice President of the United States
    D. State Senators

27. In a market economy, who decides what goods and services will be produced?

    A. consumers
    B. the government
    C. private businesses
    D. national organizations

28. Many governments in Europe have high taxes on gasoline and oil; consumers in these countries have asked their local and state governments to

    A. create more jobs.
    B. provide higher wages.
    C. provide better alternative transportation through public transit.
    D. decrease insurance costs for personal vehicles.

29. Which level of government has the ability to regulate intrastate trade?

    A. federal
    B. county
    C. local/state
    D. none of the above

30. To allow a student the opportunity to best understand how a witness experienced a historical event, the best resource would be

    A. secondary source
    B. primary source
    C. textbook passage
    D. a Webquest

31. Which article of the United States Constitution established the legislative branch of government?

    A. I
    B. II
    C. III
    D. IV

32. The College of Electors, also known as the Electoral College, was established by Article II in the United States Constitution in 1787. It is our country's system for electing the president and vice president. Which of the following is NOT true regarding the Electoral College?

    A. Electors pledge in advance to vote for the candidate of their party based on the popular vote.
    B. Electors meet after the citizen vote and cast ballots based on the public vote for president and vice president.
    C. Electors use their inside information and knowledge of our government to cast the vote that they believe is in the best interest of the country.
    D. Currently, 270 electoral votes are required to win a presidential election.

33. If no presidential candidate receives the majority of the electoral votes in a national election, who has the power to choose the President of the United States?

    A. House of Representatives
    B. Senate
    C. Supreme Court
    D. Former President may choose his successor

34. When a group of citizens claims that a bill which has gone through the process of becoming federal law is unconstitutional, which governmental body has the power to determine its constitutionality?

    A. Supreme Court
    B. President of the United States
    C. Senate
    D. Secretary of State

35. Which historical document includes the right to a trial by a jury of your peers and freedom of religion?

    A. Treaty of Paris
    B. Lewis and Clark Expedition
    C. Bill of Rights
    D. Emancipation Proclamation

36. What are the three branches of government in the United States of America?

    A. one, two, and three
    B. legislative, judicial, and executive
    C. House of Representatives, Senate, and President
    D. state, local, and federal

37. Which of the following is NOT a service provided by a local government?

    A. police and fire protection
    B. water and sewer utilities
    C. museums and libraries
    D. theme parks and restaurants

38. Which of the following is NOT considered a right of a United States citizen?

    A. right to vote
    B. right to hold office
    C. right to avoid paying taxes
    D. right to serve on juries

39. Which of the following wars led to the start of the American Revolutionary War?

    A. World War I
    B. The Civil War
    C. The French and Indian War
    D. The Industrial Revolution

40. The Axis Powers were defeated by The Allies in WWII and led to the emerging of two world superpowers and inevitably the Cold War. Which of the following countries was one of the defeated Axis Powers?

    A. Germany
    B. England
    C. France
    D. Russia

Music, Visual Arts, Physical Education, and Health

1. This music period marked the beginning of polyphony.

    A. Romantic
    B. Baroque
    C. Medieval
    D. Renaissance

2. Complete the sentence: In boys, puberty is characterized by an increase in _____.

    A. Estrogen
    B. Testosterone
    C. Body Fat
    D. Progesterone

3. The perceived fundamental frequency of a sound is

    A. timbre.
    B. rhythm.
    C. pitch.
    D. texture.

4. Which one is the element of art that involves the structure of the song or the way the song is arranged?

    A. texture
    B. form
    C. rhythm
    D. melody

5. Which of the following is used to define overweight and obese?

    A. Life expectancy
    B. Body Mass Index
    C. Medical History
    D. Muscle Tone

6. Complete the sentence: _____ involve(s) large movements like running and jumping.

    A. Gross motor skills
    B. Physical fitness
    C. Fine motor skills
    D. Academic achievement

7. Which of the following is involved when you are dividing a larger period of time into smaller rhythmic units?

    A. harmonic rhythm
    B. dynamic rhythm
    C. additive rhythm
    D. divisive rhythm

8. The emotions evoked by a piece of art are most likely products of the viewer's

    A. values.
    B. form.
    C. shape.
    D. imagination.

9. Complete the following sentence: The _____ domain deals with physical movement, coordination, and use of motor skills.

    A. Cognitive
    B. Psychomotor
    C. Affective
    D. Reactive

10. Which of the following is a gross motor skill?

    A. Tying shoes
    B. Coloring inside the lines
    C. Running
    D. Cutting on a curved line

11. Children most often lack which of the following vitamins?

    A. Vitamin C
    B. Vitamin B
    C. Vitamin K
    D. Vitamin E

12. This period is known for its balance and structure.

    A. Renaissance
    B. Baroque
    C. Romantic
    D. Classical

13. Which of the following is NOT a pillar of character?

    A. Respect
    B. Caring
    C. Trustworthiness
    D. Honesty

14. A simple flute is a type of

    A. tuning instrument.
    B. rhythmic instrument.
    C. harmonic instrument.
    D. melodic instrument.

15. In art, colors that are opposite of each other on the color wheel are considered

    A. complementary colors.
    B. secondary colors.
    C. compound colors.
    D. tertiary colors.

16. Treatment for developmental delays most often includes which of the following?

    A. Medication
    B. Occupational Therapy
    C. Speech and hearing screenings
    D. Surgery

17. Fill in the blank: _____ refers to the system of beliefs one learns and determines to be true.

    A. Self-worth
    B. Self-esteem
    C. Self-reliance
    D. Self-concept

18. A dance teacher asked his students, "Why do people in the community dance, even though they are not professionals?" The teacher is most likely helping his students to

    A. use dance as a language to represent ideas from diverse literature sources.
    B. explore forms and cultural contexts for dance.
    C. use dance vocabulary.
    D. apply the critical analysis process.

19. This Baroque period genre is a drama where the dialogue is sung rather than spoken.

    A. opera
    B. cantata
    C. motet
    D. madrigal

20. Which is NOT an aspect of physical fitness?

    A. Bone Strengthening
    B. Aerobics
    C. Flexibility
    D. Strength Training

21. The music teacher is looking for progress in the students' performance involving resonance, control, clarity, focus, consistency, and warmth. Which of the following areas is the teacher most likely assessing?

    A. tone color
    B. rhythm
    C. intonation
    D. interpretation and musicianship

22. Locomotor skills involve all of the following skills except which one?

    A. Running
    B. Twisting
    C. Skipping
    D. Jumping

23. The combination of art elements to create the appearance of action is referred to as

    A. texture.
    B. balance.
    C. movement.
    D. repetition.

24. Child development is divided into six categories. Which of the following lists these categories in order from earliest to latest?

    A. Newborn, infant, toddler, preschooler, school-aged child, adolescent
    B. Toddler, preschooler, adolescent, school-aged child, infant, newborn
    C. Adolescent, school-aged child, preschooler, toddler, infant, newborn
    D. School-aged child, adolescent, toddler, preschooler, newborn, infant

25. Which of the following lists the levels of the cognitive domain of Bloom's Taxonomy from most to least complex?

    A. Knowledge, Comprehension, Application, Analysis, Evaluation, and Synthesis
    B. Synthesis, Evaluation, Analysis, Application, Comprehension, and Knowledge
    C. Knowledge, Comprehension, Application, Evaluation, Synthesis, and Analysis
    D. Analysis, Synthesis, Evaluation, Application, Comprehension, and Knowledge

26. Character development is important for which of the following reasons?

    A. Communication of ideas
    B. Ethical decision making
    C. Self-esteem
    D. Academic achievement

27. Three or more different notes from a specific key played together are called

    A. polyphony.
    B. chord.
    C. pitch.
    D. harmony.

28. When a teacher is assessing how consistently a student sings notes with accuracy, the teacher is assessing

    A. inflection.
    B. rate.
    C. volume.
    D. pitch.

Use the picture to answer Question 29:

29. What art principle is most likely represented in this piece?

    A. form
    B. shape
    C. textures
    D. repetition

30. The nutritional category of Grains includes which of the following foods?

    A. Milk
    B. Cheese
    C. Grapes
    D. Bread

31. A kindergarten class is working on a printmaking activity. Which of the following should they be using?

    A. silk screen printing
    B. wood block printing
    C. gadget printing
    D. linoleum block printing

Use the picture to answer the question that follows:

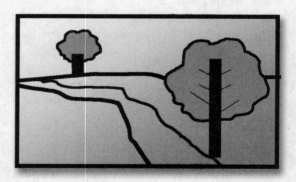

32. What type of balance is the artist most likely using?

    A. symmetrical balance
    B. asymmetrical balance
    C. radical balance
    D. horizontal balance

33. Which of the following is NOT a domain of Bloom's Taxonomy?

    A. Affective domain
    B. Psychomotor domain
    C. Reactive domain
    D. Cognitive domain

34. The music teacher is using an assessment guide to score the students' performance in a reliable, fair, and valid manner that is composed of dimensions for judging student performance, a scale for rating performances on each dimension, and standards of excellence for specified performance levels. This assessment tool is called

  A. an open-ended task.

  B. a rubric.

  C. a multiple-choice test.

  D. an essay-type test.

35. Michelangelo's Sistine Chapel frescoes were created during this period.

  A. Renaissance

  B. Romantic

  C. Classical

  D. Baroque

36. Which of the following would NOT help students to examine how music relates to personal development and enjoyment of life?

  A. define in their own words the principles of music

  B. evaluate how the study of music expands the ability to communicate with and understand others

  C. tell how music can be a joyful part of daily activities

  D. describe how making music helps to develop skills and success in working with others

37. Who is responsible for ensuring public awareness about health and nutrition?

  A. Surgeon General

  B. Attorney General

  C. Food and Drug Administration

  D. Centers for Disease Control

38. The nutritional category of Meat and Beans includes which of the following foods?

  A. Cheese

  B. Poultry

  C. Broccoli

  D. Peaches

39. This style involved opulence, grace, and lightness.

  A. Classical

  B. Baroque

  C. Rococo

  D. Renaissance

40. Which of the following is NOT a typical sign of substance abuse?

  A. Changes in school attendance

  B. Taking uncharacteristic risks

  C. Engaging in extracurricular activities

  D. Changes in physical appearance

41. A way to help children learn songs through imitation is called

  A. process of immersion.

  B. authentic teaching.

  C. rote teaching.

  D. note teaching.

42. Which of the following does NOT generally help maintain a healthy weight?

  A. Eating a balanced diet

  B. Physical activity

  C. Consuming more calories

  D. Consuming fewer calories

43. Which of the following is NOT a symptom of narcotic drug abuse?

  A. Track marks

  B. Rapid talking

  C. Red nostrils

  D. Slurred speech

44. You ask a student to restate a concept in their own words. At which level of Bloom's Taxonomy are you asking the student to perform?

  A. Analysis

  B. Comprehension

  C. Synthesis

  D. Application

45. What personal information is it important for children to know?

  A. Their address

  B. Their full name

  C. Their phone number

  D. All of the above

Science and Technology

1. What is the name for the measure of the amount of matter in a substance or object?

   A. weight
   B. volume
   C. mass
   D. density

2. The part of the crust of the Earth that contains the continents is called the

   A. Continental Crust.
   B. Oceanic Crust.
   C. Continental Drift.
   D. Pangea.

3. A teacher asked her students to measure the acceleration of toy cars rolling down a ramp. In this experiment, students should use time as what type of variable.

   A. independent variable
   B. controlled variable
   C. dependent variable
   D. observed variable

4. The process by which a plant makes food is called

   A. transpiration.
   B. respiration.
   C. photosynthesis.
   D. fertilization.

5. The necessity of a complete loop utilizing a battery, a small light bulb, and a connecting wire is an example of

   A. an electrical circuit.
   B. a mechanical circuit.
   C. a kinetic circuit.
   D. an application circuit.

6. The three layers of the Earth from inner to outer are

   A. mantle, crust, core.
   B. core, mantle, crust.
   C. crust, core, mantle.
   D. crust, mantle, core.

7. Complete the sentence: _____ is the classification of living things into categories based on physical characteristics.

   A. Taxidermy
   B. Taxonomy
   C. Topography
   D. Telegraph

8. Complete the sentence: Energy cannot be created or destroyed, but it can be _____ from one form of energy to another.

   A. transformed
   B. accumulated
   C. estimated
   D. recycled

9. Complete the sentence: _____ are the ways in which scientists answer questions and solve problems systematically.

   A. Laboratories
   B. Scientific methods
   C. Controlled experiments
   D. Hypotheses

10. A well-validated and well-supported explanation of some aspect of the natural world is called a

    A. postulate.
    B. hypothesis.
    C. law.
    D. theory.

11. Complete the sentence: A _____ moon occurs when the sun and moon are on opposite sides of the Earth.

    A. Full
    B. New
    C. First Quarter
    D. Last Quarter

12. Students select a location in Florida then search the Internet for monthly temperature data of this location for the most recent El Niño year. Students then compare monthly temperature data for the El Niño year to the average temperature data for the past 25 years in order to assess the impact of El Niño on that particular location.

    Which of the following would most likely be most efficient for recording and analyzing this information by the students?

    A. electronic mail
    B. spreadsheet
    C. LCD panel
    D. word processor

13. A traffic signal primarily involves this process.

    A. turns electrical energy into heat energy
    B. turns electrical energy into light energy
    C. turns light energy into electrical energy
    D. turns electrical energy into mechanical energy

14. The term defined as mass per unit of volume is called

    A. buoyancy.
    B. density.
    C. weight.
    D. physical change.

15. Which of the following is NOT a planet?

    A. Mercury
    B. Mars
    C. Pluto
    D. Neptune

16. Which of the following is NOT a kingdom for living things?

    A. Plants
    B. Protists
    C. Bacteria
    D. Fungi

17. What is a possible answer to a question posed in a scientific experiment?

    A. Educated guess
    B. Prediction
    C. Hypothesis
    D. Variable

18. The combustion of gasoline provokes this type of reaction.

    A. mechanical reaction
    B. magnetic reaction
    C. electrical reaction
    D. chemical reaction

19. Which type of force always causes a change in motion?

    A. balanced force
    B. neutral force
    C. unbalanced force
    D. motion force

20. The theory which attempts to account for changes in species over time is often referred to as:

    A. Survival of the fittest
    B. Evolution
    C. Adaptation
    D. Heredity

21. What type of experiment has a control and experimental group?

    A. Random experiment
    B. Quasi-experiment
    C. Nested experiment
    D. Controlled experiment

22. Alfred Wegner proposed a theory in which all the continents of the earth were once joined in a supercontinent called:

    A. Panacea
    B. Panorama
    C. Pangea
    D. Pacifica

23. A lump of sugar dissolving into water is an example of

    A. physical change.
    B. chemical change.
    C. density change.
    D. volume change.

24. What is the genetic material that contains information needed to make new cells?

    A. RNA
    B. DNA
    C. Proteins
    D. Amino Acids

25. A measurement of the total energy in a substance is called

    A. force.
    B. kinetic.
    C. heat.
    D. temperature.

26. Which of the following will NOT provide the best opportunities for inquiry-based learning?

    A. The teacher asks students to observe the Moon and record their observations. The teacher asks them to develop in small groups a model that will simulate what they have found and how the phases of the Moon change over time. They can also support their ideas with drawings of the model. They will have time to share and compare their findings, and make corrections with teacher guidance.
    B. After completing a pre-assessment activity on students' knowledge of Moon phases, a student asks about the correct order of Moon phases. The teacher challenges students to determine the sequence of phases by observing the Moon and recording their observations for one month.
    C. Students complete a Moon phase calendar by cutting out photographs of the Moon in different phases, mounting them on a monthly calendar on the proper date, and appropriately labeling each of the eight major Moon phases.
    D. The teacher begins with the question, "Does the Moon rise and set at the same time every night?" Following a brief discussion of the question, the teacher demonstrates the rising and setting of the Moon for several sequential evenings using a computer simulation. The teacher then facilitates a class discussion.

27. Cells in which a nucleus does not exist are called

    A. prokaryotic cells.
    B. eukaryotic cells.
    C. nucleolus.
    D. ribosomes.

28. What causes Tsunami?

    A. Volcanoes
    B. Earthquakes
    C. Continental Drift
    D. Richter Scale

29. Which of the following does NOT refer to a type of energy?

    A. sound
    B. electric
    C. kinetic
    D. temperature

30. Complete the sentence: _____ rock is formed when a pre-existing rock changes form into a new rock, often through burial.

    A. Metamorphic
    B. Sedimentary
    C. Igneous
    D. Compressed

31. Bacteria that cause disease are called

    A. pathogens.
    B. infections.
    C. viruses.
    D. symbiotic.

32. Which of the following is NOT an aspect of the scientific method?

    A. Predicting
    B. Observing
    C. Testing
    D. Disseminating

33. Which Apollo flight took Neil Armstrong and Edwin "Buzz" Aldrin to the surface of the moon?

    A. Apollo 7
    B. Apollo 8
    C. Apollo 11
    D. Apollo 13

34. Complete the sentence: _____ cells contain chloroplasts.

    A. Animal
    B. Bacteria
    C. Plant
    D. Fungal

35. Which type of electrical circuit uses only one electrical path?

   A. looping circuits
   B. singular circuits
   C. parallel circuits
   D. series circuits

36. Convection currents cause

   A. magnetism.
   B. plate tectonics.
   C. electricity.
   D. water flow.

37. Which one of the following terms might NOT be involved when an instrument is reliable?

   A. validity
   B. consistency
   C. repeatability
   D. precision

38. Heat is a measurement of the total energy made up of the following two energies of the molecules in a substance.

   A. temperature and potential energies
   B. kinetic and potential energies
   C. static and potential energies
   D. frictional and potential energies

39. Which is NOT a method of heat transfer?

   A. Convection
   B. Condensation
   C. Radiation
   D. Conduction

40. An organism which creates its own food is called a/an

   A. heterotroph.
   B. heterozygote.
   C. autotroph.
   D. parasite.

41. The students are involved in a scientific experiment. They want to measure the influence of different quantities of fertilizer on plant growth. They started to consider the type of plant, the type of fertilizer, the amount of sunlight the plant gets, and the size of the pots, and other factors that may influence the results. They want to plan ways to keep these factors constant. At this stage of the scientific process, what type of variables are the students dealing with?

   A. extraneous variables
   B. dependent variables
   C. independent variables
   D. controlled variables

42. Atoms with negative charge contain the following combination of electrons and protons.

   A. fewer electrons than protons
   B. an equal number of protons and electrons
   C. more electrons than protons
   D. the combination will not affect the end result

43. Who was the first American to orbit the earth?

   A. John Glenn
   B. Neil Armstrong
   C. Alan Shepard
   D. Yuri Gagarin

44. Which is not a type of vertebrate?

   A. Mammal
   B. Bird
   C. Fish
   D. Worm

45. Which of the following is NOT a good laboratory procedure?

   A. Washing hands frequently
   B. Eating in the laboratory
   C. Disposing of chemicals properly
   D. Wearing gloves

Mathematics

1. A student wrote $\frac{1}{2}$ as an answer to a fraction computation problem. What type of representation model is the student using?

   A. concrete
   B. pictorial
   C. numeral
   D. number

2. A playground has rectangular dimensions of 8 yards by 10 yards. Both dimensions are tripled to create a larger playground. The area of the playground has increased how many times?

   A. 3 times
   B. 4 times
   C. 6 times
   D. 9 times

3. The results of this type of test could help in identifying a student's specific problem areas.

   A. objective test
   B. standardized test
   C. criterion-referenced test
   D. diagnostic test

4. The number 0.77… is equal to

   A. $0.\overline{7}$
   B. 7%
   C. 77%
   D. 0.7

5. Find the next term in the pattern 3, 6, 9, 12, 15, …

   A. 17
   B. 18
   C. 19
   D. 20

6. If $\triangle ABC \sim \triangle DEF$, then which of the following is true?

   A. $\angle A \cong \angle E$
   B. $AB = DE$
   C. $\dfrac{AB}{DE} = \dfrac{BC}{EF}$
   D. $\angle C \cong \angle D$

7. The expression $b^3 \cdot b^6$ is equal to

   A. b^9
   B. $18b$
   C. $9b$
   D. b^{18}

Use the data set to answer items 8, 9, 10, and 11.

The students in a class received the following scores in a test worth 25 points:

12, 13, 10, 14, 23, 12, 13, 22, 12, 12, 10, 11, 15, 20, 10, 12, 10, 15, 22, 23

8. What is the mean of the data set?

   A. 14.55
   B. 291
   C. 12
   D. 12.5

9. What is the median of the data set?

   A. 14
   B. 12
   C. 12.5
   D. 13

10. What is the mode of the data set?

    A. 2
    B. 10 and 12
    C. 10
    D. 12

11. What is the range of the data set?

    A. 13
    B. 4
    C. 12
    D. 14

12. What is the value of x in the equation $2^{-4} \cdot -1 = x$?

    A. $\dfrac{-1}{16}$
    B. -16
    C. 16
    D. $\dfrac{1}{16}$

13. Which of the following expressions matches the description: Four times a number plus 12.

   A. $4 + 12n$
   B. $4(n + 12)$
   C. $4n + 12$
   D. $4 + 12 + n$

14. Natalie, Paul, Samuel, and Greta were comparing the distances from their houses to school. The distances were Natalie $2\frac{2}{5}$ miles, Paul $2\frac{1}{3}$ miles, Samuel $2\frac{3}{8}$ miles, and Greta $2\frac{3}{5}$ miles, respectively. What is the order of names based on these distances from least to greatest?

   A. Samuel, Paul, Greta, and Natalie
   B. Samuel, Paul, Natalie, and Greta
   C. Greta, Natalie, Samuel, and Paul
   D. Paul, Samuel, Natalie, and Greta

15. What shape could NOT be made by combining a rectangle with a triangle?

   A. Pentagon
   B. Hexagon
   C. Heptagon
   D. Octagon

16. A flag pole casts a shadow that is 12 feet. A man who is 6 feet tall casts a shadow that is 9 feet long. How tall is the flag pole?

   A. 8 feet
   B. 9 feet
   C. 15 feet
   D. 18 feet

17. Which of the following is the same as 6^{-3}?

   A. 216
   B. $\frac{-1}{216}$
   C. $\frac{1}{216}$
   D. -216

18. A form of assessment that incorporates real-life functions and applications is called

   A. alternative assessment.
   B. authentic assessment.
   C. naturalistic assessment.
   D. diagnostic assessment.

19. The following figure is created through which transformation?

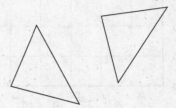

   A. Translation
   B. Reflection
   C. Rotation
   D. Dilation

20. Mary has 35 books at her home library, 21 of these books are softcover books, and the rest of the books are hardcover books. What percent of Mary's books are hardcover books?

   A. 60%
   B. 40%
   C. 166%
   D. 250%

21. A zoo sells peanuts and hot dogs. The cost of peanuts is $2 a box. The cost of a hot dog is $3.50. How much will a customer spend to buy p boxes of peanuts and h hot dogs.

   A. $2p + 3.50h$
   B. $2p - 3.50h$
   C. $2p$
   D. $3.50h$

22. The line graph that follows shows the percent of buyers at a shopping center from 1980 to 2005. Using this graph, predict the percent of buyers for the year 2010 at this shopping center.

Buyers at a Shopping Center

A. 46%
B. 42%
C. 52%
D. 55%

23. Identify the coordinates of point T in the figure shown.

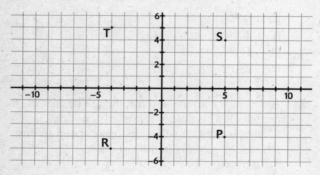

A. (5, –4)
B. (–4, 5)
C. (–4, -5)
D. (–5, –4)

24. Oranges cost $0.58 for a pound. Laura buys 13 pounds everyday from Monday to Friday for her restaurant. How much will she have spent after four weeks?

A. $150.80
B. $7.54
C. $37.70
D. $30.16

25. Select the unit of measure most appropriate for the volume of water in a bathtub.

A. Cups
B. Gallons
C. Pints
D. Quarts

26. If 4 hands are equivalent to 10 thumbs, how many thumbs are in 12 hands?

A. 30 thumbs
B. 18 thumbs
C. 5 thumbs
D. 20 thumbs

27. Solve for x: $3(2x - 5) \leq 8x - 3$.

A. $x \leq 6$
B. $x \geq 6$
C. $x \leq -6$
D. $x \geq -6$

28. Which one of the following pairs of factors does not have a Greatest Common Factor (GCF) equal to 6?

A. 24, 6
B. 42, 150
C. 54, 18
D. 18, 30

29. Which of the following can NOT be folded to make a rectangular prism?

A.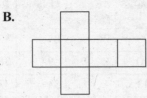

B.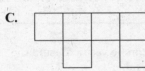

C.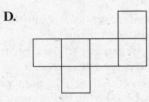

D.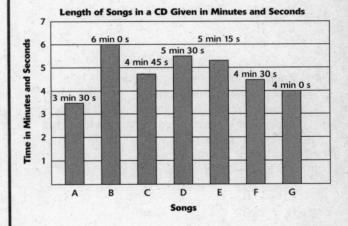

30. If the radius of a circle is cut in half, what happens to the area of that circle?

A. Cut in half
B. Cut in fourth
C. Doubled
D. Tripled

31. Which of the following is not an appropriate assessment practice?

A. Assessment should be ongoing and summative.
B. The best assessment also instructs.
C. Best instructional tasks are rich with diagnostic opportunities.
D. We should always teach then assess.

32. Find the Greatest Common Factor (GCF) of the following pair of algebraic expressions: $20x^2y$, and $50xy^2$.

A. xy
B. 10
C. $10xy$
D. $100x^2y^2$

33. What property shows that $3(x-2) = 3x - 6$?

A. Associative Property
B. Commutative Property
C. Distributive Property
D. Identity Property

34. Find the area of the figure shown.

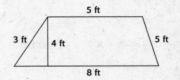

A. 26 ft²
B. 21 ft²
C. 32 ft²
D. 20 ft²

Use the following graph to answer items 35 and 36.

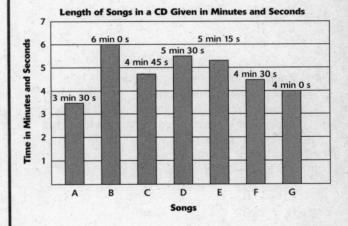

35. What is the approximate average number of minutes for the songs included in the preceding graph? (Approximate your answer to the nearest hundredth.)

A. 33.5 minutes
B. 3.5 minutes
C. 26.5 minutes
D. 4.7 minutes

36. If you want to burn a 26-minute CD using the songs given, which of the following group of songs should be selected?

A. A, B, C, D, E, and F
B. A, B, C, D, E, F, and G
C. B, C, D, E, and F
D. A, B, C, D, F, and G

37. Tashana wants to paint her kitchen wall. The dimensions of the wall are 8 feet by 9 feet. A quart of paint will cover 20 square feet. If Tashana wants to paint the wall with three coats of paint, how many quarts of paint will she need?

    A. 10
    B. 11
    C. 12
    D. 13

38. How many faces does a cube have?

    A. 4
    B. 5
    C. 6
    D. 7

39. Which one of the following is the sum of the prime factors of 120?

    A. 7
    B. 14
    C. 10
    D. 8

40. Zachary is wrapping a present which is a shoebox with dimensions 3 ft, 4 ft, and 5 ft. What is the minimum amount of wrapping paper that Zachary needs to completely wrap the box without overlap?

    A. 94 ft²
    B. 60 ft²
    C. 47 ft²
    D. 70 ft²

41. Which of the following materials would be most appropriate to help students develop area ideas?

    A. Protractor
    B. Straight edge
    C. Tangrams
    D. Compass

42. A survey of 1188 students at an elementary school was taken to find how they get to school each day. The results are shown in the following table.

How Students Get to School Each Day by Grade Level					
	Take a Bus	Walk	Adult Drives	Other	Total
3rd Grade	139	123	76	85	423
4th Grade	47	140	113	89	389
5th Grade	158	143	41	34	376
Total	344	406	230	208	1188

Which statement can be verified using the information in the table?

A. At this elementary school, fewer 4th graders use different forms of transportation than 5th graders, because fewer students attend 4th grade.

B. At this elementary school, the number of 4th graders who take the bus is greater than the number of 3rd graders who walk to school.

C. At this elementary school, more students in all grade levels take the bus to get to school than any of the other types of transportation.

D. At this elementary school, the number of 5th graders who take the bus is greater than the number of 4th graders who walk to school.

43. Which of the following is NOT a name that can be used for the figure shown.

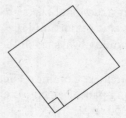

    A. Square
    B. Parallelogram
    C. Rhombus
    D. Trapezoid

44. Which of the following statements is NOT true?

   A. All squares are rectangles.
   B. All rectangles are parallelograms.
   C. All rectangles are squares.
   D. All parallelograms are quadrilaterals.

45. Solve for x: $4(2 - x) + 5 = 3(2x - 3) - 8$

   A. $x = 1$
   B. $x = 3$
   C. $x = 8$
   D. $x = 15$

Practice Test 1 Answers

Language Arts/Reading

1. C	14. C	27. D	40. B
2. C	15. B	28. B	41. A
3. D	16. D	29. B	42. B
4. A	17. D	30. A	43. D
5. D	18. B	31. C	44. B
6. C	19. C	32. A	45. D
7. D	20. A	33. C	46. D
8. B	21. A	34. A	47. D
9. B	22. D	35. D	48. A
10. C	23. C	36. D	49. C
11. A	24. B	37. A	
12. D	25. C	38. C	
13. B	26. D	39. A	

Social Science

1. C	11. D	21. C	31. A
2. D	12. C	22. D	32. C
3. A	13. B	23. B	33. A
4. D	14. A	24. B	34. A
5. C	15. C	25. B	35. C
6. D	16. D	26. A	36. B
7. A	17. B	27. A	37. D
8. A	18. C	28. C	38. C
9. B	19. B	29. C	39. C
10. D	20. A	30. B	40. A

Music, Visual Arts, Physical Education, and Health

1. C	13. D	25. B	37. A
2. B	14. D	26. B	38. B
3. C	15. A	27. B	39. C
4. B	16. B	28. D	40. C
5. B	17. D	29. D	41. C
6. A	18. B	30. D	42. C
7. D	19. A	31. C	43. B
8. D	20. C	32. B	44. C
9. B	21. A	33. C	45. D
10. C	22. B	34. B	
11. A	23. C	35. A	
12. D	24. A	36. A	

Science and Technology

1. C	13. B	25. C	37. A
2. A	14. B	26. C	38. B
3. A	15. C	27. A	39. B
4. C	16. C	28. B	40. C
5. A	17. C	29. D	41. D
6. B	18. D	30. A	42. C
7. B	19. C	31. A	43. C
8. A	20. B	32. D	44. D
9. B	21. D	33. C	45. B
10. D	22. C	34. C	
11. A	23. A	35. D	
12. B	24. B	36. B	

Mathematics

1. C	13. C	25. B	37. B
2. D	14. D	26. A	38. C
3. D	15. D	27. D	39. C
4. A	16. A	28. C	40. A
5. B	17. C	29. C	41. C
6. C	18. B	30. B	42. D
7. A	19. C	31. D	43. D
8. A	20. B	32. C	44. C
9. C	21. A	33. C	45. B
10. D	22. A	34. A	
11. A	23. B	35. D	
12. A	24. A	36. C	

Practice Test 1 Solutions

What follows are detailed solutions to the problems from practice test 1. The competency to which the test question is related is also included for reference.

Language Arts/Reading

1. **C.** Competency 1. "Talking to the text" or performing a think aloud is a strategy that supports the idea of actively reading a text.

2. **C.** Competency 2. Biography is a literary genre. All other choices are considered subsets of folklore.

3. **D.** Competency 3. Persuasive writing is writing that attempts to convince the reader that a point of view is valid or that the reader should take a specific action. Descriptive, expository, and narrative are all modes of writing as well.

4. **A.** Competency 3. Amy's use of random strings of letters shows that she knows that print conveys a message, however, her next step would be to convey that she knows that individual letters have a sound symbol relationship.

5. **D.** Competency 4. Criterion-referenced tests are assessment instruments that assess the point at which the student has achieved mastery. These tests enable educators in determining whether or not a student has met a predetermined goal.

6. **C.** Competency 6. Blogs are user-friendly web pages that allow students to post and comment on their work.

7. **D.** Competency 5. Comprehension, listening, and speaking skills are all enhanced by questioning and retelling.

8. **B.** Competency 6. Visual media is non-print media.

9. **B.** Competency 3. The teacher is truly focusing on the content, is encouraging her students to revise and improve upon what has been written, and is not yet concerned with editing for errors.

10. **C.** Competency 4. Concepts of print include that print conveys meaning, directionality (left to right progression, top to bottom), concept of a word (word boundaries), letter knowledge, phonemic awareness, and literacy language (author, illustrations, title, etc.).

11. **A.** Competency 1. The onset is defined as the first consonant or groups of consonants (sh) that come before the first vowel in a syllable. The rime unit is the first vowel sound and any others that follow it in a syllable.

12. **D.** Competency 1. Directionality (left to right progression and top to bottom) or reading, the title page, and illustrations are all examples of basic concepts of print. Captions provided to illustrations and photographs are non-fiction text features common in informational text.

13. **B.** Competency 1. Knowledge of individual words in sentences, syllables, onset-rime segments, and the awareness of individual phonemes in words is known as phonological awareness.

14. **C.** Competency 1. An onset is defined as the first consonant or groups of consonants (sh) that come before the first vowel in a syllable. A rime unit is the first vowel sound and any others that follow it in a syllable. A grapheme is a letter or group of letters that represents one sound, like *ough* in though.

15. **B.** Competency 2. Alliteration is defined as two or more words or syllables with the same beginning consonant.

16. **D.** Competency 4. Reading centers/stations allow students to co-construct meaning in a small group setting. For the teacher, this organizational format allows time to meet with guided reading groups and to differentiate instruction to meet the varying needs of students in the classroom.

17. **D.** Competency 6. Primary sources are documents or pieces of work that were written, recorded, or created during a particular time period.

18. **B.** Competency 5. Students are typically taught cursive in the third grade.

19. **C.** Competency 3. The students wish to persuade the school board to keep their music classes intact at each school site.

20. **A.** Competency 4. The workshop approach is a student-centered approach to teaching where teachers have ample time to meet and confer with small groups and individuals to best meet their academic needs.

21. **A.** Competency 2. Literature circles are a small group of children reading a chosen text and discussing that text on a routine and regular basis with a group of their peers.

22. **D.** Competency 3. Prewriting is the phase of the writing process that includes activating prior knowledge, gathering, and organizing ideas. Drafting, editing, and revising are all later phases in the writing process.

23. **C.** Competency 2. A simile is a literary device that utilizes the words *like* or *as*.

24. **B.** Competency 3. The editing phase of writing is where teachers encourage students to correct any errors they may see in their writing.

25. **C.** Competency 1. Right there or text explicit questions are literal questions where the answers are found in the text itself.

26. **D**. Competency 1. Along with the methods noted above, timed reading, readers theater, audio books, poetry readings, independent, and paired reading all aid students' reading fluency.

27. **D.** Competency 4. Oral reading fluency can be enhanced by many instructional methods like choral reading and readers theater with the key factor being repetition.

28. **B.** Competency 5. Line quality is defined in legible handwriting as the consistency of the pencil strokes.

29. **B.** Competency 4. If a student read a 200 word piece in 4:45 with 6 recorded errors, his/her accuracy rate would be as follows. $\frac{(200-6)\cdot 60}{285 \text{ seconds}} = 40.9$ WCPM. Thus, the student reads 40.9 words correct per minute.

30. **A.** Competency 1. To summarize is to simply and concisely paraphrase what has been read.

31. **C.** Competency 1. All of the choices offer terms related to the teaching of the language arts.

32. **A.** Competency 2. With the exception of A, realistic stories set in the past that usually incorporate significant time periods and/or events in history, the other choices are all nonfiction texts.

33. **C.** Competency 1. Summarizing is the ability to simply and concisely paraphrase what has been read.

34. **A.** Competency 6. Kidspiration is an example of computer software that can be used to create graphic organizers, timelines, etc., that enhance the comprehension of skills taught in the classroom through the use of technology.

35. **D.** Competency 2. Understanding the author's purpose is critical to comprehension but is not defined as a narrative literary element.

36. **D.** Competency 1. Phonological awareness, phonics, vocabulary, fluency, and comprehension are the five critical components to reading success.

37. **A.** Competency 1. A primary source is a document or piece of work, which was actually written, recorded, or created during the specific time under study.

38. **C.** Competency 2. Classroom libraries should contain a wide variety of multicultural children's literature, nonfiction resources, and various genres.

39. **A.** Competency 1. A sight word is a word that does not follow the traditional rules of the English language and must be memorized.

40. **B.** Competency 1. A vowel digraph is defined as two vowels together that make one phoneme or sound.

41. **A.** Competency 5. The teacher's daily schedule should include opportunities for whole group and small group, for students to practice their listening and speaking skills in a supportive environment.

42. **B.** Competency 1. Accuracy, prosody, rate, and automaticity are all crucial elements of fluency.

43. **D.** Competency 1. Understanding the main idea, supporting details and facts, author's purpose, fact and opinion, point of view, making inferences, and visualizing are all critical to making meaning from text, known as comprehension.

44. **B.** Competency 1. Voice-to-print match also known as one-to-one correspondence shows that Sheila now understands the concept of a word and word boundaries.

45. **D.** Competency 1. The first three choices are diagraphs or two consonants that together represent one sound. A consonant blend is two consonants that together keep their individual sounds.

46. **D.** Competency 1. Rate is defined as the speed of reading and greatly influences whether or not a student can comprehend the text. Accuracy, prosody, and automaticity are also crucial elements of fluency.

47. **D.** Competency 1. Along with accessing prior knowledge, making predictions about what is about to be read is a common strategy used to enhance comprehension.

48. **A.** Competency 1. Rhyme is the earliest developing phonological awareness skill.

49. **C.** Competency 4. Segmenting and blending are integral parts of phonological awareness.

Social Science

1. **C.** Competency 7. The attack on Pearl Harbor resulted in the United States involvement in the war. In 1945 the Allies defeated the Axis Powers with the USSR and the United States emerging as the world's superpowers.

2. **D.** Competency 7. Columbus made four voyages in an effort to find a route to the East. During his expeditions he discovered the Bahamas, Hispaniola, Cuba, Dominica, Guadeloupe, Jamaica, Central America, and South America. As illustrations and historical accounts depict, he was greeted by Native Americans who had settled the land prior to his arrival and the Vikings had also been known to have explored the area as well.

3. **A.** Competency 7. All of the listed choices are Spanish explorers; however, Juan Ponce de Leon is known for his search for the Fountain of Youth.

4. **D.** Competency 11. The use of guest speakers, high quality children's literature, learning centers, and role play/simulation activities are just some of the instructional methods that can be used in the Social Studies classroom to incite interest and comprehension of major concepts being presented.

5. **C.** Competency 8. Human systems are people or inhabitants.

6. **D.** Competency 7. Hernando de Soto discovered the Mississippi River.

7. **A.** Competency 7. The purpose of the Persian Gulf War was to liberate Kuwait and expel Iraqi forces.

8. **A.** Competency 7. Operation Desert Storm was the name for the United States land and air operations involved in the Gulf War effort.

9. **B.** Competency 7. Benjamin Franklin invented bifocals and the Franklin stove. Thomas Jefferson is considered one of the Founding Fathers of our country and the principal author of the Declaration of Independence. Abraham Lincoln implemented and signed the Emancipation Proclamation, and Clara Barton led the nursing effort for the North during the Civil War and formed the American Red Cross once the war was over.

10. **D.** Competency 7. Andrew Carnegie, John D. Rockefeller, and Cornelius Vanderbilt were all considered robber barons and made their fortunes in railroads.

11. **D.** Competency 11. Anticipation guides, K-W-H-L charts, and Venn diagrams are all graphic organizers that can be used for both instructional and assessment purposes. Chapter tests are used as assessment instruments only.

12. **C.** Competency 8. An absolute location is defined as a formal location where street names or coordinates are used to describe the locality.

13. **B.** Competency 7. Newton was an English physicist, mathematician, astronomer, natural philosopher, alchemist, and theologian known for defining gravity and the laws of motion. Copernicus placed the sun at the center of the universe. Galileo Galilei was an Italian physicist, mathematician, astronomer, and philosopher responsible for the birth of modern science. John Locke was a British Enlightenment writer whose ideas influenced the Declaration of Independence and the United States Constitution.

14. **A.** Competency 8. The essential element of geography that refers to the interaction between people and their surroundings is the Environment and Society.

15. **C.** Competency 8. Small representations, usually shapes and pictures, of real things on a map are known as symbols.

16. **D.** Competency 8. The horizontal, imaginary line that divides the Earth into its northern and southern halves is the equator.

17. **B.** Competency 9. Article III established the judicial branch of government.

18. **C.** Competency 10. One of the Supreme Court's most important powers is the power of judicial review.

19. **B.** Competency 8. Scale is when something on a map is drawn to size. In other words, compared to each other items on the map are the right size and distance apart; the larger the scale, the more detail shown (for example, theme park map), the smaller the scale, the more area shown but less detail (for example, world map).

20. **A.** Competency 9. As of 2009, the correct number of electors in the United States of America is 538.

21. **C.** Competency 8. Places and regions refers to the physical characteristics of specific places and how they form and change.

22. **D.** Competency 8. A globe, which is a small scale model, is said to be the most accurate representation of the Earth.

23. **B.** Competency 10. Policies that aid in governmental control of the economy are known as fiscal policy.

24. **B.** Competency 10. Credit unions are owned, controlled, and operated by their members.

25. **B.** Competency 10. Economic reasoning is the ability to use problem solving and strategic thinking skills in relation to economics which will help them to make better decisions in our modern global economy.

26. **A.** Competency 9. Supreme Court Justices are appointed officials in the judicial branch of government. Each of the other choices is an elected official.

27. **A.** Competency 10. Consumers, according to principles of supply and demand, decide what kinds of goods and services will be produced.

28. **C.** Competency 10. In response to increased taxes on oil and gas, consumers in Europe have asked for better public transportation.

29. **C.** Competency 9. The local and state government have the ability to regulate intrastate (between state) trade.

30. **B.** Competency 11. A primary source document is one that was created during a specific time period and accurately depicts what occurred at that time.

31. **A.** Competency 9. Article I of the United States Constitution established the legislative branch of government.

32. **C.** Competency 9. Electors are a body of elected representatives chosen by the voters in each state. While they are human beings that have their own views on who they would prefer to become the leader of this country, they pledge in advance to vote according to the wishes of the general public.

33. **A.** Competency 9. If no presidential candidate receives the majority of the electoral votes in a national election, the House of Representatives has the power to choose the President of the United States.

34. **A.** Competency 9. When a group of citizens claims that a bill that has gone through the process of becoming federal law is unconstitutional, the Supreme Court with its power of judicial review has the power to determine its constitutionality.

35. **C.** Competency 9. The historical document that includes the right to a trial by a jury of your peers and freedom of religion is the Bill of Rights.

36. **B.** Competency 9. The three branches of government are: legislative, judicial, and executive.

37. **D.** Competency 9. Local governments provide many services including but not limited to: police and fire protection, water and sewer utilities, education, public housing, transportation and road repair, libraries, museums, and sports facilities.

38. **C.** Competency 9. An accurate definition of a United States citizen is a person who is legally recognized as a member of this nation with specific inalienable rights and responsibilities which do not include tax evasion.

39. **C.** Competency 7. The French and Indian War (1754-1763), which was an extension of the European Seven Years War, was a battle over colonial territory and wealth by the French and the English. This war resulted in effectively ending French cultural and political influence in North America. In their victory, England gained massive amounts of land but also weakened their rapport with the Native Americans. In sum, although the war strengthened England's hold on the colonies, it also worsened their relationship which inevitably led to the Revolutionary War.

40. **A.** Competency 7. The Second World War (WWII) was a global military conflict between two opposing forces: The Allies (Leaders)- Great Britain (Churchill), United States (Roosevelt/Truman), Russia (Stalin), Free France (De Gaulle), China (Chiang Kai-shek) and the Axis Powers (Leaders)- Germany (Hitler), Italy (Mussolini), Japan (Hirohito).

Music, Visual Arts, Physical Education, and Health

1. **C.** Competency 14. The Medieval period marked the beginning of musical notation, rise of courtly culture, and polyphony.

2. **B.** Competency 18. Testosterone is the hormone responsible for male development.

3. **C.** Competency 12. Pitch represents the perceived fundamental frequency of a sound. It is one of the three major auditory attributes of sounds along with loudness and timbre.

4. **B.** Competency 13. Form involves the structure of the song or the way the song is arranged. For example, using a refrain that is repeated, or a chorus that is repeated after a verse.

5. **B.** Competency 17. Body Mass Index defines overweight and obese.

6. **A.** Competency 18. Gross motor skills involve large movements; fine motor skills involve specific and detailed movements.

7. **D.** Competency 12. Divisive rhythms involve dividing a larger period of time into smaller rhythmic units. Additive rhythms are involved when larger periods of time are constructed from smaller rhythmic units added at the end of the previous unit.

8. **D.** Competency 13. When viewing a work of art (like *Mona Lisa* by Leonardo Da Vinci), the formal elements involved might be color, dimension, lines, mass, shape, perspective, and others, but the emotions evoked by these works of art are products of the viewer's imagination and reaction to the work of art.

9. **B.** Competency 20. The affective domain deals with emotions. The cognitive domain deals with knowledge. The psychomotor domain deals with physical skills.

10. **C.** Competency 18. Tying shoes, coloring inside the lines, and cutting on a curved line are fine motor skills. Running is a gross motor skill.

11. **A.** Competency 17. Children most often lack vitamins A, C, and D.

12. **D.** Competency 14. The Classical period is known for its balance and structure.

13. **D.** Competency 18. The six pillars of character are trustworthiness, respect, responsibility, fairness, caring, and citizenship.

14. **D.** Competency 12. Melody bells and simple flutes are considered melodic instruments.

15. **A.** Competency 13. Complementary colors are opposite of each other on the color wheel.

16. **B.** Competency 18. Developmental delays are most often treated with various types of therapies including speech therapy, physical therapy, and/or occupational therapy. Speech and hearing screenings are used to identify delays, not treat them. Medication and surgery are not usually used to treat developmental delays.

17. **D.** Competency 18. Self-concept is the cognitive aspect of self and refers to the system of beliefs, attitudes, and opinions which a person learns and determines to be true.

18. **B.** Competency 15. The teacher is most likely allowing his students to explore forms and cultural contexts for dance and to identify and describe the role of dance in the community.

19. **A.** Competency 12. Opera is a drama where the dialogue is sung rather than spoken.

20. **C.** Competency 17. Physical fitness is comprised of three aspects—aerobics, strength training, and bone strengthening. Although important, flexibility is not one of those aspects.

21. **A.** Competency 16. Tone color involves resonance, control, clarity, focus, consistency, and warmth. Intonation involves accuracy to printed pitch. Interpretation and musicianship includes style, phrasing, tempo, dynamics, and emotional involvement. Rhythm involves accuracy of note and rest values, duration, pulse, steadiness, and correctness of meter.

22. **B.** Competency 18. Locomotor skills include efficiency in walking, running, and jumping. Twisting is a nonlocomotor skill.

23. **C.** Competency 13. Movement refers to the combination of art elements to create the appearance of action or suggestion or implication of motion.

24. **A.** Competency 18. The stages of development in order are newborn, infant, toddler, preschooler, school-aged child, and adolescent.

25. **B.** Competency 20. The levels of Bloom's Taxonomy from least complex to most complex are Knowledge, Comprehension, Application, Analysis, Evaluation, and Synthesis.

26. **B.** Competency 18. Character development provides a basis for making ethical decisions.

27. **B.** Competency 12. Three or more different notes from a specific key played together are called a chord.

28. **D.** Competency 16. When a teacher is assessing how consistently a student sings notes with accuracy, the teacher is assessing pitch.

29. **D.** Competency 13. In an artwork, repetition is created when elements like objects, patterns, shapes, space, light, direction, and lines are repeated.

30. **D.** Competency 17. Milk and cheese fall in the Milk category. Grapes falls in the Fruit category. Bread falls in the Grains category.

31. **C.** Competency 12. Gadget printing involves the use of materials like a potato masher, plastic cup, meat pounder, grater, funnel and other, as well as tempera paints, and paper. The children make prints on their paper. This is a more appropriate type of printing method for kindergarten students than silk-screen, linoleum, or wood block printing, which require a higher skill level.

32. **B.** Competency 13. In asymmetrical balance, the elements are placed unevenly in the work of art, but work together to produce overall harmony.

33. **C.** Competency 20. The three domains of Bloom's Taxonomy are Cognitive, Affective, and Psychomotor.

34. **B.** Competency 16. The music teacher is using an assessment guide to score the students' performance in a reliable, fair, and valid manner that is composed of dimensions for judging student performance, a scale for rating performances on each dimension, and standards of excellence for specified performance levels. It is an assessment tool that allows for more standardized evaluation according to specified criteria, making grading simpler and more transparent.

35. **A.** Competency 14. The Early Renaissance included religious themes. The Renaissance classicism included realistic painting. The changes in style during this era were not uniform across the board. In general, art was more emotional and dramatic in nature; for example, Michelangelo's Sistine Chapel frescoes and sculptures of David and Moses.

36. **A.** Competency 15. The activity of students defining in their own words the principles of music does not necessarily help them to examine how music relates to personal development and enjoyment of life. The other activities could support students' examination of how music relates to their personal development and enjoyment of life.

37. **A.** Competency 19. Surgeon General is responsible for public awareness about health and nutrition.

38. **B.** Competency 17. Cheese is in the Milk category. Poultry is in the Meat and Beans category. Broccoli is in the vegetable category. Peaches are in the Fruit category.

39. **C.** Competency 14. The Eighteenth Century era included the Rococo style, which involved opulence, grace, and lightness (in contrast to the Baroque era).

40. **C.** Competency 19. Signs and symptoms of substance abuse typically include ceasing familiar activities like sports, homework, or hobbies; sudden changes in school attendance and quality of work; doing things you would not normally do like borrowing money or stealing; taking uncharacteristic risks; attitude change; changes in physical appearance and grooming; engaging in suspicious behavior; and feeling exhausted, depressed, hopeless, or suicidal.

41. **C.** Competency 16. Rote teaching is a way of helping children learn songs through imitation (usually presented sequentially and repeated back by the children). The process of immersion is another way in which children hear songs sung by parents, teachers, or on recordings (as the songs become more and more familiar, they will begin to join in and sing). In note teaching, students gradually and systematically learn to read music notation.

42. **C.** Competency 17. Consuming more calories will lead to increasing weight unless accompanied by physical activity. Eating a balanced diet, engaging in physical activity, and eating fewer calories are methods for obtaining and maintaining a healthy weight.

43. **B.** Competency 19. Rapid talking is not a symptom of narcotic drug abuse.

44. **B.** Competency 20. You are asking the student to perform at the level of comprehension.

45. **D.** Competency 19. It is important for students to know their full name, address, and phone number.

Science and Technology

1. **C.** Competency 21. Mass is a measure of the amount of matter in a substance or object. It is different than weight. It is also a measure of an object's resistance to acceleration.

2. **A.** Competency 23. The crust is divided into two sections—continental crust and oceanic crust. The continental crust contains the continents. The oceanic crust lies under the oceans.

3. **A.** Competency 27. In this case, time is usually the independent variable, while speed is the dependent variable. This is because when taking measurements, times are usually predetermined, and the resulting speed of the toy cars is recorded at those times. As far as the experiment is concerned, the speed is dependent on the time. Since the decision is made to measure the speed at certain times, time is the independent variable.

4. **C.** Competency 24. Photosynthesis is the process by which a plant makes food. Transpiration is the loss of water through the plant's leaves. Respiration is the process by which the cells convert sugar molecules into energy. Fertilization is the process by which the plant reproduces.

5. **A.** Competency 22. An electrical circuit must have a continuous flow of electricity going through a complete loop (circuit), returning to their original position and cycling through again. An example that illustrates the necessity of a complete loop utilizes a battery, a small light bulb, and a connecting wire.

6. **B.** Competency 23. The layers of the earth are the core, mantle, and crust. The core is the innermost layer. The crust is the outermost layer.

7. **B.** Competency 24. Taxonomy is the classification of living things into categories based on physical characteristics.

8. **A.** Competency 22. Energy cannot be created or destroyed, but it can be transformed from one form of energy to another.

9. **B.** Competency 25. Scientific methods are the ways in which scientists answer questions and solve problems systematically.

10. **D.** Competency 26. A well-validated and well-supported explanation of some aspect of the natural world is called a theory. A hypothesis is a tentative and testable insight into the natural world, which is not yet verified but if it were found to be true it would explain certain aspects of the natural world, and might become a scientific theory. A law is a truthful explanation of different events that happen with uniformity under certain conditions.

11. **A.** Competency 23. A full moon occurs when the moon and sun are on opposite sides of the earth and the surface of the moon is entirely visible.

12. **B.** Competency 27. Spreadsheets allow tabulation and performance of simple and complicated calculations, mathematical manipulations, and plots and graphs on various types of data, such as numbers, names, alphabetical information, scientific measurements, statistical information, and budget information. This will provide a very effective way to organize the data collected by the students.

13. **B.** Competency 22. The traffic signal turns electrical energy into light energy. Notice that there is a heat energy byproduct, but this is not the primary purpose of the process.

14. **B.** Competency 21. Density (symbol: ρ, which is the Greek "rho") is defined as mass per unit of volume, or the ratio of total mass (m) to total volume (V): $\rho = \frac{m}{V}$ (for example, kilogram per cubic meter or kg/m^3, and grams per cubic centimeter or g/cm^3). In other words, it defines how closely the molecules are packed together.

15. **C.** Competency 23. The eight planets are Mercury, Venus, Earth, Mars, Jupiter, Saturn, Uranus, and Neptune. Pluto is no longer considered a planet.

16. **C.** Competency 24. The six kingdoms are Archaebacteria, Eubacteria, Protists, Fungi, Plants, and Animals. Bacteria is a domain.

17. **C.** Competency 25. A hypothesis is the possible answer a scientist predicts in a scientific experiment.

18. **D.** Competency 22. Chemical energy is the energy stored in the chemical bonds of molecules; for example, the combustion (burning) of gasoline provokes a chemical reaction that releases chemical energy. The molecules are broken to produce heat and light.

19. **C.** Competency 22. Balanced forces do not cause a change in motion. They are in opposite directions and equal in size. In contrast to balanced forces, unbalanced forces always cause a change in motion. They are in opposite direction and not equal in size. Motion and neutral forces are not terms used to describe forces.

20. **B.** Competency 24. The theory of evolution attempts to account for changes in species and the creation of new species over time. Survival of the fittest is an aspect of evolution which explains why some adaptations remain and some fall out of the fossil record.

21. **D.** Competency 25. A controlled experiment is one in which a treatment (experimental) group and control group exist. The treatment group receives a treatment while the control group does not. This provides a method for comparison.

22. **C.** Competency 23. The supercontinent proposed by Wegner was called Pangea.

23. **A.** Competency 21. A lump of sugar dissolving into water is an example of physical change. Matter is in constant change. A physical change does not produce a new substance (for example, freezing and melting water), and a chemical change or reaction does produce one or more substances.

24. **B.** Competency 24. DNA contains the genetic material that contains the information to make new cells.

25. **C.** Competency 22. Heat is a measurement of the total energy in a substance. That total energy is made up of the kinetic, and the potential energies of the molecules of the substance. Temperature does not tell you anything about the potential energy.

26. **C.** Competency 27. In alternative C, students completing a Moon phase calendar by cutting out photographs of the Moon in different phases, mounting them on a monthly calendar on the proper date, and appropriately labeling each of the eight major Moon phases does not provide the best opportunities for inquiry-based learning. Alternatives A, B, and D provide opportunities for both a research question and data analysis, which support inquiry-based learning.

27. **A.** Competency 24. Prokaryotic cells do not contain a nucleus. Eukaryotic cells contain a nucleus. The nucleolus is inside the nucleus of many cells and creates ribosomes.

28. **B.** Competency 23. Tsunami are tidal waves caused by earthquakes which occur under water.

29. **D.** Competency 22. Temperature is not energy, but it is a number that relates to the kinetic energy possessed by the molecules of a substance (measured in Kelvin, Fahrenheit, or Celsius degrees).

30. **A.** Competency 23. Metamorphic rocks are formed when pre-existing rocks change form through changes like burial.

31. **A.** Competency 24. Bacteria that cause disease are pathogens. Infections are the result of bacteria causing disease. Viruses are a different cause of disease.

32. **D.** Competency 25. The steps of the scientific method include 1) ask a question, 2) make observations, 3) hypothesize, 4) predict, 5) test, and 6) conclude.

33. **C.** Competency 23. Apollo 7 was the first manned mission. Apollo 8 was the first manned mission to orbit the moon. Apollo 11 was the first mission to land on the moon. Apollo 13 mission was aborted due to the explosion of oxygen tanks and was called a "successful failure" when all astronauts returned safely to Earth.

34. **C.** Competency 24. Plant cells contain chloroplasts. Chloroplasts allow the plant to harness energy from the sun. Photosynthesis takes place in the chloroplasts.

35. **D.** Competency 22. Series circuits use only one electrical path. Parallel circuits use several electrical paths. For example, parallel circuits allow the distribution of the electric current throughout a house. Singular and looping circuits are not terms used to describe electrical circuits.

36. **B.** Competency 23. Convection currents move the plates of the earth's crusts. This phenomena is referred to as plate tectonics.

37. **A.** Competency 26. Reliability refers to the consistency of a set of measurements or measuring instrument. This can refer to whether the measurements of the same instrument provide the same measurement (test-retest), or whether two independent investigators give consistently similar scores (this is called inter-rater reliability). An instrument could be reliable but not valid. A reliable instrument might be measuring something consistently, but not necessarily what it is supposed to be measuring validly. Reliability refers to the precision of the instrument. Validity refers to the degree to which a measure accurately assesses the specific concept it is designed to measure. A good instrument should be both reliable and valid.

38. **B.** Competency 22. Heat is a measurement of the total energy made up of kinetic and potential energies of the molecules in a substance. Temperature is a measure related to the average kinetic energy of the molecules of a substance. Temperature is not a type of energy.

39. **B.** Competency 23. Three methods of heat transfer are convection, radiation, and conduction.

40. **C.** Competency 24. A heterotroph consumes its food from its environment. An autotroph creates its own food.

41. **D.** Competency 27. The students are dealing with controlled variables. This involves the type of plant, the type of fertilizer, the amount of sunlight the plant gets, the size of the pots, and any other variables or factors that need to be controlled. These are variables or factors that would otherwise influence the dependent variable if they were not controlled. The independent variable would be the amount of fertilizer used (the changing factor of the experiment). The dependent variables would be the growth in height and/or mass of the plant (the factors that are influenced in the experiment).

42. **C.** Competency 22. Atoms with negative charge contain more electrons than protons, and atoms with a positive charge contain fewer electrons than protons.

43. **A.** Competency 23. Alan Shepard was the first American to be launched into space. He completed a sub-orbital flight of 15 minutes and achieved weightlessness for about 5 minutes. Yuri Gagarin was the first human being in space; Gagarin was Russian. John Glenn was the first American to orbit the Earth and Neil Armstrong was the first American to walk on the moon.

44. **D.** Competency 24. The types of vertebrates (animals with a backbone) are fish, amphibians, reptiles, birds, and mammals. Worms are invertebrates (animals without a backbone).

45. **B.** Competency 25. Eating and drinking in the laboratory space is not a good procedure. A laboratory should be free of food and drink.

Mathematics

1. **C.** Competency 28. The student is using $\frac{1}{2}$ for the answer, which is a numeral or abstract representation (also known as symbolic) representation. A numeral is a symbolic or written representation of a number. The concrete level would require the use of manipulative materials, like cubes. The pictorial model would need the use of pictures or drawings. Number is the actual cardinality, value, or numberness of the representation, which is understood mentally. It is the idea represented by the abstract (numeral), pictorial, or concrete models. The idea of ½ can be modeled in these ways.

2. **D.** Competency 29. If the length and width are tripled, the area will be increased by 3×3 times, or 9 times. The original area of the playground was 80 square yards. If both dimensions are tripled, the dimensions would then be 24 yards × 30 yards. This is an area of 720 square yards. This is an increase of 9 times.

3. **D.** Competency 32. The results of diagnostic tests could help in identifying specific problem areas. Diagnostic tests are used within the diagnostic-prescriptive teaching of mathematics. This process is an instructional model that consists of diagnosis, prescription, instruction, and ongoing assessment.

4. **A.** Competency 28. A non-terminating repeating decimal like 0.77… is equal to $0.\overline{7}$, where the line on top of the 7 indicates that 7 is repeating, which is the same as using "…". The other options are approximations of this number.

5. **B.** Competency 30. The pattern is adding three to the term below. The next term is $15 + 3 = 18$.

6. **C.** Competency 29. The triangles are similar. This means corresponding angles are congruent and corresponding sides are proportional. Angle A corresponds with Angle D; Angle B corresponds with Angle E; and Angle C corresponds with Angle F. AB corresponds with DE; BC corresponds with EF; and AC corresponds with DF. Choice C is a proportion of corresponding sides.

7. **A.** Competency 28. The expression $b^3 \cdot b^6$ is equal to b^9 (add exponents).

8. **A.** Competency 31. To find the mean of this data set, you need to add the scores and divide by 20 (number of scores): $291 \div 20 = 14.55$.

9. **C.** Competency 31. To find the median, you need to order the data set and find the middle score.

   10, 10, 10, 10, 11, 12, 12, 12, 12, 12, 13, 13, 14, 15, 15, 20, 22, 22, 23, 23

   Scores 12 and 13 are in the middle because we have an even number of scores or entries in this data set. You need to average these two scores to find the median: $(12 + 13) \cdot 2 = 25 \cdot 2 = 12.5$.

10. **D.** Competency 31. The mode is the most frequent score. A frequency table should be used to organize the data.

Scores	Frequency
10	4
11	1
12	5
13	2
14	1
15	2
20	1
22	2
23	2

The most frequent score for this data set is 12.

11. **A.** Competency 31. The range of the data set is the highest score minus the lowest score: $23 - 10 = 13$.

12. **A.** Competency 28. You need to solve the negative exponent first and then multiply for negative one, and 2^{-4} is equal to $\frac{1}{2^4} = \frac{1}{16}$, and $\frac{1}{16} \cdot -1 = \frac{-1}{16}$.

13. **C.** Competency 30. Four times a number is 4n. This plus 12 is 4n + 12.

14. **D.** Competency 28. Start by ordering the fractions from least to greatest. One way to do this ordering is by changing all the possible answers to decimal form, comparing to each other, and ordering them accordingly from least to greatest: $2\frac{1}{3} = 2.333\ldots$, $2\frac{3}{8} = 2.375$, $2\frac{2}{5} = 2.4$, $2\frac{3}{5} = 2.6$. Another way is to compare them as fractions, and order them accordingly. Finally, look at the names and decide who lives closer and who lives the farthest. In this case the order would be Paul $\left(2\frac{1}{3}\right)$, Samuel $\left(2\frac{3}{8}\right)$, Natalie $\left(2\frac{2}{5}\right)$, and Greta $\left(2\frac{3}{5}\right)$.

15. **D.** Competency 29. A pentagon is a five sided figure. If one side of the triangle matches one side of the rectangle, the figure has five sides. If one side of the triangle does not match one side of the rectangle and it is matched to the end of one side, the figure would have six sides making it a hexagon. If one side of the triangle does not match one side of the rectangle, and the triangle was placed in the middle of a side the final figure would have seven sides, making it a heptagon. An octagon is not possible.

16. **A.** Competency 29. Set up a proportion. $\frac{x \text{ feet}}{12 \text{ feet}} = \frac{6 \text{ feet}}{9 \text{ feet}}$. Solve this proportion by cross multiplication. $9x = 12(6)$. So $9x = 72$. Therefore, $x = 8$ feet.

17. **C.** Competency 28. $6^{-3} = \frac{1}{6^3} = \frac{1}{(6 \cdot 6 \cdot 6)} = \frac{1}{216}$.

18. **B.** Competency 32. Authentic assessment is a form of alternative assessment that incorporates real-life functions and applications. Alternative assessment refers to other (non-traditional) options used to assess students' learning, which are not necessarily a form of authentic assessment. However, authentic assessments are usually based on alternative forms of assessment. Naturalistic assessment involves evaluation that is based on the natural setting of the classroom. It involves the observation of students' performance and behavior in an informal context. They also are not necessarily a form of authentic assessment.

19. **C.** Competency 29. A rotation is a turn. A translation is a slide. A reflection is a flip. A dilation is making smaller or larger.

20. **B.** Competency 28. First, we need to find the number of hardcover books by subtracting 21 from 35, which results in 14 hardcover books. Then, divide 14 by 35 to calculate the percent of hardcover books in this case: 40%.

21. **A.** Competency 30. The cost of peanuts is $2 a box. *P* boxes of peanuts would cost 2p dollars. Hot dogs cost $3.50 each. *H* hot dogs would cost 3.50h dollars. The total of these is 2p + 3.50h.

22. **A.** Competency 31. There seems to be a pattern of increasing the amount of buyers every five years. There is also a bigger increase every 10 years. The year 2010 seems to be included in one of those cycles. That is why 46 percent seems to be the best prediction.

23. **B.** Competency 29. Point T is to the left and above the origin (point (0,0)). To get from (0,0) to point T, you move left 4 and up 5. This gives the coordinates of (–4, 5).

24. **A.** Competency 28. You need to translate the word problem into a mathematical sentence. You have 13 pounds of oranges for $0.58 times fives days for four weeks: $4(5(13 \cdot \$0.58)) = 4(5(7.54)) = 4(37.70) = \$150.80$.

25. **B.** Competency 29. The volume of water in a bathtub is a large amount. Use a large unit. Gallon is the largest unit, so it is most appropriate for the volume of water in a bathtub.

26. **A.** Competency 29. 12 hands $\times \frac{10 \text{ thumbs}}{4 \text{ hands}} = 30$ thumbs.

27. **D.** Competency 30. First distribute across the parentheses. This gives $6x - 15 \leq 8x - 3$. Then isolate the variable on one side of the inequality by subtracting 8x from both sides and adding 15 to both sides. This gives $-2x \leq 12$. Divide both sides by -2 which reverses the inequality. This gives $x \geq -6$.

28. **C.** Competency 28. One way to solve this problem is finding the factors of each pair of numbers, and then using these factors to find the GCF. Look for the GCF within each pair (shown in **bold text** for each pair below).

    A. 24: 1, 2, 3, 4, **6**, 8, 12, 24   and 6: 1, 2, 3, **6**   GCF = 6   Yes, they have 6 as GCF.

    B. 42: 1, 2, 3, **6**, 7, 14, 21, 42   and 150: 1, 2, 3,   GCF = 6   Yes, they have 6 as GCF.
    5, **6**, 10, 15, 25,
    30, 50, 75, 150

    C. 54: 1. 2. 3, 6, 9, **18**, 27, 54   and **18**: 1, 2, 3,   GCF = 18   No, they don't have 6 as GCF.
    6, 9, 18

    D. 18: 1, 2, 3, **6**, 9, 18   and 30: 1, 2, 3, 5, **6**   GCF = 6   Yes, they have 6 as GCF.

    Another way to solve this problem is by using prime factorization. Find the prime factorization of each pair of numbers and then use these prime factorizations to find the GCF. Look at the common prime factors within each pair (shown in **bold text** for each pair below).

    A. $24 = \mathbf{2} \cdot 2 \cdot 2 \cdot \mathbf{3}$,   and $6 = \mathbf{2} \cdot \mathbf{3}$ GCF $= 2 \cdot 3 = 6$ Yes, they have 6 as GCF.

    B. $42 = \mathbf{2} \cdot \mathbf{3} \cdot 7$,   and $150 = \mathbf{2} \cdot \mathbf{3} \cdot 5 \cdot 5$ GCF $= 2 \cdot 3 = 6$ Yes, they have 6 as GCF.

    C. $54 = \mathbf{2} \cdot \mathbf{3} \cdot \mathbf{3} \cdot 3$,   and $18 = \mathbf{2} \cdot \mathbf{3} \cdot \mathbf{3}$ GCF $= 2 \cdot 3 \cdot 3 = 18$ No, they don't have 6 as GCF.

    D. $18 = \mathbf{2} \cdot \mathbf{3} \cdot 3$,   and $30 = \mathbf{2} \cdot \mathbf{3} \cdot 5$ GCF $= 2 \cdot 3 = 6$ Yes, they have 6 as GCF.

29. **C.** Competency 29. In option C, the front and back squares will overlap, and a face is missing. All other choices give each face.

30. **B.** Competency 29. The radius is squared to find the area of the circle. If the radius is cut in half, the area would be divided by 2^2 or cut in fourth. For example, if the radius of the circle was 4 inches, the area would be $A = \pi(4)^2 = 16\pi$. If the radius were cut in half, the new radius would be 2 inches. The area would then be $A = \pi(2)^2 = 4\pi$. Since 4 is one fourth of 16, the new area is one fourth of the old area.

31. **D.** Competency 32. We should not teach then assess. Assessment should be ongoing and summative. The best assessment also instructs and the best instructional tasks are rich with diagnostic opportunities.

32. **C.** Competency 28. Look at the common factors within this pair of expressions (shown in **bold text** below).

    $20x^2y = \mathbf{2} \cdot 2 \cdot \mathbf{5} \cdot \mathbf{x} \cdot x \cdot \mathbf{y}$

    $50xy^2 = \mathbf{2} \cdot \mathbf{5} \cdot 5 \cdot \mathbf{x} \cdot \mathbf{y} \cdot y$

    GCF $= 2 \cdot 5 \cdot x \cdot y = 10xy$

33. **C.** Competency 30. The associative property says you can multiply or add three numbers together in any order. The commutative property says you can add or multiply two numbers in either order. The distributive property allows for multiplication across parentheses with addition or subtraction. This is the distributive property.

34. **A.** Competency 29. The figure is a trapezoid. The formula for the area of a trapezoid is $A = \frac{1}{2}(b_1 + b_2)h$. Base 1 is 5 feet; base 2 is 8 feet; height is 4 feet. Therefore, the area is $A = \frac{1}{2}(5 + 8)(4) = \frac{1}{2}(13)(4) = 26$ ft^2.

35. **D.** Competency 31. The sum of the minutes and seconds is 33 minutes and 30 seconds, which is approximately 33.5 (30 seconds is about 0.5 of a minute). The average number of minutes is this number divided by 7: $33.5 \div 7 = 4.7$ minutes.

36. **C.** Competency 31. Remember to be careful with the addition of the seconds (60 seconds equals a minute). You need to check the sum for each one to see which is nearest or equal to 26 minutes:

A. A, B, C, D, E, and F: The sum is equal to 25 minutes 30 seconds.

B. A, B, C, D, E, F, and G: The sum is equal to 33 minutes 30 seconds.

C. B, C, D, E, and F: The sum is equal to 26 minutes.

D. A, B, C, D, F, and G: Sum equal to 28 minutes 15 seconds.

37. **B.** Competency 29. The area of the wall is 72 square feet. Three coats will then cover $72 \times 3 = 216$ square feet. If each quart covers 20 square feet, then 10 quarts will cover 200 square feet. This is not enough. If you add one more quart, or 11 quarts, then you can cover 220 square feet. You need 11 quarts.

38. **C.** Competency 29. Faces are the surfaces of the cube. There are six faces on a cube.

39. **C.** Competency 28. The prime factors of 120 are 2, 3, and 5. The sum of these prime factors is $2 + 3 + 5 = 10$. There are several ways to find the prime factors of 120. One of them is to use the divisibility rules, when possible, using prime numbers less than 11 (the square root of 120 is approximately less than 11) or 2, 3, 5, and 7:

Since 120 is an even number then it is divisible by 2.

Since the sum of the digits of 120 ($1 + 2 + 0 = 3$) is divisible by 3, then 120 is also divisible by 3.

Since the last digit of 120 is 0, then 120 is divisible by 5.

There is no divisibility rule for 7, but we know that 120 is not divisible by 7.

40. **A.** Competency 29. The amount of wrapping paper that Zachary needs is the surface area of the present. The box has faces which have dimensions 3×4, 3×5, and 4×5. The area of each of these faces is 12, 15, and 20 respectively. There are two of each face. Therefore, the surface area is $2 \times (12 + 15 + 20) = 2 \times 47 = 94$ ft².

41. **C.** Competency 32. Tangrams would be most appropriate to help students develop area ideas. The Tangram puzzle is based on a solid square divided in seven smaller pieces (two small triangles, one medium triangle, two large triangles, one square, and one parallelogram).

42. **D.** Competency 31. The best way to find the best choice for this item is by analyzing each alternative. Choice A indicates that there are more 5th graders than 4th graders attending this elementary school, but this is not true. There are more 4th graders (389) than 5th graders (376). Choice B indicates that more 4th graders take the bus than 3rd graders who walk to school, but this is not true. The number of 4th graders who take the bus is 47, and the number of 3rd graders who walk to school is 123, which indicates that there are more 3rd graders walking than 4th graders taking the bus. Choice C indicates that more students take the bus than students who use any of the other types of transportation. This is not true because fewer students (344) take the bus than students who walk to school (406). More students walk to school than any of the other types of transportation. Choice D for this item indicates that more 5th graders (158) take the bus than 4th graders who walk to school (140). This is true, and is the only alternative that can be verified by the information provided in the table.

43. **D.** Competency 29. The figure shown is a square. Squares can also be called parallelograms, rhombuses, and rectangles. It cannot be called a trapezoid.

44. **C.** Competency 29. Squares are rectangles with four equal sides. Therefore, all squares are rectangles. Rectangles are parallelograms with ninety degree angles. Therefore, all rectangles are parallelograms. Squares, rectangles, and parallelograms have four sides, therefore, all parallelograms are quadrilaterals. Not all rectangles are squares, so choice C is not true.

45. **B.** Competency 30. First distribute through the parentheses which gives $8 - 4x + 5 = 6x - 9 - 8$. Then combine like terms to give $13 - 4x = 6x - 17$. Isolate the x variable on one side of the equation by adding 17 to both sides and adding $4x$ to both sides. This gives $30 = 10x$. Divide both sides by 10, so $x = 3$.

Practice Test 2

The test which follows is approximately the length of the FTCE: Elementary Education (K–6) Subject Area Examination. Allow yourself 2 hours and 30 minutes to complete the practice test. Record your answers on the Answer Sheet. When you are finished, check your answers. Detailed solutions follow the test.

Language Arts and Reading

1	Ⓐ Ⓑ Ⓒ Ⓓ	41	Ⓐ Ⓑ Ⓒ Ⓓ
2	Ⓐ Ⓑ Ⓒ Ⓓ	42	Ⓐ Ⓑ Ⓒ Ⓓ
3	Ⓐ Ⓑ Ⓒ Ⓓ	43	Ⓐ Ⓑ Ⓒ Ⓓ
4	Ⓐ Ⓑ Ⓒ Ⓓ	44	Ⓐ Ⓑ Ⓒ Ⓓ
5	Ⓐ Ⓑ Ⓒ Ⓓ	45	Ⓐ Ⓑ Ⓒ Ⓓ
6	Ⓐ Ⓑ Ⓒ Ⓓ	46	Ⓐ Ⓑ Ⓒ Ⓓ
7	Ⓐ Ⓑ Ⓒ Ⓓ	47	Ⓐ Ⓑ Ⓒ Ⓓ
8	Ⓐ Ⓑ Ⓒ Ⓓ	48	Ⓐ Ⓑ Ⓒ Ⓓ
9	Ⓐ Ⓑ Ⓒ Ⓓ	49	Ⓐ Ⓑ Ⓒ Ⓓ
10	Ⓐ Ⓑ Ⓒ Ⓓ		
11	Ⓐ Ⓑ Ⓒ Ⓓ		
12	Ⓐ Ⓑ Ⓒ Ⓓ		
13	Ⓐ Ⓑ Ⓒ Ⓓ		
14	Ⓐ Ⓑ Ⓒ Ⓓ		
15	Ⓐ Ⓑ Ⓒ Ⓓ		
16	Ⓐ Ⓑ Ⓒ Ⓓ		
17	Ⓐ Ⓑ Ⓒ Ⓓ		
18	Ⓐ Ⓑ Ⓒ Ⓓ		
19	Ⓐ Ⓑ Ⓒ Ⓓ		
20	Ⓐ Ⓑ Ⓒ Ⓓ		
21	Ⓐ Ⓑ Ⓒ Ⓓ		
22	Ⓐ Ⓑ Ⓒ Ⓓ		
23	Ⓐ Ⓑ Ⓒ Ⓓ		
24	Ⓐ Ⓑ Ⓒ Ⓓ		
25	Ⓐ Ⓑ Ⓒ Ⓓ		
26	Ⓐ Ⓑ Ⓒ Ⓓ		
27	Ⓐ Ⓑ Ⓒ Ⓓ		
28	Ⓐ Ⓑ Ⓒ Ⓓ		
29	Ⓐ Ⓑ Ⓒ Ⓓ		
30	Ⓐ Ⓑ Ⓒ Ⓓ		
31	Ⓐ Ⓑ Ⓒ Ⓓ		
32	Ⓐ Ⓑ Ⓒ Ⓓ		
33	Ⓐ Ⓑ Ⓒ Ⓓ		
34	Ⓐ Ⓑ Ⓒ Ⓓ		
35	Ⓐ Ⓑ Ⓒ Ⓓ		
36	Ⓐ Ⓑ Ⓒ Ⓓ		
37	Ⓐ Ⓑ Ⓒ Ⓓ		
38	Ⓐ Ⓑ Ⓒ Ⓓ		
39	Ⓐ Ⓑ Ⓒ Ⓓ		
40	Ⓐ Ⓑ Ⓒ Ⓓ		

Social Science

1	Ⓐ Ⓑ Ⓒ Ⓓ
2	Ⓐ Ⓑ Ⓒ Ⓓ
3	Ⓐ Ⓑ Ⓒ Ⓓ
4	Ⓐ Ⓑ Ⓒ Ⓓ
5	Ⓐ Ⓑ Ⓒ Ⓓ
6	Ⓐ Ⓑ Ⓒ Ⓓ
7	Ⓐ Ⓑ Ⓒ Ⓓ
8	Ⓐ Ⓑ Ⓒ Ⓓ
9	Ⓐ Ⓑ Ⓒ Ⓓ
10	Ⓐ Ⓑ Ⓒ Ⓓ
11	Ⓐ Ⓑ Ⓒ Ⓓ
12	Ⓐ Ⓑ Ⓒ Ⓓ
13	Ⓐ Ⓑ Ⓒ Ⓓ
14	Ⓐ Ⓑ Ⓒ Ⓓ
15	Ⓐ Ⓑ Ⓒ Ⓓ
16	Ⓐ Ⓑ Ⓒ Ⓓ
17	Ⓐ Ⓑ Ⓒ Ⓓ
18	Ⓐ Ⓑ Ⓒ Ⓓ
19	Ⓐ Ⓑ Ⓒ Ⓓ
20	Ⓐ Ⓑ Ⓒ Ⓓ
21	Ⓐ Ⓑ Ⓒ Ⓓ
22	Ⓐ Ⓑ Ⓒ Ⓓ
23	Ⓐ Ⓑ Ⓒ Ⓓ
24	Ⓐ Ⓑ Ⓒ Ⓓ
25	Ⓐ Ⓑ Ⓒ Ⓓ
26	Ⓐ Ⓑ Ⓒ Ⓓ
27	Ⓐ Ⓑ Ⓒ Ⓓ
28	Ⓐ Ⓑ Ⓒ Ⓓ
29	Ⓐ Ⓑ Ⓒ Ⓓ
30	Ⓐ Ⓑ Ⓒ Ⓓ
31	Ⓐ Ⓑ Ⓒ Ⓓ
32	Ⓐ Ⓑ Ⓒ Ⓓ
33	Ⓐ Ⓑ Ⓒ Ⓓ
34	Ⓐ Ⓑ Ⓒ Ⓓ
35	Ⓐ Ⓑ Ⓒ Ⓓ
36	Ⓐ Ⓑ Ⓒ Ⓓ
37	Ⓐ Ⓑ Ⓒ Ⓓ
38	Ⓐ Ⓑ Ⓒ Ⓓ
39	Ⓐ Ⓑ Ⓒ Ⓓ
40	Ⓐ Ⓑ Ⓒ Ⓓ

Music, Visual Arts, Physical Education, and Health

1	Ⓐ Ⓑ Ⓒ Ⓓ	41	Ⓐ Ⓑ Ⓒ Ⓓ
2	Ⓐ Ⓑ Ⓒ Ⓓ	42	Ⓐ Ⓑ Ⓒ Ⓓ
3	Ⓐ Ⓑ Ⓒ Ⓓ	43	Ⓐ Ⓑ Ⓒ Ⓓ
4	Ⓐ Ⓑ Ⓒ Ⓓ	44	Ⓐ Ⓑ Ⓒ Ⓓ
5	Ⓐ Ⓑ Ⓒ Ⓓ	45	Ⓐ Ⓑ Ⓒ Ⓓ
6	Ⓐ Ⓑ Ⓒ Ⓓ		
7	Ⓐ Ⓑ Ⓒ Ⓓ		
8	Ⓐ Ⓑ Ⓒ Ⓓ		
9	Ⓐ Ⓑ Ⓒ Ⓓ		
10	Ⓐ Ⓑ Ⓒ Ⓓ		
11	Ⓐ Ⓑ Ⓒ Ⓓ		
12	Ⓐ Ⓑ Ⓒ Ⓓ		
13	Ⓐ Ⓑ Ⓒ Ⓓ		
14	Ⓐ Ⓑ Ⓒ Ⓓ		
15	Ⓐ Ⓑ Ⓒ Ⓓ		
16	Ⓐ Ⓑ Ⓒ Ⓓ		
17	Ⓐ Ⓑ Ⓒ Ⓓ		
18	Ⓐ Ⓑ Ⓒ Ⓓ		
19	Ⓐ Ⓑ Ⓒ Ⓓ		
20	Ⓐ Ⓑ Ⓒ Ⓓ		
21	Ⓐ Ⓑ Ⓒ Ⓓ		
22	Ⓐ Ⓑ Ⓒ Ⓓ		
23	Ⓐ Ⓑ Ⓒ Ⓓ		
24	Ⓐ Ⓑ Ⓒ Ⓓ		
25	Ⓐ Ⓑ Ⓒ Ⓓ		
26	Ⓐ Ⓑ Ⓒ Ⓓ		
27	Ⓐ Ⓑ Ⓒ Ⓓ		
28	Ⓐ Ⓑ Ⓒ Ⓓ		
29	Ⓐ Ⓑ Ⓒ Ⓓ		
30	Ⓐ Ⓑ Ⓒ Ⓓ		
31	Ⓐ Ⓑ Ⓒ Ⓓ		
32	Ⓐ Ⓑ Ⓒ Ⓓ		
33	Ⓐ Ⓑ Ⓒ Ⓓ		
34	Ⓐ Ⓑ Ⓒ Ⓓ		
35	Ⓐ Ⓑ Ⓒ Ⓓ		
36	Ⓐ Ⓑ Ⓒ Ⓓ		
37	Ⓐ Ⓑ Ⓒ Ⓓ		
38	Ⓐ Ⓑ Ⓒ Ⓓ		
39	Ⓐ Ⓑ Ⓒ Ⓓ		
40	Ⓐ Ⓑ Ⓒ Ⓓ		

Science and Technology

1 Ⓐ Ⓑ Ⓒ Ⓓ	41 Ⓐ Ⓑ Ⓒ Ⓓ	1 Ⓐ Ⓑ Ⓒ Ⓓ	41 Ⓐ Ⓑ Ⓒ Ⓓ
2 Ⓐ Ⓑ Ⓒ Ⓓ	42 Ⓐ Ⓑ Ⓒ Ⓓ	2 Ⓐ Ⓑ Ⓒ Ⓓ	42 Ⓐ Ⓑ Ⓒ Ⓓ
3 Ⓐ Ⓑ Ⓒ Ⓓ	43 Ⓐ Ⓑ Ⓒ Ⓓ	3 Ⓐ Ⓑ Ⓒ Ⓓ	43 Ⓐ Ⓑ Ⓒ Ⓓ
4 Ⓐ Ⓑ Ⓒ Ⓓ	44 Ⓐ Ⓑ Ⓒ Ⓓ	4 Ⓐ Ⓑ Ⓒ Ⓓ	44 Ⓐ Ⓑ Ⓒ Ⓓ
5 Ⓐ Ⓑ Ⓒ Ⓓ	45 Ⓐ Ⓑ Ⓒ Ⓓ	5 Ⓐ Ⓑ Ⓒ Ⓓ	45 Ⓐ Ⓑ Ⓒ Ⓓ

Mathematics

6 Ⓐ Ⓑ Ⓒ Ⓓ	6 Ⓐ Ⓑ Ⓒ Ⓓ
7 Ⓐ Ⓑ Ⓒ Ⓓ	7 Ⓐ Ⓑ Ⓒ Ⓓ
8 Ⓐ Ⓑ Ⓒ Ⓓ	8 Ⓐ Ⓑ Ⓒ Ⓓ
9 Ⓐ Ⓑ Ⓒ Ⓓ	9 Ⓐ Ⓑ Ⓒ Ⓓ
10 Ⓐ Ⓑ Ⓒ Ⓓ	10 Ⓐ Ⓑ Ⓒ Ⓓ
11 Ⓐ Ⓑ Ⓒ Ⓓ	11 Ⓐ Ⓑ Ⓒ Ⓓ
12 Ⓐ Ⓑ Ⓒ Ⓓ	12 Ⓐ Ⓑ Ⓒ Ⓓ
13 Ⓐ Ⓑ Ⓒ Ⓓ	13 Ⓐ Ⓑ Ⓒ Ⓓ
14 Ⓐ Ⓑ Ⓒ Ⓓ	14 Ⓐ Ⓑ Ⓒ Ⓓ
15 Ⓐ Ⓑ Ⓒ Ⓓ	15 Ⓐ Ⓑ Ⓒ Ⓓ
16 Ⓐ Ⓑ Ⓒ Ⓓ	16 Ⓐ Ⓑ Ⓒ Ⓓ
17 Ⓐ Ⓑ Ⓒ Ⓓ	17 Ⓐ Ⓑ Ⓒ Ⓓ
18 Ⓐ Ⓑ Ⓒ Ⓓ	18 Ⓐ Ⓑ Ⓒ Ⓓ
19 Ⓐ Ⓑ Ⓒ Ⓓ	19 Ⓐ Ⓑ Ⓒ Ⓓ
20 Ⓐ Ⓑ Ⓒ Ⓓ	20 Ⓐ Ⓑ Ⓒ Ⓓ
21 Ⓐ Ⓑ Ⓒ Ⓓ	21 Ⓐ Ⓑ Ⓒ Ⓓ
22 Ⓐ Ⓑ Ⓒ Ⓓ	22 Ⓐ Ⓑ Ⓒ Ⓓ
23 Ⓐ Ⓑ Ⓒ Ⓓ	23 Ⓐ Ⓑ Ⓒ Ⓓ
24 Ⓐ Ⓑ Ⓒ Ⓓ	24 Ⓐ Ⓑ Ⓒ Ⓓ
25 Ⓐ Ⓑ Ⓒ Ⓓ	25 Ⓐ Ⓑ Ⓒ Ⓓ
26 Ⓐ Ⓑ Ⓒ Ⓓ	26 Ⓐ Ⓑ Ⓒ Ⓓ
27 Ⓐ Ⓑ Ⓒ Ⓓ	27 Ⓐ Ⓑ Ⓒ Ⓓ
28 Ⓐ Ⓑ Ⓒ Ⓓ	28 Ⓐ Ⓑ Ⓒ Ⓓ
29 Ⓐ Ⓑ Ⓒ Ⓓ	29 Ⓐ Ⓑ Ⓒ Ⓓ
30 Ⓐ Ⓑ Ⓒ Ⓓ	30 Ⓐ Ⓑ Ⓒ Ⓓ
31 Ⓐ Ⓑ Ⓒ Ⓓ	31 Ⓐ Ⓑ Ⓒ Ⓓ
32 Ⓐ Ⓑ Ⓒ Ⓓ	32 Ⓐ Ⓑ Ⓒ Ⓓ
33 Ⓐ Ⓑ Ⓒ Ⓓ	33 Ⓐ Ⓑ Ⓒ Ⓓ
34 Ⓐ Ⓑ Ⓒ Ⓓ	34 Ⓐ Ⓑ Ⓒ Ⓓ
35 Ⓐ Ⓑ Ⓒ Ⓓ	35 Ⓐ Ⓑ Ⓒ Ⓓ
36 Ⓐ Ⓑ Ⓒ Ⓓ	36 Ⓐ Ⓑ Ⓒ Ⓓ
37 Ⓐ Ⓑ Ⓒ Ⓓ	37 Ⓐ Ⓑ Ⓒ Ⓓ
38 Ⓐ Ⓑ Ⓒ Ⓓ	38 Ⓐ Ⓑ Ⓒ Ⓓ
39 Ⓐ Ⓑ Ⓒ Ⓓ	39 Ⓐ Ⓑ Ⓒ Ⓓ
40 Ⓐ Ⓑ Ⓒ Ⓓ	40 Ⓐ Ⓑ Ⓒ Ⓓ

Language Arts and Reading

1. Which of the following would be not considered a biography?

   A. Martin's (Luther King, Jr.) Big Words
   B. The Picture Book of Sacagawea
   C. Helen Keller
   D. Graham's Best Baseball Game Ever

2. When an author attempts to explain something to the reader, they are using what mode of writing?

   A. descriptive
   B. expository
   C. narrative
   D. persuasive

3. The Florida Comprehensive Assessment Test (FCAT) is a(n)

   A. norm-referenced test.
   B. informal reading inventory.
   C. criterion-referenced test.
   D. performance based assessment.

4. In order to communicate in writing, penmanship must be legible. Which of the following contributes to legible handwriting?

   A. spacing
   B. letter formation
   C. letter alignment
   D. all of the above

5. Which of the following choices would be considered a consonant blend?

   A. sch
   B. str
   C. sh
   D. wh

6. Jade is experiencing reading difficulties as noted on her recent timed, fluency check. It takes her an extended amount of time to say the words presented on the page. This shows a weakness in which area of fluency?

   A. prosody
   B. accuracy
   C. automaticity
   D. rate

7. When an author presents his thoughts in his writing in the form of a story, what mode of writing is he using?

   A. descriptive
   B. expository
   C. narrative
   D. persuasive

8. Knowledge of individual words in sentences, syllables, onset-rime segments, and the awareness of individual phonemes in words is known as

   A. phonics
   B. phonological awareness
   C. phoneme segmentation
   D. phoneme manipulation

9. Text explicit questions are also known as

   A. think and search questions.
   B. inferences.
   C. right there questions.
   D. reader and author questions.

10. Which of the following instructional methods aid fluency?

    A. repetitive or repeated reading
    B. echo reading
    C. choral reading
    D. all of the above

11. Which of the following is NOT a critical element of narrative writing?

    A. plot structure
    B. setting
    C. fluency
    D. characterization

12. Identify the literary device used in the following example:

The teenager stole some soap from the grocery store. The police said he made a clean getaway.

  A. pun
  B. hyperbole
  C. simile
  D. alliteration

13. All of following should be included in a classroom library except

  A. books from a variety of genres.
  B. a plethora of nonfiction resources.
  C. books that promote stereotypes of various races and ethnicities.
  D. a wide array of multicultural children's literature.

14. A teacher asks her students, "Which two words rhyme: hat, back, cat?" Which area of emergent literacy does this illustrate?

  A. vocabulary
  B. concepts of print
  C. fluency
  D. phonological awareness

15. During a whole group lesson, a first grade teacher asks her students to do the following task: "I am going to segment a word into parts and pause between each sound. I want you to say the whole word together."

Which progress monitoring assessment is the teacher using?

  A. test of nonsense word fluency
  B. informal reading inventory
  C. test of phonological awareness
  D. test of alphabet knowledge

16. The teacher has organized her classroom to allow for small groups. Students are listening to books on tape or cd, reading poetry, and responding to quality literature in writing. This is an example of what organizational format?

  A. literature circles
  B. shared reading
  C. interactive writing
  D. reading centers/stations

17. An authentic arrowhead found on a Native American reservation is

  A. a valuable teaching tool.
  B. an example of a primary source.
  C. an artifact.
  D. all of the above

18. In what grade are students typically taught to write in cursive?

  A. first
  B. third
  C. fourth
  D. Kindergarten

19. The local school board has announced that they plan to do away with art classes in all of the district's elementary schools. The students and teachers at each school are outraged. What would be the best form of written communication to share their thoughts with the school board?

  A. narrative
  B. descriptive
  C. expository
  D. persuasive

20. The workshop approach to organizing your classroom provides time to

  A. work on your lesson plans.
  B. offer a great deal of whole group instruction.
  C. meet with small groups of students to meet individual and small group needs.
  D. meet briefly with every student in your classroom.

21. Literature circles usually consist of four to six children

  A. all reading the same book they each chose based upon interest.
  B. completing worksheets about a book they are reading while sitting at a round table.
  C. all reading a text on the same reading level, with teacher assistance.
  D. reading different books but talking about them in a small group.

22. A teacher encourages her students to brainstorm ideas about a topic of interest that they might like to write about. Brainstorming takes place during what phase of the writing process?

    A. drafting
    B. revising
    C. editing
    D. prewriting

23. Which of the following is an example of onset-rime segments?

    A. c-at
    B. home-run
    C. hold-ing
    D. pre-view

24. Accuracy, rate, prosody, and automaticity are all components of reading _____.

    A. comprehension
    B. fluency
    C. speed
    D. words correct per minute

25. Which of the following choices are essential elements of reading comprehension?

    A. inferring and questioning
    B. understanding author's purpose and point of view
    C. visualizing the text
    D. all of the above

26. Gavin, a Kindergarten student, made approximations while reading at the beginning and middle of the school year. However, by the end of the year, he was pointing to each word on the page as he read his guide reading books. What concept of print is Gavin exhibiting?

    A. directionality
    B. voice-to-print match
    C. return sweep
    D. sight word recognition

27. A group of third graders are finishing up *narrative biographies* about a historical figure of their choosing that they had learned about during a social studies thematic unit. To encourage them to revise their work and include appropriate content, the teacher provides each child with a rubric. Which of the following rubrics would assist students in the revision of their content?

    A. a rubric focusing on punctuation and grammar
    B. a rubric that ensures each sentence has subject-verb agreement
    C. a rubric that encourages them to check all words for correct spelling
    D. a rubric focusing on the traits of writing like organization, word choice, and the use of supporting details

28. During a read aloud, a kindergarten student comments that the teacher is reading the pictures and not the words in the book. This child is demonstrating a lack of understanding in

    A. letter knowledge.
    B. alphabetic principle.
    C. concepts of print.
    D. phonemic awareness.

29. Which of the following choices would be considered a consonant blend?

    A. ch
    B. th
    C. wh
    D. bl

30. John is experiencing reading difficulties as noted on his recent timed, fluency check. His reading speed is slow and halted. This shows a weakness in which area of fluency?

    A. prosody
    B. accuracy
    C. automaticity
    D. rate

31. Making predictions about what a particular text is going to be about aids student

    A. automaticity.
    B. sight word recognition.
    C. analysis of cause and effect.
    D. comprehension.

32. A hyperbole is an exaggerated statement used for effect and is not meant to be taken literally. Which of the following is a hyperbole?

    A. The elephant was enormous!
    B. She ran as fast as a race car.
    C. Her nose was red like a strawberry.
    D. She must have weighed 1,000 pounds!

33. Where can you easily access a wide array of multicultural literature, free of charge, for use in your elementary classroom?

    A. school library
    B. college library
    C. Library of Congress
    D. the internet

34. The purpose of anecdotal notes is

    A. to make note of everything a student is doing wrong.
    B. to observe students while they work and record the observations for later study.
    C. to make notes of student work and stick strictly to your lesson plan regardless of these notes.
    D. none of the above

35. The National Reading Panel identified five critical areas for success in reading. Which of the following is not one of the five critical areas?

    A. comprehension
    B. fluency
    C. phonics
    D. motivation

36. During what stage of reading have students mastered basic concepts of print and are beginning to use various strategies for problem solving in reading?

    A. early
    B. pre-reading
    C. fluent
    D. emergent

37. What cueing system focuses on meaning that is associated with language through prior knowledge and experience?

    A. graphophonemic
    B. semantic
    C. visual
    D. auditory

38. An example of visual media is

    A. an online article.
    B. a journal.
    C. the newspaper.
    D. an atlas.

39. Questioning and retelling enhance communication skills among students in the classroom. What critical reading skill is most enhanced by these strategies?

    A. fluency
    B. word recognition
    C. phonics
    D. comprehension

40. Which of the following is a web-based activity that could take place in the classroom?

    A. blog
    B. online newsletter
    C. wiki page
    D. all of the above

41. Which of the following teaching methods does NOT enhance oral language development in students in the classroom?

    A. literature circles
    B. paired reading
    C. silent reading
    D. choral reading

42. Prior to a read aloud, setting a purpose aids what specific language art that is often neglected?

    A. reading
    B. writing
    C. speaking
    D. listening

43. Which of the following is not a basic concept of print?

    A. captions
    B. directionality
    C. title page
    D. illustrations

44. Information and media literacy would be enhanced by which of the following instructional aides?

    A. primary sources
    B. printed material (magazines, textbooks, etc.)
    C. the internet
    D. all of the above

45. Which of the following statements best describes how an educator should use the internet in her primary (K–2) classroom?

    A. Students should be provided preselected sites to choose from in order to avoid exposure to inappropriate web content.
    B. Students can be provided preselected sites but should be taught advanced search skills to collect information helpful to their learning.
    C. Students should be taught to critically question and evaluate the site based on its content and their needs.
    D. Students should be left to surf the web as they desire.

46. To summarize either orally or in written form is to

    A. concisely paraphrase what has been read.
    B. expand upon the author's main idea.
    C. to infer the author's purpose.
    D. none of the above

47. What are the three cueing systems?

    A. Emergent, Early, and Fluent
    B. Word identification, oral language development, and letter identification
    C. Graphophonemic, semantic, and syntactic
    D. Pre-Alphabetic, Alphabetic, and Conventional

48. A word that is recalled by memory only is known as a(n)

    A. sight word.
    B. high frequency word.
    C. alliterative phrase.
    D. phonogram.

49. Which of the following words contains a vowel digraph?

    A. bar
    B. boast
    C. batch
    D. bunt

Social Science

1. Japanese forces launched an attack on the United States naval base at Pearl Harbor in Hawaii on what date?

   A. December 7, 1991
   B. December 7, 1492
   C. December 7, 1941
   D. December 7, 1931

2. Operation Desert Storm was

   A. the name for the United States land and air operations involved in the Gulf War effort.
   B. the other name for the Gulf War.
   C. the name the media used for the Persian Gulf War.
   D. the name for a video game and had nothing to do with the Gulf War effort.

3. Which of the following statements describes the historical figure Thomas Jefferson?

   A. Invented bifocals and the Franklin stove
   B. Implemented and signed the Emancipation Proclamation
   C. Led the nursing effort for the North during the Civil War and formed the American Red Cross after the war
   D. Considered one of the Founding Fathers of our country and the principal author of the Declaration of Independence

4. During the Gilded Age, or the years following the Civil War, the Industrial Revolution made it possible for "robber barons" to accumulate gigantic fortunes. Which of the following people were considered "robber barons" during this time period?

   A. Andrew Carnegie
   B. John D. Rockefeller
   C. Cornelius Vanderbilt
   D. All of the above

5. Human beings tend to live in environments that meet their needs. Which essential element of geography refers to the interaction between people and their surroundings?

   A. Environment and Society
   B. Human Systems
   C. Process that shapes the Earth
   D. World in Spatial terms

6. Small representations, usually shapes and pictures, of real things on a map are known as

   A. a legend.
   B. cartographers.
   C. symbols.
   D. keys.

7. Which of the following is the horizontal, imaginary line that divides the Earth into its northern and southern halves?

   A. Prime Meridian
   B. Tropic of Capricorn
   C. International Date Line
   D. Equator

8. What article of the Constitution established the judicial branch of government in the United States of America?

   A. I
   B. III
   C. X
   D. V

9. The Supreme Court is the highest court of appeals in the United States. One of its most important powers is the power of

   A. legislative review.
   B. executive review.
   C. judicial review.
   D. legal review.

10. On a theme park map, features like bathrooms and restaurants are drawn the right size and distance apart in an effort to represent, in a smaller form, the park's amenities accurately. This map is known as being drawn to

    A. legend.
    B. scale.
    C. coordinates.
    D. hemispheres.

11. Prior to Columbus's arrival in the New World, native populations had settled the land. What happened to the native populations as a result of his discovery?

    A. The native populations were decimated by disease and warfare.
    B. The native populations flourished under the European influence.
    C. The native populations warmly welcomed all assistance provided by the Europeans.
    D. The native populations fought for their land and were victorious in their efforts.

12. The concept that events in history are linked to one another through a series of cause and effect occurrences is known as historic causation. Which of the following events would NOT be considered to possess historic causation?

    A. Columbus's discovery of the New World
    B. Industrial Revolution
    C. Japanese attack on Pearl Harbor
    D. Signing any bill into law

13. The ancient civilization of the Sumerians invented

    A. the wheel.
    B. cuneiform writing.
    C. initial forms of irrigation.
    D. all of the above

14. The use of what teaching strategy can assist students in synthesizing and summarizing informational text?

    A. fill-in-the-blank tests
    B. graphic organizers
    C. independent worksheets
    D. silent reading with no group discussion

15. An absolute location is defined as

    A. an informal location.
    B. a location where local landmarks are used to describe the place.
    C. a difficult location to access.
    D. a formal location where street names or coordinates are used to describe the locality.

16. When one company or institution has exclusive control of a particular good or service in a market, this is known as

    A. oligopoly
    B. roly-poly
    C. capitalism
    D. monopoly

17. How many electoral votes are required to win the presidency?

    A. 270
    B. 260
    C. 280
    D. 240

18. Electors are representatives of the people that actually elect the president and vice president. As of 2009, how many electors are there in the United States of America?

    A. 535
    B. 536
    C. 537
    D. 538

19. Policies that aid in governmental control of the economy are known as

    A. financial policy.
    B. fiscal policy.
    C. inflation policy.
    D. trade policy.

20. What article of the Constitution established the legislative branch of government in the United States of America?

    A. II
    B. III
    C. I
    D. IV

21. Which of the following people advises the President on matters of foreign policy?

    A. Secretary of State
    B. Secretary of the Treasury
    C. Press Secretary
    D. First Lady

22. The Supreme Court is the highest court of appeals in the United States. Who is responsible for appointing Supreme Court justices?

    A. the Senate
    B. the President
    C. the House of Representatives
    D. the public

23. What financial institution is owned, controlled, and operated by its members?

    A. federal reserve banks
    B. stock market
    C. Wall Street
    D. credit unions

24. Ancient Egyptians made many contributions to the world including

    A. cuneiform writing.
    B. the division of time.
    C. preservation of bodies after death.
    D. devising the famous Code of Hammurabi.

25. If no presidential candidate receives the majority of the electoral votes in a national election, who has the power to choose the President of the United States?

    A. House of Representatives
    B. Senate
    C. Supreme Court
    D. Former President may choose his successor

26. When a group of citizens claims that a bill which has gone through the process of becoming federal law is unconstitutional, which governmental body has the power to determine its constitutionality?

    A. President of the United States
    B. Supreme Court
    C. Senate
    D. Secretary of State

27. Which of the following wars led to the start of the American Revolutionary War?

    A. World War I
    B. The Civil War
    C. The Industrial Revolution
    D. The French and Indian War

28. The Axis Powers were defeated by The Allies in WWII and led to the emerging of two world superpowers and inevitably the Cold War. Which of the following countries was one of the defeated Axis Powers?

    A. Germany
    B. England
    C. France
    D. Russia

29. The ancient Phoenicians were well known for

    A. their manufacturing of glass.
    B. their manufacturing of metals.
    C. the development of their famous purple dye.
    D. all of the above

30. Which of the following is the vertical, imaginary line that divides the Earth into its eastern and western halves?

    A. Prime Meridian
    B. Tropic of Capricorn
    C. International Date Line
    D. Equator

31. In a market economy, who decides what goods and services will be produced?

    A. the government
    B. private businesses
    C. national organizations
    D. consumers

32. Many governments in Europe have high taxes on gasoline and oil; consumers in these countries have asked their local and state governments to

    A. create more jobs.
    B. provide higher wages.
    C. provide better alternative transportation through public transit.
    D. decrease insurance costs for personal vehicles.

33. The NCSS is a specialized organization in this content area. What does NCSS stand for?

    A. National Council for Safe Start
    B. National Council for Student Studies
    C. National Council for the Social Studies
    D. National Council for the Social Sciences

34. The belief that the United States should control all of North America was known as _____. This idea fueled much of the warfare that took place against the Native Americans.

    A. Manifest Destiny
    B. Louisiana Purchase
    C. Westward Expansion
    D. the arrival of the Mayflower

35. What element on the map shows the viewer the map's orientation in terms of cardinal directions?

    A. the legend
    B. the scale
    C. the compass rose
    D. the key

36. The Magna Carta of 1215(England) is

    A. considered the very first modern document which sought to limit the powers of the governing body.
    B. an English legal charter.
    C. the most significant early influence on the extensive historical process that led to the rule of constitutional law today.
    D. all of the above

37. Who is considered the leader of the local government?

    A. city council
    B. mayor
    C. governor
    D. president

38. What are the three levels of government in the United States?

    A. local, state, and federal
    B. legislative, judicial, and executive
    C. domestic, national, and international
    D. local, federal, and abroad

39. What famous American gave a speech that so eloquently began with the phrase: *Four score and seven years ago, our fathers brought forth on this continent, a new nation, conceived in liberty and dedicated to the proposition that all men are created equal.*

    A. Martin Luther King, Jr.
    B. John F. Kennedy, Jr.
    C. Abraham Lincoln
    D. Susan B. Anthony

40. The following image identifies what imaginary line that designates the official change of each day?

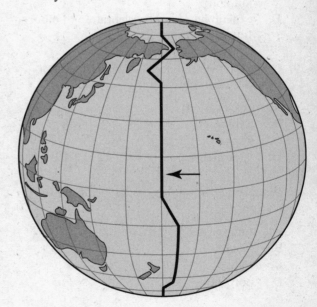

    A. International Date Line
    B. Prime Meridian
    C. equator
    D. Tropic of Cancer

Music, Visual Arts, Physical Education, and Health

1. The basic element of music used to describe the amount of rhythms played at a specific time, and overall quality of sound of a music composition is

    A. pitch.
    B. rhythm.
    C. timbre.
    D. texture.

2. Which of the following is NOT most likely to help students to examine how music relates to their community?

    A. describe how they have used music to be of service to someone
    B. explain how participation in music can become a lifetime pursuit
    C. play the melody of a song using the autoharp
    D. explain how people celebrate, and mourn, through music

3. Complete the sentence: The highest level of Bloom's Taxonomy is

    A. Application.
    B. Synthesis.
    C. Evaluation.
    D. Comprehension.

4. Which one the following is a type of music texture?

    A. timbre
    B. tempo
    C. tone
    D. polyphony

5. This era is distinguished by being emotional, large, and programmatic.

    A. Classical
    B. Baroque
    C. Modern
    D. Romantic

6. Obesity increases the risk of all of the medical conditions listed EXCEPT which one?

    A. Heart Disease
    B. Stroke
    C. Diabetes
    D. Anorexia

7. A series of strikes on a percussion instrument is called

    A. rhythmic pattern.
    B. melodic pattern.
    C. pitch pattern.
    D. harmonic pattern.

8. Which of the following is NOT an aspect of gross motor skill development?

    A. Locomotor skills
    B. Manipulative Skills
    C. Nonlocomotor skills
    D. Athleticism

9. To assess recognition of instrument timbres, students listen to recorded examples and indicate what instrument is played. What type of assessment is the teacher most likely using?

    A. authentic assessment items
    B. multiple-choice or simple completion items
    C. performance-based assessment items
    D. alternative assessment items

10. A collection of work that exhibits an individual's efforts, progress, and achievement is a

    A. reflection task.
    B. self-assessment task.
    C. portfolio.
    D. traditional task.

11. Fill in the blank: _____ is the overindulgence in and dependence on an addictive substance.

    A. Domestic abuse
    B. Substance abuse
    C. Apathy
    D. Compulsion

12. Complete the sentence: _____ involve(s) specific and detailed movements like cutting with scissors.

  A. Gross motor skills
  B. Physical fitness
  C. Fine motor skills
  D. Academic achievement

13. Claudio Monteverdi, an Italian composer, was the first great composer and is considered to be the father of this type of music genre.

  A. Oratorio
  B. Opera
  C. Cantata
  D. Chorale

14. Which one of the following art activities would NOT provide opportunities to enhance students' engagement with art?

  A. Copy a drawing from a specific genre presented in a book
  B. Work independently in decorating a card for a family member
  C. Work collaboratively in decorating a mural
  D. Work with creative individuals and in creative environments where possible

15. It is important to keep safety in mind when planning physical activities. Which of the following should a teacher do when planning a physical activity which would help prevent accidents and injuries?

  A. Stop misbehavior before it spreads
  B. Restrict the physical activity in the lesson
  C. Review rules prior to beginning activity
  D. Encourage students to experiment with equipment

16. A teacher asked her students to create movements in response to music. This activity will most likely help students connect music and dance in terms of

  A. speed.
  B. visual image.
  C. timbre.
  D. rhythm.

17. The succession of notes in a music piece is called a

  A. rhythm.
  B. melody.
  C. cadence.
  D. tempo.

18. Which of the following is considered a school-based prevention program?

  A. Recovery support group
  B. Drug awareness program
  C. Narcotics anonymous
  D. Drug treatment program

19. Which of the following is the highest locomotor skill?

  A. Walking
  B. Skipping
  C. Crawling
  D. Galloping

20. Some people consider this composer as the first composer or the Romantic era.

  A. Ludwig van Beethoven
  B. Niccoló Paganini
  C. Wolfgang Amadeus Mozart
  D. Johann Sebastian Bach

21. Which of the following is an aerobic activity?

  A. Lifting weights
  B. Jogging
  C. Stretching
  D. Sit-ups

22. Improvisation is a shared characteristic between jazz and music from

  A. the Renaissance period.
  B. the Classical period.
  C. the Baroque period.
  D. the Romantic period.

23. Which of the following is a fine motor skill?

  A. Skipping
  B. Holding a pencil
  C. Jumping
  D. Twisting

24. Which of the following is NOT a style of the Nineteenth Century?

    A. Romanticism
    B. Rococo
    C. Realism
    D. Impressionism

25. A teacher intentionally and regularly involves students in music and dance routines. This practice serves to develop students'

    A. contrast.
    B. dissonance.
    C. rhythm.
    D. dominance.

26. Which of the following lists the levels of the cognitive domain of Bloom's Taxonomy from least to most complex?

    A. Knowledge, Comprehension, Application, Analysis, Evaluation, and Synthesis
    B. Synthesis, Evaluation, Analysis, Application, Comprehension, and Knowledge
    C. Knowledge, Comprehension, Application, Evaluation, Synthesis, and Analysis
    D. Analysis, Synthesis, Evaluation, Application, Comprehension, and Knowledge

27. Which of the following best describes the use of a student's art portfolio?

    A. The artwork collected by a student that is representative of the student's work and progress.
    B. The artwork collected by a student that is used to compare the student with other students.
    C. The artwork collected by a student that is used to grade on a scale.
    D. The artwork collected by a student that contains the student's work.

28. Child development is divided into six categories. Which of the following lists these categories in order from latest to earliest?

    A. Newborn, infant, toddler, preschooler, school-aged child, adolescent
    B. Toddler, preschooler, adolescent, school-aged child, infant, newborn
    C. Adolescent, school-aged child, preschooler, toddler, infant, newborn
    D. School-aged child, adolescent, toddler, preschooler, newborn, infant

29. You have become concerned about the physical development of a child in your care. The child has not begun to walk unassisted and cannot hold a cup or bottle on his/her own. What age might this child be?

    A. 6 months
    B. 9 months
    C. 12 months
    D. 18 months

30. Which of the following is an example of strength training?

    A. Swimming
    B. Yoga
    C. Running
    D. Lifting weights

31. Putting parts together to form a whole is which level of Bloom's Taxonomy?

    A. Analysis
    B. Evaluation
    C. Synthesis
    D. Application

32. During a particular reporting period students in a fifth-grade music class have played recorders. The teacher assesses recorder proficiency by requiring each student to practice and play a piece of music chosen from the instructional repertoire. What type of assessment is the teacher most likely using?

    A. traditional form of assessment
    B. rubric assessment
    C. criterion reference assessment
    D. performance-based assessment

33. Which of the following is NOT a symptom of abuse of inhalants like glue?

    A. Watery eyes
    B. Slurred speech
    C. Runny nose
    D. Drowsiness

34. A basic principle of art design that refers to the ways in which the art elements like lines, shapes, colors, and textures of a piece of art are arranged is called

    A. value.
    B. balance.
    C. repetition.
    D. movement.

35. Picasso's style of fragmenting the forms of people, still life, and landscapes into geometric forms is called

    A. cubism.
    B. impressionism.
    C. realism.
    D. pointillism.

36. Fill in the blank: There are _____ pillars of character.

    A. four
    B. five
    C. six
    D. seven

37. The nutritional category of Vegetables includes which of the following foods?

    A. Broccoli
    B. Strawberries
    C. Fish
    D. Yogurt

38. This style involved total destruction of realistic depiction.

    A. Realism
    B. Romanticism
    C. Cubism
    D. Rococo

39. Which of the following is NOT considered an important principle of art design?

    A. repetition
    B. unity
    C. color
    D. style

40. Complete the sentence: In girls, puberty is characterized by an increase in _____.

    A. Estrogen
    B. Testosterone
    C. Body Fat
    D. Progesterone

41. The nutritional category of Fruits includes which of the following foods?

    A. Sweet Potato
    B. Carrots
    C. Blueberries
    D. Chicken

42. In art, the color red is considered a

    A. secondary color.
    B. compound color.
    C. primary color.
    D. tertiary color.

43. Which of the following is NOT a nutritional category in the USDA Food Pyramid?

    A. Milk
    B. Grains
    C. Vegetables
    D. Soda

44. Good communication skills involves all of the following skills EXCEPT which one?

    A. Active Listening
    B. Conflict Resolution
    C. Good grammar
    D. Communicating without attacking

45. Who is responsible for regulating food labels?

    A. Surgeon General
    B. Attorney General
    C. Food and Drug Administration
    D. Centers for Disease Control

Science and Technology

1. What is the name for the amount of cubic space that an object occupies?

   A. volume
   B. mass
   C. density
   D. weight

2. What creates the Earth's magnetism?

   A. The rotation of the Earth around the sun.
   B. The rotation of the moon around the Earth.
   C. The rotation of the outer core around the inner core.
   D. The rotation of the solar system.

3. Temperature is a measure related to the average of this type of energy of the molecules of a substance.

   A. kinetic energy
   B. heat energy
   C. static energy
   D. frictional energy

4. Which is NOT a property of a living thing?

   A. Grows and develops
   B. Reproduces
   C. Has a skeleton
   D. Made up of cells

5. What causes seasons?

   A. The tilt of the Earth
   B. The distance of the Earth from the sun
   C. The rotation of the moon around the Earth
   D. The gravitational pull of the moon

6. Which of the following provides the best opportunities for inquiry-based learning?

   A. Students define and describe the El Niño effect by using text and images they find on the Internet.
   B. Students select a location in the U.S. then search the Internet for monthly temperature data of this location for the most recent El Niño year. Students then compare monthly temperature data for the El Niño year to the average temperature data for the past 50 years in order to assess the impact of El Niño on that particular location.
   C. Students read an article about El Niño provided in their textbook, and complete a test based on their reading.
   D. Students go to the library to find newspaper accounts describing the impact of El Niño on the California coast. They then summarize what they find in a two-page written report.

7. Which is the least specific level of taxonomy?

   A. Species
   B. Genus
   C. Domain
   D. Kingdom

8. Which of the following is NOT a type of contact force?

   A. frictional force
   B. tension force
   C. electrical force
   D. mechanical force

9. Complete the sentence: The _____ makes up the majority of the Earth's volume.

   A. crust
   B. core
   C. moon
   D. mantle

10. A truthful explanation of different events that happen with uniformity under certain conditions is called a

   A. law.
   B. theory.
   C. hypothesis.
   D. postulate.

11. Complete the sentence: _____ are the ways in which scientists answer questions and solve problems systematically.

   A. Laboratories
   B. Scientific methods
   C. Controlled experiments
   D. Hypotheses

12. Complete the sentence: A _____ moon occurs when the sun and moon are on the same side of the earth.

   A. Full
   B. New
   C. First Quarter
   D. Last Quarter

13. The sun provides this type of energy.

   A. Magnetic energy
   B. Radiant energy
   C. Nuclear force
   D. Acoustic force

14. Which Apollo flight was considered a "successful failure" when its mission had to be aborted due to the explosion of oxygen tanks?

   A. Apollo 7
   B. Apollo 8
   C. Apollo 11
   D. Apollo 13

15. The iron in an iron bar combining with oxygen in the air to produce rust is an example of

   A. volume change.
   B. density change.
   C. chemical change.
   D. physical change.

16. What is a possible answer to a question posed in a scientific experiment?

   A. Educated guess
   B. Prediction
   C. Hypothesis
   D. Variable

17. Which of the following is NOT a domain for living things?

   A. Archaea
   B. Fungi
   C. Eukarya
   D. Bacteria

18. Which of the following is NOT a continent?

   A. South America
   B. Antarctica
   C. Arctic Circle
   D. Australia

19. This type of energy travels in a straight line.

   A. Magnetic energy
   B. Acoustic energy
   C. Light energy
   D. Nuclear energy

20. Which of the following is NOT a stage in the water cycle?

   A. Evaporation
   B. Perspiration
   C. Condensation
   D. Collection

21. All cells contain the following parts EXCEPT which one?

   A. DNA
   B. cell walls
   C. organelles
   D. cell membranes

22. Which of the following occurs when light passes through a transparent material like water at a slant angle?

   A. Refraction
   B. Diffraction
   C. Transformation
   D. Dislocation

23. What part of the cell breaks down sugar to create energy?

    A. Endoplasmic Reticulum
    B. Ribosomes
    C. Golgi Complex
    D. Mitochondrion

24. In an experiment, students have not yet determined exactly what data will be collected. The perspective and objective of the study determine which data are important. The students are most likely involved in

    A. planning a controlled experiment.
    B. identifying a research question.
    C. formulating a hypothesis.
    D. revisiting the hypothesis to answer a question.

25. What type of experiment has a control and experimental group?

    A. random experiment
    B. quasi-experiment
    C. nested experiment
    D. controlled experiment

26. Optics is a branch of physics that studies the physical properties of

    A. sound.
    B. eyes.
    C. vision.
    D. light.

27. Who proposed the theory that the continents were once joined in a supercontinent called pangea?

    A. Alfred Wegner
    B. Albert Einstein
    C. Benjamin Franklin
    D. Neil Armstrong

28. Which of the following is NOT a shape of bacteria?

    A. Rods
    B. Cones
    C. Spheres
    D. Spirals

29. A transparent object with flat polished surfaces that refracts or diffuses light is called

    A. prism.
    B. diamond.
    C. pyramid.
    D. plastic.

30. Complete the sentence: _____ rock is formed when debris is compressed and fused together.

    A. Metamorphic
    B. Sedimentary
    C. Igneous
    D. Compressed

31. Complete the sentence: _____ reproduction requires two parents.

    A. Asexual
    B. Nonsexual
    C. Conjugation
    D. Sexual

32. A phase change that involves changing from a solid to a liquid can be called

    A. sublimation.
    B. freezing.
    C. evaporating.
    D. fusion.

33. Which of the following is NOT considered an electromagnetic wave?

    A. ultraviolet rays
    B. X-rays
    C. radio waves
    D. sound waves

34. Which of the following is NOT an aspect of the scientific method?

    A. Predicting
    B. Observing
    C. Testing
    D. Disseminating

35. Which is NOT a group of fungi?

    A. Perfect fungi
    B. Club fungi
    C. Imperfect fungi
    D. Threadlike fungi

36. Does an instrument that is considered valid also have to be reliable?

   A. No, it is valid so it does not need to be reliable.
   B. No, they are two separate issues.
   C. Yes, you need it to be valid as well as consistent. You cannot have a valid instrument without reliability.
   D. Yes, if the instrument is valid we can assume it is also reliable.

37. A physical occurrence related to stationary and moving electrons and protons is called

   A. vibration.
   B. electricity.
   C. light.
   D. sound.

38. An organism which consumes food from its environment is called a/an

   A. heterotroph.
   B. heterozygote.
   C. autotroph.
   D. parasite.

39. Which of the following occurs when two plates slide against each other in opposite directions?

   A. Earthquakes
   B. Canyons
   C. Mountains
   D. Volcanoes

40. Students are exploring the relationship between two variables, and will either manually enter the data for each variable into a table of values or import them using a link cable. In this experiment, the students are most likely using

   A. word processors.
   B. spreadsheets.
   C. online databases.
   D. graphing calculators.

41. Which of the following is NOT an example of a conductor?

   A. aluminum
   B. copper
   C. rubber
   D. graphite

42. Which of the following is NOT a good laboratory procedure?

   A. Washing hands frequently
   B. Eating in the laboratory
   C. Disposing of chemicals properly
   D. Wearing gloves

43. In an investigation activity, students generate questions about a topic they are following. They identify the questions they can answer themselves. Which of the following sources should they most likely use to answer the questions they cannot answer themselves?

   A. Visit online science video Websites
   B. Visit science related Ask the Expert Websites
   C. Visit social network Websites
   D. Visit online science databases

44. Which of the following is NOT a type of rock?

   A. Metamorphic rock
   B. Sedimentary rock
   C. Hard rock
   D. Igneous rock

45. The process by which a plant converts glucose into energy is called

   A. transpiration.
   B. respiration.
   C. photosynthesis.
   D. fertilization.

Mathematics

1. A student is using a number line to represent fractional number values. What type or types of representation models is the student using?

   A. pictorial and abstract models
   B. concrete and abstract models
   C. only the abstract model
   D. only the pictorial model

2. Find the next term in the pattern 1, 3, 4, 7, 11, 18, 29, …

   A. 36
   B. 40
   C. 47
   D. 50

3. Which one of the following assessment practices could least likely help in identifying a student's specific problem areas?

   A. alternative test
   B. diagnostic test
   C. standardized test
   D. authentic test

4. A bedroom is rectangular and has dimensions 12 feet and 10 feet. If one dimension is doubled and the other dimension is tripled, the area of the bedroom floor has increased by how many times?

   A. 2 times
   B. 3 times
   C. 5 times
   D. 6 times

5. Sue found the following set of measures for a project she was doing. Which one of these sets of fractions is arranged in ascending order (from least to greatest)?

   A. $\dfrac{3}{16}, \dfrac{3}{8}, \dfrac{5}{8}, \dfrac{1}{4}$

   B. $\dfrac{5}{8}, \dfrac{3}{8}, \dfrac{1}{4}, \dfrac{3}{16}$

   C. $\dfrac{3}{16}, \dfrac{1}{4}, \dfrac{3}{8}, \dfrac{5}{8}$

   D. $\dfrac{1}{4}, \dfrac{5}{8}, \dfrac{3}{8}, \dfrac{3}{16}$

6. What is the value of $4.1 \cdot 10^{-2}$?

   A. 0.41
   B. 0.041
   C. 410
   D. 41

7. If $\triangle ABC \cong \triangle DEF$, then which of the following is true?

   A. $\angle A \cong \angle E$
   B. $AB = DE$
   C. $AC = EF$
   D. $\angle C \cong \angle D$

8. A tree that is 8 feet tall casts a shadow that is 4 feet long. A girl casts a shadow that is 2.5 feet long. How tall is the girl?

   A. 1.25 feet
   B. 4 feet
   C. 5 feet
   D. 6.5 feet

9. Which of the following equations matches the description: The difference of a number and 4 is two times the number.

   A. $N - 4 = 2N$
   B. $4 - N = 2N$
   C. $N + 4 = 2N$
   D. $N - 4 = 2 - N$

Use the figure for items 10, 11, and 12.

This is a line plot representing students' scores on an exam with 35 items.

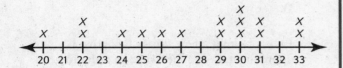

10. What is the mean of the data set? Round your answer to the nearest ones.

    A. 31
    B. 30
    C. 442
    D. 28

11. What is the mode of the data set?

    A. 33
    B. 30
    C. 29
    D. 31

12. What is the median of the data set?

    A. 29
    B. 26.5
    C. 29.5
    D. 30

13. Which of the following is NOT an example of alternative assessment?

    A. multiple-choice assessment item
    B. portfolio assessment task
    C. rubric
    D. performance assessment task

14. Select the unit of measure that is most appropriate for the length of time it may take to run a mile.

    A. Minutes
    B. Seconds
    C. Hours
    D. Days

15. The figure shown is an example of what transformation?

    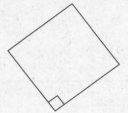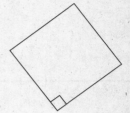

    A. translation
    B. reflection
    C. rotation
    D. dilation

16. Select the number that will result in a smaller product after it is squared.

    A. 3
    B. −0.03
    C. 1.3
    D. 0.3

17. A train takes 3 hours to travel 225 miles. Assuming there are no stops, how many miles will this train travel in 12 hours?

    A. 825 miles
    B. 56.25 miles
    C. 900 miles
    D. 1125 miles

18. Which expression can be used for the table below?

X	Y
1	5
2	7
3	9
4	11

    A. $Y = 2x - 3$
    B. $Y = x + 4$
    C. $Y = 2x + 3$
    D. $Y = 3x + 2$

19. Identify the coordinates of point S in the figure shown.

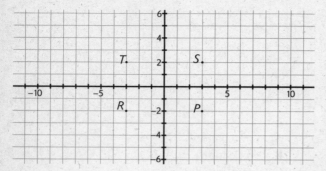

A. (3, 2)
B. (2, 3)
C. (–3, –2)
D. (–2, –3)

20. The box-and-whisker plot below displays the list of Peter's test scores this semester in a math class. What is the median of Peter's test scores?

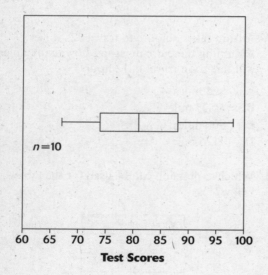

A. 67
B. 72
C. 87
D. 81

21. How many meters are in 120 centimeters?

A. 12 meters
B. 1200 meters
C. 12 meters
D. 1.2 meters

22. Solve for x: $4x - 3 = 2x + 9$.

A. $x = 1$
B. $x = 2$
C. $x = 3$
D. $x = 6$

23. Parker bought a new square table that is approximately $4\sqrt{2}$ feet wide. In order to get a box for this table, how wide must the box at least approximately be?

A. 6 feet
B. 5.5 feet
C. 5 feet
D. 4.5 feet

24. A car dealer was selling a used car for a 10 percent discount of the original price. If you paid $9,000.00 for this car, what was the original price of the car? This problem does not include taxes and other fees.

A. $10,000
B. $900
C. $8,100
D. $90,000

25. Find the area of the figure shown.

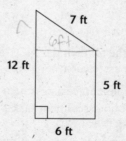

A. 30 ft²
B. 51 ft²
C. 55 ft²
D. 102 ft²

26. Which one of the following ideas related to mathematics teaching is true?

    A. Mastery of skills is the key for teaching mathematics and problem solving is not appropriate for elementary school level.

    B. Problem solving should come only before mastery of skills.

    C. Problem solving does not come only after mastery of skills.

    D. Problem solving should come only after mastery of skills.

27. Which of the following is a unit of area?

    A. Ft^3
    B. In^2
    C. M^3
    D. Cm

28. Simplify the following expression: $300 - 40 \div 5 \cdot (2^3 - 2) \cdot 3 + 8$.

    A. 164
    B. 308.44
    C. 148
    D. 944

29. Solve for x: $2x - 5 > 5x + 4$

    A. $x > -3$
    B. $x > 3$
    C. $x < -3$
    D. $x < 3$

30. At a supermarket, Samuel needs to arrange cans of food (all the same size) in seven shelves. He estimated that he could fit about 45 cans of food in half a shelf. The cans of food come in boxes of 30 cans each. Approximately how many boxes of cans of food will Samuel need to fill up the seven shelves?

    A. 10.5 boxes
    B. 21 boxes
    C. 3 boxes
    D. 630 cans

31. Sarah has a swimming pool which has rectangular dimensions of 5 meters, 12 meters, and 20 meters. What amount of water will fill the swimming pool?

    A. 60 m^3
    B. 240 m^3
    C. 600 m^3
    D. 1200 m^3

32. How many faces does a triangular prism have?

    A. 3
    B. 4
    C. 5
    D. 6

33. At a local school, Carlos decided to develop and administer a survey for a school project. He wanted to know whether the students in the school county were in favor of a new rule mandated by the school board. At the end of the school day, he stood outside the school exit and asked a few students to complete the survey as they went out. Some students participated, and others did not. He gathered and analyzed the data and concluded that the students in the school county were not in favor of the new rule mandated by the school board. Did Carlos interpret the results of the survey correctly?

    A. The procedures used by Carlos to develop the survey were valid, but the interpretation of the survey's results is not correct.

    B. The procedures used by Carlos to develop the survey were sufficiently systematic and valid, and the interpretation of the survey's results is basically correct. Asking students in one school is enough of a sample to make some generalizations about a whole school county.

    C. The procedures used by Carlos to develop the survey were not systematic and valid, and the interpretation of the survey's results is not correct.

    D. The procedures used by Carlos to develop the survey were not systematic and valid, but the interpretation of the survey's results is probably correct.

34. Robert painted $\frac{3}{4}$ of a wall yesterday, and 25 percent of the same wall today. What percent of the wall did Robert paint in these two days?

   A. 25%
   B. 50%
   C. 75%
   D. 100%

35. Maria made the following table based on the numbers of hours she worked per day last month. Find the mean number of hours per day that she worked last month.

Number of Hours	Tally	Frequency
7	ℋℋ ℋℋ //	12
8	///	3
9	//	2
10	ℋℋ //	7

   A. about 6 hours per day
   B. about 8 hours per day
   C. about 48.5 hours per day
   D. about 7.5 hours per day

36. A parallelogram must have which of the following properties?

   A. All equal sides
   B. Two sets of parallel sides
   C. All right angles
   D. Five sides

37. What is the approximate percent for a $9.50 payment out of $350?

   A. 3%
   B. 0.3%
   C. 30%
   D. 0.03%

Use the following table to answer items 38 and 39.

Number of Hours	Frequency
1	21
2	15
3	2
4	7

38. Find the median for the data set given in the table above. Round your answer to the nearest tenth.

   A. 2 hours
   B. 2.5 hours
   C. 1.9 hour
   D. 1 hour

39. Find the range of the data set given in the table.

   A. 3
   B. 14
   C. 2
   D. Not possible.

40. Jillian has a toy box which has dimensions of 4 feet, 6 feet, and 3 feet. What is the volume of her toy box?

   A. 72 ft³
   B. 72 ft²
   C. 108 ft³
   D. 108 ft²

41. Elizabeth is painting her bedroom wall. The dimensions of the wall are 8 feet tall by 14 feet wide. A gallon of paint will cover 50 square feet. If Elizabeth wants to paint her room with two coats of paint, how many gallons of paint will she need?

   A. 2
   B. 3
   C. 5
   D. 6

42. Which of the following demonstrates the commutative property of multiplication?

 A. $(3 \times 4) \times 5 = 3 \times (4 \times 5)$
 B. $3 \times 4 = 4 \times 3$
 C. $4 \times 1 = 4$
 D. $0 \times 4 = 0$

43. Which of the following is not a necessary skill or concept for the effective learning of addition computation involving two- and three-digit whole numbers?

 A. Addition concept with cubes
 B. Addition facts memorization
 C. Place value up to hundreds with base-ten blocks
 D. All of the above skills and concepts are necessary

44. The figure shown can be called which of the following names?

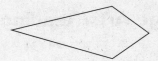

 A. Rhombus
 B. Kite
 C. Trapezoid
 D. Rectangle

45. If the base of a triangle is cut in one fourth and the height is not changed, what happens to the area of that triangle?

 A. Cut in one-half
 B. Cut in one-fourth
 C. Doubled
 D. Tripled

Practice Test 2 Answers

Language Arts/Reading

1. D	14. D	27. D	40. D
2. B	15. C	28. C	41. C
3. C	16. D	29. D	42. D
4. D	17. D	30. D	43. A
5. B	18. B	31. D	44. D
6. C	19. D	32. D	45. A
7. C	20. C	33. A	46. A
8. B	21. A	34. B	47. C
9. C	22. D	35. D	48. A
10. D	23. A	36. A	49. B
11. C	24. B	37. B	
12. A	25. D	38. A	
13. C	26. B	39. D	

Social Science

1. C	11. A	21. A	31. D
2. A	12. D	22. B	32. C
3. D	13. D	23. D	33. C
4. D	14. B	24. C	34. A
5. A	15. D	25. A	35. C
6. C	16. D	26. B	36. D
7. D	17. A	27. D	37. B
8. B	18. D	28. A	38. A
9. C	19. B	29. D	39. C
10. B	20. C	30. A	40. A

Music, Visual Arts, Physical Education, and Health

1. D	13. B	25. C	37. A
2. C	14. A	26. A	38. C
3. B	15. C	27. A	39. D
4. D	16. D	28. C	40. A
5. D	17. B	29. D	41. C
6. D	18. B	30. D	42. C
7. A	19. B	31. C	43. D
8. D	20. A	32. D	44. C
9. B	21. B	33. B	45. C
10. C	22. C	34. B	
11. B	23. B	35. A	
12. C	24. B	36. C	

Science and Technology

1. A	13. B	25. D	37. B
2. C	14. D	26. D	38. A
3. A	15. C	27. A	39. A
4. C	16. C	28. B	40. D
5. A	17. B	29. A	41. C
6. B	18. C	30. B	42. B
7. C	19. C	31. D	43. B
8. C	20. B	32. D	44. C
9. D	21. B	33. D	45. B
10. A	22. A	34. D	
11. B	23. D	35. A	
12. B	24. A	36. C	

Mathematics

1. A	13. A	25. B	37. A
2. C	14. A	26. C	38. A
3. C	15. A	27. B	39. A
4. D	16. D	28. A	40. A
5. C	17. C	29. C	41. C
6. B	18. C	30. B	42. B
7. B	19. A	31. D	43. D
8. C	20. D	32. C	44. B
9. A	21. D	33. C	45. B
10. D	22. D	34. D	
11. B	23. A	35. B	
12. A	24. A	36. B	

Practice Test 2 Solutions

What follows are detailed solutions to the problems from practice test 2. The competency to which the test question is related is also included for reference.

Language Arts/Reading

1. **D.** Competency 2. Biographies are books written about important, famous, or infamous people.

2. **B.** Competency 3. Expository writing is writing that attempts to explain, describe, or inform. Descriptive, persuasive, and narrative are all modes of writing as well.

3. **C.** Competency 4. FCAT is a criterion-referenced test. These types of tests are assessment instruments that assess the point at which the student has achieved mastery.

4. **D.** Competency 5. Letter formation, spacing, letter size and alignment, along with line quality all contribute to legible handwriting or penmanship.

5. **B.** Competency 1. A consonant blend is two or three consonants that together keep their individual sounds.

6. **C.** Competency 1. Automaticity is the ability to say the words quickly and easily. Accuracy, prosody, and rate are also crucial elements of fluency.

7. **C.** Competency 3. Narrative writing is writing that tells a story.

8. **B.** Competency 1. Knowledge of individual words in sentences, syllables, onset-rime segments, and the awareness of individual phonemes in words is known as phonological awareness.

9. **C.** Competency 1. Right there or text explicit questions are literal questions where the answers are found in the text itself.

10. **D.** Competency 1. Along with the methods noted above, timed reading, readers theater, audio books, poetry readings, independent, and paired reading all aid a student's reading fluency.

11. **C.** Competency 3. Narrative writing should include the following elements: plot structure, conflict, characterization, setting, theme, point of view, sequencing, and transitions. Fluency is a critical skill in reading.

12. **A.** Competency 2. A pun is defined as a play on words.

13. **C.** Competency 2. Classroom libraries should contain a wide variety of multicultural children's literature, nonfiction resources, and various genres.

14. **D.** Competency 1. Rhyme is the earliest developing phonological awareness skill.

15. **C.** Competency 4. Segmenting and blending are integral parts of phonological awareness.

16. **D.** Competency 4. Reading centers/stations allow students to co-construct meaning in a small group setting. For the teacher, this organizational format allows time to meet with guided reading groups and to differentiate instruction to meet the varying needs of students in the classroom.

17. **D.** Competency 6. Primary sources are documents or pieces of work that were written, recorded, or created during a particular time period.

18. **B.** Competency 5. Students are typically taught cursive in the third grade.

19. **D.** Competency 3. The students wish to persuade the school board to keep their art classes intact at each school site.

20. **C.** Competency 4. The workshop approach is a student-centered approach to teaching where teachers have ample time to meet and confer with small groups and individuals to best meet their academic needs.

21. **A.** Competency 2. Literature circles are a small group of children reading a chosen text and discussing that text on a routine and regular basis with a group of their peers.

22. **D.** Competency 3. Prewriting is the phase of the writing process that includes activating prior knowledge, gathering, and organizing ideas. Drafting, editing, and revising are all later phases in the writing process.

23. **A.** Competency 1. The onset is defined as the first consonant or groups of consonants that come before the first vowel in a syllable. The rime unit is the first vowel sound and any others that follow it in a syllable.

24. **B.** Competency 1. Accuracy, prosody, rate, and automaticity are all crucial elements of fluency.

25. **D.** Competency 1. Understanding the main idea, supporting details and facts, author's purpose, fact and opinion, point of view, making inferences, and visualizing are all critical to making meaning from text, known as comprehension.

26. **B.** Competency 1. Voice-to-print match, also known as one-to-one correspondence, shows that Sheila now understands the concept of a word and word boundaries.

27. **D.** Competency 3. If truly focusing on the content, the teacher is encouraging her students to revise and improve upon what has been written and is not *yet* concerned with editing for errors.

28. **C.** Competency 4. Concepts of print includes that print conveys meaning, directionality (left to right progression, top to bottom), concept of a word (word boundaries), letter knowledge, phonemic awareness, and literacy language (author, illustrations, title, etc.).

29. **D.** Competency 1. The first three choices are digraphs or two consonants that together represent one sound. A consonant blend is two consonants that together keep their individual sounds.

30. **D.** Competency 1. Rate is defined as the speed of reading and greatly influences whether or not a student can comprehend the text. Accuracy, prosody, and automaticity are also crucial elements of fluency.

31. **D.** Competency 1. Along with accessing prior knowledge, making predictions about what is about to be read is a common strategy used to enhance comprehension.

32. **D.** Competency 2. A hyperbole is an exaggerated statement used for effect and is not meant to be taken literally. A person weighing a thousand pounds would be an example of a hyperbole.

33. **A.** Competency 2. Along with your classroom library, your school library is the easiest place to access a wide array of multicultural literature, free of charge.

34. **B.** Competency 4. The purpose of using anecdotal notes is to observe students while they work and record the observations for later study

35. **D.** Competency 1. The five critical skill areas noted by the National Reading Panel (NRP) are phonics, phonological awareness, vocabulary, fluency, and comprehension. Although motivation is a key component to reading engagement, this was not specifically identified by the NRP.

36. **A.** Competency 1. During pre-reading/emergent reading phases, young children are being exposed to basic concepts of print and may approximate the text. During the Early phase of reading, children have mastered basic concepts of print and are now attempting to apply reading strategies that they have been taught in the classroom. Fluent readers are proficient readers and employ the necessary reading strategies when needed to gain meaning from text.

37. **B.** Competency 1. Of the three cueing systems (graphophonemic, syntactic, semantic), semantic refers to the meaning of the text.

38. **A.** Competency 6. Visual media is non-print media.

39. **D.** Competency 5. The critical reading skill most enhanced by questioning and retelling is comprehension.

40. **D.** Competency 6. Blogs, online newsletters, wiki pages, online book clubs, webquests, etc., are all examples of web-based activities that could take place in the elementary classroom.

41. **C.** Competency 5. Oral language development would be enhanced by any teaching methods where students were encouraged to speak to one another regarding the learning taking place in the classroom.

42. **D.** Competency 5. Listening is the language art used most often yet it is also the one most often neglected. Listening requires the student to take in or receive what has been heard and seen, attend to what is most important, and then comprehend the message. Setting a purpose for listening ensures that students understand the objective of the lesson.

43. **A.** Competency 1. Directionality (left to right progression and top to bottom) or reading, the title page, and illustrations are all examples of basic concepts of print. Captions provided to illustrations and photographs are non-fiction text features common in informational text.

44. **D.** Competency 6. Information and media literacy are aided by the use of artifacts, primary sources, internet, printed material, and visual media.

45. **A.** Competency 6. Primary students should be provided preselected sites to choose from in order to avoid exposure to inappropriate web content.

46. **A.** Competency 1. To summarize is to simply and concisely paraphrase what has been read.

47. **C.** Competency 1. All of the choices offer terms related to the teaching of the language arts.

48. **A.** Competency 1. A sight word is a word that does not follow the traditional rules of the English language and must be memorized.

49. **B.** Competency 1. A vowel digraph is defined as two vowels together that make one phoneme or sound.

Social Science

1. **C.** Competency 7. Japanese forces launched an attack on the United States naval base at Pearl Harbor in Hawaii on December 7, 1941. This event prompted the United Sates involvement in World War II and undoubtedly contributed to the victory of the Allied forces.

2. **A.** Competency 7. Operation Desert Storm was the name for the United States land and air operations involved in the Gulf War effort.

3. **D.** Competency 7. Benjamin Franklin invented bifocals and the Franklin stove. Thomas Jefferson is considered one of the Founding Fathers of our country and the principal author of the Declaration of Independence. Abraham Lincoln implemented and signed the Emancipation Proclamation and Clara Barton led the nursing effort for the North during the Civil War and formed the American Red Cross once the war was over.

4. **D.** Competency 7. Andrew Carnegie, John D. Rockefeller, and Cornelius Vanderbilt were all considered robber barons and made their fortunes in railroads.

5. **A.** Competency 8. The essential element of geography that refers to the interaction between people and their surroundings is the Environment and Society.

6. **C.** Competency 8. Small representations, usually shapes and pictures, of real things on a map are known as symbols.

7. **D.** Competency 8. The horizontal, imaginary line that divides the Earth into its northern and southern halves is the equator.

8. **B.** Competency 9. Article III established the judicial branch of government.

9. **C.** Competency 10. One of the Supreme Court's most important powers is the power of judicial review.

10. **B.** Competency 8. Scale is when something on a map is drawn to size. In other words, compared to each other items on the map are the right size and distance apart; the larger the scale, the more detail shown (i.e. theme park map), the smaller the scale, the more area shown but less detail (i.e. world map).

11. **A.** Competency 7. Prior to Christopher Columbus's arrival in the New World, native populations had settled the land. As a result of his "discovery", these native populations were decimated by disease and warfare.

12. **D.** Competency 7. Columbus's discovery of the New World opened up the western hemisphere to economic and political development. The Industrial Revolution was a technological development which led to the use of machinery over manual labor. The Japanese attack on Pearl Harbor forced the United States to become involved in WWII.

13. **D.** Competency 7. The ancient civilization of the Sumerians invented the wheel, cuneiform writing, and initial forms of irrigation by using the dikes and canals.

14. **B.** Competency 11. The use of graphic organizers can assist students in synthesizing and summarizing informational text.

15. **D.** Competency 8. An absolute location is defined as a formal location where street names or coordinates are used to describe the locality.

16. **D.** Competency 10. A monopoly is when one company or institution has exclusive control of a particular good or service in a market.

17. **A.** Competency 9. There are 538 electors. In order for the candidate to win with the majority of the vote, they would have to receive 270 electoral votes.

18. **D.** Competency 9. As of 2009, there were 538 electors in the United States of America.

19. **B.** Competency 10. Fiscal policy aids governmental control of the economy.

20. **C.** Competency 9. Article I of the Constitution established the legislative branch of government in the United States of America.

21. **A.** Competency 9. The Secretary of State advises the President on matters of foreign policy.

22. **B.** Competency 10. The President appoints Supreme Court justices.

23. **D.** Competency 10. Credit unions are financial institutions that are owned, controlled, and operated by their members.

24. **C.** Competency 7. Ancient Egyptians made many contributions to the world including the construction of the great pyramids, hieroglyphic writing, preservation of bodies after death, and completion of the solar calendar.

25. **A.** Competency 9. If no presidential candidate receives the majority of the electoral votes in a national election, the House of Representatives has the power to choose the President of the United States.

26. **B.** Competency 9. When a group of citizens claims that a bill that has gone through the process of becoming federal law is unconstitutional, the Supreme Court with its power of judicial review has the power to determine its constitutionality.

27. **D.** Competency 7. The French and Indian War (1754-1763) which was an extension of the European Seven Years War, was a battle over colonial territory and wealth by the French and the English. This war resulted in effectively ending French cultural and political influence in North America. In their victory, England gained massive amounts of land but also weakened their rapport with the Native Americans. In sum, although the war strengthened England's hold on the colonies, it also worsened their relationship which inevitably led to the Revolutionary War.

28. **A.** Competency 7. The Second World War (WWII) was a global military conflict between two opposing forces: The Allies (Leaders)- Great Britain (Churchill), United States (Roosevelt/Truman), Russia (Stalin), Free France (De Gaulle), China (Chiang Kai-shek) and the Axis Powers (Leaders)- Germany (Hitler), Italy (Mussolini), Japan (Hirohito).

29. **D.** Competency 7. The ancient Phoenicians were sea traders that were proficient in sailing at night using the stars as their guide. They were also well known for their manufacturing of glass, metals, and the development of their famous purple dye.

30. **A.** Competency 8. The vertical, imaginary line that divides the Earth into its eastern and western halves is the Prime Meridian.

31. **D.** Competency 10. Consumers, according to principles of supply and demand, decide what kinds of goods and services will be produced.

32. **C.** Competency 10. In response to increased taxes on oil and gas, consumers in Europe have asked for better public transportation.

33. **C.** Competency 11. Specialized organizations, like the National Council for the Social Studies (NCSS), have a website with multiple links to other reputable websites that assist educators in teaching in this content area.

34. **A.** Competency 7. The belief that the United States should control all of North America fueled much of the warfare that took place against the Native Americans. This belief was called Manifest Destiny.

35. **C.** Competency 8. The compass rose identifies the cardinal directions on the map.

36. **D.** Competency 9. The Magna Carta of 1215 (England) is considered the very first modern document which sought to limit the powers of the governing body, an English legal charter and the most significant early influence on the extensive historical process that led to the rule of constitutional law today.

37. **B.** Competency 9. The leader of the local government is the mayor.

38. **A.** Competency 9. The three levels of government in the United States are: local, state, and federal.

39. **C.** Competency 7. Abraham Lincoln gave the Gettysburg Address on November 19, at the dedication of the Soldiers' National Cemetery in Gettysburg, Pennsylvania.

40. **A.** Competency 8. The day officially changes each day according to the International Date Line. The line follows 180° longitude except where it crosses land so there are some departures from the meridian.

Music, Visual Arts, Physical Education, and Health

1. **D.** Competency 12. Texture is considered one of the basic elements of music, and used to describe the amount of rhythms played at a specific time, and overall quality of sound of a music composition. The number, timbre, harmony, tempo, and rhythms of the instruments being used may affect a music composition texture.

2. **C.** Competency 15. The activity of students playing the melody of a song using the autoharp is not likely to help them to examine how music relates to their community. The other activities could support students' examination of how music relates to their community.

3. **B.** Competency 20. The levels of Bloom's Taxonomy are Knowledge, Comprehension, Application, Analysis, Evaluation, and Synthesis.

4. **A.** Competency 12. Monophony, homophony, and polyphony are types of music textures.

5. **D.** Competency 14. The Romantic era is distinguished by being emotional, large, and programmatic.

6. **D.** Competency 17. Obesity increases the risk for diabetes, stroke, and heart disease. Anorexia is an eating disorder. Most people with anorexia are not obese.

7. **A.** Competency 12. A series of strikes on a percussion instrument is called rhythmic pattern or drum beat.

8. **D.** Competency 18. Gross motor skill development is divided into locomotor skills. Nonlocomotor skills, and manipulative skills. Athleticism is not an aspect of gross motor skill development.

9. **B.** Competency 16. In the case presented in this item, the teacher is most likely using multiple-choice or simple completion items, which is a more traditional approach than authentic or performance-based assessment.

10. **C.** Competency 16. A collection of work that exhibits an individual's efforts, progress, and achievement is a portfolio.

11. **B.** Competency 19. Substance abuse is the overindulgence in and dependence on an addictive substance. Substances most commonly abused include alcohol and narcotic drugs.

12. **C.** Competency 18. Gross motor skills involve large movements; fine motor skills involve specific and detailed movements.

13. **B.** Competency 12. Claudio Monteverdi, an Italian composer, is considered the first great composer of the opera and has come to be known as the "Father of Opera".

14. **A.** Competency 15. The activity of copying a drawing from a specific genre presented in a book would not provide opportunities to enhance students' engagement with art. The other activities could provide opportunities to enhance students' engagement with art.

15. **C.** Competency 20. Reviewing rules prior to beginning an activity is the best way to prevent accidents and injuries. If misbehavior is already happening, an accident could occur. Students' physical activity should not be restricted and students should not, in most cases, be encouraged to experiment.

16. **D.** Competency 13. The activity helps students understand movement and music are related to each other by rhythm.

17. **B.** Competency 13. Melody is the succession of notes in a music piece.

18. **B.** Competency 19. Recovery support groups, narcotics anonymous, and drug treatment programs are treatment programs. A drug awareness program is a prevention program.

19. **B.** Competency 18. Children learn to crawl, then walk, then gallop, then skip. Skipping is the highest level locomotor skill.

20. A. Competency 14. One of the composers of the Romantic era was Ludwig van Beethoven, German, considered by some people as the first Romantic composer. Niccoló Paganini was another composer of this era, but was not considered the first. Wolfgang Amadeus Mozart and Johann Sebastian Bach were Classical period composers.

21. B. Competency 17. Aerobic activity is when the body is engaged in rhythmic activity for a sustained period of time. It is cardiovascular fitness. Lifting weights and sit-ups are examples of strength training; stretching is flexibility training. Jogging is aerobic activity.

22. C. Competency 13. The Baroque period (1600-1760) was known for its intricate ornamentation. The word "baroque" was derived from the Portuguese word barroco, which means "misshapen pearl" (irregular in shape).

23. B. Competency 18. Holding a pencil is a fine motor skill. Jumping, twisting, and skipping are gross motor skills.

24. B. Competency 14. The Nineteenth century included the following: Romanticism (idealistic style, focused on emotion rather than reason and on spontaneous expression, and painted energetically with brilliant colors), Realism (everyday characters, situations, and dilemmas), Naturalism (realistic subjects in natural settings), and Impressionism (visible brushstrokes with an emphasis on light and color, and layers of oil paints added without waiting for other layers to dry). Rococo style was part of the Eighteenth century, and involved opulence, grace, and lightness.

25. C. Competency 12. Students need practice and repetition in order to develop rhythm, which is the basis of dance.

26. A. Competency 20. The levels of Bloom's Taxonomy from least complex to most complex are Knowledge, Comprehension, Application, Analysis, Evaluation, and Synthesis.

27. A. Competency 16. A portfolio should be used to represent the artwork collected by a student that is representative of the student's work and progress. It should provide more than a way to assign a grade at the end of the academic year.

28. C. Competency 18. The stages of development in order from earliest to latest are newborn, infant, toddler, preschooler, school-aged child, and adolescent.

29. D. Competency 18. Children will typically develop the ability to walk and hold a cup or bottle between the ages of 9 months and 15 months. If a child has not begun to walk unassisted by the time he/she is 18 months old, there is reason to be concerned.

30. D. Competency 17. Strength training activities focus on improving muscular strength. Lifting weights improves muscular strength. Swimming and running are aerobic activities. Yoga is for flexibility and relaxation.

31. C. Competency 20. Putting parts together is synthesis.

32. D. Competency 16. In performance-based assessment, the teacher observes and makes a judgment about the student's demonstration of a skill or competency in creating a product, constructing a response, or making a presentation. In the case presented in this item, the teacher is most likely using performance-based assessment.

33. B. Competency 19. Typical symptoms of the abuse of inhalants are runny nose, watery eyes, drowsiness, and poor muscle control.

34. B. Competency 12. Balance is a basic principle of art design. It is similar to the idea of balance in physics. It refers to the ways in which the art elements (for example, lines, shapes, colors, textures) of a piece of art are arranged.

35. **A.** Competency 13. *Cubism* is a revolutionary movement begun in the early twentieth century (Picasso and Braque). It employs an analytic vision based on fragmentation and multiple viewpoints. *Impressionism* is a late-nineteenth-century French school of painting, which focused on transitory visual impressions, often painted directly from nature, with an emphasis on the changing effects of light and color (Monet, Renoir, and Pissarro). *Realism* is a Nineteenth century movement, especially in France, which refers to objective representation. It rejected idealized academic styles in favor of everyday subjects (Daumier, Millet, and Courbet). *Pointillism* is a method of painting developed by Seurat and Paul Signac in the 1880s, which used dabs of pure color that were intended to mix in the eyes of viewers rather than on the canvas. It is also known as divisionism or neoimpressionism.

36. **C.** Competency 18. There are six pillars of character, namely, trustworthiness, respect, responsibility, fairness, caring, and citizenship.

37. **A.** Competency 17. Broccoli is in the vegetable group. Strawberries are fruit. Fish are meat and beans. Yogurt is in the milk category.

38. **C.** Competency 14. The Twentieth era included Cubism, which involved total destruction of realistic depiction. Picasso and Braque were representatives of this style in the early twentieth century.

39. **D.** Competency 13. Style is the manner of expression of an artist, which is sometimes known as genre. It is not a principle of design. Several principles of design are very important: line, unity, color, shape, form, texture, balance, repetition, movement, and value.

40. **A.** Competency 18. Estrogen is the hormone responsible for female development.

41. **C.** Competency 17. Sweet potato and carrots are in the vegetable category. Blueberries are in the Fruit category. Chicken is in the meat and beans category.

42. **C.** Competency 13. The primary colors are red, yellow, and blue.

43. **D.** Competency 17. The nutritional categories are Grains; Vegetables; Fruits; Oils; Milk; and Meat and Beans. Soda is not a nutritional category.

44. **C.** Competency 18. Good communication skills including active listening, conflict resolution, and communication without attacking the other person. Good grammar, although important, is not critical for communication.

45. **C.** Competency 19. Surgeon General is responsible for public awareness about health and nutrition. The Food and Drug Administration is responsible for food labeling.

Science and Technology

1. **A.** Competency 21. Volume is another property of matter together with mass. The amount of cubic space that an object occupies is called volume.

2. **C.** Competency 23. The rotation of the earth causes the outer core to rotate around the inner core, creating the earth's magnetism.

3. **A.** Competency 22. Temperature is a measure related to the average kinetic energy of the molecules of a substance. Heat is a measurement of the total energy in a substance. That total energy is made up of the kinetic, and the potential energies of the molecules of the substance.

4. **C.** Competency 24. There are six properties of living things. They are: made up of cells, obtain and use energy, grow and develop, reproduce, respond to stimuli in environment, adapt to environment.

5. **A.** Competency 23. The tilt of the earth causes seasons.

6. **B.** Competency 27. In alternative B, the students are challenged to answer the question, "What is El Niño's impact on the climate at a given locality?" Students answer that question based on analysis of data collected on the Internet. This provides a good opportunity for inquiry-based learning.

7. **C.** Competency 24. The levels of taxonomy from broadest to most specific are Domain, Kingdom, Phylum, Class, Order, Family, Genus, Species.

8. **C.** Competency 22. Electrical forces are action-at-a-distance forces. They are involved when the protons in the nucleus of an atom and the electrons outside the nucleus exert an electrical pull towards each other despite the spatial separation. The other forces included in this item are contact forces.

9. **D.** Competency 23. The mantle is the largest layer of the earth and makes up the majority of the earth's volume.

10. **A.** Competency 26. A law is a truthful explanation of different events that happen with uniformity under certain conditions; for example, laws of nature, laws of gravitation.

11. **B.** Competency 25. Scientific methods are the ways in which scientists answer questions and solve problems systematically.

12. **B.** Competency 23. A new moon occurs when the moon and sun are on the same side of the earth and no reflection of the sun off the earth's surface is visible.

13. **B.** Competency 22. The sun provides radiant or light energy. Magnetic force is the force (pull or push) of a magnet. Nuclear force is present in the nucleus of atoms. Dividing, combining, or colliding of nuclei can result in the release of nuclear energy. Acoustic energy is the energy in the form of mechanical waves that are transmitted through materials (like plastic or air). They can be an audible or inaudible wave.

14. **D.** Competency 23. Apollo 7 was the first manned mission. Apollo 8 was the first manned mission to orbit the moon. Apollo 11 was the first mission to land on the moon. Apollo 13 mission was aborted due to the explosion of oxygen tanks and was called a "successful failure" when all astronauts returned safely to earth.

15. **C.** Competency 21. The iron in an iron bar combining with oxygen in the air to produce rust is an example of chemical change. The chemical properties of a substance indicate the ability of a substance to be altered into new ones, and involve changes in the molecular structure of the substance or object. These chemical changes may include burning, rusting, and digestion. Under some conditions, a chemical reaction may involve breaking apart, combining, recombining, or decomposing substances.

16. **C.** Competency 25. A hypothesis is the possible answer a scientist predicts in a scientific experiment.

17. **B.** Competency 24. The three domains are Archaea, Bacteria, and Eukarya. Fungi is a kingdom.

18. **C.** Competency 23. The six continents are Eurasia, North America, South America, Africa, Australia, and Antarctica. The Arctic Circle is not a continent.

19. **C.** Competency 22. Light travels in a straight line. It can change direction, but still keeps traveling in a straight line; for example, when a light ray strikes a mirror, it changes direction, but continues traveling in a straight line. In this case, the mirror *reflects* light.

20. **B.** Competency 23. The stages in the water cycle are evaporation, condensation, precipitation, and collection.

21. **B.** Competency 24. All cells contain Cell Membranes, Cytoplasm, DNA, and Organelles. Only Eukaryotic cells contain cell walls.

22. **A.** Competency 22. Refraction occurs when light passes through a transparent material like water at a slant angle, the ray of light bends or changes speed. Diffraction occurs when a ray of light bends around the edges of an object, the ray of light has been diffracted.

23. **D.** Competency 24. The mitochondrion breaks down sugar to create energy. The Endoplasmic Reticulum creates proteins, lipids, and other materials. The Golgi Complex packages and distributes proteins. The ribosomes build proteins.

24. **A.** Competency 27. The students are most likely involved in planning a controlled experiment.

25. **D.** Competency 25. A controlled experiment is one in which a treatment (experimental) group and control group exist. The treatment group receives a treatment while the control group does not. This provides a method for comparison.

26. **D.** Competency 22. Optics is a branch of physics that studies the physical properties of light. It provides information about the behavior and properties of light and its interaction with matter.

27. **A.** Competency 23. Alfred Wegner proposed the concept of pangea.

28. **B.** Competency 24. The three shapes of bacteria are rods, spheres, and spirals. Bacteria are not cone shaped.

29. **A.** Competency 22. A transparent object with flat polished surfaces that refracts or diffuses (breaks apart) light is called a prism.

30. **B.** Competency 23. Sedimentary rocks are formed when debris settles and is compressed and fused together forming rocks.

31. **D.** Competency 24. Sexual reproduction requires two parents. Asexual reproduction requires only one parent.

32. **D.** Competency 21. A phase change that involves changing from a solid to a liquid can be called fusion. It can also be called melting. Transformations might not be apparent by just looking at a substance. The transformations are processes that take place over time and might develop slowly. The different phases of matter are related to each other in terms of changes in temperature and/or pressure. Therefore, matter can undergo a phase change through heating and cooling, shifting from one form to another; for example, melting (changing from a solid to a liquid), freezing (changing from a liquid to a solid), evaporating (changing from a liquid to a gas), boiling (past the boiling point, which is the temperature at which a liquid boils at a fixed pressure; for example boiling of water to form steam), and condensing (changing from a gas to a liquid).

33. **D.** Competency 22. Light is considered an electromagnetic radiation that has a wavelength (electromagnetic waves); for example, radiant waves, X-rays, radio waves, and ultraviolet rays. A sound wave is not considered an electromagnetic wave.

34. **D.** Competency 25. The steps of the scientific method include 1) ask a question, 2) make observations, 3) hypothesize, 4) predict, 5) test, and 6) conclude.

35. **A.** Competency 24. The four groups of fungi are Threadlike fungi, Club fungi, Imperfect fungi, and Sac fungi.

36. **C.** Competency 26. Yes, you need it to be valid as well as consistent. You cannot have a valid instrument without reliability. You cannot assume that an instrument is reliable if it is considered valid.

37. **B.** Competency 22. A physical occurrence related to stationary and moving electrons and protons is called electricity.

38. **A.** Competency 24. A heterotroph consumes its food from its environment. An autotroph creates its own food.

39. **A.** Competency 23. Earthquakes are formed when plates intersect and slide against each other in opposite directions.

40. **D.** Competency 27. In this experiment, because of the use of the link cable, the students are most likely using graphing calculators.

41. **C.** Competency 22. Electric current is the flow of electricity through a conductor. Electrical cables are usually made of conductors (for example, copper) and insulation (for example, rubber on the outside part). An electrical circuit is a path or combination of paths that allow the flow of the electrical current from one place to another. Most familiar conductors are metallic: copper (the most common material used for electrical wiring), silver (the best conductor, but expensive), and gold (used for high-quality surface-to-surface contacts). There are also many non-metallic conductors, including graphite, solutions of salts, and all plasmas.

42. **B.** Competency 25. Eating and drinking in the laboratory space is not a good procedure. A laboratory should be free of food and drink.

43. **B.** Competency 27. Out of the choices provided for this item, students should most likely use the science related Ask the Expert Websites to answer the questions they cannot answer themselves. At these Websites, students can ask questions in any topic and have them answered for free by science experts or scientists. The other choices might not be as appropriate or effective for this purpose.

44. **C.** Competency 23. The three types of rock are igneous, sedimentary, and metamorphic.

45. **B.** Competency 24. Photosynthesis is the process by which a plant makes food. Transpiration is the loss of water through the plant's leaves. Respiration is the process by which the cells convert sugar molecules into energy. Fertilization is the process by which the plant reproduces.

Mathematics

1. **A.** Competency 28. The number line involves both the pictorial (line and tick mark drawings), and abstract (the numerals under the line and tick mark drawings for number values) models.

2. **C.** Competency 30. The pattern is the sum of the previous two terms makes the next term. The previous two terms are 18 and 29. Their sum is 47.

3. **C.** Competency 32. Standardized tests are least likely to provide information to help in identifying a student's specific problem areas. Their validity and reliability depends on three basic assumptions: students have been equally exposed to the test content in an instructional program, students know the language of the test directions and the test responses, and students just like those taking the test have been included in the standardization samples to establish norms and make inferences. These are better for making programmatic decisions.

4. **D.** Competency 29. The area of a rectangle is length times width. If the length is doubled and the width is tripled, the area is now $(2 \times \text{length})(3 \times \text{width}) = 6 \times \text{length} \times \text{width}$. Alternatively, the original area of the bedroom would be $12 \times 10 = 120 \text{ ft}^2$. If one dimension is doubled and the other is tripled, the dimensions become either $24 \text{ ft} \times 30 \text{ ft}$ or $36 \text{ ft} \times 20 \text{ ft}$. Either way, the new area is 720 ft^2. This is six times the original area of 120 ft^2.

5. **C.** Competency 28. One way to solve this problem is by changing all the fractions to common denominators and arranging them from there. The denominators involved in this case are 4, 8, and 16. The least common multiple (LCM) or denominator (LCD) is 16 (marked in bold type below). You can find this by finding the nonzero multiples of these denominators and selecting the LCM:

   4: 4, 8, 12, **16**, 20, 24, 28, 32, 36, 40, 44, 48, …

   8: 8, **16**, 24, 32, 40, 48, …

   16: **16**, 32, 48, …

   Notice that there are other common multiples, but you want to select the least common multiple (or denominator). Another way to find the least common multiple is by using prime factorization: $4 = 2^2$, $8 = 2^3$, and $16 = 2^4$. You select the common and noncommon multiples out of the prime factorizations. In this case $2^4 = 16$ is the least common multiple (denominator). You still need to use this denominator to change each fraction to its equivalent fractions (whenever needed) and then arrange them in order from least to greatest: $\frac{5}{8} = \frac{10}{16}$, $\frac{3}{8} = \frac{6}{16}$, $\frac{1}{4} = \frac{40}{16}$, and $\frac{3}{16}$. The order is the following: $\frac{3}{16}, \frac{4}{16}, \frac{6}{16}, \frac{10}{16}$ or $\frac{3}{16}, \frac{1}{4}, \frac{3}{8}, \frac{5}{8}$.

   You can also change all the fractions to their equivalent decimal form and arrange them from least to greatest using this information: $\frac{5}{8} = 0.625$, $\frac{3}{8} = 0.375$, $\frac{1}{4} = 0.25$, and 0.1875. Order these decimal numbers from least to greatest and then convert back to the reduced fractions. The order of the fractions is still the same.

   A number line could also be a useful and proper representation for these fractions. The following figure presents this alternative.

6. **B.** Competency 28. You have that $4.1 \cdot 10^{-2} = 4.1 \cdot \frac{1}{100} = 0.041$ (move the decimal point twice to the left as a result of multiplying by 1/100 or 0.01).

7. **B.** Competency 29. The triangles are congruent. This means corresponding angles are congruent and corresponding sides are congruent. Angle A corresponds with Angle D; Angle B corresponds with Angle E; and Angle C corresponds with Angle F. AB corresponds with DE; BC corresponds with EF; and AC corresponds with DF. Choice B provides corresponding sides which are congruent or equal in length.

8. **C.** Competency 29. Set up a proportion. $\frac{8 \text{ feet}}{4 \text{ feet}} = \frac{x}{2.5 \text{ feet}}$. Since $\frac{8}{4}$ is 2, then $x = (2.5)(2) = 5$ feet.

9. **A.** Competency 30. The difference of a number and 4 is $N - 4$. Two times the number is $2N$. These expressions are equal, so the equation is $N - 4 = 2N$.

10. **D.** Competency 31. The mean of this data set is 27.625, which is approximately 28 (to the nearest ones). This is the sum of all the measures divided by the total number of measures: $442 \div 16$.

11. **B.** Competency 31. The mode of this data set is 30, which is the most frequent measure with three scores.

12. **A.** Competency 31. The median is the middle of the data set. Since we have 16 measures, the middle is the 8th measure. You need to count 8 from left to right and 8 from right to left. The middle measure is 29.

13. **A.** Competency 32. Multiple-choice assessment item is not an example of alternative assessment. It is an example of traditional assessment.

14. **A.** Competency 29. Running a mile generally take less than one hour. Seconds are too small a unit to use. Minutes is the most appropriate unit.

15. **A.** Competency 29. A translation is a slide. A rotation is a turn. A reflection is a flip. A dilation is an expansion or compression.

16. **D.** Competency 28. You need to examine each of the alternatives:

    A. 3: $3^2 = 9$, and $9 > 3$

    B. –0.03: $(-0.03)^2 = 0.0009$ (negative · negative = positive), and $0.0009 > -0.03$

    C. 1.3: $(1.3)^2 = 1.69$, and $1.69 > 1.3$

    D. 0.3: $(0.3)^2 = 0.09$, and $0.09 < 0.3$

17. **C.** Competency 28. You might notice that 12 hours is four times as long as a three hour trip. Then you have that $225 \cdot 4 = 900$, or the train will travel 900 miles in 10 hours.

    Another way to solve this problem is by establishing a proportion: 225 hours to 3 hours = x to 12 hours. By cross multiplying and solving for x, you have $225 \cdot 12 = 3x$; $2700 \cdot 3 = x$; and $900 = x$.

    You can also notice the ratio for miles per hour is 75 miles/1 hour. For 12 hours, you have $75 \cdot 12 = 900$. The following table illustrates different increments in terms of miles and hours.

Miles	75	150	225	450	675	900
Hours	1	2	3	6	9	12

18. **C.** Competency 30. Each term in the "y" column increases by 2. This is the slope. If you subtract 2 from 5, you will get the value of the expression when x is 0. This value is 3. When x is 0, y will be 3. This is the y-intercept. The expression is then $Y = 2x + 3$.

19. **A.** Competency 29. The point is 3 points to the right and 2 points up from the origin. This makes the coordinates (3, 2).

20. D. Competency 31. In a box-and-whisker plot, the median is the middle line of the box, which divides the data set in half. In this case, the median is 81.

The following figure illustrates the different parts of a box-and-whisker plot:

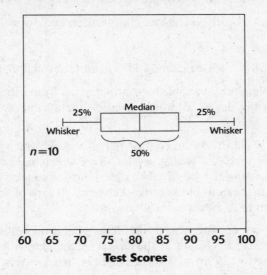

The lowest number is the left whisker. The highest number is the right whisker. The median is in the middle of the box. In this case, the median is 81, lowest score is 67, highest score is 98, lower quartile is 73, and upper quartile 88. The lower quartile is the middle of the lower half of the numbers. The upper quartile is the middle of the upper half of the numbers. Joining the lower quartile, upper quartile, and median forms the box. Joining the box to the high number on the right and the low number on the left forms the whiskers.

21. D. Competency 29. There are 100 centimeters in a meter. $120 \text{ cm} \times \left(\dfrac{1 \text{ meter}}{100 \text{ centimeters}}\right) = 1.2 \text{ meters}$.

22. D. Competency 30. First isolate the x variable by subtracting $2x$ from each side and adding 3 to each side. This gives $2x = 12$. Divide both sides by 2 to give $x = 6$.

23. A. Competency 28. The table is approximately $4\sqrt{2}$ feet wide or $4 \cdot 1.4$, which is equal to 5.6. The choice is that the box needs to be approximately 6 feet wide. The other choices (5.5, 5, or 4.5 feet) are too small.

24. A. Competency 28. There are several correct ways to solve this problem. One way to solve this problem is by noticing that if you paid a 10 percent discount of the original price, then the new price is 90 percent of the original price (100% – 10% = 90%). This implies that 90 percent · original price = new discount price, or 90 percent · original price = $9,000. You can find the original price by dividing $9,000 by 90 percent or 0.90 or 0.9. This will give you the original price: $10,000.

25. B. Competency 29. The figure can be viewed two main ways—as a trapezoid or as a rectangle with a triangle on top. If you view it as a trapezoid, the bases are 12 and 5 and the height is 6. The area, then, is $A = \dfrac{1}{2}(12+5)(6) = \dfrac{1}{2}(17)(6) = (17)(3) = 51 \text{ ft}^2$.

26. C. Competency 32. Problem solving does not come only after mastery of skills. You do not need to wait until skills or concepts are mastered or formalized in order to present problem solving tasks. In many cases, problem solving and application of mathematics should be used as a context for presenting ideas, and skills and concepts are learned as a need for solving a problem. According to the National Council of Teachers of Mathematics (NCTM) problem solving should be the key for teaching mathematics.

27. B. Competency 29. Area is a square unit. The only unit that is squared is choice B.

28. A. Competency 28. You need to use the correct order of operations for this expression:

$300 - 40 \div 5 \cdot (2^3 - 2) \cdot 3 + 8$:   1st, calculate exponentials: $2^3 = 8$.

$300 - 40 \div 5 \cdot (8 - 2) \cdot 3 + 8$:   2nd, solve parentheses: $(8 - 2) = (6)$.

$300 - 40 \div 5 \cdot (6) \cdot 3 + 8$:   3rd, calculate multiplication and division, from left to right:

$40 \div 5 \cdot (6) \cdot 3 = 144$.

$300 - 144 + 8 = 156 + 8 = 164$ 4th, calculate addition and subtraction, as they appear, from left to right.

29. C. Competency 30. First isolate the x variable by subtracting $5x$ from each side and adding 5 to each side. This gives $-3x > 9$. Divide both sides by -3, which, in an inequality will reverse the inequality sign. This gives $x < -3$.

30. B. Competency 28. Samuel could fit 45 cans of food in half a shelf, which means that he can fit about 90 cans in a full shelf (45 cans of food · 2). He has seven shelves, which means he could fit up to 630 cans of food altogether (7 shelves · 90 cans of food per shelf). Each box of cans of food has 30 cans. You need to divide total number of cans that can fit in the seven shelves by 30 cans of food for each box: $630 \div 30 = 21$ boxes. This means that he can fit 21 boxes in the seven shelves.

31. D. Competency 29. The amount of water which will fill the pool is the volume. The volume of a rectangular prism is the area of the base times the height. If the base is rectangular with dimensions 12 meters by 20 meters, the area of the base is $(12)(20) = 240$. The height is then 5 meters. So $240 \times 5 = 1200 \text{ m}^3$.

32. C. Competency 29. A triangular prism has two triangular bases and three rectangular faces. This is a total of five faces.

33. C. Competency 31. The procedures used by Carlos to develop the survey were not systematic and valid, and the interpretation of the survey's results is not correct. Asking students in one school is not enough of a sample to make generalizations about a whole school county. This is not representative of the whole intended population.

34. D. Competency 28. You need to convert $\frac{3}{4}$ to a percent ($3 \div 4 = 0.75$), which is 75%. Then add this to 25%: $75\% + 25\% = 100\%$.

35. B. Competency 31. The mean is a measure of central tendency of data. The mean of a set of data is the sum of the measures divided by the total frequency: $\frac{196}{24} = 8.17$.

36. B. Competency 29. A parallelogram is a quadrilateral (four sided figure) with two sets of parallel sides. It could have all equal sides and/or right (90 degree) angles, but it is not required in order to be a parallelogram.

37. A. Competency 28. You can solve this problem by using a proportion.

$\frac{9.50}{350} = \frac{x}{100}$ $x\%$ or $\frac{x}{100}$

$9.50 \cdot 100 = 350 \cdot x$ Cross multiply.

$950 = 350x$

$950 \div 350 = 350x \div 350$ Divide by 350 on both sides of the equality to isolate x, and get the percent.

$2.7\% = x$ Approximate the answer as 3%.

38. A. Competency 31. The median is a measure of central tendency. You need to have the data in order from least to greatest or from greatest to least. The median is the number that falls in the middle of the data set. In this case, you have 45 numbers, and the middle of the data set is the 23rd number. The median is 2 hours.

39. A. Competency 31. The range of the data set is the highest score minus the lowest score: $4 - 1 = 3$.

40. A. Competency 29. The volume of a box is length x width x height or Area of the base × height of box. The volume of this box, then, is $4 \times 6 \times 3 = 72$ ft^3.

41. C. Competency 29. The area of the wall is $8 \times 14 = 112$ square feet. Since she wants to paint two coats, she needs to cover 224 square feet. Each gallon of paint will cover 50 square feet, so 4 gallons would cover 200 square feet. Five gallons will cover 250 square feet. She needs 5 gallons.

42. B. Competency 30. The commutative property of multiplication states that the order of multiplication can be reversed, so $ab = ba$. This is demonstrated by choice B. Choice A is the associative property of multiplication; choice C is the identity property of multiplication; choice D is the zero property of multiplication.

43. D. Competency 32. All of the skills and concepts included in this item are necessary for effective learning of addition computation involving two- and three-digit whole numbers. The addition concept with cubes provides the basic model for demonstrating and development of the proper computation algorithm (step-by-step systematic process to attain a goal, which is usually memorized and carried out using paper and pencil procedures). It would help students to have their addition facts memorized. This would help with speed and accuracy, but not with understanding of the algorithm. Place value up to hundreds with base-ten blocks is a very important concept. Place value is considered the key for understanding computation.

44. B. Competency 29. The figure shown is a kite. A kite is a four sided figure which has adjacent sides of equal length, but opposite sides are not equal length.

45. B. Competency 29. If the base is cut in one fourth and the height is not changed, the area will be cut in one fourth as well.

Resources

Books

Armbruster, B. B., Lehr, F., and Osborn, J. (2003). *Put Reading First. The Research Building Blocks for Teaching Children to Read. (K–3)* Free: www.nifl.gov.

Bear, D., Ivernizzi, M., Templeton, S., and Johnston, F. (2007) *Word Their Way,* 4th ed. NJ: Prentice Hall, Inc.

Beck, I., McKeown, M., and Kucan, L. (2002). *Bringing Words to Life.* NY: Guilford Press.

Blair, T. R. (2007). *Teaching Children to Read in Diverse Communities.* St. Paul, MN: Freeload Press. Also available at www.freeloadpress.com.

Buxton, C. A., Provenzo, E.F., and Others (2007). *Teaching Science in Elementary and Middle School: A Cognitive And Cultural Approach.* CA: Sage Publications.

Carin, A. A., Bass, T. J. E., and Contant, T. L. (2004). *Teaching Science As Inquiry.* NJ: Prentice-Hall, Inc.

Carpenter, T. P., Fennema, E., Franke, M. L., Levi, L., and Empson, S. (1999). *Children's Mathematics: Cognitively Guided Instruction.* Portsmouth, NH: Heinemann.

Carpenter, T. P., and Moser, J. M. (1982). The development of addition and subtraction problem-solving skills. In T. P. Carpenter, J. M. Moser, and T. A. Romberg (eds.), *Addition and Subtraction: A Cognitive Perspective,* pp. 9–24. Hillsdale, NJ: Erlbaum.

Cathcart, G. W., Pothier, Y. M., Vance, J. H., and Bezuk, N. S. (2001). *Learning Mathematics in Elementary and Middle Schools,* 4th ed. NJ: Prentice-Hall, Inc.

Chapin, J. R. (2009). *Elementary Social Studies: A Practical Guide.* Boston, MA: Allyn and Bacon.

Cunningham, P. (2004). *Phonics They Use.* Allyn and Bacon.

DeVries, B. A. (2008*). Literacy assessment and intervention for the elementary school classroom,* 2d ed. Scottsdale, AZ: Holcomb Hathaway Publishers.

Dorn, L. J., and Soffos, C. (2001). *Scaffolding Young Writers; A Writers' Workshop Approach.* Portland, MI: Stenhouse Publishers.

Fountas, I. and Pinnell, G. S. (2006). *Teaching for Comprehending and Fluency.* NH: Heinemann.

Fountas, I. and Pinnell, G. S. (2000) *Guiding Readers and Writers.* NH: Heinemann.

Freeman, D. E. and Freeman, Y. (2004*). Essential Linguistics.* Heinemann.

Fritzer, P. J. and Brewer, E. A. (2010). *Social Studies Content for Elementary and Middle School Teachers.* Boston, MA: Allyn and Bacon.

Galda, L. and Cullinan, B. E. (2006). *Literature and the Child,* 6th ed. Mason, OH: Thomson Wadsworth.

Gelineau (2003). *Integrating the Arts Across the Elementary School Curriculum.* CA: Wadsworth Publication Company.

Greer, B. (1992). Multiplication and division as models of situations. In D. A. Grouws (ed.), *Handbook of Research on Mathematics Teaching and Learning,* pp. 276–299. New York: MacMillan.

Harvey, S. and Daniels, H. (2009). *Inquiry Circles in Action.* Portsmouth, NH: Heinemann.

Harvey, S. and Goudvis, A. (2007). *Strategies that Work,* 2d ed. ME: Stenhouse Publishers.

Heddens, J. W. and Speer, W. R. (2005). *Today's Mathematics, Concepts, and Classroom Methods, and Instructional Activities.* NJ: John Wiley and Sons, Inc.

Heilman, A. (2005). *Phonics in Proper Perspective,* 10th ed. NJ: Prentice Hall, Inc.

Heilman, A., Blair, T., and Rupley, W. (2002). *Principles and Practices of Teaching Reading,* 10th ed. NJ: Prentice Hall.

Herberholz, B. J., and Herberholz, D. W. (2001). *Artworks for Elementary Teachers: Developing Artistic and Perceptual Awareness.* NY: McGraw-Hill College.

Hurwitz, A., and Day, M. (2006). *Children and Their Art: Methods for the Elementary School.* CA: Wadsworth Publication Company.

Johnson, A., Kennedy, L. M., and Tipps, S. (2007). *Guiding Children's Learning of Mathematics.* KY: Wadsworth Publication Company.

Lambdin, D. V., Suydam, M. N., Lindquist, M. M., and Smith, N. L. (2006). *Helping Children Learn Mathematics.* NJ: John Wiley and Sons, Inc.

Lawrence, J. E., and Anderson, W. M. (2006). *Integrating Music into the Elementary Classroom.* NY: Schirmer Books.

Lawrence, J. E., and Anderson, W. M. (2009). *Integrating Music into the Elementary Classroom + Resource Center Printed Access Card.* NY: Schirmer Books.

Leu, D., Kinzer, C., Wilson, R., and Hall, M. A. (2005). *Phonics, Phonemic Awareness, and Word Analysis for Teachers: An Interactive Tutorial,* 8th ed. NJ: Merrill/Prentice Hall, Inc.

Lindeman, C. A., and Hackett, P. (2006). *The Musical Classroom: Backgrounds, Models, and Skills for Elementary Teaching.* NJ: Prentice-Hall, Inc.

Lindquist, Tarry (2002). *Seeing the Whole Through Social Studies,* 2d ed. Portsmouth, NH: Heinemann.

Lott, J. W., Billstein, R., and Libeskind, S. (2009). *A Problem Solving Approach to Mathematics for Elementary School Teachers.* MA: Addison-Wesley.

Ma, L. (1999). *Knowing and Teaching Elementary Mathematics: Teachers' Understanding of Fundamental Mathematics in China and the United States.* PA: Lawrence Erlbaum Assoc., Inc.

Mayesky, M. (2005). *Creative Activities for Young Children.* NY: Delmar Publications.

Norton, D. E. (2009). *Multicultural Children's Literature; Through the Eyes of Many Children.* Boston, MA: Allyn and Bacon.

Opitz, M. and Rasinski, T. (1998). *Good-bye Round Robin.* NH: Heinemann.

Payne, R. (2005). *A Framework for Understanding Poverty,* 4th ed. TX: Aha! Process, Inc.

Prescott-Griffin, M., and Witerall, N. (2004). *Fluency in FOCUS.* NJ: Heinemann.

Rasinski, T. (2003). *The Fluent Reader.* NY: Scholastic.

Rasinski, T. and Padak, N. (2000). *From Phonics to Fluency*. NJ: Allyn and Bacon.

Sexton, C., Mcelroy, D., Gerlovich, J., and Martin, R. E., Jr. (2008). *Teaching Science for All Children: An Inquiry Approach*. NJ: Allyn and Bacon.

Taberski, S. (2000). *On Solid Ground*. NH: Heinemann.

Tompkins, G. E. (2006). *Language Arts Essentials*. Upper Saddle River, NJ: Pearson Prentice Hall, Inc.

Tompkins, G. (2005). *Literacy for the 21st Century,* 4th ed. NJ: Prentice Hall, Inc.

Vacca, J., Vacca, R., Gove, M. K., Burkey, L., Lenhart, L., and McKeon, C. (2005). *Reading and Learning to Read*, 6th ed. NJ: Allyn and Bacon.

Van De Walle, J. A., Karp, K. S., and Bay-Williams, J. M. (2009). *Elementary and Middle School Mathematics: Teaching Developmentally,* 7th ed. NJ: Allyn and Bacon.

Wachowiak, F., and Clements, R. D. (2005). *Emphasis Art: A Qualitative Art Program For Elementary And Middle Schools*. NJ: Allyn and Bacon.

Wasylyk, T. A. (2006). *Handwriting*. Honesdale, PA: Universal Publishing.

Weaver, C. (2002). Word Perception and Reading Process. In *Reading Process and Practice,* 3d ed. NH: Heinemann.

Helpful Websites

www.acei.org—The Association for Childhood Education International

www.aahperd.org—The American Alliance for Health, Physical Education, Recreation and Dance

www.flreads.org—The Florida Reading Association

www.ncte.org—The National Council for the Teachers of English

www.nctm.org—The National Council of Teachers of Mathematics

www.nlvm.usu.edu—The National Library of Virtual Manipulatives

www.nsta.org—The National Science Teachers Association

www.reading.org—The International Reading Association

www.socialstudies.org—The National Council for the Social Studies

References

CDC. (n.d.). Centers for Disease Control and Prevention. Retrieved May 26, 2009, from http://www.cdc.gov/nccdphp/dnpa/obesity/index.htm.

Chapin, J. R. (2009). Elementary Social Studies: A Practical Guide. Boston, MA: Allyn and Bacon.

DeVries, B. A. (2004). Literacy Assessment and Intervention for the Elementary Classroom. Scottsdale, AZ: Holcomb Hathaway Publishers.

Dorn, L. J., and Soffos, C. (2001). Scaffolding Young Writers; A Writers' Workshop Approach. Portland, MI: Stenhouse Publishers.

Fritzer, P. J. and Brewer, E. A. (2010). Social Studies Content for Elementary and Middle School Teachers. Boston, MA: Allyn and Bacon.

Galda, L. and Cullinan, B. E. (2006). Literature and the Child, 6th ed. Mason, OH: Thomson Wadsworth.

Geometry. (n.d.). In *Dictionary.com* online. Retrieved May 13, 2009, from http://dictionary.reference.com/browse/ Geometry.

Harvey, S. and Daniels, H. (2009). Inquiry Circles in Action. Portsmouth, NH: Heinemann.

Norton, D. E. (2009). Multicultural Children's Literature; *Through the Eyes of Many Children*. Boston, MA: Allyn and Bacon.

Tompkins, G. E. (2006). Language Arts Essentials. Upper Saddle River, NJ: Pearson Prentice Hall, Inc.

USDA. (n.d.) United States Department of Agriculture. Retrieved May 26, 2009, from http://www.mypyramid.gov/.

Wasylyk, T. A. (2006). Handwriting. Honesdale, PA: Universal Publishing.

Glossary

absolute location: Formal location; street names or coordinates are used to describe location

abstract level: *See* symbolic

acute triangle: A triangle in which all three angles measure less than 90 degrees

adaptation: A trait which is advantageous to a species

aerobics: Physical activity which engages the body in rhythmic activity for a sustained period of time

algae: One category of plant-like protists

alleles: A form that a gene can take; received from parents in sexual reproduction

alliteration: Two or more words or syllables, near each other, with the same beginning consonant

amino acids: Building blocks of proteins

amniotic egg: Eggs of reptiles; hold a fluid that protects the embryo

amphibians: One type of vertebrate; live part of life in water and part of life on land

angiosperms: Another name for flowering seed plants

animals: Eukaryotic, multicellular heterotrophs

anther: Part of the stamen which makes pollen

aquifer: A formation that transmits water under the surface of the earth

archaea: One of three domains of taxonomy; single-celled organisms

archaeabacteria: Single-celled microorganisms

area: The amount of surface which a shape covers; measured in square units

art movement: A phrase used to describe a group of artists who have a specific style during a specific period of time (months, years, or decades)

arthropod: The largest group of animals; invertebrates with a segmented body with specialized parts, jointed limbs, an exoskeleton, and a well-developed nervous system; examples include centipedes, lobsters, spiders, and insects

asexual reproduction: Reproduction which depends on one parent; a duplicate copy of the parent is made

associative property: Of addition – mathematical property which states that the sum of three or more addends can be found in any order $(a + (b + c) = (a + b) + c)$; of multiplication – mathematical property which states that the product of three or more factors can be found in any order $(a \cdot (b \cdot c) = (a \cdot b) \cdot c)$; when more than two terms are added together or multiplied together, the order in which the terms are paired does not affect the sum or product

asteroid: Made up of rock, metal, or ice and are like planets in that they orbit the sun. A belt of asteroids exists between Mars and Jupiter and separates the planets

asymmetry: When there is no symmetry in the structure of the body

at-a-distance forces: They result even when the interacting objects are not in physical contact, but they exert a push or pull despite the physical separation; for example, gravitational, electrical, and magnetic forces.

atom: The smallest particle of the element, which retains the properties of that element

ATP: Made by mitochondrion; form of energy cells can use

attributes: Aspects of a shape that are particular to a specific shape

automaticity: The ability to recognize a large bank of words by sight; ability to decode unfamiliar words quickly; includes the ability to comprehend the words

autotroph: Organisms which create their own food

average: The sum of a set of quantities divided by the total number of quantities; also known as mean

bacilli: Rod-shaped bacteria

bacteria: One of three domains of taxonomy; single-celled organisms

balance: It is a basic principle of art design. It is similar to the idea of balance in physics. It refers to the ways in which the art elements (for example, lines, shapes, colors, textures) of a piece of art are arranged

balanced forces: They do not cause a change in motion. They are equal in size and opposite in direction; as illustrated by the following two arrows →←

bar graph: A statistical graph used to compare quantities; may be made up of all vertical bars or all horizontal bars; used mainly for purposes of comparison

base: Side of a polygon in relation to a height; side of a polygon which forms a 90 degree angle with the height

beat: The basic time unit of music in a selection, the pulse of the beat level. In some cases, it identifies the tempo of a piece or a particular sequence of individual beats. It may also refer to particular beats in the measure.

bilateral symmetry: The two sides of the body mirror each other

Bill of Rights: Formal statement of the rights belonging to people of the United Sates; amendments 1 through 10 of the United States Constitution; added in 1791 to protect the rights of citizens

birds: One type of vertebrate; generally fliers; have feathers and wings

birds of prey: Birds which hunt and eat other animals; have sharp claws and a sharp beak; include eagles, hawks, and owls

bladder: Holds urine until it can be removed from the body

body mass index: A measurement of the relative percentages of fat and muscle mass in the body; an index of obesity

bone strengthening: Physical activity in which the goal is to strengthen bones in the body

bones: Part of the skeletal system

bony fish: One type of fish; includes goldfish, tuna, and cod

caecilians: A type of amphibian; live in tropical areas of Asia, Africa, and South America and look like earthworms or snakes with the thin, moist skin of amphibians

calories: A quantity of food capable of producing a specific amount of energy; a measure of the nutritional value of foods

canyon: Geologic formation which occurs when erosion changes the face of the earth's surface

cardiac muscle: The heart

cardiovascular and circulatory system: Transports materials in the blood throughout the body

carnivore: Meat eater

cartilage: Part of the skeletal system; between bones

cartilaginous fish: One type of fish; includes sharks and rays

cartographer: Mapmaker

cell membrane: Surround the cell and provide a protective layer that covers the surface of the cell and acts as a barrier to its environment

cell wall: Rigid structures which give support to cells

cellular respiration: The process by which plants convert the energy that is stored in glucose molecules into energy that cells can use; occurs in the mitochondrion

cellulose: A complex sugar that animals cannot digest without help

central nervous system: Brain and spinal cord

centripetal force: Involved when an object moves in a circular path and force is directed toward the center of the circle in order to keep the motion going; for example, gravitational force keeping a satellite circling Earth

Charles Darwin: Father of Evolution

chemical change or reaction: Produces one or more substances (for example, burning)

chemical rocks: Sedimentary rocks which form when standing water evaporates and leaves dissolved minerals behind

chlorophyll: Green pigment found inside the inner membrane of a chloroplast

chloroplasts: Organelles present in plant and algae cells and allow the plant to harness energy from the sun

chords: Three or more different notes from a specific key played together

cilia: Hairlike structures which beat back and forth causing the ciliate to move

ciliates: Complex protists that have hundreds of tiny, hairlike structures called cilia, which beat back and forth causing the ciliate to move

circumference: The distance around a circle

cirrus: Clouds which are wispy and feathery

city council: Group of people elected to serve as part of the city government

classifications: Use the properties of shapes to lead to a hierarchical structure

classifying: Categorizing based on observable traits

clastic rocks: Basic sedimentary rocks that are accumulations of broken pieces of rocks

club fungi: Fungi which include mushrooms

cnidarians: Invertebrates which have stinging cells; more complex than sponges; examples include jellyfish, sea anemone, and coral

cocci: Spherical-shaped bacteria

cognitive levels: The cognitive levels are divided in three, namely, concrete, pictorial (also known as representational), and symbolic (also known as abstract. See individual definition of each level for more details)

collaborative learning: See cooperative learning

collection: Part of the water cycle which occurs when the water returns to the surface of the earth and falls back into water sources like oceans, lakes, or rivers

color: An element of art; the visual perceptual property corresponding to the categories that we call red, or yellow, among others

comet: Bodies in space made of rocks, frozen water, frozen gases, and dust. Comets orbit the sun and contain a tail that follows the comet. The most famous comet is Halley's comet.

communicating: Conveying information

commutative property: Of addition – mathematical property which states that the order of addition can be reversed $(a + b = b + a)$; of multiplication – mathematical property which states that the order of multiplication can be reversed $(a \cdot b = b \cdot a)$; the order in which you add two terms together or multiply two terms together does not affect the sum or product

composite numbers: They are numbers composed of several whole-number factors. For example, 30 is a composite number because it is composed of several whole-number number factors other than 1 and itself, like 2, 3, 5, 6, 10, and 15.

compound: Matter that combines atoms chemically in definite weight proportions. Water is an example of a compound of oxygen and hydrogen.

comprehension: The ability to understand what one has read

concrete level: Cognitive level that involves the use of manipulative materials or other real-live objects to represent mathematical ideas; for example, using five cubes to represent the numerical value of number five

condensation: Part of the water cycle in which water vapor in the air cools and changes back into liquid forming clouds

conduction: When heat transfers through molecular movement. For example, when you pick up a metal bar, it is cold. As you hold it, the warmth of your body conducts heat to the metal bar

conductor: Allows electricity to flow freely through it; for example, copper is a good conductor of electricity

cones: A three-dimensional figure which has one circular base and a separate face which comes to a vertex point; similar to a pyramid with a circular base

Congress: National, legislative body of the United States; consists of the Senate and the House of Representatives

congruent: Exactly the same; congruent figures are the same shape and same size

conjugation: Process in which two individuals join together and exchange genetic material using a second nucleus

contact forces: They are the result of the physical interaction between objects; for example, frictional forces, tensional forces, normal forces, air resistance forces, and applied forces

continent: Six regions of continental crust; Eurasia (Europe and Asia), Africa, North America, South America, Antarctica, and Australia

continental arctic: Air mass which bring extremely cold temperatures and little moisture. They generally originate in the arctic circle and move south across Canada and the United States during winter.

continental crust: The part of the crust which is not under the oceans; the part of the crust which forms the continents

continental polar: Air mass which brings cold and dry weather, but not as cold as Continental Arctic masses. They generally form south of the Arctic circle and affect the weather in the United States in the winter. In the summer, Continental Polar air masses affect only the northern portion of the United States.

continental tropical: Air masses which form over the Desert Southwest and northern Mexico in the summer. They begin over the equator where moist air is heated and rises. As this air moves away from the equator, it begins to cool causing precipitation in the tropics and leaving the air dry. This dry air then forms a Continental Tropical air mass creating the deserts of the Southwest and Mexico. These air masses rarely form in the winter but keep temperatures in the Southwest above 100 degrees in the summer.

controlled experiment: Experiment in which there is a treatment and control group

convection: Occurs through the movement of masses, either air or water. Convection occurs when hot air rises, cools, and then falls

convection current: The transfer of heat by movement of heated particles into an area of cooler fluid

cooperative learning: It is a way of organizing the classroom, supporting and facilitating students' development. In these approaches, the classroom is organized in small groups of two, three, four, or five students each. The students are also assigned roles or duties to perform during activities.

coordinate system: A system of two or three dimensions which allows for positioning points, lines, and shapes in space

core: Innermost layer of the earth; made up of two sections – the inner core and the outer core

crocodiles and alligators: One group of reptiles; spend most of time in water; have a flat head with eyes and nostrils on the top of the head

crust: The top layer of the earth

cumulus: Clouds which are puffy and look like cotton balls; produce heavy thunderstorms in summer

Curwen hand signs: A set of hand symbols that correspond with Solfege. The song "Do a Deer" from the movie *The Sound of Music* is a basic song that illustrates the use of Solfege — Do, Re, Mi, Fa, So, La, and Ti, and start over again at Do.

cuticle: A waxy layer that coats the surfaces of plants which are exposed to air

cylinder: A three-dimensional figure which has two circular bases and a curved rectangular face between them; Similar to a prism with circular bases

cytoplasm: Fluid found inside a cell

cytoskeleton: Web of proteins inside the cytoplasm

decagon: Ten sided polygon

deciduous trees: Trees which lose most or all of their leaves, typically in the fall

decimals: A set of numbers based on powers of ten. They are fractions expressed in a decimal notation. The denominators of these fractions are powers of 10 (like 10, 100, or 1000). For example, 0.6 (read six tenths) is equivalent to 6/10 (dividing the numerator by the denominator).

decode: To sound out words; segmenting and blending phonemes

denominator: In a fraction of the form *a/b*, where *a* is any integer and *b* is any integer except zero, *b* represents the denominator of the fraction. It expresses the number of equal part in which the whole is divided. For example, in the fraction 4/8, the 8 indicates that the whole was divided into eight equal parts.

density: It is defined as mass per unit of volume, or the ratio of total mass (*m*) to total volume (*V*) – $\rho = m/V$ (for example, kilogram per cubic meter or kg/m^3). In other words, it defines how closely the molecules are packed together.

depository: A firm entrusted with the safe-keeping of valuable assets like funds (money)

dermis: Bottom layer of the skin

descriptive: Writing that describes a person, place, thing, or idea

developmental delay: Physical development which has not occurred in a normal timeframe; when a child has not reached specific developmental milestones they are said to have a developmental delay

diffusion: Method by which Nonvascular plants move materials from one part of the plant to another

digestive system: Digests food into small particles so that nutrients can be absorbed

dilation: A shrinking or expanding of a figure

distributive property: Mathematical property which states that a number multiplied by a sum/difference can be found by multiplying each term of the sum/difference by the multiplier (a · (b + c) = a · b + a · c); when a sum or difference is multiplied by a common term, each part of the sum or difference can be multiplied by the common term and then added or subtracted

dodecagon: Twelve sided polygon

doldrums: Regions of little steady air movement

dominant traits: Traits which appear more frequently in a population

dynamics: In science, it is the branch of mechanics that study the relationship between motion and the forces affecting motion of bodies; in music, it refers to the volume or loudness of a sound or note in a song

Earth: Third planet from the sun; the planet which we live upon

earthquakes: Shaking of the earth's crust; occurs when two continental plates slide against each other in opposite directions; the earthquake occurs when there is a large slippage which shakes the continental plates at their border or fault-line

echinoderm: Spiny-skinned invertebrates that include sea stars, sea urchins, and sand dollars

economic reasoning: Problem solving and strategic thinking skills

ectotherm: Cold-blooded animals; animals which are unable to regulate their own body temperatures

edges: Intersection of two faces of a polyhedron

educational coaching: See scaffolding

electric current: It is the flow of electricity through a conductor.

electrical circuit: A continuous flow of electricity going through a complete loop (circuit), returning to the original position and cycling through again

electricity: A physical occurrence related to stationary and moving electrons and protons

electrons: Part of an atom located in the outer part of the atom

element: Consists of only one type of atom; for example, iron and carbon

embryos: Fertilized eggs

encode: The process of changing oral language into writing

endocrine system: Controls glands that send out hormones

endoplasmic reticulum: A system of folded membranes in which proteins, lipids, and other materials are made

endotherm: Warm-blooded animals; animals which are able to regulate their own body temperatures

energy: The ability to move other matter or provoke a chemical change in other matter; also the ability to do work; for example, heat energy, mechanical energy, electrical energy, wave energy, chemical energy, and nuclear energy

epicenter: The point on a fault-line in which the slippage occurs causing the earthquake

epidermis: Top layer of the skin

equilateral triangle: A triangle in which all three sides are the same length

erosion: The movement of earth due to water movement

eubacteria: Large groups of single-celled organisms; bacteria

eukarya: One of three domains of taxonomy; multi-celled organisms

eukaryote: Cells in which a nucleus exists; organisms whose cells contain complex structures including membrane-bound organelles and a nucleus containing DNA

evaporation: Part of the water cycle in which the sun heats up water on the surface of the earth turning it into steam which goes into the air

evergreen trees: Trees which keep most of their leaves year round

evolution: Change over time; the process of species adapting and creating new species

exoskeleton: A hard outer skeleton

exponent: An exponent is a number or symbol (like a letter), placed above and to the right of the expression, which is called the base of the expression to which the exponent applies. The exponent indicates the number of times the base is used as a factor multiplied by itself. For example, the exponent 3 in the expression 8^3 indicates the 8 is multiplied by itself three times: $8 \times 8 \times 8$. The exponent x in the expression $(a + b)^x$ indicates $(a + b)$ is multiplied by itself x times.

exponential notation: This is a way to represent repeated multiplication in a simpler manner. For example, three multiplied by itself four times or $3 \times 3 \times 3 \times 3$ can be represented as 3^4, which is equal to 81. Remember that 3^4 is *not* equivalent to 3×4 or 4×3.

expository: Writing that gives information, explains why or how, clarifies a process, or defines a concept

fable: Folklore that includes a moral to the story or the teaching of a lesson

faces: Surfaces of a polyhedron

factors: Factors are any of the numbers or symbols that you multiply together to get another number or product. For example, 5 and 6 are factors of 30, because $5 \times 6 = 30$; similarly, 1 and 30 are factors of 30 because $1 \times 30 = 30$.

fertilization: When a sperm fuses with an egg

filament: Part of the stamen which holds up the anther

fine motor skills: Motor skills which include small muscle movements including holding a pencil and cutting with scissors; movements which are detailed and specific

fins: Fan-shaped structures that help fish to steer, stop, and balance in the water

fish: One type of vertebrate; live in water; contain gills that allow fish to breathe under water

flagella: Whiplike strands extending out from a cell which move back and forth to move the cell

flatworm: Invertebrates; simplest kind of worms; have bilateral symmetry

flightless birds: Birds which cannot fly; examples include penguins, kiwi, and ostriches

flowering seed plants: One type of vascular plant; also called angiosperm

fluency: The ability to read quickly, accurately, and with proper expression

food pyramid: Developed by the U.S. Department of Agriculture (USDA) as a guide for good nutrition; visual and written representation of quantities and types of foods necessary for good nutrition

force: A pull or a push; necessary to make a machine work

form: In music, it refers to the structure of the song. It is the way the song is arranged, like a refrain that is repeated or a chorus that is used after a verse. As an element of art, it refers to a total structure, including all the visible aspects of a structure or design and the way they are united, and all the elements of a work of art independent of their meaning. It allows us to mentally capture the work of art and understand it. For example, when viewing a work of art, the formal elements involved are color, dimension, lines, mass, shape, perspective, shape, and others, but the emotions evoked by the work of art are products of the viewer's imagination.

forming hypotheses: Predicting the outcome of a scientific inquiry

fossil record: The timeline of life gathered from examining fossils

fossils: Imprints of once-living organisms found in rock layers

fractions: Can be expressed as a ratio of two whole numbers, a/b, where $b > 0$; for example, 1/2, 2/3, and 12/4

frequency: For a collection of data, the number of items in a given category

frequency table: A table for organizing a set of data that shows the number of pieces of data that fall within given intervals or categories

friction: Happens when surfaces that touch each other have a certain resistance to motion

frogs and toads: The largest type of amphibian; have strong leg muscles for jumping and well-developed ears and vocal cords for hearing and calling

fungi: Eukaryotic heterotrophs that have rigid cell walls and no chlorophyll

fur: Thick coats of hair; generally on animals who live in cold climates

gametes: Egg and sperm

gametophyte stage: Stage of plant's life cycle in which male and female parts make gametes

gas: It is one of the three main states of matter that is distinguished from liquid and solid by its relatively low density and viscosity, relatively great expansion and contraction with changes in pressure and temperature, ability to diffuse easily, and spontaneous tendency to distribute uniformly throughout space. It has no definite volume or shape; for example, water vapor or steam.

genes: Factors which determine genetic traits

genre: It is a set of principles or conditions and styles within a particular media. In music, genres are categories for established forms of compositions, like Classical music. In art, western, horror, and romantic comedy are recognized genres in the film industry. In painting, genres include still life, and pastoral landscape. A particular artwork may combine genres, but each genre has a recognizable group of principles. In literature, a category of composition with defining characteristics and overall form

geology: The study of the earth; science which deals with the physical history of the earth

geometry: The branch of mathematics that deals with the deduction of the properties, measurement, and relationships of points, lines, angles, and figures in space from their defining conditions by means of certain assumed properties of space

germination: When the seed is dropped or planted in a suitable environment and the seed sprouts and forms a new plant

gills: An organ that removes oxygen from the water allowing fish to breathe under water

golgi complex: Organelle that packages and distributes proteins

graphic organizers: Synthesizing and summarizing tools that aid comprehension

greatest common factor: The greatest common factor (GCF) of a set of numbers is the largest whole-number number that is a factor of all the given numbers. For example, the GCF of 30 and 20 is 10, which is the largest whole-number common factor that divides both numbers evenly

Gregor Mendel: Discovered the principles of heredity

gross motor skills: Motor skills which include large muscle movements including running, galloping, and skipping; movements which involve large muscle groups

gymnosperms: Another name for nonflowering seed plants

harmony: The resulting sound from the simultaneous sounding of two or more tones consonant with each other

heat: A measurement of the total energy in a substance. That total energy is made up of the kinetic, and the potential energies of the molecules of the substance.

height: Minimum distance between two bases; perpendicular distance from one base to another; perpendicular distance from a vertex to a base

heptagon: Seven sided polygon

herbivore: Plant eater

heredity: Passing of traits from parents to their offspring

heterogeneous: Differing in kind

heterotrophs: Organisms which consume food from their environment

hexagon: Six sided polygon

homophony: A type of music texture that involves two or more parts moving together in harmony

House of Representatives: Lower house of the United States Congress; sometimes known as the most representative body in the federal government

hyphae: Chains of cells which make up multi-cellular fungi

hypothesis: An educated guess

igneous rocks: Rocks which are formed by the cooling of magma

imperfect fungi: All species of fungi which are not threadlike, sac, or club fungi

inferring: Making conclusions based on observed data

inner core: The innermost part of the core; solid and thick

insulator: Does not allow the electrons to flow freely; for example, glass, rubber, and air

integers: Integers represent whole numbers that can be positive, negative, or zero. For example, 23, –23, or 0 are negative integers. On a number line, negative numbers are on the left side of zero, and the positive numbers on the right. An integer without a sign is assumed to be a positive number. All integers can be expressed as fractions, but not all fractions can be expressed as integers (–25/5 is a fraction that can be expressed as the integer –5)

integumentary system: Skin, hair, and nails

interactive writing: Students and teachers collaborate on constructing a written work and write it together

invertebrate: Animals that do not have a backbone

irrational numbers: This set of numbers includes real numbers that cannot be written as the ratio of two integers. This includes infinite and non-repeating decimals. For example, square root of $2 = \sqrt{2} = 1.414213 \ldots$, and pi $= \pi = 3.141592 \ldots$

isosceles triangle: A triangle in which at least two sides are the same length

jawless fish: One type of fish; includes hagfish and lampreys

judicial review: Includes the power of the courts to declare laws invalid if they violate the Constitution, supremacy of federal laws or treaties when they differ from state/local laws, and the role of the Court as the final authority on the meaning of the Constitution

Jupiter: Fifth planet from the sun; known for its large red spot; largest planet

kidney: Filters waste from the blood; regulates body's water balance

kinetic energy: It is energy of motion of a mechanical system. For example, a moving car has mechanical energy because of its motion (kinetic energy), and a moving baseball has mechanical energy because of both its high speed (kinetic energy) and its vertical position above the ground (gravitational potential energy)

kite: A quadrilateral with adjacent sides of equal length and opposite sides of different lengths

lava: Magma which has reached the surface of the earth

leaching: The process by which materials in the soil are transferred into the water

learner-centered instruction: A learning approach that is being advocated and supported by the constructivist learning approach to teaching. This is based on the premise that the student actively constructs knowledge, not in a passive manner. The process of solving problems and applying mathematics ideas becomes very relevant.

least common multiple: The least common multiple (LCM) of a set of numbers is the smallest non-zero number that all of the given numbers divide into. For example, the LCM of 30 and 20 is 60.

legend: A story passed down over time that is believed to be true but cannot be proven

ligaments: Part of the skeletal system; connects bones to other bones

light: A type of energy, which has a comparatively low level of physical weight or density; considered an electro-magnetic radiation that has a wavelength (electromagnetic waves)

line: A thin continuous mark from a pen, pencil, or brush applied to a work of art surface; shape and thickness may be used to express movement or tone

line graph: A type of statistical graph using lines to show how values change over time

lipids: With proteins, control the movement of larger materials into and out of the cell

liquid: One of the three main states of matter that is distinguished from gas and solid by its readiness to flow and little or no tendency to disperse; has a definite volume, but no shape; for example, water

literary element: Essential parts of narratives; setting, character, plot, theme, and style

literature circles: Small, temporary, and heterogeneous groups of students that gather together to discuss a book that each of them are reading with the goal of enhancing comprehension

lizards and snakes: One group of reptiles; most common reptiles

locomotor motor skills: An aspect of gross motor skills which includes movements across distances like walking, running, and skipping

lung: Organ that removes oxygen from the air and delivers it to the blood

lymph: Fluid that moves through the lymphatic system

lymph nodes: Small bean-shaped masses of tissue that remove pathogens from the lymph

lymphatic system: Removes excess fluid from around cells; eliminates bacteria and waste

lysosomes: Vesicles responsible for digestion inside a cell

magma: Hot material that forms below the Earth's surface

magma chamber: The accumulation of magma in one location under the surface of the Earth

mammals: Type of vertebrate; all mammals have hair and mammary glands

mammary glands: Structures that make milk

manipulating variables: Causing a change in one variable to determine effect

manipulative motor skills: An aspect of gross motor skills that includes manipulating other objects like kicking or throwing a ball

manipulatives: They are small objects that can be touched and moved about by students in ways that enable descriptions and learning to come alive. They are used to help students internalize mathematics concepts, and work with abstract ideas at a concrete level; for example, base-ten blocks used to help students understand place value ideas.

mantle: The layer of the Earth that is above the core; makes up the majority of the Earth's volume

maritime polar: Air masses which are cool and moist and bring cloudy, damp weather to the United States. They form over the northern Atlantic and Pacific oceans and can form at any time of the year. They are usually warmer than Continental Polar air masses

maritime tropical: Air masses which bring warm temperatures and moisture. They are most common over the eastern United States and are created over the southern Atlantic Ocean and Gulf of Mexico. They can form year round but are most common in the summer

Mars: Fourth planet from the sun; the red planet

marsupials: Mammals which carry their young in a pouch

mass: A measure of the amount of matter in a substance or object; different than weight; also a measure of an object's resistance to acceleration

matter: Makes up everything in our world — rocks, people, chairs, buildings, animals, and chemical substances, among others. It takes up space and has mass.

mayor: Elected official; leader of the local government

mean: The sum of a set of quantities divided by the total number of quantities

measurement: The act of measuring; using a standard or non-standard unit to describe an aspect of a shape

mechanical force: The application of force to bend, dent, scratch, compress, or break something; for example, machines in general multiply force or change the direction of force

median: The middle score of a set of scores when arranged according to size (or numerical order); for an even number of scores or quantities, the median is the average of the middle two scores

meiosis: In sexual reproduction, the process which creates gametes; cells are produced that contain half the genetic material of the parent sex cells

melody: The succession of notes in a music piece; also the horizontal development of the notes; sometimes referred to as tune

Mercury: The closest planet to the sun

metamorphic rocks: Rocks which form when a pre-existing rock is moved into an environment in which the minerals that make up the rock become unstable, often burial

metamorphosis: A transformation in which an animal changes form; examples include a tadpole becoming a frog or toad or a caterpillar becoming a butterfly

meteor: Objects that rotate around the sun but are too small to be called asteroids or comets. They are made from bits and pieces of the solar system that have fallen into Earth's atmosphere.

Milky Way: Our solar system

mitochondrion: Power source of the cell; the organelle in which sugar is broken down to produce energy

mitosis: Asexual reproduction in which structures of the cell are copied identically

mixture: Refers to any combination of two or more substances; the substances keep their own chemical properties. It may be homogeneous or heterogeneous. A homogeneous mixture is uniform and consistent throughout. A heterogeneous mixture consists of dissimilar elements or parts.

mode: The number that occurs with the greatest frequency in a set of scores. There may be one or more modes or no mode for a set of data.

models: Representations

molecules: They are the smallest particle of substance that may exist independently and maintain all the properties of the substance. Molecules of most elements are made of one atom, but the molecules of oxygen, hydrogen, nitrogen, and chlorine are made of two atoms each.

mollusk: Invertebrate which has at least one shell; examples include snails, squids, and octopi

molten: Melted

monophony: This is the simplest of music texture that involves a single vocal part (with or without accompaniment). It consists of melody without accompanying harmony. This may be accomplished by producing one note at a time.

monotremes: Mammals that lay eggs

moon: Satellites of planets. They generally orbit around a planet

motor skill: Skills which involve movement of specific muscle groups

mountain: Geologic formation which occurs when plates collide and push each other upward

movement: Refers to the combination of art elements to create the appearance of action or suggestion of motion

multicultural: Related to or representative of diverse cultures

multimedia: Composed of more than one form of communication

multiples: The products of any numbers or symbols that you multiply together; for example, 30 is a multiple of 5 and 6 because $5 \times 6 = 30$; similarly, 30 is a multiple of 1 and 30 because $1 \times 30 = 30$

muscular system: System of muscles in the body

music: The art of arranging sounds in time in order to produce a continuous, balanced, unified, and evocative composition, such as through melody, harmony, rhythm, pitch, and the sound qualities of timbre (tone) and texture

mycelium: Twisted mass of hyphae

myth: A story often describing the adventures of superhuman beings in order to describe a people's customs or beliefs

narrative: Writing that recounts a personal or fictional experience or tells a story based on a real or imagined event

natural selection: Theory that explains how evolution occurs over time to create new species from existing species

Neptune: Eighth planet from the sun; fourth largest planet

nervous system: Senses the environment and controls the body; receives and sends electrical signals throughout the body

neurons: Used to send and receive electrical signals throughout the body

neutrons: Part of an atom located in the nucleus (or solid center) of an atom together with protons

nimbus: Clouds which produce precipitation

nonagon: Nine-sided polygon

nonfiction: Informational text about real people, places, events, and things

nonflowering seed plants: One type of vascular plant; also called gymnosperms

nonlocomotor motor skills: An aspect of gross motor skills that includes movements not involving distances like twisting and turning

nonvascular plants: Plants that do not have specialized tissues to move water and nutrients through the plant

Northern hemisphere: The northern half of the earth

nucleolus: A dark area in which the cell begins to make ribosomes

nucleus: Organelle which contains DNA

number: A number represents the cardinality or the idea of how many objects are contained in a set

numeral: A numeral is the symbolic representation of a numerical quantity; for example, the numeral written as "5" represents symbolically how many objects are contained in a set, in this case five objects

numerator: In a fraction of the form a/b, where a is any integer and b is any integer except zero, a represents the numerator of the fraction. It expresses the number of equal parts taken from the whole after the whole is divided into equal parts. For example, in the fraction 4/8, the 4 indicates the number of equal parts that were taken from a whole that was divided into 8 equal parts.

nutrition: The process by which animals eat and use food

observing: Part of the scientific process

obtuse triangle: A triangle in which one angle measures more than 90 degrees

oceanic crust: The part of the crust which is under the oceans

octagon: Eight sided polygon

operations: The operations indicate what is to be done with the numbers involved in a given mathematical situation. The main four operations are addition, subtraction, multiplication, and division.

optics: A branch of physics that studies the physical properties of light; provides information about the behavior and properties of light and its interaction with matter

organ: Two or more tissues working together to carry out a specific function

organ system: Organs working together

organelle: "Little organs", which carry out the life processes within the cell

organic rocks: Sedimentary rocks that are formed by organic material such as calcium from shells, bones, and teeth

organs: A group of tissues that carries out a specific function within the body

outer core: The outermost part of the core; molten material

ovary: Part of the pistil

ovule: Inside the ovary; contains an egg

Pangea: Supercontinent believed to have once existed; a supercontinent which included all the continental crust in one region

parallelogram: A quadrilateral with exactly two pairs of parallel sides

parasite: Organisms that invade other organisms called hosts to obtain the nutrients they need

peer tutoring: In peer tutoring, students work together on a subject that is giving them trouble. They help and support each other as they learn. One student can be the tutor and assist another student in learning a subject. The students benefit from the shared insights and individual attention they get in this environment.

pentagon: Five-sided polygon

percent: Refers to the number of parts out of one hundred parts; for example, 76 percent (written 76%) indicates that you have 76 parts out of 100 parts

perching birds: Birds that have adaptations for landing on branches; include songbirds like robins and sparrows

percolation: The downward movement of water through the soil and rock in the ground

perimeter: The distance around a polygon

peripheral nervous system: Nerves of the body that connect all parts of the body to the central nervous system

persuasive: Writing that attempts to convince the reader that a point of view is valid or that the reader should take a specific action

phase change: Matter can undergo a phase change through heating and cooling, shifting from one form to another; for example, melting (changing from a solid to a liquid), freezing (changing from a liquid to a solid), evaporation (changing from a liquid to a gas), boiling (past the boiling point, which is the temperature at which a liquid boils at a fixed pressure; for example boiling of water to form steam), and condensation (changing from a gas to a liquid).

phloem: One type of vascular tissue

phonemic awareness: Ability to hear and manipulate the sounds of spoken language; includes noticing rhyme and recognizing the separate, small sounds in words (phonemes)

phonics: The understanding of the relationships between the written letters of the alphabet and the sounds of spoken language

phospholipids: A group of fatty compounds found in living cells

photosynthesis: Process which allows plants and algae to use sunlight, carbon dioxide, and water to make sugar and oxygen

physical change: Does not produce a new substance (for example, freezing and melting water)

physical fitness: Physical condition; ability to engage in physical activity; contains three aspects – aerobics, strength training, and bone strengthening

phytoplankton: Free-floating single-celled protists; microscopic and usually float near the water's surface

pictograph: A diagram or graph using pictured objects, icons, or symbols to convey ideas or information.

pictorial: This cognitive level involves the use of pictures or drawings to represent mathematical ideas. For example, using the drawings of five cubes to represent the numerical value of number five

pistil: Female part of the plant

pitch: Represents the perceived fundamental frequency of a sound; one of the three major auditory attributes of sounds along with loudness and timbre

placental mammals: Mammals whose embryos develop inside the mother's body and are attached to the mother through a placenta

plantlets: A type of asexual reproduction in plants when tiny plants grow along the edges of a plant's leaves

plants: Eukaryotic, multicellular autotroph

plate tectonics: The movement of the plates of the earth's crust

Pluto: Celestial body which was once considered a planet; now is considered a dwarf planet

polygon: A two dimensional figure which is closed and contains at least three straight sides which meet only at corners

polyhedron: Three-dimensional figures in which all faces are polygons

polyphony: A type of music texture that involves two or more melodic voices in harmony; instead of one voice (monophony), or one dominant melodic voice accompanied by chords (homophony)

portfolio: Purposeful collections of student work samples that when viewed in its entirety provides a picture of the individual's range of abilities

potential energy: Stored energy of position; for example, a moving baseball has mechanical energy because of both its high speed (kinetic energy) and its vertical position above the ground (gravitational potential energy)

Preamble: The introductory statement of the United States Constitution

precipitation: Part of the water cycle which occurs when the amount of water that has condensed in the air is too much for the air to hold. The clouds that hold the water become heavy and the water falls back to the surface of the earth in the form of rain, hail, sleet, or snow

predicting: An educated guess

prevailing westerlies: Winds which move towards the poles. They appear to curve to the east, but come out of the west

prime number: A number with exactly two whole number factors (1 and the number itself). The first few prime numbers are 1, 2, 3, 5, 7, 11, 13, and 17.

prisms: A polyhedron which has two congruent and parallel faces with all other faces parallelograms

prokaryote: Cells in which a nucleus does not exist

properties: Aspects of a shape that define the shape

proportion: A statement indicating that two ratios are equal; for example, at the market today, four apples cost $1.20, then eight apples should cost $2.40

prosody: Ability to read with appropriate rhythm, intonation, and expression

proteins: With lipids, control the movement of larger materials into and out of the cell

protists: One of the kingdoms; organisms which are similar to plants, fungi, and animals, but do not fit neatly into those kingdoms

protons: Part of an atom located in the nucleus (or solid center) of an atom together with neutrons

protozoans: Animal-like protists

pseudopodia: False feet

pyramids: A polyhedron with one base; all other faces are triangles which intersect at a common point called a vertex

quadrilateral: Four sided polygon

radial symmetry: When the body is organized around a center

radiation: When heat is transferred through electromagnetic waves. Examples of radiation are the heating of the skin by the sun and the heat of a bonfire. The heat is transferred through the movement of electromagnetic waves

range: The difference between the highest score and lowest score in the data set

rate: In mathematics, a rate is a type of ratio. A ratio is called a rate when the measuring units describing two quantities being compared are different. For example, Gill drove the car at 65 miles per hour, or you can get 12 cans for $3.00. Also see unit rate. In reading, the speed of reading

ratio: Another use of fractions; the comparison of two numbers or quantities

rational numbers: A set of numbers that contains integers and positive and negative fractions; expressed as the ratio of two integers, a/b; where b > 0; for example, 2/5, ‾3/8, or 7/1 = 7

Readers Theater: Script reading that focuses the reader on the key elements of fluency, accuracy, rate, and prosody

real numbers: This set of numbers includes both rational (such as 42, –42, ½, and 0.25) and irrational numbers (such as pi (π) or the square root of 2). It can be thought of as points in an infinite long number line.

recessive trait: Traits which appear less frequently in a population

recording and interpreting data: Part of the scientific process; collection of data to answer hypothesis

rectangle: A parallelogram with one right angle

reflection: A flip; moving a figure by flipping it over a mirror line; mirror image

relative location: Informal location; local landmarks are used to identify location (i.e., near schools and shopping mall)

repetition: In an artwork, created when elements like objects, patterns, shapes, space, light, direction, and lines are repeated. For example, a pattern on a rug could be repeated to form a work of art.

representational: See pictorial

reproductive system: Provides the components for making new life

reptiles: One type of vertebrate; live entirely on land; have lungs and thick, dry skin

reservoir: A lake-like area where water is kept until needed

respiratory system: Transports oxygen to the blood and removes carbon dioxide from the blood

rhombus: A parallelogram with all equal sides

rhythm: The variation of the length and accentuation of a series of sounds or other events; for example, variations in the length of musical tones indicated by using musical notation involving various types of notes and rests

ribosomes: The smallest of all organelles; protein builders

Richter scale: A scale which indicates the intensity of an earthquake's magnitude

right triangle: A triangle in which one angle measures exactly 90 degrees

rotation: A turn; moving a figure by turning it around a given point

rough ER: Endoplasmic reticulum that is covered in ribosomes and is usually found near the nucleus

roundworm: Invertebrate worms with bodies that are long, slim, and round; have bilateral symmetry and a simple nervous system

runners: Above-ground stems that form new plants

runoff: Occurs when rain water falls to land and moves across the land to rivers, streams, or other water sites

sac fungi: Fungi which include yeasts, mildews, truffles, and morels

salamanders: A type of amphibian; live in the woods of North America; have four strong legs and a long tail

Saturn: Sixth planet from the sun; known for its rings; second largest planet

scaffolding: Used to provide guidance and support to a student as he or she learns, without limiting the student's investigation abilities, provides the basic support and accommodations to facilitate a student's social, academic, emotional, and mental development

scalene triangle: A triangle in which all three sides are different lengths

scales: Structures covering the bodies of fish to protect them and lower friction as they swim through the water

scientific inquiry: Process of developing and answering scientific questions

sedimentary rocks: Rocks which are created when layers of debris, or sediment, are compacted and fuse together

seedless plants: One type of vascular plant; includes ferns and horsetails

segmented worm: Invertebrates; have bilateral symmetry but are more complex than flatworms and roundworms; have a closed circulatory system and a complex nervous system

seismometer: An instrument which measures the magnitude or strength of an earthquake

self-concept: Cognitive aspect of self and generally refers to the system of beliefs, attitudes, and opinions learned and that each person determines to be true

self-esteem: An emotional aspect of self and generally refers to how one feels about him/herself

Senate: Upper house of the United States Congress

senses: Structures which allow the brain to collect information; includes sight, sound, taste, touch, and smell

sex cells: Cells responsible for sexual reproduction in fungi

sexual reproduction: Reproduction which requires two parents; offspring contain a combination of DNA from both parents

shape: It is an element of art. It is an enclosed space and limited to two dimensions (length and width), which boundaries are defined by other elements of art (for example, lines, colors, values, and textures). Some geometric shapes that have clear edges are circles, rectangles, squares, and triangles. Some natural shapes are amoebas and clouds.

similar: Same shape but different size

sinkhole: Formed when cavities form under the surface of the earth. These cavities are formed when water filling the space is removed through evaporation or absorption. The weight of the soil or other material above the cavity collapses it, forming a sinkhole. Sinkholes are very common in Florida.

Six Pillars of Character: Standards of character which form a foundation for ethics and ethical decision-making; trustworthiness, respect, responsibility, fairness, caring, and citizenship

skeletal muscle: Attaches to bones with tendons for body movement

skeletal system: Provides the frame for the body and protects body parts

slope: Rate of change of one variable in relation to a second variable; how one variable changes with respect to a second variable

smooth ER: Endoplasmic reticulum which does not contain ribosomes, makes lipids, and breaks down toxic material that could damage the cell

smooth muscle: Moves food through digestive system

solid: One of the three main states of matter that is different from gas and liquid; has definite volume and shape; for example, ice

solution: A type of mixture that is homogeneous; uniform and consistent throughout. For example, seawater is a solution containing water and salt, which could be separated through the evaporation process

Southern hemisphere: The southern half of the earth

spheres: A three-dimensional figure in which all points on the surface are the same distance from the center of the sphere; a ball

spirilla: Spiral-shaped bacteria

sponge: The simplest invertebrates; asymmetrical and have no tissues; marine animals

sporangia: Spore cases which are used when threadlike fungi reproduce asexually

spores: Asexual reproduction in which a fungi breaks apart forming new fungi

sporophyte stage: Stage of plant's life cycle in which plants make spores, which then can grow in a suitable environment

square: A parallelogram with all equal sides and one right angle

stamen: Male part of the plant

star: Made up entirely of gases and are mostly made of hydrogen. Stars are born in hot gas and dust. Color, temperature, and size depend on the star's mass. Star colors can vary from slightly reddish, orange, and yellow to white and blue. These colors are easy to see especially on dark nights

stigma: Part of the pistil

stomata (stoma): Openings in the leaf's surface which can open and close allowing carbon dioxide to enter the plant's leaves

stratus: Clouds which are horizontal, layered clouds that appear to blanket the sky

strength training: Physical activity in which the goal is to strengthen muscles in the body

stress: The impact of a continually changing environment on the body

style: In science, a part of the pistil of a plant. In art, the manner of expression of an artist. *Also see* genre

substance abuse: Overindulgence in and dependence on an addictive substance, especially alcohol or narcotic drugs

survival of the fittest: Those with the most advantageous adaptations survive

symbolic: This cognitive level involves the use of symbols to represent mathematical ideas. In this case you either read or say the words representing the mathematical idea. For example, using the numeral "5" or the number name "five" to represent the numerical value of number five

tadpole: An early stage of a frog or toad; must live in water; has gills and a tail; develops lungs and limbs which allow the frog or toad to live on water

taxonomy: Classification of living things based on physical characteristics

temperature: It is a measure related to the average kinetic energy of the molecules of a substance. For example, in Kelvin degrees, this measure is directly proportional to the average kinetic energy of the molecules.

tempo: The speed of underlying beat (Allegro, Allegretto, Presto, Moderato, Lento, and Largo) used singly or in combination within a music selection

texture: In music, it is considered one of the basic elements of music, and used to describe the amount of rhythms played at a specific time, and overall quality of sound of a music composition. The number, timbre, harmony, tempo, and rhythms of the instruments being used may affect a music composition texture. Monophony, homophony, and polyphony are types of music textures. In art, it refers to the surface tactile quality of a shape or structure — rough, smooth, soft, hard, and glossy. It may refer to the physical texture felt with the hands, or visual texture that gives the illusion of texture, like the use of paint to give the impression of rough texture when the surface remains smooth.

theory: Scientific belief

think alouds: They help in making visible the mental processes that might be invisible to students in the reading or problem-solving process. Using this approach, a teacher reads a passage or solves a problem and models his or her thinking by voicing all the things they are noticing, doing, seeing, feeling, and asking as they process the text in the passage. Students are then encouraged to "borrow" and practice the various strategies the teacher used, and apply them in their own reading or problem-solving process.

threadlike fungi: Fungi that live in soil and are decomposers

timbre: The quality of a musical note or sound or tone that distinguishes different types of sound production, such as voices or musical instruments. For example, a person uses timbre to distinguish the saxophone from the trumpet in a jazz band even when they are playing the same notes at the same pitch and loudness.

tissues: When different kinds of cells combine

tone: *See* timbre

trachea: Top of the respiratory system; air enters the body through the trachea

trade winds: Warm, steady winds that blow continuously

translation: A slide; moving a figure along a straight line from one location to another

transpiration: Loss of water through leaves

trapezoid: A quadrilateral with exactly one pair of parallel sides

triangle: Three sided polygon

tsunami: A tidal wave which occurs as a result of an earthquake occurring under water

tuataras: One group of reptiles; live on a few islands off the coast of New Zealand; similar to lizards

tubers: Underground stems that can produce new plants

tune: *See* melody

turtles and tortoises: One group of reptiles; have a protective shell

unbalanced forces: They always cause a change in motion. They are in opposite direction to each other, and not equal in size. When two unbalanced forces are exerted in opposite directions, their combined force is equal to the difference between the two forces and exerted in the direction of the larger force.

unit rate: When the second term in the rate is 1, the rate is referred to as unit rate. For example, Natalie types 36 words per minute, or Samuel earns $14.00 per hour.

United States Constitution: Fundamental law of the United States; effective date March 4, 1789

unity: A principle of art that occurs when all of the elements of a piece combine to make a balanced, pleasing, harmonious, and complete whole or unit

Uranus: Seventh planet from the sun; the third largest planet

urinary system: Removes waste from the body

vacuoles: Large vesicles

value: In art, a relative darkness or lightness of a color

variable: A quantity which may assume any numerical value or set of numerical values

vascular plants: Plants that have tissues, called vascular tissues, which move water and nutrients from one part of the plant to another

vascular tissues: Tissues which move water and nutrients from one part of a plant to another

Venus: Second planet from the sun

vertebrate: Animals that have a backbone

vertices: Intersection of two edges of a polyhedron

vesicle: Piece of the Golgi complex's membrane that pinches off in a small bubble which transports the lipids and proteins to other parts of the cell or outside the cell

visual arts: Art forms focusing on the creation of works that are primarily visual in nature; for example two-dimensional art (drawing, painting, photography, printmaking, and filmmaking), and three-dimensional art (sculpture and architecture)

vocabulary: Includes all the words the reader can understand and use. The more words a child knows, the better he or she will understand what is read. Knowing how words relate to each other is a building block that leads to comprehension

vocal range: The measure of the extent of pitches that a human voice can produce; the highest to the lowest note a person's voice can produce — Soprano, Alto or Contralto, Tenor, Baritone, and Bass

volcano: Geologic formation which occurs when magma rises from below the earth's surface in an eruption

volume: Another property of matter; the amount of cubic space that an object occupies

water birds: Birds that live in the water; have webbed feet for swimming or long legs for wading; examples include cranes, ducks, and loons

Webquest: Web-based learning experience

weight: The measure of the Earth's pull of gravity on an object. It is measured in pounds (English or traditional system), or grams (metric system). An object's weight on Earth is the force that Earth's gravity exerts on an object with a specific mass.

whole numbers Whole numbers are natural numbers and zero. Natural numbers are the counting numbers (1, 2, 3, 4, 5, …).

Wiki: Collaboratively authored searchable documents linked internally and externally; like mini-web pages

wind: Horizontal movement of air

xylem: One type of vascular tissue

zooflagellate: Protozoan which moves with flagella